*The Making of New Zealanders*

# THE MAKING OF NEW ZEALANDERS

## RON PALENSKI

AUCKLAND
UNIVERSITY
PRESS

First published 2012

Auckland University Press
University of Auckland
Private Bag 92019
Auckland 1142
New Zealand
www.press.auckland.ac.nz

ISBN 978 1 86940 726 1

Publication is kindly assisted by ⓈＣreative *nz*
ARTS COUNCIL OF NEW ZEALAND TOI AOTEAROA

**National Library of New Zealand Cataloguing-in-Publication Data**
Palenski, Ron.
The making of New Zealanders / by Ron Palenski.
Includes bibliographical references and index.
ISBN 978-1-86940-726-1
1. National characteristics, New Zealand—History. 2. Nationalism—
New Zealand—History. 3. New Zealanders—Ethnic identity—History.
4. New Zealand—Social life and customs—19th century. I. Title.
993.02—dc 23

Cover design: Spencer Levine

Printed in China by 1010 Printing International Ltd

# CONTENTS

# PREFACE

I cannot remember when first the light bulb appeared above my head that shone brightly with the thought that I must write about the evolution of the national identity of New Zealanders. When I first mentioned it, some people tried to persuade me otherwise because it had been done already or because there was too much contention associated with it. I discussed nationalism and parochialism and postmodernism and a whole basket of other 'isms' with various people and eventually took a proposal to the postgraduate committee of the History and Art History Department of the University of Otago. The idea became a doctoral thesis and now it has become a book.

No book can be the product of just one person, especially not an academic book. This one draws on the works of a great many people, some of them still active historians and other professionals, some of them not, some of them gone but certainly not forgotten. Some of them knew their expertise was being drawn on, some did not. Some of those I have consulted and whose work I have studied disagree with my views, but willingly tendered their advice anyway.

The thesis that has become a book would not have been started, let alone finished, without the support and encouragement of the History and Art History staff at Otago University. They, like academic historians at other institutions, do their invaluable work largely away from the public's gaze, yet all are leading experts in their particular fields and have a profound influence on students who pass their way. The department head, Professor Barbara Brookes, had the ultimate say on whether my plan became a reality, and my supervisors, Professor Tom Brooking, Associate Professor Alexander Trapeznik and Dr Rani Kerin, held my hand through the process. Others in the department who provided invaluable advice and support were Professor Tony Ballantyne and Professor Judy Bennett, though I am loath to name names because everyone with whom I came into contact was unfailingly supportive. I could name the whole staff and not be overdoing it. The department's Student and Academic Support Administrator, Mrs Frances Couch, was especially helpful. Academic staff in other areas also kept me headed in the right direction, especially the Dean of the School of Physical Education, Professor Douglas Booth, and Whakarongotai Hokowhitu of Te Tumu, the School of Māori, Pacific and Indigenous Studies. Professor Brian Moloughney, now the Pro-Vice-Chancellor, Division of Humanities at Otago, was more responsible than he knew for my pursuit of academic endeavours. Emeritus Professor Erik Olssen and, outside of Otago, Professor James Belich at Victoria University of Wellington provided valuable ideas. Word of the thesis reached the ears of Dr Sam Elworthy of Auckland University Press and he added his support and encouragement to that of all the rest.

But careful readers should not blame any of these people for any omissions or errors; I am wholly responsible.

Academic researchers are extremely well served in New Zealand. The various institutions which preserve the past for the present and the future deserve the gratitude of all, and they certainly have mine. In particular, I thank the respective staffs of Hocken Collections Uare Taoka o Hākena, University of Otago, and the university's Central Library; Archives New Zealand Te Rua Mahara o te Kāwanatanga; the Alexander Turnbull Library and the National Library of New Zealand Te Puna Mātauranga o Aotearoa which among many priceless assets has the best multi-newspaper archive website in the world – New Zealanders do not know how lucky they are until they try searching newspaper archives in other countries.

My family, especially Kathy, knows how grateful I am for their support.

*Ron Palenski*
*March 2012*

# ORTHOGRAPHICAL NOTE

Rather than using the Latin term 'sic', which can be intrusive and disrupt the flow for readers, quotations are true to their original and footnotes when necessary clarify or correct. Odd spellings, misspellings and letter case are retained as they first appeared. The macron in Māori words in quotations is used when it appeared in the originals.

# Introduction

*... let a man trouble himself little about the decadence of*
*England but think much of the rise of New Zealand*
*—Anthony Trollope,* The New Zealander [1]

In 1877 a son of Scottish immigrants wrote to the editor of the
*Auckland Star* because he was concerned about his nationality.[2] His
parents were Scottish, he said, or 'Scotch' in the manner of the
time, but he had been born in Auckland. 'Now, am I Scotch or am
I a young colonial?' he asked. An agony uncle letter may seem an
odd way to have the matter resolved, but the editor of the *Star* – or
someone acting for him – led the correspondent out of his quandary.
The young man was fully entitled to call himself a colonial in prefer-
ence to the perpetuation of 'old country' distinctions:

> The sinking of national identity in the first generation of native born
> population is followed in all the colonies and is fully warranted by the
> fact that the colony has become the adopted country of the parents
> and the children know no other.

In other words, the erstwhile Scot had become a New Zealander.
This metamorphosis lies at the heart of this book. At what point in
the nineteenth century did transplanted English, Scots or Irish, or
people from anywhere else, make the mental leap to considering

themselves New Zealanders? At what point did they acknowledge to themselves, and have it acknowledged by others, that 'Home' was part of a distant and increasingly nostalgic past and that 'home' was where the heart literally was? And what brought about this transformation?

This book suggests that identity was established in New Zealand much earlier than most historians have previously thought. The catalyst was not the debate, such as it was, about whether New Zealand should be part of the Australian Commonwealth; it was not the concurrent sending of troops off to fight in South Africa in the Boer War; it was not the New Zealand rugby team's tour of the British Isles, France and North America in 1905–06 – and, if it was none of those things, it certainly could not have been New Zealand's role in the Gallipoli campaign in 1915.

In the beginning, 'New Zealander' meant Māori – the indigenous people as opposed to the settlers. But over time, and as the country developed and more and more people were born in New Zealand, the meaning changed. The country for a time, in the words of historian and twentieth-century man of letters Eric Hall McCormick, 'became the focus of a stock Romantic sentiment that though Europe might be decadent or even doomed, in the newer countries across the ocean its civilisation would be renewed and perpetuated'.[3] New Zealand in the nineteenth century became a place of a distant hope. So Charles Dickens, after a poor review in *The Times* in 1847, wrote to a friend: 'Inimitable very mouldy and dull. Disposed to go to New Zealand and start a magazine.'[4]

In the same vein, the great nineteenth-century English historian Thomas Babington (Lord) Macaulay in 1840 introduced a subsequently much-quoted 'New Zealander'. Macaulay had plucked this individual from his imagination when writing of Leopold von Ranke's history of the papacy for the *Edinburgh Review*. Talking of the enduring strength of the Roman Catholic Church, Macaulay was of the view that that institution 'may still exist in undiminished vigour when some traveller from New Zealand shall, in the midst

*New Zealander* by French
illustrator Gustave Doré.
From B. Jerrold, ed., *London:
A Pilgrimage* (London: Grant
& Co., 1872)

of a vast solitude, take his stand on a broken arch of London Bridge
to sketch the ruins of St Paul's'.[5] Macaulay's 'traveller from New
Zealand' became, in the retelling, 'a New Zealander'.

The image stuck.[6] During Queen Victoria's jubilee celebrations
in 1897, the *Westminster Gazette* remarked that the New Zealander
came and stood on London Bridge without disastrous results.[7] One
of the jubilee celebrants was the New Zealand premier, Richard
John Seddon, who was quoted as quipping that in view of the fine
physique of the Māori, no broken arch would support his weight.[8]
Two years later, when Seddon urged the House of Representatives
to support his proposal to dispatch troops to South Africa, he again
invoked the Macaulay image:

It has been said by the historian Macaulay that it would be a New-
Zealander who, on a broken arch of London Bridge would recount
the ruin of London and the downfall of the Empire. I am sorry

for Macaulay; he little knew the New-Zealander. The history of the future will show that the New-Zealander will not recount the downfall of the Empire, but will fight to maintain it.[9]

The 'death-watch' New Zealander came up in a sporting context too. In 1883, remarking on the success of New Zealand provincial rugby teams against the New South Wales side the year before, the London *Sporting Life* said: 'It will be strange if Macaulay's New Zealander should be realised in the shape of a footballer. It is quite within the bounds of possibility that in the course of time we may have to chronicle the doings of a New Zealand football team on English grounds.'[10] The conjecture proved prophetic. After the landmark tour of the United Kingdom by the New Zealand rugby union team in 1905–06, *Athletic News* in England had this to say: 'So far as the Rugby game is concerned Macaulay's New Zealander has come, and conquered.'[11]

Clearly, by the turn of the century, a sense of national identity had become well established in the minds of New Zealanders and, through various outward manifestations, to the rest of the world. There was no eureka moment in this evolution of New Zealand identity, either in the Archimedean sense or in the sense of the Victorian goldfields rebellion that has been held up as a symbol of democratic protest and national identity in Australia.[12] Rather, a sense of identity evolved in New Zealand through the latter half of the nineteenth century via a multiplicity of agencies and actions. As one New Zealand writer, Alan Mulgan, recalled of his nineteenth-century schooldays: 'New Zealand was not yet a nation, indeed scarcely conscious that she might or should be one . . . all the time influences were working within us. We could not see them then, but we can now – little things and big things.'[13]

Two historians, W. P. Morrell and D. O. W. Hall, saw the emergence of identity around the same time. 'By the eighteen eighties there was growing up a new generation of men and women who had been born in New Zealand', they wrote. 'Increasing knowledge

*Emigrants reading mail from home*, an 1852 painting by E. (Elisha?) Noyce. E-079-003, Alexander Turnbull Library, Wellington, New Zealand (ATL)

of their country and its possibilities all contributed to kindle in New Zealanders a proper feeling of self-respect.'[14] Rather than events such as the Boer War or the federation debate formulating a national New Zealand identity, it is apparent that the identity was formed earlier and these two events, and others, simply reflected and affirmed its existence. It follows, therefore, that later events, and particularly New Zealanders' role at Gallipoli, were affirmations and expressions of an identity already well established.[15]

What were the roots of that identity? Geography and the physical environment were important factors which led to the gradual definition of New Zealand and New Zealanders, drawing them toward thinking of their country as their prime point of allegiance instead of some distant place of birth. The influence of geography was asserted early on in the debate about whether New Zealand should follow the colonies on the other side of the Tasman into federation. One of the New Zealand delegates at an 1890 conference in Melbourne, Sir John Hall, uttered a phrase that became much repeated: 'Nature has made 1200 impediments to the inclusion of New Zealand in any such Federation in the 1200 miles of stormy ocean which lie between us and our brethren in Australia.'[16] The other New Zealand delegate, Captain William Russell, added the nationalist argument to that of distance: 'A remarkable individuality must spring up in this country, and . . . I think we should endeavour to form a distinct race for ourselves in the colony of New Zealand, rather than amalgamate with other colonies and have our characteristics probably very materially changed by so doing.'[17] When the lyricists of what became the national anthems of New Zealand and Australia wrote their words, they neither extolled an individual (as in 'God Save the Queen') nor sounded a call to arms (as in 'La Marseillaise'), but embraced the physical nature of the lands in which they settled. 'May our mountains ever be / Freedom's ramparts on the sea', urged Thomas Bracken in New Zealand; 'We've golden soil and wealth for toil / Our home is girt by sea', enthused Peter Dodds McCormick in Australia.

If identification with the new-found land was one of the foundations of a sense of belonging, another was time – time in the basic sense of knowing and understanding what time of day it was; and time in relationship between one place and another. New Zealand was a world leader in standardising time on a national basis, fixed by longitude in relation to Greenwich.[18] Its adoption of a uniform time, New Zealand Mean Time, in 1868 was for pragmatic reasons, but the move also had a unifying, centralising effect. It was a stride toward national identity and modernity that has seldom been remarked upon. It put national advantages ahead of parochial considerations and enhanced the country's sense of itself, separate and distinct from the other Australasian colonies. As an editorial in the Wellington *Evening Post* remarked, the advent of one time for the

An 1888 painting by Charles Blomfield of the White Terrace, one of the many scenic attractions that contributed to the uniqueness of New Zealand. G-472, ATL

whole of New Zealand was 'one which marks the progress made by the colony and the extension of the many settlements towards what they will one day become – one harmonious and great country'.[19]

The uniformity of time and an affinity with the land contributed to the bedrock of a burgeoning sense of identity, as did the abolition of provincial governments in 1876 – New Zealand's own version of federalism – and the introduction of pioneering legislative initiatives under the Liberal government from 1893. In that year New Zealand became the first country in the world to give women the vote (after failing narrowly at an earlier attempt in 1878) and, under the premiership (if not the authorship) of Seddon for the next thirteen years, enacted a range of social legislation which was seen as daring and ground-breaking and eventually imitated in one form or another by other countries.[20] New Zealand was thus gradually moulding its own image as a distinct (and enlightened) nation, neither dependent on nor obsequious to the imperial government in London or the 'mother colony' of New South Wales.

New Zealand, of course, had issues common to other countries, especially the temperance movement, which was allied with the arguments for equal rights for women. In Patricia Grimshaw's memorable phrase: 'The struggle to make men sober proved the catalyst for feminism.'[21] It was an aggregation of the issues, and New Zealand's way of dealing with them, that spurred the development of national identity. But New Zealand also had conditions unique to itself. The most crucial difference between New Zealand and other settler colonies was that Māori were legally acknowledged, if not totally embraced. Māori were not wholly marginalised as Aboriginals were in Australia or any of the native peoples of southern Africa or North or South America. Colonial New Zealand was as much imbued with the fashionable social Darwinist notions of white supremacy as other white settler colonies of the time and passed a range of increasingly prohibitive laws aimed at reducing the prevalence of Asians (specifically Chinese).[22] But at the same time, Māori gained representation in the national parliament from as early as 1867 and played significant roles in the underpinning and affirmation of New Zealand identity. The Māori, as with other strands of nationalism, were a point of positive difference between New Zealand and, especially, the Australian colonies; as much a distinctive part of New Zealand as its mountains and rivers.

Perhaps the single most important overt manifestation of New Zealand identity was the decision not to follow the other antipodean colonies into forming the Australian federation. William Parker Morrell called it 'another milestone on the road to national self-consciousness'.[23] Had New Zealand lined up with the six other colonies, there would now be no such thing as a New Zealand national identity; there would be state parochialism, just as there is now in Australia as substrata in Australian life. Wellington would be a state capital; New Zealand's leading politicians for more than a century would have been members of either a state legislature in Wellington or of the federal parliament, first in Melbourne and later in Canberra. In terms of the future of what was then the colony of

New Zealand, the decision was a momentous, indeed portentous, one. However, the decision not to federate did not bring about a national identity; quite the reverse – it was an extant national identity that brought about the decision. It has been said that 'we usually decide who we are by reference to who and what we are not'.[24] New Zealanders decided they were not Australians.

The advent of the South African war – the first opportunity for New Zealand to display its martial mettle to Britain and for the wider benefit of the Empire – was a time of national fervour: a time of, in the phraseology of the day, 'jingoism'. But beneath the imperial loyalty lay the newly acquired sense of national identity, a sense of being New Zealanders first; and the war, like the federation debate, allowed outward expression of that sense. During the Boer War, as in the brief federation debate, Māori again proved to be a telling factor in New Zealand attitudes, providing both a point of difference and another underpinning plank in national identity. The British, with the ready agreement, even encouragement, of their enemies, declared the war to be 'a white man's war' and there was mutual abhorrence at the prospect of natives fighting against the white man (whether Briton or Boer). But Māori – with or without official approval – fought with distinction alongside Pākehā.[25]

If Māori were peripheral, but no less pivotal, to the national identity confirmed by the Boer War, they were central to the impetus the sport of rugby had in giving New Zealanders a sense of self and of national pride. Rugby had been introduced into New Zealand in 1870 and Māori took the New Zealand game onto the world stage with the organisation and formation of the Native team that toured New Zealand, Australia and Britain in 1888–89. Greg Ryan called them 'the forerunners of the All Blacks', but they were more than that: their uniform was a black jersey with a silver fernleaf on the breast; they adopted tactics which were later wrongly said to have begun with the 1905–06 official New Zealand team in Britain; and they implemented the practice of a haka before each encounter, something which later became a distinctive pre-match ritual of the

Spectators in 1908 at a rugby match at Athletic Park in Wellington – the benefits of national identity redounded on all. Author's collection

New Zealand game.[26] The Native team's success led indirectly to the formation of the New Zealand Rugby Football Union in 1892, and one of its members, Tāmati Rangiwahia ('Tom') Ellison, successfully proposed at the NZRFU's first annual meeting that the Natives' uniform be adopted as the national team uniform. Ellison himself captained the first official New Zealand team to wear the uniform and it became the first to be known as the All Blacks.[27]

The visit to Britain by the 1905–06 All Blacks has been held up as a critical contributor to national identity – Keith Sinclair called it 'the game's Gallipoli' – but the Natives of 1888–89 were the real standard-bearers and precedent setters.[28] As Scott Crawford has argued: 'For New Zealanders, the image of themselves as belonging to a country devoted to sport has been an important foundation for the development of national identity.'[29] Using sport as a marker of national identity in a wider sense, Matti Goksøyr remarked: 'Sports were a means to call attention and respect to the existence of a small nation, to establish the small nation's place in the consciousness of the big world.'[30] While sport may be deprecated by certain thinkers as being superficial and of no lasting importance in the affairs of a nation-state, to deny its wider impact on the people is to deny an enduring reality.

Taken on its own and in isolation, sport may have just fleeting importance. But in the context of how the people of a country think about themselves, about what they regard as important to their collective make-up, sport becomes another building block of national identity. And as this book shows, re-examination of all such building blocks, both individually and collectively, leads to the conclusion that in New Zealand they were put in place a great deal earlier than has generally been supposed.

So what is meant by national identity? Probably the most well-known contemporary account comes from Benedict Anderson's *Imagined Communities*. A nation, he suggested, is: 'An imagined political community . . . it is imagined because the members of even the smallest nation will never know most of their fellow-members, meet them, or even hear of them, yet in the minds of each lives the image of their communion.'[31] Keith Sinclair, whose landmark work *A Destiny Apart* laid down the parameters of national identity and identified the Boer War and the 1905–06 rugby tour as critical, came to a similar definition – years before:

> What, many people have asked, is a nation. My answer is that
> a nation is a people most of whom think that they are a nation.
> Usually they have a country and sometimes, but not always, their
> own language. Usually they have, to some degree, their own
> distinctive culture. *A people becomes a nation when it grows aware that
> its existence differs from that of other peoples and comes to feel, as it were,
> set apart.* It is a social process, history, that leads to this sense of
> identity.[32] [italics added]

That self-awareness – that imagined community – does not mean that all people espousing a national identity must be the same, or think or act the same. Differences can, in fact do, exist within an overarching nationalism. Diversity is as much a part of 'the group' as sameness. In a New Zealand context, John Cawte Beaglehole acknowledged this diversity within unity another way:

> We must consider New Zealand not merely as an example of, or an item in, constitutional growth, nor merely as an individual – however minor an individual – on the international stage, but as a community of mixed feelings that have, in course of time and varied pressures, run into a national channel. As with other nations, therefore, its historian, however much he would prefer the solid ground of constitutional decisions or overt acts, cannot avoid the psychological. The feeling and the act go somehow together.[33]

The sense of being a New Zealander is something that is 'felt' by individuals rather than prescribed from without. It is this book's contention that national identity is shaped by common concerns and a shared sense of belonging to a nation-state or geographical area. This is what an individual feels, or at least felt, in the nineteenth century. It should not be confused with a New Zealand nationalism, a state nationalism, which is when the country asserted its own interests over those of others; when New Zealand stopped paying obeisance to mother Britain. This may have been after the Empire conference of 1926 that determined all members were autonomous and equal in status; it may have been with the passing of the Statute of Westminster by the House of Commons and its eventual adoption by New Zealand; and it may even have been as late as the 1970s when Britain joined the European Economic Community, as it then was. But none of those things was about an individual's national identity.[34]

There is a postmodernist view that the concept of national identity is flawed, if not downright misleading, because it is based on a nineteenth-century world that was essentially dominated by white males. Any national identity that then took root therefore paid little or no heed to a great number of people for whom it was supposed to apply, women and indigenous people especially. New Zealander Giselle Byrnes wrote that national identity 'has been exposed as an artificial device'.[35] As Katie Pickles argues, 'The primacy of masculinity in colonial, imperial and then national identity has endured in New Zealand historiography'.[36] She relates how feminist historians in New Zealand and Australia 'began to challenge the place of gender in a national identity that was influenced by colonisation'.[37] This led, she believes, to calls to move beyond nationalist histories and seek transnational comparisons with other parts of the British world.[38]

If an individual's sense of national identity can be taken to mean allegiance to a nation-state, it can be explained by saying there are various levels of allegiance, which are not mutually exclusive. Imagine an archery target: the inner ring represents loyalty to family, the next to friends, the next to town or city and other immediate or local commitments, the next to province, the next to country, perhaps the next to country of origin (although this allegiance diminished as native-born numbers grew), and the outer ring to Empire.[39] Linda Colley, among the foremost of historians of the complexities of British nationalisms and identities, wrote:

> In practice, men and women often had double, triple, or even quadruple loyalties, mentally locating themselves, according to the circumstances, in a village, in a particular landscape, in a region, and in one or even two countries. It was quite possible for an individual to see himself as being, at one and the same time, a citizen of Edinburgh, a Lowlander, a Scott, and a Briton.[40]

She also put it more whimsically: 'Identities are not like hats. Human beings can and do put on several at a time.'[41]

People's allegiances also often extend beyond the village, the province, the country. History, as Australians Ann Curthoys and John Docker have noted, is 'constantly bursting through national barriers'.[42] This is not a new phenomenon, but it is one that is gaining more scholarly attention as historians reach beyond national borders to understand regional and global trends. It may be that, both now and in the future, national boundaries become less important than they once were and perhaps as irrelevant as they were before the rise of the nation-state, although this is doubtful. For instance, if transnationalism in some politically idyllic future requires citizens of France to regard themselves firstly as borderless Europeans – or, to take the ideal to its ultimate, world citizens – and secondly as French, would that necessarily diminish their 'Frenchness'?

New Zealand and other British Empire settler colonies such as those in Australia and Canada managed such a dual allegiance without any diminution of their sense of self or their sense of belonging. New Zealand national identity developed in tandem with the concept of imperial nationalism under which citizens of New Zealand saw themselves as both New Zealander and British, or at least, felt a sense of belonging to both the country in which they lived and the empire of which their country was then a part. Morrell, writing as an expatriate New Zealander in the 1930s, saw logic in the dichotomy:

> If we see eye to eye so much with Great Britain in imperial matters, it is partly because we are not only the youngest of the daughter countries but also the daughter that takes most after her mother. Yet a word of caution is necessary: as always in such cases, first acquaintance sees the family resemblance but longer and fuller knowledge brings out the traits of difference.[43]

It was not a contradiction that New Zealand identity slowly asserted itself while at the same time those living in New Zealand continued to profess an allegiance to Britain and, more specifically, the Empire and, more specifically still, its monarch. It was not a contradiction for the same reason that allegiance to and pride in a region of New Zealand did not and does not contradict or override an allegiance to the country as a whole – for what is nationalism but parochialism writ large?

To burst through national barriers, as Curthoys and Docker put it, is not to deny either their existence or their effectiveness. Indeed, a move away from the concept of nationalism could have the opposite effect to that intended. The forces of multiculturalism and globalisation, according to Alice Brittan, 'have heightened our desire for examples of untainted, authentic or pure embodiments of local culture'.[44] A New Zealand historian, Peter Hempenstall, noted similar interactions between global and local forces:

> Trans-nationalism as an explanatory force seems to be running out of steam, one of the criticisms being that it does not really escape making the nation state the beginning and end point of most studies. The emphasis today is much more on tracing the messy entanglements of people and groups and ideas across local, regional, national and international boundaries. There are spaces where truly trans-national transactions occur, but more frequently people live within their local communities, and their local histories, and find the meanings they give to their lives there.[45]

People in New Zealand in the nineteenth century – or indeed at any other time – could not rationally deny who and where they were and what factors influenced their daily lives, however unrecognised such factors may have been. Those who immigrated and stayed came to think of themselves as nationals – the native-born were nothing else. Together, they laid the foundations for the making of New Zealanders this book is about to trace.

THE NEW ZEALAND

GRAND TOUR

by STEAMSHIP RAIL COACH HORSE & FOOT

1890

N.Z. SURVEY, WELLINGTON.

A brochure from 1890 that advertised the New Zealand grand tour by steamship, rail, coach, horse and foot. Eph-A-Tourism-NZ-1890-01-front, ATL

# ONE

# From Many to One:
# Linking the 'Fishing Villages'

*The ruthless years roll on and all is changed!* – Evening Post[1]

New Zealand in its toddler years was once likened to six little fishing villages, creating the image of disparate settlements dotted around the coast with little in common and even less connecting one with another.[2] It was a valid point to make and one also noted by an early man of many parts (including premier), William Fox, who wrote that each settlement 'had a distinct origin and a separate aim, which, combined with their local separation, makes them more truly distinct colonies than Virginia and Maryland or Delaware and New Jersey'.[3] The point was reinforced by the title of Fox's 1851 book, *The Six Colonies of New Zealand*. Over the succeeding years, the separateness became togetherness.

New Zealand in Fox's time was not the New Zealand it came to be. He once took six days to get from Nelson to Wellington; overland mail by 'native runner' from Wellington to Auckland took three weeks; sea mail between the two North Island cities frequently went via Sydney or Melbourne; often the quickest route from Dunedin to Auckland was via Bluff and a dash across the Tasman to Hobart. Distance was, to paraphrase Geoffrey Blainey, tyrannical;[4] communication between settlements was haphazard and slow; transport was either by wind-powered vessel or by foot or horse on unformed roads over uncertain country.

Gradually – and it must have seemed oh so painfully gradually to people at the time, although it was all remarkably rapid in historical terms – New Zealand took shape; the immigrants who arrived, mainly from Britain and the Australian colonies (and they were still separate colonies), set to building their new homes and their new country. When Wellington and New Zealand marked 50 years of European settlement in 1890, a local poet burst into verse: 'The ruthless years roll on and all is changed!' It certainly had. New Zealand was not six little fishing villages any longer; the inhabitants were not transplanted English or Scots or Irish or from anywhere else – they had become New Zealanders.

Of the many factors in the transformation from infant country to adult, communication was critical. 'The history of communications is a vital part of our story', an eminent jurist, Sir Frederick Chapman, told the first meeting of the Otago branch of the New Zealand Historical Association in 1928.[5] He was mainly talking about the significant external links established, especially by the home-grown Union Steam Ship Company, but his comments could have covered the whole gamut of communication. Chapman had personal knowledge of the privations of the past – his father, Sir Henry Chapman, was with Fox on the harrowing six-day Nelson to Wellington voyage in 1850.[6] From the time of one Chapman to the time of the next, a web of linkages had drawn New Zealand and New Zealanders together. The telegraph, the railways, shipping and other enterprises which were national rather than local all transformed New Zealand, all led to a sense of 'oneness', to a recognisable and recognised national identity.

Keith Sinclair thought that 'undoubtedly one of the most important' circumstances in the rise of national identity was the establishment of communications networks: 'Vogel's roads and bridges and railways, the establishment of post offices, the electric telegraph and the telephone enabled people to communicate nationally. Previously people lived in provinces and thought provincially.'[7] In a global sense, Niall Ferguson described the telegraph as one of the metal networks that shrank the world. Messages from country to country that not long before took months could now take minutes; Ferguson quoted 'an apostle' of the new technology, Charles Bright, as calling the telegraph 'the world's system of electrical nerves'. It was the nineteenth century's 'information highway'.[8] It was no less so in New Zealand; it was the portal to the future.

## The joining of the dots

The introduction of the telegraph led directly to the decision to standardise time in New Zealand – a world first for the fledgling country that is hardly ever acknowledged. The joining of the dots – the increased interaction between the 'six little fishing villages' – also led to irrevocable change in the governance of New Zealand. The *Otago Daily Times* correspondent in Christchurch began a dispatch dated 24 June 1862 about news and events: 'The principal event of last week was the sitting of the Supreme Court.' The sitting gained the correspondent's attention not just because of the court's workload – 'the heaviest ever known in Canterbury' – but also 'the atrocity' of the cases under review: two of rape, one of which also involved burglary and robbery, and one of arson.[9] But for all the fleeting notoriety, and even allowing for the fact the death sentence was passed for the first time in Canterbury in the arson case, an event of far more portentous significance also occurred in Christchurch in the week under the correspondent's review. The lengthy dispatch included toward its end the sentence: 'The electric telegraph, between Lyttelton and Christchurch, is now an accomplished fact.'

Thus buried beneath the minutiae of the court proceedings was news of the first telegraph link in New Zealand, the first step in a communication chain that over the following months and years

This Auckland view, west along Shortland Street toward Queen Street, shows the new
– the Shortland Street Post Office and the laden telegraph pole – mixing with the old.
4-2415, Sir George Grey Special Collections, Auckland Libraries

bound the scattered settlements of the young colony together and
helped create a cohesive national identity. As A. C. Wilson pointed
out in his 1994 history of telecommunications in New Zealand,
the telegraph brought 'greater community cohesion and prosperity,
greater awareness of outside regions and access to them as well
as the consequent breakdown of parochialism within regions'.[10]
A. S. Helm in a mid-twentieth-century master's thesis considered
'[t]he telegraph . . . to be of enormous significance to New Zealand
as it facilitated the unification of the country in a manner previously
impossible'.[11] The opening of the first telegraph line heralded the
beginnings of a national identity as opposed to settlers continuing
to identify themselves only with their own familiar surroundings.[12]

According to Wilson, one of the leading advocates of the
Lyttelton–Christchurch line was the *Lyttelton Times*, which wanted
to relay shipping and other news more quickly across the Port Hills
to its more populous readership in Christchurch. That paper's

advocacy may explain why its main rival, the *Press*, accorded only scant coverage to a development of such significance. 'Want of space will not permit giving a detailed report', the *Press* sniffed, though it noted that 200 men attended a public dinner to mark the occasion and many 'seemed disposed to prefer "making a night of it" to venturing out in the mist that was descending outside'.[13] ('Want of space' did not prevent that newspaper from publishing on the same page a lengthy report of an illegal boxing bout on the banks of the Waimakariri River.)[14]

The second line in New Zealand, between Port Chalmers and Dunedin, was completed a few weeks later, and within five months the *Otago Witness* noted that the 'public utility [of the lines] has been apparent enough . . . to induce a disposition on the part of the different Provincial Governments to extend the system over the country'.[15] Lines between Bluff and Nelson and Christchurch and Hokitika followed within the next four years and, on 28 August 1866, telegraphic communication between the South and North Islands (though the South was then referred to as the 'Middle Island') was established. The Canterbury provincial engineer, Edward Dobson, reflected on the progress – and the difference – that had been made:

> Within the last few weeks we have witnessed the successful laying
> of the Cook's Straits cable, connecting the seat of Government in
> the North Island with all the principal towns of the Middle Island;
> and have had laid on our breakfast tables the printed reports of
> the debates with which the walls of the legislative chambers at
> Wellington were echoing but a few hours previously.[16]

The success of the inauguration of the interisland telegraph was noted in Wellington by the *Evening Post*:

> Now that the . . . troubled waters of Cook's Strait are cleft by the
> thin line of wire, we may hope at no distant date to see the length
> and breadth of the colony intersected by threads of metal carrying

civilisation into the most remote places and now little known districts in the heart of the country.[17]

The newspaper reproduced copies of the first messages transmitted across the strait and they were wholly congratulatory rather than heavy with meaning, unlike Samuel Morse's first message in his new transmission code between Washington and Baltimore 22 years previously: 'What hath God wrought.'[18]

The Governor, Sir George Grey, was even more matter-of-fact in his congratulations: 'The Governor of New Zealand congratulates the Superintendent and inhabitants of ____ on the establishment of telegraphic communication between the two islands of New Zealand.'[19] The same telegram was sent to each provincial superintendent, with the province's name in place of the dash. Typical of the replies was this from the deputy superintendent of Otago, Brian Haggitt: 'The Superintendent of Otago reciprocates His Excellency's congratulations on the establishment of telegraphic communication between the two islands of New Zealand.'[20] The following table demonstrates how rapid was the expansion of the telegraph and its use by the government in Wellington as well as the provincial governments and newspapers.

The telegraph was not, of course, purely an internal benefit. Its full advantages could be appreciated only when it linked New Zealand with other countries. England was joined with France by undersea cable in 1850, with the United States in 1858, and with India in 1865.[21] Darwin was linked with Java in 1871, bringing a direct link between the core and the periphery of the Empire closer. The lack of a cable connection with Australia was, according to Wilson, putting New Zealand behind the times.[22] It was also putting pressure on the New Zealand domestic service because it was being dominated by lengthy press messages of news garnered from newspapers and shipped across the Tasman before being telegraphed around the country. By early 1876, cable vessels started laying a cable from La Perouse in Botany Bay and after eleven days they were off Nelson.

TABLE 1.1 COMPARATIVE TABLE SHOWING TELEGRAPH PROGRESS

| June year | Miles of line (kilometres) | Telegraph stations | Private, press, provincial government | General government | Totals | Annual percentage increases |
|---|---|---|---|---|---|---|
| TELEGRAMS SENT ANNUALLY | | | | | | |
| 1866 | 699 (1125) | 13 | 24,761 | 2476 | 27,237 | |
| 1867 | 757 (1218) | 21 | 55,261 | 15,331 | 70,952 | 260 |
| 1868 | 1110 (1786) | 31 | 72,241 | 26,244 | 98,485 | 138 |
| 1869 | 1329 (2139) | 45 | 106,070 | 50,097 | 156,157 | 158 |
| 1870 | 1661 (2673) | 56 | 122,545 | 62,878 | 185,423 | 118 |
| 1871 | 1676 (2697) | 72 | 253,582 | 59,292 | 312,874 | 168 |
| 1872 | 2185 (3516) | 81 | 344,524 | 67,243 | 411,767 | 131 |
| 1873 | 2356 (3791) | 93 | 485,507 | 83,453 | 568,960 | 138 |
| 1874 | 2530 (4072) | 105 | 645,067 | 107,832 | 752,899 | 132 |
| 1875 | 2986 (4805) | 127 | 786,237 | 130,891 | 917,128 | 121 |

Source: *AJHR*, vol. 2, 1875, F-1A.

The cable was landed at Wakapuaka, which came to be known as Cable Bay, and on 21 February 1876 the line was open for business. As Howard Robinson in *A History of the Post Office in New Zealand* remarked:

> The Tasman cable was particularly valuable because of the quick communication with Britain and other parts of the Empire.
> The transmission of messages in a matter of minutes over 12,000 miles [19,000 km] separating Britain from the antipodes was far different from the time, not more than two decades earlier, when six to eight months were required for letters to traverse the same route.[23]

New Zealanders also significantly contributed to the technical development of the telegraph, a projection of New Zealand expertise upon the world that has been rarely noticed in their

How the *New York Times* reported on Donald Murray's pioneering telegraph work. *New York Times*, 25 January 1914, p. 48

own country. The most innovative was a former journalist, Donald Murray, who while working in Sydney developed what was said to be an idea of the first Sydney manager of the New Zealand Press Association, Alick Fraser. Murray's system, devised in Sydney and refined by him in London and New York, employed a keyboard perforator which allowed an operator to prepare ('punch', in tele-communications language) a paper tape, which was then fed into a tape transmitter. At the receiving end of the line, a printing mechanism 'read' the tape transmission and printed it on paper. This became the basis for teletype and teleprinter machines. The rights to Murray's system were bought in Britain, France and the United States, though there is no mention of him in Wilson's history of the industry in New Zealand.[24]

Another telegraphic innovator was John Gell, who for a time was an electrical engineer at Wakapuaka, the trans-Tasman cable terminal. He developed an automatic perforator, which could transmit at between 50 and 72 words a minute compared with about 20 for the manual system that had been developed in England. As the *Observer* remarked: 'With John Gell and Donald Murray . . . both in the field as telegraphic instrument inventors, New Zealand bulks somewhat large before the electrical world just now.'[25] Gell's system was taken up by the Australian and New Zealand governments.[26] The scientific and architectural journal of the early twentieth century, *Progress*, remarked that a New Zealander visited Gell in London and reported him to be 'on the high road to success', his manufacturing plant employing 20 people.[27] While neither Murray nor Gell gained the widespread overseas publicity that other New Zealanders did on fields of battle or sports, or through publishing houses, their largely unsung achievements also contributed to a New Zealand sense of identity.

## A time for all

The *West Coast Times*, which was transformed from a weekly to a daily newspaper in Hokitika in 1866 as a direct beneficiary of the rapid increase in population because of the discovery of gold on the Coast, raised another issue accentuated by the advent of the telegraph. In an editorial, it complained about secrecy of communication between the Coast and 'the Eastland civilization' and worried about telegraph charges.[28] In addition, it raised the question of time – a factor which, when resolved, also had the effect of solidifying and unifying identity in New Zealand:

> There is only one other of the present arrangements to which we deem it necessary to make reference. The [telegraph] office closes at five o'clock – that is, at some hour which the presiding official chooses to "make" five – for there is no time in Hokitika. Not only closes against the further reception of messages to be transmitted, but as it appears against the receipt for delivery of messages on their way from other destinations . . . the idea of a telegraph office, the

The town that had no time: Hokitika in the 1870s. Pa7-51-05-1, ATL

bureau of a department charged with the special mission of annihilating time and space, going to sleep from five o'clock in the afternoon
to lazy hours the next morning is on the face of it exquisitely absurd.[29]

Concerns had already been expressed in the 'Eastland civilization'
two years before. In an editorial, the *Press* in Christchurch said it
had received many complaints about the lack of a common time
between the city and its port, Lyttelton.

> Some time ago this was of no very great consequence, but now that
> we have got on so far as to carry on our communication by means of
> railway and telegraph, we really ought no longer to put up with the
> inconvenience of having a different time between two towns sepa-
> rated by so short a distance and brought into such close connection.[30]

Christchurch had 'a good Government clock' which could be heard
throughout the town, and it regulated time up to the foot of the
Port Hills, the paper noted. But time in Lyttelton was regulated

by ships with the result that it varied considerably from day to day – 'one week Christchurch may be a quarter of an hour faster than Lyttelton, and next week Lyttelton may have gained as much as Christchurch'.[31] A New Zealand geographer, Eric Pawson, noted that an appreciation of the time differences between towns could be gauged by the reporting of earthquakes, events which excited interest due to their unfamiliarity. One of the most significant earthquakes in Wellington, in 1855, was reported by newspapers to have occurred ten minutes later in Nelson and New Plymouth than it was in Wellington. Similarly, an earthquake centred on the southern North Island in 1863 was recorded by newspapers to have occurred at four different times in four different towns.[32]

New Zealand's adoption of a uniform time, New Zealand Mean Time, in 1868 was for pragmatic reasons, but it also had a centralising effect that hastened a national sense of identity. Identification with the new-found land was one of the foundations of nationalism, a sense of belonging; another was time – time in the basic sense of knowing and understanding what time of day it was as well as time in relationship between one place and another. New Zealand was one of the first countries in the world – some say *the* first – to standardise time on a national basis, fixed by longitude in relation to what later came to be recognised as the prime meridian, Greenwich.[33] In so doing it put national advantages ahead of parochial considerations and enhanced the country's sense of itself as separate and distinct from the other Australasian colonies. As the Wellington *Evening Post* editorial tellingly remarked, the dawning of one time for the whole colony was one which marked its progress 'and the extension of the many settlements towards what they will one day become – one harmonious and great country'.[34]

The catalyst for the need to determine a common time was the rapid expansion of telegraph links and the more gradual expansion of railway connections. If it was confusing and inconvenient for telegraph offices to observe differing opening and closing times, then for railways it was not just a matter of convenience but also one of safety.[35] As the *Press* also complained of the confused time difference between Christchurch and Lyttelton: 'It is impossible for the people of Lyttelton to calculate when precisely to catch the railway trains, and in telegraphing from either end about the closing hours of business, the unlucky operator is never certain that he will find the office at the other end open.'[36]

New Zealand towns previously observed times set locally according to their longitudes.[37] In an era when pocket watches were a status symbol and public clocks a rarity, time was signalled to townspeople and visiting sailors by means of a time gun (the firing of a cannon at a set time, usually noon) or the dropping of a time ball (a ball fixed to a mast that dropped at a predetermined time). Some places observed two different times, one set locally and the other set centrally for government offices. The latter was set according to Wellington Mean Time, which did not find favour with those who saw no good reason why Wellington should decide such things.[38] The 'intimation' that Wellington time would be imposed on Dunedin was 'a fresh instance of the tyrannical caprice which actuates our rulers at Wellington', the *Otago Daily Times* protested.[39] It was said to cause great inconvenience in Invercargill, whose longitude was six degrees west of Wellington's, and in Dunedin a Supreme Court judge, the aforementioned Sir Henry Chapman, arrived for a sitting at Wellington time when the court had been ready at Otago time 34 minutes before.[40] But it was not the fault of the learned judge, who remarked that a clerk had altered the clock without authority.[41] According to the *Evening Post*, government officials were under orders to 'regulate their labors according to Wellington time' but the court in Otago chose otherwise and continued 'under the old system'.

It was to overcome such inconsistencies and confusion that a Dunedin member of Parliament, William Reynolds, proposed in the House of Representatives that Christchurch Mean Time – Christchurch because it was considered to be longitudinally more central – be observed throughout the country.[42] Among the opponents was another Otago member, James Macandrew (who was also the Otago provincial government superintendent), who said he saw no need for a standard time because New Zealand was not intersected by railway lines as Britain was.[43] Reynolds' proposal was successful and the government turned to its pre-eminent scientist, James Hector, for an opinion on the appropriate longitude on which to determine New Zealand time.[44] 'This resolution', Hector remarked, 'had so many advantages that it was needless to discuss them; the only question to be decided was, what time should be used.'[45] His recommendation of a meridian of 172 degrees 30 minutes east (because it was close to the average for the whole colony and because it set the time at a neat 11 hours and 30 minutes ahead of Greenwich) was accepted by Parliament and gazetted on 31 October 1868.[46] New Zealand Mean Time – 9 minutes 11.5 seconds in advance of the discarded Wellington Mean Time – came into effect on 2 November 1868.[47]

New Zealand was fifteen years ahead of any other country in setting a standard time, according to Thomas King, of the Colonial Observatory, who noted that Hector had been a pioneer in the field through earlier work in Canada, where he suggested the first methods for fixing time zones for the benefit of the Canadian Pacific Railway.[48] King related how Hector, who had been on Captain John Palliser's four-year exploration in western Canada, advised its government of the need to modify existing methods of time reckoning.[49] He suggested time be fixed by hourly meridians across the American continent, the method later adopted by the railway and by the Canadian government. 'I do not know if Sir James Hector is disposed to claim that his prediction may have been the germ from which the movement in North America originated', commented King, 'but whether the hint was fruitful or not it would appear as if in point of fact he was the first in the field.'[50]

Scottish-born Hector was doctor, naturalist, geologist and principal cartographer on the expedition and has been described as ranking with Mungo Park and David Livingstone as Scottish

The Government's pre-
eminent scientist of the
nineteenth century, James
Hector. *Proceedings of the Royal
Society of New Zealand*, vol. 54, 1923

medical doctors who made a wider mark.[51] During the expedition, he discovered five passes through the Rocky Mountains, one of which later became the route for the Canadian Pacific Railway. As a result of his work with Palliser, Hector was offered a job in 1861 as geologist to the Otago Provincial Council and four years later moved to Wellington to become director of the Geological Survey of New Zealand and of the Colonial Museum, two of many government posts he held for the next 30 years.[52] Hector appears to have written little about his remarkably prescient recommendation to the Canadian government eight years before of splitting that country into time zones. In an exercise book containing notes about the 1868 adoption of mean time in New Zealand, he merely recorded on the second page: 'Note: No reference in these pages to zonal time system as recommended to the Canadian Government in 1860.'[53]

When the new time came into effect late in 1868, various newspapers published comparisons between New Zealand Mean Time and what they called 'true' time.[54] The *Evening Post* in Wellington pointed out how to convert mean time to 'true' time but hoped the latter would fall generally into disuse.[55] Among the examples given were:

| | |
|---|---|
| Auckland | add 9 minutes 16.7 seconds |
| Napier | add 17 minutes 31.7 seconds |
| Taranaki | add 6 minutes 13.9 seconds |
| Wellington | add 9 minutes 11.5 seconds |
| Nelson | add 3 minutes 7.2 seconds |
| Picton | add 7 minutes 11 seconds |
| Lyttelton | add 57.1 seconds |
| Westport | subtract 3 minutes |
| Port Chalmers | subtract 6 minutes 43.3 seconds |
| Bluff | subtract 12 minutes 35 seconds |

The *Otago Witness* was perhaps less informative for its readers, remarking: 'As many of our readers may doubtless wonder what New Zealand mean time . . . means, we may inform them that it is the time corresponding to the longitude of 170 30 East, being exactly eleven hours and a half in advance of Greenwich time.'[56] A writer of a letter to the editor of the *Evening Post*, identified only as A. Stock, was more succinct: 'The Time Ball will drop on Monday at 12 o'clock New Zealand mean time. This time is 9min 17sec slower than Wellington mean time. All the clocks and watches should be put back 9½ min on Monday morning.'[57] Speaking to the Wellington Philosophical Society in 1903, King reflected on the change:

It may be said that the idea is a very obvious one, and that any country might have arranged to follow it in deciding upon the basis

Colonial Secretary's Office,
Wellington, 30th October, 1868.

IN accordance with a Resolution of the House of Representatives to the effect that New Zealand Mean Time be adopted throughout the Colony, it is hereby notified for public information, that the time corresponding to the longitude of 172° 30' East from Greenwich—which is exactly 11½ hours in advance of Greenwich time—has been adopted as the Mean Time for the Colony ; and that from and after the second day of November, the Public Offices of the General Government will be opened and closed in accordance therewith.

E. W. STAFFORD.

The *Gazette* notice proclaiming one time for all. *New Zealand Gazette*, 31 October 1868, p. 507

of a time system. This is perfectly true; it is obvious enough – after it has been adopted; but the fact remains that no other country did take it up for something like fifteen years after it had been adopted for New Zealand.[58]

The setting of New Zealand Mean Time was a significant although rarely recognised step forward to a national identity by the young colony. Wilson, in his history of telecommunications in New Zealand, believed town and country users of the embryonic telegraph service benefited from the 'often overlooked change'.[59] While Guy Scholefield included Reynolds in the *Dictionary of New Zealand Biography* in 1940, no mention was made of his role in standardising New Zealand time; the later multi-volume *Dictionary of New Zealand Biography* does not include him at all.[60] The *Otago Witness*, of which Reynolds was briefly editor and for a time on the board of its publisher, the Otago Daily Times and Witness Newspaper Company, said on his death that he was one of the most prominent pioneer settlers of Otago and had a 'not inconsiderable share in making the political history of the colony', but again no mention was made of his role in standardising time.[61]

While New Zealand had set a uniform time, the other Australasian colonies had not. In a study of time in Australia,

Graeme Davison called timekeeping until 1895 'a haphazard affair'.[62] Sydney, for example, was 25 minutes ahead of Melbourne; within Victoria, times differed from town to town; three different railway systems operated in Queensland and three different times were kept; in South Australia, Port Pirie and Port Augusta were a minute apart despite both towns being in the same geographical region, the northern Spencer Gulf. New Zealand continued to take part in conferences at which the Australian colonies debated standardising their time. An intercolonial postal conference in Sydney in 1891 supported the 'desirableness of adopting one uniform standard time throughout'; and a year later a conference of surveyors recommended one time zone based on the 150th meridian for New South Wales, Tasmania, Victoria and Queensland, the 135th meridian for South Australia, and the 120th for Western Australia. 'The adoption of such a standard would not only facilitate the internal business of each province, but would be a great convenience in connection with railway and telegraphic communication between the colonies', the conference report noted.[63]

The debate continued at a postal and telegraph conference in Brisbane in 1893, and the leader of the New Zealand delegation, Postmaster-General Joseph Ward, said he had long been impressed with the need for the Australian colonies to reach some agreement on time:

> The practical result of it is that when a man arrives in Melbourne and starts for Sydney, Adelaide or Brisbane, his watch becomes almost useless to him, and he has to inquire at the different stations as he goes along to know how much he has to put his watch backwards or forwards, as the case may be. In New Zealand at one time we laboured under a similar disability in the matter of recording the time. We had no less than four times in different parts of the colony. We found that system inconvenient and unsuitable and we made up our minds to change it. We have now adopted one mean time and it has worked admirably.[64]

The Australian colonies subsequently passed the Standard of Time Bill and local times were replaced by standard time zones across the continent from 1 February 1895.[65] The United States followed with the adoption of railway-imposed time zones in 1899 which were eventually given full legal effect in 1918.[66]

The impetus for increased attention to timekeeping through the eighteenth and nineteenth centuries came through burgeoning trade and the resultant beginnings of what is now known as globalisation. The industrial revolution, as well as what Dutch historian Jan de Vries coined the 'industrious revolution', ordered people's lives by fixing times rather than by simply obeying natural dictates such as the movement of the sun, the phases of the moon and the changing of the seasons. This change was noted by C. A. Bayly as a 'significant bodily discipline' alongside an increased uniformity in clothing, citing the work of Hans-Joachim Voth who demonstrated 'how the whole society [of England] was pervaded by a new sense of time discipline between 1750 and 1830'.[67] Villages and communities operated on their own times, as later in New Zealand and elsewhere, but more precision in timekeeping came to be required as labour became more specialised.

In New Zealand, a need for uniformity was also 'reinforced by the technical imperatives of coordinating people and machines within increasingly specialised divisions of labour', as Eric Pawson wrote.[68] Time became more of the essence as the telegraph and railways brought about increased contact both within national borders and externally. During the mid-nineteenth century after the introduction of New Zealand Mean Time, the 'village and globe' pattern of settler New Zealand, as Rollo Arnold put it, gave the country an odd, 'facing both ways, traditional/modern stance'.[69] This Janus-like attitude was made manifest, in Arnold's view, by New Zealand society on the one hand adhering to the methods of 'traditional societies' and on the other being governed by carefully measured time. The time-ordered change to society, and with it changes in spatial perceptions, brought about what David Harvey called 'contradictory reactions'.[70] While he was writing in the late twentieth century, his views would nevertheless have been as valid for the nineteenth century, or perhaps even more valid, when the changes he recounted were unfolding:

> The more global interrelations become, the more internationalized our dinner ingredients and our money flows, and the more spatial barriers disintegrate, so more rather than less of the world's population clings to place and neighborhood or to nation, religion, ethnic grouping or religious belief as specific marks of identity. Such a quest for visible and tangible marks of identity is readily understandable in the midst of fierce time-space compression.[71]

In a nineteenth-century New Zealand context, two different types of identity were expressed: first, by such views as those of public commentators in Otago who wanted to continue with their ways of doing things rather than to obey the dictates of Wellington; second, by the view of the *Evening Post* (and echoed later by others) that a common time for all was a step toward 'a great and harmonious country'. One may be regarded as a parochial view, itself a lower layer of allegiance than the other, a sense of national identity. This was, to paraphrase John Cawte Beaglehole's words, a 'community of mixed feelings' running into a national channel.[72]

## By rail and a sea change

One of the catalysts for the introduction of a standard time was the railways, which had an impact on nineteenth-century New Zealand that is difficult to overstate. The iron horse, as its most active political proponent, Julius Vogel, called it, brought change in two broad ways.[73] It opened up opportunities for people to see beyond their own regions, to travel distances over land which they previously could not contemplate. And it shaped modern New Zealand. As a

Rail brought the provinces and their people together. An artist's view of the
first rail bridge across the Waitaki River that separates Canterbury from Otago.
*Illustrated London News*, 26 October 1872

chronicler of New Zealand's rail history, Neill Atkinson, remarked,
'first and foremost rail was an engine of colonisation'.[74] The railways
opened up regions where settlers had not reached, especially in the
North Island, and its mere presence helped develop agriculture, for-
estry, mining and other industries, not to mention the rail industry
itself. For the rest of the nineteenth century and for at least half of
the twentieth, trains were the traveller's choice in New Zealand and
they were the tie that bound New Zealanders.

The first steam train operated between Christchurch and
Ferrymead in 1863 and was extended to Lyttelton with the opening
of the tunnel four years later. By that time, provincial governments
were building lines as quickly as they could find the cash to pay
for the land on which they were laid, but in 1870 the energetic
Julius Vogel embarked on his ambitious public works plan that was
dependent on heavy overseas borrowing. Although Vogel had his
critics, he largely got his own way, and in the words of William
Pember Reeves became 'one of the short list of statesmen whose

work has left a permanent mark on the Dominion and one of whom it may be said that almost all that he did or tried to do was wise'.[75]

By 1873, the first line operated in Auckland, although its arrival had been for so long talked about that its debut was almost overlooked. As the *Evening Star* noted: 'This morning one of the most important events in the history of the province took place with so little attendant display or ceremony that probably few are at this moment aware that the event has taken place at all.'[76] The line, built by private contractors until taken over by the government, was from the centre of the city to Onehunga. The first train rolled out at 8 a.m. and reached Newmarket fifteen minutes later and Onehunga at 8.45. 'This is not very fast', the *Star* reporter thought, 'but it is perhaps as well to begin slow and get faster than to begin fast and come to grief.'

There was a great deal more enthusiasm in the South Island five years later when the line from Amberley, just north of Christchurch, to Invercargill was completed (aside from a brief section near Clinton in South Otago). The ceremonial first train from Christchurch to Dunedin had twelve carriages carrying about

The railways allowed people to see how others lived. Ngatira station in the western Bay of Plenty. *New Zealand Graphic*, 9 December 1893

300 passengers, including the Governor, the Marquis of Normanby. About 12,000 people crowded around the station in Dunedin to see the arrival.

> There appeared to be but one opinion regarding the vast importance of the occasion and from embellished addresses officially presented, to the huzzas of labouring men, and the fantastic expressions of pleasure with which the Maoris hailed the passing train, every possible means appeared to be used to demonstrate the general opinion that the great fact of completed railway communication was of absorbing interest.[77]

Throughout the 1870s, the central government's Public Works Department laid hundreds of miles of track in both islands, linking Auckland with Hamilton in 1877 and Wellington with both Taranaki and Hawke's Bay. Private railways continued and were either expanded or taken over by the government which had standardised all lines at the 1067 mm narrow gauge. The railway, Atkinson wrote, was a timely invention: 'Together with the electric telegraph and the steamship, it facilitated the eradication of space by time and radically altered the way people understood their world.'[78]

It was during this period of New Zealand's development, when metal strips throughout the land were drawing New Zealanders closer together, that James Mills in Dunedin launched the Union Steam Ship Company, a hugely successful commercial venture as it turned out, and one that was also of enduring significance in the establishment of a New Zealand identity. It also signalled the beginning of what business historian Ian Hunter has called the 'age of enterprise', a period in which entrepreneurial New Zealanders began to make a lasting impression on the economy of the country, sometimes in defiance of economic trends either in New Zealand or elsewhere.[79] The USS Co, which became emblematic of New Zealand and in which New Zealanders showed a proprietorial pride, began with five small vessels of an aggregate gross tonnage of 2126; 50 years later, by which time it had been sold to the British Peninsular and Oriental Steam Navigation Company, or P&O, its fleet comprised 73 vessels with a gross tonnage of 253,988. In 1875, its largest ship was just 721 tons; in 1925, its newest passenger liner and one of the best-equipped in the world, the *Aorangi*, was 17,491 tons.

The company's own account of its first 50 years expressed no doubt about its role in the shaping of New Zealand: 'The comprehensive system of regular services which it established in place of the former haphazard communications was of immense value to the growing community.'[80] Its national importance was also underlined by its first historian, Sydney Waters: 'The story of the . . . company is closely bound up with that of the economic progress of New Zealand over three-quarters of a century.'[81] The company's most recent historian, Gavin McLean, who looked beyond the ships and who sailed in them (and organised them from the shore), was similarly impressed with its significance and reach:

. . . although a minnow in comparison with the US Steel Corporation or the vast American railroad corporations, it was nevertheless a significant shipping line by international standards. Its large fleet, centralised management and world-wide operations made it a modern enterprise in every sense of the word and . . . its influence on the tiny New Zealand economy of the era undoubtedly exceeded that of the Brierley Investments and Fletcher Challenges of today [1990].[82]

For the ordinary New Zealander, who looked at the company through contemporary eyes, it had modern steamships at a time (in its earliest days) when others still swore by sail and its ships could be relied on for regular sailings around the coast or across the Tasman (or later on, further afield). With the vision of its building and purchase programme, there was innovation in its marketing too. A visitor from Britain, H. G. Spearing, who wrote of his travels for the readers of the weekly British magazine the *Graphic*, recorded that New Zealand was 'not a country to be rushed through, though you may see a good deal of it by taking one of those wonderfully cheap tickets issued by the Union Steam Ship Company'.[83] A voyage of about three weeks, a round trip from Melbourne to Sydney and including the main New Zealand ports, cost him about £18; its additional value was that passengers could stop over at any of the ports and catch a later ship at no further cost.[84] To a later generation of New Zealanders, the company was best known for its interisland steamers, which from their beginning late in the nineteenth century were so popular that the Union company persuaded the Railways Department to co-ordinate its train times in Lyttelton and Wellington with ferry sailings and to deposit passengers, freight and mail directly on the wharf.

The company and the name of its founder, Sir James Mills, were almost inseparable from 1875 until 1936, the year he died. He laid down its first building blocks in Dunedin when he was 27 and took over the Harbour Steam Company that was founded by his erstwhile employer and Otago pioneer, Johnny Jones. Glowing phrases flowed when Mills died in London in 1936:

Sir James Mills, K.C.M.G., Chairman.

Sir James Mills, the
man who revolutionised
New Zealand shipping.
From the Union Steam
Ship Company's 50th
anniversary book, 1925

[T]he enterprise . . . he founded, developed, and extended was
always first among shipping companies in the adoption of new ideas
in shipping construction. . . . The whole history of the company
indicates that Sir James must have been born with a larger amount
of personal courage than most men, for he was never perturbed by
the untried experiments if he thought it would add to the efficiency
and smooth running of the shipping line he had built up. . . . While
much of Sir James's success in the shipping world was undoubtedly
due to his farsighted policy and his personal courage, he had a lovable
disposition that endeared him to all who worked with him.[85]

The founding of national organisations was a factor in assum-
ing a national identity. The Union company was only one example,

although a leading one, of commercial enterprises playing their part in drawing New Zealanders together. From the mid-1880s, the Dunedin music store founded by Charles Begg opened branches throughout the country (and bought the rights to 'God Defend New Zealand'); the New Zealand Express Company was formed in Dunedin in 1867 and rapidly expanded; New Zealand's biggest company in the twentieth century, Fletcher Challenge, could trace its roots back to a drapery business called Levin & Co founded in Wellington in 1841; Wright Stephenson was established in 1861 and National Mortgage and Agency three years later. A well-established brand in the twenty-first century, Speight's, began in Dunedin a year after the Union company and became one of the bedrocks of another commercial heavyweight, the Lion Nathan group.

Rapid advances in communications led to an era in which people began to think nationally: the engines of state followed. The Post Office was reorganised nationally in 1879 and took over the Telegraph Department in 1881. By the beginning of the 1880s, New Zealand Railways had a national general manager rather than island-based commissioners, and for the first time a North Island Main Trunk line was talked about (although it took 26 years to complete). None of these nationally embracing events could have taken place without the communications webs which now had New Zealand in their grip.

## Voices over the wires

Another piece of the unifying telecommunications jigsaw was gradually put in place during the last third of the nineteenth century – the telephone. It was developed in the United States in the 1870s. Alexander Graham Bell was granted a patent in 1876 and within eighteen months New Zealanders began experimenting with the scheme that had been described in the February 1877 edition of *Scientific American*.[86] As A. C. Wilson noted, 'competing parochial interests and pride have led to conflicting claims over where exactly the telephone was first publicly demonstrated in New Zealand' and he highlighted one such demonstration in Blenheim that occurred in March 1878.[87] It was evident that telegraph engineers were active over the summer of 1877–78 trying to turn the theory into practice and some succeeded, including an earlier experiment in Blenheim to the one mentioned by Wilson.[88] The general manager of telegraphs, Charles Lemon, oversaw an experiment in which the Governor, the Marquis of Normanby, listened to an operator talking and singing from a room at the other end of the Blenheim telegraph building, a virtual 170 km away.[89] The Governor was serenaded with the operator's rendition of 'Ah! che la morte' from Verdi's *Il Trovatore*. It was not recorded whether he sang in English or Italian but it was perhaps an ironic choice given the song is about pending death while the experiment was about giving life to a new communications tool. By April 1878, what appears to have been the first practical use of the telephone occurred when two Wellington companies had lines installed (by a plumber) between their head offices and workshops.[90]

Politicians grasped the possibilities of the telephone for communication and a further bringing together of New Zealanders. One, Samuel Andrews, who suggested its usefulness for connections between railway stations, nevertheless indicated his reservations about whether everyone was convinced:

> He hoped the Premier would not treat him on this occasion, as Lord Derby treated George Stephenson's expression of opinion that one day a vessel would be driven by steam across the Atlantic, when that statesman offered to eat the boiler of the first steamer that crossed to America.[91]

The Premier, Sir John Hall, showed he was not as incredulous as Derby, affirming: 'The Telegraph Department had more information about this subject than almost any other establishment in the colony.'[92] Two years later, a member of the Legislative Council,

Henry Chamberlin, suggested the use of telephones as a monitoring device rather than for pure communication, arguing that authorities could better check on inmates in prisons and mental institutions. This elicited the response from a cabinet minister, Richard Oliver, that the government would 'avail themselves of the use of the telephone in all circumstances where it might be found desirable'.[93]

By then, the government had taken control of all 'electric communication by telephone', making it illegal for anyone to construct their own lines without permission.[94] As Wilson noted, this was a departure from the existing practice in the United States and the Australian colonies where private companies led telephone development. The Post and Telegraph Department's annual report noted that the government anticipated 'that the telephone would be an important factor in the future extension of the telegraph system of the colony'.[95] It reported that the first telephone exchange opened on 1 October 1880 in Christchurch with 27 subscribers, a second opened in Auckland ten days later with 26 subscribers, and there were 56 subscribers when the third exchange opened in Dunedin on 26 April 1881.[96] By the end of March 1902, there were 26 central and 44 sub-exchanges in New Zealand catering for 9260 subscribers.[97] By 1925, New Zealand, with 8.1 telephones per 100 head of population, was listed fourth in a table of telephones per capita after the United States (13.1), Canada (10.4) and Denmark (8.3).[98] At the time of the opening of the first automatic exchange in Auckland in 1925, an unidentified writer in the *New Zealand Herald* – itself the fourteenth subscriber in Auckland – described the advent of the telephone in the early 1880s both as one of the 'wonders' and one of the 'milestones' of the 'new age'.[99]

As the first 'information highway', the introduction of the telegraph was an integral step in the gradual process of New Zealand's evolution from a disparate collection of settlements, each with their

News from home – or perhaps another colony. The Auckland Post Office in 1864.
*Illustrated London News*, 13 August 1864

own ways of doing things and each with their own governments, into a national entity. The lines of copper wire slung between poles not only enabled communication where hitherto there had been little, or even none, they also had the effect of binding together New Zealanders wherever they were. This unifying effect of the telegraph led to the need for a uniform time throughout the country which enhanced the sense of 'oneness' and commonality among what had been characterised previously as 'six little fishing villages'. Improved transport through the railways and the Union Steam Ship Company further added to the communications web enveloping New Zealand and New Zealanders. The cumulative benefits of the unifying process, the creation of one whole from disparate parts, led to a national outlook supplementing parochial concerns which in itself heightened the sense of national identity. No longer would William Fox be able to talk about six separate colonies.

While the country as a whole benefited from the enhanced communications, especially the telegraph, the change was most pronounced for newspapers (and therefore their readers). These served during the nineteenth century and for the first quarter of the twentieth before the arrival of radio as the prime means of disseminating news within communities, and from one community to another, or from one country to another. Their role was as a mirror, imperfect as it may have been at times, of the society in which they operated and of the country and world beyond. With the advent of the telegraph changing the manner in which they operated, newspapers were a major factor in solidifying the country's evolving sense of national identity in the latter part of the nineteenth century.

TWO

# The Press
# Stirred into New Life

*Surely all of this must have rapidly led to a
predominantly 'New Zealand' consciousness?* [1]

If transport networks represented, in Rollo Arnold's expressive
phrasing, 'strong sinews [which] were knitting the colony together',
the telegraph, the post office and newspapers represented the
'nerves'.[2] No one could doubt, he said, that the country's economic
activities were shaped by the 'speedy exchange of telegraphed information', which surely 'must have rapidly led to a predominantly
"New Zealand" consciousness'.[3] Yet the opinion-shaping role of
newspapers as contributory agents to this process of social change
in nineteenth-century New Zealand has seldom been considered.

While the coming of the telegraph to New Zealand brought
the direct benefits of quicker communication and gave a sense of
drawing communities together, it also had unintended – or, at least,
unforeseen – consequences for newspapers, one of its main users and
beneficiaries. According to Guy Scholefield, the telegraph 'wrought
a radical change in the character and tempo of New Zealand journalism'.[4] The discovery of gold in Otago at about the same time
also contributed to the change which enveloped the New Zealand
press. Newspapers gradually emerged from what Scholefield called

the 'horse and buggy era' of the first 25 years of the colony when they were the vehicles for political views, depended on their own correspondents in other centres for news, and clipped what they could from English or Australian newspapers. The enhanced communications afforded by the telegraph led to the formation of news agencies, and especially what later came to be known as the New Zealand Press Association, and newspapers gradually looked more to their own backyards rather than the previous focus on 'Home' for news. Whether newspapers reflected public opinion or led it, their greater role in the fledgling New Zealand society helped create a feeling of identity with community and country.

The story of New Zealand newspapers in the nineteenth century can be encapsulated into two distinct eras: the first period from 1840 when newspapers were more vehicles for political proselytising and the perpetuation of parochial interests; and the second when they began to be organised on a more commercial basis governed by the imperatives of advertising and circulation. It is with the beginnings of the second period that the role of the newspaper in helping shape a national identity is most relevant. Two examples will serve to illustrate the change in style of the press. A surgeon serving with British forces in New Zealand, Arthur Saunders Thomson – 'an upright and kind-hearted gentleman', according to Scholefield – wrote *The Story of New Zealand* in 1859.[5] He commented on newspapers:

> All the papers were in the habit of using strong language; indeed, savage scurrility supplied the place of wit, and harshness of expression the want of keenness. Many articles were actuated by personal feelings, but, as some excuse for this state of things, it is to be remembered that the press was the only check the people had on their rulers.

Contrast that with the recollection of James (later Sir James) Hutchison, who noted that 'hitting below the belt or bad taste or bad sportsmanship' was anathema to his predecessor as editor of the *Otago Daily Times*, Sir George Fenwick: 'I recall vividly one Saturday morning when he was annoyed at a somewhat personal allusion to Mr Seddon in "Passing Notes" [a column in the newspaper]. "I hate that sort of thing," he exclaimed. It was an education in the ethics of journalism to work directly under him.'[6]

While printing presses and other paraphernalia connected with the trade formed part of the colonial baggage carted to New Zealand in the 1840s, there was not a wholesale transfer across the seas of the British style of newspaper. As Ross Harvey observed, the British–North American rhetoric of the press as a vital defender of public interests and as a mouthpiece for different classes was not matched in New Zealand, aside from the immediate post-1940 period.[7] 'Commercial, local and regional interests, not class struggle or opposition to censorship, seem to be the best way of interpreting the nineteenth-century New Zealand press.'[8]

Arnold also noted that New Zealand did not follow the British example of a national press: 'There was no colonial "London" from which the press could claim to speak with a national voice.'[9] Neither did many other countries follow the British example. The absence of a national press and of even a single national newspaper was another example of New Zealand being different and being developed according to its needs and shape rather than being an English clone on the other side of the world. A national press, and a multiplicity of nationally circulated newspapers, developed in England because it had London as a hub from which railway lines and roads extended. London was not just the geographic centre but also the fount of political and commercial direction and happened to have vastly more people than any other city. Such circumstances were not replicated in New Zealand where no one city, especially not in the nineteenth century, could lay claim to being the centre of the country's being. But even if one could, there were practical arguments against a national newspaper. Distribution would have been the most obvious and immediate problem: there was no

THE

# NEW ZEALAND GAZETTE.

No. I. WEDNESDAY, AUGUST 21, 1839. [PRICE 9D.

NO. I, a Specimen Number of the NEW ZEALAND GAZETTE, a Newspaper for the First and Principal Settlement of the New Zealand Land Company, which it is supposed will be at *Port Nicholson*, in *Cook's Straits*, is now presented to the public. It will be found to contain various information interesting to the Colony now on the eve of departing, to their friends, and to those who may wish to be acquainted with the principles, objects, and local circumstances of the Colony, and the actual proceedings of the Colonists to the present time. The *Second Number* will be published in New Zealand as soon after the arrival of the Colony as it may be found possible to print it, which, it is hoped, will be within a fortnight of the disembarkation of the Colonists; and as ships pass through Cook's Straits almost daily, on their return from Australia to Europe, it is expected that immediate and frequent opportunity will be afforded for transmitting the second and subsequent numbers to England.

Price of this specimen number, 9d.; annual subscription, £1 10s., in advance.

Orders received by Mr D. Ramsay, at the New Zealand Agency Office and Subscription Reading Rooms, 5 Adam street, Adelphi.

---

Under engagement to sail, 15th September, for

SOUTH AUSTRALIA and PORT PHILIP,

Calling at Plymouth, and having three-fourths of her cargo engaged, will be dispatched with the same punctuality as the "Caroline,"

THE FAST-SAILING SHIP, ORISSA, A 1, 450 Tons, James Brown, Commander, lying in the St Katherine's Docks.

Has a poop, lofty between decks, first rate accommodation, and will carry a Surgeon.

For freight or passage apply to Richards, Wood, and Co., 117 Bishopsgate street Within; or to Charles Dod and Co., 17, Mark lane.

---

FIRST SCOTCH COLONY FOR NEW ZEALAND.

THE ship BENGAL MERCHANT, of 503 tons, having been chartered to sail from Greenock in September next, parties intending to join the Colony are requested to do so on or before the 20th August current, in order that the necessary preliminary arrangements may be made for the Voyage.

The selection of Emigrants from the applicants for a free passage will be proceeded with as soon as possible. Each applicant will receive a printed circular, mentioning the day on which he is to attend, before the 20th current, at the Company's Office.

JOHN CRAWFORD, Secretary.
New Zealand Land Company's Office,
24 Queen street, Glasgow, 13th August, 1839.

---

EMIGRANT SHIPS FOR NEW ZEALAND.

THE Directors of the New Zealand Land Company hereby give notice that the Company's Ships will sail for the First and Principal Settlement, as under mentioned:—

The *Oriental*, 506 Tons,
The *Aurora*, 550 Tons,
The *Adelaide*, 640 Tons,

from London, on Tuesday, the 10th of September next.

The *Duke of Roxburgh*, 417 Tons,

from London, on Tuesday, the 10th of September and from Plymouth, on Saturday, the 14th of September next.

The *Bengal Merchant*, 503 Tons,

from London, on Tuesday, the 10th of September, and from the Clyde, on Tuesday, the 17th of September next.

By order of the Directors,
JOHN WARD, Secretary.
New Zealand Land Company's Office,
1 Adam street, Adelphi,
20th August, 1839.

---

SOUTH AUSTRALIAN & NEW ZEALAND EMIGRATION BOARDING HOUSE,
No. 20 Burr street, St Katherine's Docks,

IS most conveniently situated, and neatly furnished for Families; and Gentlemen about to emigrate to either of the above Colonies will find every attention paid to their comfort, combined with very moderate charges, having the advantage of being in the immediate neighbourhood of the London and St Katherine's Docks, a respectable and quiet neighbourhood.

Private sitting rooms, and large warehouses, packing rooms, &c. &c.

P.S.—A letter addressed as above will be punctually attended to.

---

TO INTENDING EMIGRANTS.

A YOUNG MAN of respectability, practically experienced in the breeding, rearing, fattening, and general management of Sheep, Cattle, Horses, and other Live Stock, tenders his services to any gentleman about to proceed to Australia, Van Diemen's Land, or New Zealand, STOCK MAN, HEAD SHEPHERD, or GENERAL SUPERINTENDENT.

Apply, post-paid, to H. B., care of Mr. W. ...nes, bookseller, Hanover-street, Edinburgh.

---

UNION BANK OF AUSTRALIA,
London Office, 38 Old Broad street.

*Directors*—George Fife Angas, Esq.; Robert Brooks, Esq.; James John Cummins, Esq.; Robert Gardner, Esq., Manchester; John Gore, Esq.; Charles Hindley, Esq., M.P.; Benjamin Ephraim Lindo, Esq.; Charles Edward Mangles, Esq.; Christopher Rawson, Esq., Halifax; Thomas Sands, Esq., Liverpool; James Bogle Smith, Esq.; James Ruddell Todd, Esq.

*Trustees*—George Carr Glyn, Esq.; John Gore, Esq.; James John Cummins, Esq.

*Bankers*—Messrs Glyn, Hallifax, Mills, and Co.

*Solicitors*—Messrs Bartlett and Beddome.

*Secretary*—Samuel Jackson, Esq.

COLONIAL ESTABLISHMENTS.

*Colonial Inspector*—John Cunningham Maclaren, Esq.

At Sydney, New South Wales.

*Local Directors*—Thomas Gore, Esq.; Ranulph Dacre, Esq.; Philip Flower, Esq.; S. K. Salting, Esq.

*Manager*—Mr Maclaren.

*Accountant*—Mr James Sea.

At Hobart Town, Van Diemen's Land.

*Local Directors*—Alfred Garrett, Esq.; Joseph G. Jennings, Esq.; Atkin Morrison, Esq.

*Manager*—Cornelius Driscoll, Esq.

*Accountant*—Mr David Kennedy.

At Launceston.

*Local Directors*—Michael Conolly, Esq.; William Fletcher, Esq.; Philip Oakden, Esq.; Thomas Williams, Esq.

*Manager*—Lewis W. Gilles, Esq.

*Accountant*—Mr John Hartridge.

At Campbleton—Sub-branch.

*Agent*—John McLeod, Esq.

At Melbourne, Port Philip.

*Local Directors*—John Gardner, Esq.; — Rucker, Esq.

*Manager*—William Highett, Esq.

BANK IN NEW ZEALAND.

The Directors of the New Zealand Land Company hereby give notice that they have effected an arrangement with the Directors of the Union Bank of Australia; in pursuance of which, a Branch of the Union Bank will be established forthwith on the Company's First and Principal Settlement.

The Directors therefore recommend to the Colonists the Union Bank of Australia, as a means of effecting their pecuniary transactions with convenience and security.

By order of the Directors,
JOHN WARD, Secretary.
New Zealand Land Company's Office,
1 Adam street, Adelphi,
20th August, 1839.

---

NEW ZEALAND BANKING COMPANY.
Capital—£100,000 sterling, in 5,000 shares of £20 each.
Deposit—One pound per share.

ARRANGEMENTS are in progress for the immediate formation of this Bank, and for the commencement of business in THE FIRST OR PRINCIPAL SETTLEMENT about to be founded by the New Zealand Land Company.

One half of the subscribed capital to be called up in quarterly instalments of £2 10s. per share, and the deposit of 1*l.* per share to make part of the first instalment.

A more detailed prospectus will be issued in a short time: in the meantime, applications for shares will be received by Mr David Ramsay, the New Zealand Subscription Rooms, No. 5 Adam street, Adelphi; James Bridges, Esq., W.S., Hanover street, Edinburgh; and John Crawford, 24 Queen street, Glasgow.

15th August, 1839.

---

TENDERS FOR HAMBURGH BEEF AND PORK.

THE Directors of the New Zealand Land Company hereby give notice that they will be ready on Wednesday, 21st day of August inst., at two o'clock in the afternoon precisely, to receive Tenders from persons willing to supply for shipment the under-mentioned articles, viz.:—

260 barrels prime Hamburgh Beef, in bond.
200 barrels prime Hamburgh Pork, in bond.

The terms and particulars of the Contract may be seen, on application to the Secretary, at the Company's Office.

By order of the Board,
JOHN WARD, Secretary.
New Zealand Land Company's Office,
1 Adam street, Adelphi,
14th August, 1839.

---

FREE PASSAGE.

EMIGRATION to NEW ZEALAND.

The Directors of the New Zealand Land Company hereby give notice that they are ready to receive applications for a Free Passage to their FIRST and PRINCIPAL SETTLEMENT, from Mechanics, Gardeners, and Agricultural Labourers, being married, and not exceeding 30 years of age. Strict inquiry will be made as to qualifications and character. The Company's Emigrant Ships will sail from England early in September next.

Further particulars and printed forms of application may be obtained at the Company's Offices.

By order of the Directors,
JOHN WARD, Secretary.
No. 1 Adam street, Adelphi,
June 15, 1839.

---

EPISCOPAL CHURCH IN NEW ZEALAND.

COMMITTEE.

Hon. Francis Baring, M.P.
Sir G. Sinclair, Bart., M.P.
J. Ivatt Briscoe, Esq., M.P.
William Hutt, Esq., M.P.
J. Abel Smith, Esq., M.P.
Rev. Samuel Hinds, D.D.
G. S. Evans, Esq., D.C.L.
Rev. W. Selwyn, M.A.
E. Halswell, Esq., M.A.
W. Swainson, Esq., F.R.S.
H. Moreing, Esq., F.A.S.
Captain Daniell.
Henry St Hill, Esq.
E. B. Hopper, Esq.

BANKERS.

Messrs SMITH, PAYNE, and SMITHS.

At a meeting of intending Colonists and others interested in establishing a branch of the Church of England in New Zealand, held this day at the Offices of the New Zealand Land Company, JOHN IVATT BRISCOE, Esq., M.P. in the Chair, the following Resolutions were passed unanimously.

1. "The Society for the Propagation of the Gospel in Foreign Parts" having consented "to grant a salary of 100*l.* per annum for three years, together with a grant for outfit, to any well-qualified Clergyman who shall be willing to undertake the duty of Chaplain to the Colony which is about proceeding to New Zealand;" Resolved, that this liberality on the part of the Society be met by a corresponding measure on the part of the friends of the Colony and the Emigrants.
2. That 200*l.* per annum be guaranteed to the Clergyman, in addition to the salary allowed by the Society.
3. That a House and Glebe be provided for the Clergyman for the time being.
4. That every exertion be made to complete the subscriptions required for building the Church.
5. That the foregoing Resolutions be published in the newspapers, for the information of those Clergymen of the Church of England who may be disposed to become Candidates for the appointment.

Subscriptions received by members of the Committee, or by the Bankers, Messrs SMITH, PAYNE, and SMITHS.

---

OUTFITTING WAREHOUSE.

JAMES RICHARDSON and SONS, 72 High street, Wapping, near the London Dock Bridge.

Gentlemen proceeding to India, Australia, and New Zealand, are fully equipped with every article requisite for the voyage, on the shortest notice.

---

TO EMIGRANTS.—MEDICINE CHESTS, &c.

T. W. HORDER, of 20 Fenchurch street, begs to call the attention of those parties who may be in want of Medicine Chests to a large assortment at his Establishment, which he begs most respectfully to offer to the Public on such terms as will defy competition.

A great variety of Seidletz Cases, filled, at 4s. 6d. each; Seidletz Powders, 1s. 6d. a box, or two for 2s. 6d.; Carbonate of Soda, 1s. per lb.; Tartaric Acid, 3s. 6d. per lb.

A liberal allowance to Captains and Shippers.

---

TO BUILDERS, WHARFINGERS, AND OTHER CAPITALISTS PROCEEDING TO NEW ZEALAND.

TO BE SOLD or LET on Building Leases a Town and Country Section, being the second in the order of choice, in the first British settlement in New Zealand. For the convenience of Purchasers or Tenants, these sections will be sold or let either wholly or in part; and it is proposed that the right of selection shall be confided to the largest purchaser or holder. Apply to Mr George Morphett, 3 Bream's buildings, Chancery lane.

---

EAMONSON'S INODOROUS CHAMBER CONVENIENCE, at little more than the cost of the common slop-pail, may be had fitted up with a taste suitable to the most elegant bed-rooms; will be found well worthy the inspection of the Nobility and Gentry, at the sole manufacturers, Eamonson and Company, the Exeter Hall Bedding and Cabinet Factory, 393 Strand, between the Adelphi Theatre and Exeter Hall.

To Emigrants and Settlers in particular, during the passage, it will be found invaluable. A liberal allowance made by taking a quantity.

---

PORTABLE COLONIAL COTTAGES.

L. R. PEACOCK, Manufacturer, West street, Walworth, Surrey, on the most improved principles, to pack up in a small compass. May be fitted with doors, windows, &c., complete.

L. R. P. made those occupied in the Colony of Port Adelaide, Port Philip, &c., by Col. Litchfield, I. M. Litchfield, M.D., R. Williams, T. J. Higgins, R. Davis, T. Adams, T. Orr, Esqrs., and others; and is also erecting large houses for the Hon. H. Petre, F. A. Molesworth, G. Duppa, Captain Edward Daniell, E. B. Hopper, G. Hunter, Esq., and others about to proceed to New Zealand, Van Diemen's Land, and the Colonies.

Plans and models may be seen as above. Let-

---

AGENCY.

THE SUBSCRIBERS having formed a Co-partnership, purpose proceeding with the FIRST COLONY on the 25th of AUGUST to NEW ZEALAND, where they will establish themselves.

They take the present opportunity to offer their services to their friends and others as Agents for the Management of Landed Property, the Purchase and Sale of Merchandise, and the Superintendence of Shipping and other Agency Business.

Their Correspondents in London are Messrs Buckle, Bagster, and Buckle.

DANIELL and RIDDIFORD.
London, August 19, 1839.

---

COLONY OF NEW ZEALAND AGENCY.

A GENTLEMAN of active business habits, possessing a practical knowledge of the art of Surveying, and being well acquainted with the value of Land, is about to establish himself in the above Colony, and would be willing to undertake the local management of an Estate for any Gentleman who has invested Capital in the purchase of Land there, and who may require a confidential Agent to superintend the choice of location—to see that the allotment is from time to time disposed of in the most advantageous manner—and generally to preserve the rights and interests of the Proprietor. Unexceptionable references will be given and required.

Address, by letter (post paid), to P. K. R., 38 Queen street, Cheapside.

*** None but Principals need apply.

---

NEW ZEALAND AGENCY.

THE BRITISH AND COLONIAL EXPORT COMPANY, 98 Leadenhall street, in addition to their other Colonial Agencies have been requested by several influential parties proceeding as Settlers to that country, to act as Commercial Agents for the First Colony of New Zealand. The Export Company, whose Manager has been a good deal in New Zealand and the neighbouring British Colonies in Australia, are ready, therefore, to undertake any commission business which intending Emigrants may require previous to sailing, as well as during their absence from Great Britain, especially purchasing and shipping goods adapted to the Colony; whilst to such parties as may favour them with their business, the most unreserved information will be afforded as to the nature of the country they are going to,—the employment and prospects of the Settlers,—together with the best modes of investing capital, &c. &c. &c.

As these valuable Islands eminently possess in their soil and climate, rivers and harbours, flax fisheries, and forests, the materials of a great and powerful people, there is no reason to doubt the immediate success of the First Colony, and, with the usual energies of Englishmen, that New Zealand will become, in process of time, one of the proudest possessions of the British Crown. Applications to be made to

British and Colonial Export Company,
98, Leadenhall street.
T. HORTON JAMES,
Resident Manager.

---

D. RAMSAY, Agent to the New Zealand Land Company for the Sale of Land.

D. Ramsay, one of the earliest advocates in the cause of Emigration, has been induced, at the earnest solicitation of various friends (patrons of the present colony), to open an Office in the immediate neighbourhood of the New Zealand Land Company, where gentlemen who may wish to purchase Lands, and those who think of emigrating, may be supplied with the prospectus, and all the publications of the Company relative to the Colonization of New Zealand.

D. Ramsay is prepared to contract with Gentlemen for the supply of Portable Cottages, to be manufactured on his own premises under the immediate inspection of any Gentleman who may honour him with his patronage; and for the purpose of affording the best practical information, he has engaged a skilful and intelligent mechanic to superintend that department.

D. Ramsay having opened accounts upon an extensive scale with the principal manufacturers of Wolverhampton, Birmingham, Manchester, Sheffield, &c. &c., will undertake to supply every description of goods, furniture, and stores, to any extent requisite for the Colony or Settlement about to be formed in New Zealand, on the lowest possible terms.

A list of articles in general requisition, with the prices affixed, will be furnished in a few days.

No. 5 Adam street, Adelphi,
15th August, 1839.

---

T. AND C. LOCKHART, SEEDSMEN and FLORISTS, 156 Cheapside, London, beg most respectfully to call the attention of the Company and Emigrants to New Zealand to their stock of Agricultural, Garden, and Flower Seeds, catalogues of which may be had gratis on post-paid application.

---

AGRICULTURAL and KITCHEN GARDEN SEEDS in large or small Assortments for Settlers in New Zealand, and all other Colonies, carefully packed by Gordon, Thomson, and Co., Seedsmen, 25 Fenchurch

The first issue of New Zealand's first newspaper, the *New Zealand Gazette*, 21 August 1839. It was published in London; the second issue in Petone.

rail link between Wellington and Auckland until 1908 and roads were such that a newspaper printed in Wellington at midnight, for example, could not possibly have reached Aucklanders at a saleable time the next morning; southbound newspapers would have had to take overnight shipping. New Zealanders seemed happily content with their local newspapers providing news locally, from elsewhere within New Zealand and from overseas. It is instructive in this regard that Australia did not have a national newspaper until 1964 (the *Australian*) and that the first truly national newspaper in the United States, *USA Today*, did not begin until 1982.

The New Zealand newspaper industry in the nineteenth century was vibrant, if volatile. As examples, Scholefield records that in Otago between 1860 and 1879, 44 newspapers were established. On the West Coast between 1865 and 1879, 23 were founded. For all New Zealand, between 1860 and 1879, 181 newspapers commenced publication and 87 ceased.[10] The first daily newspaper was the *Otago Daily Times* in 1861; in 1905 there were 209 newspapers, 61 of them dailies.[11] Newspapers served to promote the interests of the regions they served as well as the political ambitions of their owners. A new settlement in New Zealand without a newspaper was at a disadvantage, as one of the early settlers in New Plymouth, Charles Hursthouse, made clear: 'From the first, Wellington and Nelson have had their papers for the publication of their individual claims . . . but Taranaki has never enjoyed the advantage of a paper.'[12] Hursthouse was also quoted as saying: 'Nothing has tended to retard the progress of the settlement more than the absence of a newspaper.'[13]

## Harbingers of change

Two events in the early 1860s served to change the nature of the New Zealand press and to set it on its path as a key driver of a distinctive national identity. The first was the discovery of gold in

# "OTAGO WITNESS"
## PRICE SIXPENCE

A point-of-sale sign for the *Otago Witness*, the weekly offshoot of the *Otago Daily Times* that was aimed at country readers. Author's collection

Otago in 1861 and the second the introduction of the telegraph the following year. An itinerant Tasmanian, Gabriel Read, worked for a farmer and member of the Otago Provincial Council, John Hardy, in the early winter of 1861 and was encouraged by his employer to search for gold in the Tuapeka district inland from Dunedin. It was Hardy who reported Read's initial find to the council of, in Read's words, 'a beautiful soft slate . . . the gold shining like the stars in Orient on a dark frosty night'.[14] Hardy's grandson, Guy Scholefield, later recorded:

> On the material wealth flowing into the province, the Scots founded their primary and grammar schools, their libraries in goldfield towns, their finely-built capital city and the first university in New Zealand . . . equally fruitful was the dower of leaders, political and intellectual, who were to influence the history of the next half-century.[15]

As Patrick Day noted: 'The discovery of gold was followed by a population increase and business growth that, among other matters, transformed the press.'[16] The discovery of gold in Otago, remarked Ian Hunter, 'witnessed an incredible influx of population and enthusiasm – immigrants and speculators poured into the region by the thousands'.[17] Gold exports from Otago in 1860 were valued at £17,585 but increased by a factor of 90 to £1,591,389 in 1862.[18]

The newspaper industry was one of the beneficiaries of the increased commercial activity and of the vastly increased population: more people meant more potential readers and advertisers.

The first issue of the first daily newspaper in New Zealand, the *Otago Daily Times*, edited and part-owned by one of the New Zealand men of the century, Julius Vogel.

Among the 'dower of leaders' who followed the gold was Julius Vogel, a Londoner of English Jewish and Dutch Christian background who had been both a gold assayer and a journalist on the Victorian goldfields.[19] His impact on the press of the newly rich province was remarkable for its immediacy. He arrived in Dunedin in October 1861 and began work at once for the *Otago Colonist and Dunedin and Invercargill Advertiser*, a weekly better known just as the *Colonist* and owned by the Otago superintendent, James Macandrew.[20] Within a few weeks, as Scholefield put it, he bought a share in the *Colonist*'s rival, the *Otago Witness*, became its editor and persuaded its owner, William Cutten, another of the era's newspapermen-politicians, that a daily would better serve the increasing population.[21] On 15 November, barely a month after Vogel arrived, the *Otago Daily Times* was published for the first time. It was the first daily newspaper in New Zealand.

GOLD-DIGGERS OUT PROSPECTING.

The discovery of gold in Otago in 1861 and later on the West Coast added greatly to the population, the economy, and to the sale of newspapers. *Illustrated London News*, 1863

The coincidence of the introduction of the telegraph with the population influx, at least in Otago, and the increased commercial activity led to fundamental change in the way newspapers operated. Just as the telegraph wires linked distant communities together, so they linked newspapers, creating an information web that embraced the whole of New Zealand. Previously, newspapers relied heavily on 'Home' news, but with the telegraph they could more rapidly print news from other centres in New Zealand. This also came at a time when the population was boosted from immigrants, whether permanent or transitory, and when the native-born population began to be more numerous and influential as well as one for whom 'Home' was a generation removed. Table 2.1 shows the progressive population increase, according to census, for the second half of the nineteenth century, demonstrating the spike caused by the discovery of gold (1861–64 increase), and steadily increasing figures for potential future newspaper readers.

## TABLE 2.1 RISE OF THE NATIVE-BORN

| YEAR | POPULATION | NATIVE-BORN | % OF POPULATION |
|---|---|---|---|
| 1858 | 59,328 | 18,202 | 31.52 |
| 1861 | 96,100 | 27,604 | 28.72 |
| 1864 | 171,016 | 41,235 | 24.11 |
| 1867 | 217,899 | 64,052 | 29.40 |
| 1871 | 255,853 | 93,474 | 36.53 |
| 1874 | 299,008 | 122,635 | 41.01 |
| 1878 | 413,464 | 174,126 | 42.11 |
| 1881 | 489,100 | 223,404 | 45.68 |
| 1886 | 576,453 | 300,190 | 52.08 |
| 1891 | 625,641 | 366,716 | 58.61 |
| 1896 | 702,756 | 441,661 | 62.85 |
| 1901 | 772,277 | 516,016 | 66.83 |

Source: *Population Census 1926, Vol. VII, Native-Born and Foreign-Born* (Wellington: Government Printer, 1929), p. 7.

## TABLE 2.2 LITERACY (%)

| Census | MALES | | | FEMALES | | | BOTH SEXES | | |
|---|---|---|---|---|---|---|---|---|---|
| | Read & write | Read only | Cannot read | Read & write | Read only | Cannot read | Read & write | Read only | Cannot read |
| 1858 | 66.86 | 9.59 | 23.55 | 59.13 | 13.53 | 27.34 | 63.51 | 11.30 | 25.19 |
| 1861 | 73.45 | 7.12 | 19.43 | 61.36 | 11.89 | 26.75 | 68.67 | 9.01 | 22.32 |
| 1864 | 77.27 | 5.64 | 17.09 | 65.27 | 9.65 | 25.08 | 72.07 | 7.17 | 20.13 |
| 1867 | 75.62 | 5.95 | 18.43 | 64.86 | 9.24 | 25.90 | 71.35 | 7.25 | 21.40 |
| 1871 | 73.10 | 6.36 | 20.54 | 63.75 | 9.10 | 27.15 | 69.20 | 7.50 | 23.30 |
| 1874 | 71.40 | 6.96 | 21.64 | 63.94 | 9.56 | 26.50 | 68.15 | 8.09 | 23.76 |
| 1878 | 72.11 | 5.91 | 21.98 | 66.33 | 7.80 | 25.87 | 69.52 | 6.76 | 23.72 |
| 1881 | 73.31 | 5.01 | 21.68 | 68.94 | 6.39 | 24.67 | 71.32 | 5.63 | 23.05 |
| 1886 | 75.40 | 4.36 | 20.24 | 72.41 | 5.31 | 22.28 | 74.01 | 4.80 | 21.19 |
| 1891 | 77.97 | 3.74 | 18.29 | 76.48 | 4.24 | 19.28 | 77.27 | 3.97 | 18.76 |
| 1896 | 81.06 | 2.71 | 16.23 | 80.09 | 3.08 | 16.83 | 80.60 | 2.89 | 16.51 |
| 1901 | 83.08 | 1.81 | 15.11 | 82.44 | 2.10 | 15.46 | 82.78 | 1.95 | 15.27 |
| 1906 | 84.03 | 1.48 | 14.49 | 82.91 | 1.73 | 15.36 | 83.5 | 1.60 | 14.90 |
| 1911 | 84.30 | 0.78 | 14.92 | 83.20 | 0.95 | 15.85 | 83.78 | 0.86 | 15.36 |

Source: *Results of a Census of New Zealand taken on 15th October 1916 – Part V, Education* (Wellington: Malcolm Fraser, Government Statistician, 1920), p. 1.

Increasing literacy rates also helped newspaper circulations, readership and influence. The figures in Table 2.2 show a general trend toward an increased number of people with the ability to both read and write, especially after the introduction of compulsory education in 1877. A future Roman Catholic archbishop and metropolitan of New Zealand for nearly 50 years, Francis Redwood, recalled how he learned to read and write in the 1840s: 'My brother-in-law, Mr Joseph Ward, was a surveyor and a good scholar. For a suitable remuneration he . . . undertook our schooling and right well he did it. He taught us reading, writing and arithmetic admirably. I learnt my alphabet from Mrs Ward, my sister Martha . . . I was a well taught boy.'[22] Until state-funded universal education, not all children would have had such access to learning, or their parents to the money to pay for it.

In the earlier days, the first period of newspaper development, when ships from 'Home' arrived, newspapermen vied with each other to be first on board to claim the newspapers and thus gain an edge on their rivals. The practice was to pore over the English and Australian papers and prepare a summary of the foreign news. An Auckland editor from the 1850s, David Burn, explained his duties in his diary:

Thursday 27th: Penned a letter on Archdeacon Williams affair. Off with it to town and found the "Shamrock" had arrived in port from Honolulu. More disastrous intelligence on the state of the Californian markets . . . kept back my leader [editorial] and made a good summary.

Monday 1st: Yesterdays brig proved to be the "Moa," fifteen days from Sydney, and with English news to the 8th of March. At work all day preparing a Summary.[23]

In its centenary publication, the *New Zealand Herald* remarked that, until the 1870s, 'nearly all news of great events came to the

How the *Auckland Star* in 1970 depicted its early owner and pioneer Henry Brett rowing out to sailing ships to gain an edge by getting the news first. *Auckland Star* Centennial Supplement, 8 January 1970

*Herald* by ship'. The first news the paper received of the assassination of Abraham Lincoln in 1865 was when a reporter boarded a schooner from Australia and interviewed a passenger, who had in his baggage a newspaper report of the assassination in Washington. 'Lincoln was shot dead on April 15 1865; the *Herald* got the news on July 9.'[24] Similarly, the *Evening Star* in Dunedin reflected on the early days of news-gathering when it marked its centenary in 1963. Rather than waiting for ships to berth at Port Chalmers or Dunedin, any harbour transport to hand was used to reach the ship as soon as it was inside the Heads. The reporter's first duty was to pay respects to the captain and the second was to 'claim his share of any newspapers that had come with the ship. When he returned to the office, these would be carefully combed for news.'[25]

The race to be first with the news, no matter how old it was, was fiercely competitive and not always ethical. As the *Evening Post* noted when it marked its 50th anniversary: 'Even in 1865 the hunt for news was associated with ways that are dark and tricks that are vain.'[26] It recorded that in the third issue of the paper, on 10 February 1865, the owners, Blundell and Company, advertised a £10 reward 'for evidence leading to the conviction of someone who, by impersonation, obtained from the intercolonial steamer (the *Albion*) files of papers intended for the *Evening Post*'.

## Newspapers 'join hands'

The advent of the telegraph not only consigned this rudimentary method of reportage to history but transformed coverage from localised into national. Anticipating the potential advantage of the innovation, the co-owner of the *Southland Times* in Invercargill, Gerard George FitzGerald, set up the New Zealand General Telegraphic Agency to 'supply the press throughout New Zealand with the latest English and Australasian intelligence'.[27] He was a younger brother of the owner of the *Press* in Christchurch, James Edward FitzGerald, who had become increasingly concerned that newspapers in Invercargill and Dunedin could obtain news from ships which had not yet arrived at Lyttelton and have their papers available for sale in Christchurch before the *Press* could match them with the news.[28] It was the first news agency in New Zealand and took advantage of Invercargill's proximity to Bluff (or Campbelltown as it then was), which for many shipping lines was the first port of call in New Zealand or the last of departure. Mindful of the cost, the elder FitzGerald drew his city rivals, the *Lyttelton Times* and the *Canterbury Standard*, into the venture. The new agency began operating in May 1865 with the completion of the Dunedin–Christchurch telegraph line and the *Press* noted that it was now assured of being able to print the latest news from overseas at least three days before the southern newspapers could reach Lyttelton.[29]

Julius Vogel, as the editor of the *Otago Daily Times*, began a similar news-sharing agency to that of the brothers FitzGerald but, unlike the *Press*, chose not to share with his direct rivals in Dunedin and sold telegrams only to newspapers further afield.[30] Other ventures in the bulk supplying of news throughout the country followed, including an arrangement introduced by Vogel when he was post-master-general that the government organise the compilation of news reports in Melbourne and that these be made available to all New Zealand newspapers willing to pay. This initiative had a desultory life and ceased altogether when Vogel realised there was more money in the news business for the government if it were the recipient of revenue from press telegrams.[31] The *Otago Daily Times* then reintroduced a service that involved several other newspapers, and a Wellington-based service, known as the Holt and McCarthy agency, catered for the rest. Vogel, by then living in Wellington but owner of the *Southern Cross* in Auckland, was said to have been the impetus behind the new agency. Holt was known to Vogel through being private secretary to James Brogden, who was contracted to build railways in New Zealand; Florence McCarthy was a journalist who was also a director of the Wellington *Independent*, a newspaper that supported Vogel.[32]

Commercial competitiveness between the rival services, with overtones of political motivation, led to friction and, ultimately, to court. The *Otago Daily Times* in 1870 accused the government of violating the confidentiality of telegrams and of giving a digest of news to the pro-government *Independent* in Wellington before it reached its intended recipient, the *Evening Post*. It was a head-on collision on the new information highway between the press and government. The particular telegrams that raised the newspapers' ire were digests of news about the war between France and Prussia and which included the declaration of France as a republic and the imprisonment of Napoleon III in Prussia. A few days later, when it had established to its satisfaction why the telegrams to the *Evening Post* were delayed, the *Otago Daily Times* fulminated: 'We are in a position to prove that the telegraph, as it is now conducted, is subject to Ministerial influences of the most reprehensible character; and that so far from being devoted exclusively to the business of the public, its most important function is that of a political tool.'[33]

The leader was written by the editor, George Burnett Barton, and he left no room for doubt about his feelings: 'It was suppressed in Wellington for eight hours in order to suit the convenience of the *Independent*.'[34] The following week, the *Otago Witness* said in an editorial that the management of the telegraph was 'neither honest nor honourable' and it accused the government of an 'unscrupulous abuse of power'.[35] Adding piquancy to the issue was the role of Vogel, the founding editor of the *Otago Daily Times*, being the minister in charge of the Telegraph Department. He had been replaced as editor by Barton two years before in 1868 because directors of the controlling company were increasingly concerned with Vogel's politicking. Raewyn Dalziel described Vogel as being 'quite unmanageable by any board and his views were alienating advertisers as well as some readers'.[36] An earlier biographer of Vogel's, Randall Burdon, wrote that Vogel expressed 'opinions which the directors and the shareholders blushed to read in the columns of their own newspaper'.[37] Foremost among Vogel's opinions which the board did not share was his advocacy of the abolition of provincial government.

Barton was subsequently sued for criminal libel by the government, which denied any interference in the passage or confidentiality of the telegrams. He faced two charges of publishing 'a false and malicious libel of and concerning the Government of New Zealand' in relation to two separate stories in the *Otago Daily Times*. Although he was committed for trial in the Supreme Court on both, the government decided against proceeding. This was held to have been because of constitutional confusion about the validity of a governor's pardon granted to a sub-editor, Charles Muston, to allow him, without fear of prosecution, to identify Barton as the author.[38] The *Evening Post* commented that the withdrawal was:

> [a] practical admission that to suit political ends Ministers did not hesitate to misuse the Royal prerogative, and that they obtained Mr Barton's committal by illegal and unconstitutional means. It would be difficult to conceive a position more humiliating or contemptible than that which the Ministry now occupies in relation to this remarkable case.[39]

The abandoning of proceedings was generally regarded as a victory for the newspaper and vindicated its stand.[40] The case also had the effect of widening the gap between press and government, especially given the decreasing number of editors or owners who also held government office. 'Government and press began to be not only publicly defined as distinct domains', commented Day, 'but also acceptable limits to their cooperative endeavours began to be acknowledged.'[41] While there is no evidence that public faith in the confidentiality of telegrams may have been shaken by this celebrated case, John Davies Ormond may well have had it in mind when he wrote to Sir Donald McLean the following year: 'There are some things it is better to telegraph about and some better to write about. I have telegraphed you about general matters and will now write about other things.'[42]

Competing groups of newspapers continued to share telegraphed stories until the mid-1870s when George Fenwick and business partner George Reed bought the *Otago Daily Times*. Fenwick persuaded directors to reduce the daily cost of the newspaper to a penny to ward off opposition from the *Morning Herald*, the first penny paper in Dunedin and one started by workers not hired when Fenwick took over the *Times*.[43] Within two years of taking over, Fenwick arranged to lease a special wire from the government for press telegrams and organised a meeting of other newspaper proprietors to form a national agency to use it.[44] This was the birth of the United Press Association which in 1942 became the New Zealand Press Association. Its original intentions, as drafted at a meeting in Dunedin on 17 November 1878 were:

- That the association be formed for the mutual exchange among its members of telegraphic intelligence and for the procuring of cable news from overseas.
- That the association should be of a strictly non-political character.
- That the association should include only one morning and one evening paper in each of the towns and cities of the colony.
- That cable messages, for which satisfactory arrangements had been made with Reuter and the *Sydney Morning Herald*, should be supplied to members at a reduction of 25 per cent on the charge of one penny per word hitherto made.[45]

Its limitation on one morning and one evening paper in each town excluded some of the country's leading papers of the time. For example, the *Lyttelton Times* was an original member of the association which meant that its morning paper rival, the *Press*, was not. Other significant papers left out were the *Auckland Star*, the *Evening Post* in Wellington, and the *Evening Star* in Dunedin. The government initially denied this latter group the same ability as the association to lease a special wire, leading to charges of bribery and corruption which were 'so embarrassing that the Government capitulated and granted the protesting newspapers the lease of a second wire on the same terms as the association'.[46] The competing agencies so clogged the telegraph offices that the Telegraph Department report in 1873 complained:

It must be noticed that the arrangements made by two competing Press Associations for supplying intelligence to newspapers were among the chief producers of public dissatisfaction. On the arrival of a steamer from Australia, the Associations endeavoured to excel each other in supplying their customers English and Australian news; consequently there was a substantial repetition of very long messages to each of the principal stations, and it was precisely when the Department was temporarily overweighted by those long repetitions that the commercial public sent in messages and was most sensitive if the delivery of any of them was at all delayed.[47]

Perhaps ironically, given his previous roles in news agencies, the report to the Governor, Sir James Fergusson, was written by the Commissioner of Telegraphs, Julius Vogel. By late 1879, the association agreed the agency 'war' was costly to both sides and the *Press* was admitted on payment of a joining fee of £250 (because it was seen as the leading paper of the opposition). The others which had been excluded were allowed to join for £50 each and, by October 1880, the United Press Association, comprising 48 papers, was registered.[48]

The effect of the association was to create a news umbrella for the whole of New Zealand in which newspapers, aside from purely local news, published the same news wherever they were. As the telegraph was a scientific link between communities, the association became the information link, each adding to the sense of national identity, drawing disparate communities into a unified whole. The gradual development of the association reduced the reliance by individual newspapers on clipping overseas papers, and by the end of the century New Zealand news made up the bulk of content with foreign stories generally contained upon one page known within newspapers then, as now, as 'the cable page'. The association forged links with the principal domestic agency in New South Wales (now Australian Associated Press) and became a part-owner of the London-based international agency, Reuter, while also subscribing to others such as Associated Press of America (AP) and Agence France-Presse of France (AFP). The association also began assigning either its own reporters or seconding staff from newspapers to overseas events of particular interest to New Zealand, reasoning they could best provide what their readers wanted. This practice began with the Boer War (1899–1902), involved sport for the first time with the New Zealand rugby team's inaugural tour of the United Kingdom and France in 1905–06, and continued into the twenty-first century. The association also maintained an office in Sydney from 1888 and later had correspondents in London, Washington, Singapore and Hong Kong.[49] 'In effect a national institution, the Press Association has profoundly contributed to the character and integrity of New Zealand journalism', wrote Scholefield.[50]

Membership of the association did not prevent newspapers from having their own correspondents outside of their circulation areas: the principal dailies maintained correspondents in Wellington, for example, mainly for parliamentary news-gathering. They also maintained a string of part-time correspondents within their circulation areas. Arnold remarked that the 'Our Own Correspondent' resident in rural areas supplying news to urban newspapers achieved 'influence and prestige': 'Despite the pretence of anonymity, the community knew its correspondent's identity and admired his achievements. It fed him news, and no doubt debated his published views with him. If he had ambitions in public life, his newspaper role would have helped him advance them.'[51]

Three of the UPA/NZPA members – the *Otago Daily Times*, the *Press* and the *New Zealand Herald* – joined together as New Zealand Associated Press to station a correspondent in London from 1892.[52] The first appointee was a former editor of the *Evening Post* and the *New Zealand Times*, Charles Rous-Marten.[53] The *Evening Post* later joined the group, which had its own correspondent in London until 1989. The intention of this group, just as it had been for the Press Association itself, was to provide its newspapers with news tailored for New Zealand and which would not otherwise be provided by either British newspapers or the international agencies. As Rous-Marten's replacement in 1908, Guy Scholefield, explained, the position provided a supplementary service by mail to the cabled news supplied through the Press Association.[54] Beyond their national borders, such correspondents and other expatriate New Zealanders took it upon themselves to act as advocates of New Zealand: 'Since the retirement of [William Pember] Reeves from New Zealand House, there were few qualified to speak on behalf of the Dominion.'[55] Scholefield said he regularly wrote to British newspapers espousing the New Zealand cause, as did New Zealanders who worked for London papers, Evelyn Isitt and Constance Barnicoat. Percy Vaile, an expatriate Auckland lawyer, was another who wrote regular letters to the editor expressing a New Zealand view or extolling what he saw as the country's virtues.[56] These individuals were unofficial publicists for their country, advancing New Zealand another step in its journey from vassal state to separate identity.

The increasing maturity of the colony and its changing interests were reflected in the content of newspapers, which themselves were an evolving entity. Metropolitan newspapers were those defined as being published in Auckland, Wellington, Christchurch and Dunedin (whether daily or weekly), and others were described as provincial newspapers. A good example of the latter was the *Timaru Herald*, which was established as a weekly in 1864 with its main aim to serve the settlers of South Canterbury and to gain devolved government from Canterbury.[57] On one level its purpose was to serve the local interests of its readers, on another its role was to provide news from elsewhere, and on another to provide news from 'Home'. In one issue in 1865, for example, its main editorial went over three of the four columns available on the one page and was the editor's general view of the efficacy or otherwise of the region's parliamentary representatives. Shipping news on the same page reported the safe arrival of the *Blue Jacket* off Falmouth 81 days out of Lyttelton, and what goods for sale had come in the latest ships to arrive in Timaru. As was the practice, news – sometimes with comment – was added to the end of the editorial and spilled onto the following page. The arrival of the English mail at Bluff was reported, but the *Herald* could not explain to its readers why intelligence thus gained was not available to them but was to readers of rival newspapers in Dunedin and Christchurch. A potpourri of news from the *Herald*'s correspondent in Christchurch was accorded a sentence an item: the road to the West Coast was to be pushed forward; there was a favourable response to a Canterbury railway debenture in London; a child was seriously injured by a fall of stone in Lyttelton; a presbytery meeting was held and 1322 acres of land were sold. Such reporting raised more questions than it answered.[58]

Thirty years later, the design of the newspaper had changed from four columns a page to eight and it used a smaller body type. The *Herald*'s look, however, was still akin to that of most other newspapers until well into the twentieth century: classified advertisements on the front page and spreading inside (the Auckland and Dunedin *Evening Stars* occasionally published a column of news on their front pages); items all arranged in single columns with modular layout still a feature of the future (meaning stories continued from the bottom of one column to the top of the next); news stories, often of just one paragraph and occasionally just one sentence, added on to the end of the leading article. The *Herald* in 1895 carried more telegraphed news from around New Zealand and its British news was less extensive. Coverage of a general election in Britain consisted of a list of who was elected rather than any comment; but even so, a report of a school football match in Timaru was almost of the same length and both were vastly outweighed by the three full columns devoted to a public meeting on the frozen meat trade (and essentially, whether farmers were getting enough money for their carcasses).[59] Telegraphed news from Australia was more evident than it had been 30 years earlier (and than it is now) and run at greater length than news from further afield. Items from countries other than Britain and Australia were generally confined to a sentence or two, which may have been all that was sent (given the cost of cabling). Newspapers did not 'sectionalise' their product – that is, politics, trade, sport, racing and general news were all laid side by side according to no apparent selection process (although possibly determined by the time of arrival by telegraph).

The *Evening Post* in Wellington on the same day, fittingly for a metropolitan paper, especially one based in the capital, provided more national news, even though it was still just four pages. The Knights of Labour, as a national organisation, was given lengthy space for its latest urgings that the poll tax on Chinese immigrants be increased. The *Post*'s overseas coverage rested under the general heading of 'cable news' and seemed to be heading for a pattern more familiar in the twentieth century. It was only cable news of greater import – the Boer War four years later or the death of Queen Victoria, as examples – which broke the stylistic mould.

Advertisements in both Timaru and Wellington were almost wholly local, in the sense they related to local companies or individuals urging their services and goods on readers. Advertisements for national companies such as the Union Steam Ship Company carried information related to Wellington only, in the case of the *Post*. 'Display ads' – multi-column advertisements, usually illustrated – for big firms did not begin appearing until around the time of World War I.

## Political alignment of newspapers

While the practice of politicians owning and running newspapers for their own benefit had practically ceased by the late nineteenth century, it did not mean newspapers were politically neutral. They were not, despite some at times lofty claims made for their independence of thought. For instance, the *Evening Post*'s first editor was described as 'dignified, temperate and judicial, and his criticisms . . . inclined to be merciful'.[60] Its first issue claimed it would endeavour, 'faithfully and concisely', to narrate the news of the day, to pursue a liberal course and not overstep the bounds of moderation. Likewise, the first issue of the *Press* in Christchurch promised: 'It is not our intention to support or to attack the Government as a matter of party, but we shall assault and expose abuses wherever we shall find them; not enviously and vindictively, but earnestly and faithfully, as the peculiar and especial duty of the press.'[61]

Even so, newspapers were generally in one or other of two political camps during the late nineteenth and early twentieth century: they were either supporters of the Liberal government or they were not. The *New Zealand Times*, the successor to the *Independent*, was the pro-government paper in Wellington, for example, while the *Evening Post* was opposed (although under editor Edward Thomas Gillon from 1884 until 1896, the *Post*'s 'normal stance was one of opposition to the government of the day, whatever its colour'.)[62] The pattern continued throughout New Zealand in two-paper towns, with one favouring the Liberals and the other, if not favouring the fragmented opposition, then at least not an enthusiastic supporter of Richard Seddon. This political alignment was confined, however, to editorial columns. Scholefield, who worked for the *New Zealand Times*, wrote: 'It was an axiom, understood by all, that the news columns should be strictly non-party and objective. That convention grew out of the cooperative character of the Press Association.'[63] He also noted that the employment policies of newspapers did not reflect their political allegiance: 'In most offices, both upstairs and down, were staff members opposed to the policy of their paper. New Zealand had acquired a reputation for offering haven to journalists from abroad, journalists whose opinions were disapproved by their employers.'[64] Scholefield gave as examples the pioneering Labour activist John Thomas Paul, as editor of the *Otago Witness*; the founder of the first socialist party in Wellington, Robert Hogg, who worked for the *New Zealand Times*; and in what he called 'a classic example', a senior editorial position at the *New Zealand Herald* given to the Australian trade unionist and Utopian, William Lane.[65]

68

Editorials are deemed to be the view of the newspaper; the editorial, or leading article or leader, is historically the platform from which a newspaper expresses its opinion. They are not necessarily written by an editor, although often are. Newspapers employ leader writers who write the editorials, usually after consultation with the editor, but other staff members and occasionally outsiders are also assigned the task from time to time. In Leslie Verry's view, Edward Thomas Gillon was 'the most celebrated, if not necessarily the greatest', editor the *Evening Post* had.[66] For all his time on the paper, Gillon was practically the sole author of editorials: 'None of his associates was encouraged to write a leader; on the rare occasions when Gillon took a holiday he wrote the leaders in advance, each labelled for the day when it was to be published. Often he came to work at 8.30am with the leader for the day already written.'[67]

This was in marked contrast to a later era of the *Evening Post*. It was an open secret, according to the *Otago Daily Times* editor, James Hutchison, that a politician and nephew of a former premier, Arthur Atkinson, 'for a long period' wrote leading articles for the *Post*. 'The subject of them was discussed by telephone between him and the editor of this paper in their respective beds after the morning paper had reached them.'[68] Atkinson was described by Scholefield as 'a brilliant and at times bitter critic of the Seddon administration'.[69]

For all its opposition to Seddon, the *Evening Post* was held to be a politically independent paper, and conservatives felt they needed a morning paper to oppose the *New Zealand Times* and better represent their views.[70] Accordingly, the Wellington Publishing Company was formed by a group of opponents of the Liberals, including the opposition leader, Sir William Russell, to launch a new morning newspaper with an *Evening Post* sub-editor, Charles Earle, as its editor. Apparently the choice of title was between *Morning News* and *New Zealand News*, but when the launch date approached and Sir Joseph Ward announced that New Zealand's constitutional status had been elevated from colony to dominion, the directors

This attractive photo of the *Evening Herald* printing office in Wanganui reflects the period – and includes the newspaper-owning future Liberal premier, John Ballance, third from left. 1/1-000139-G, ATL

opted first of all for *Dominion News* and then, later the same day, the *Dominion*. It has been called an outstanding example of a newspaper established originally with a political motive.[71]

Outstanding it may have been, but many other newspapers were established for political reasons, usually as a vehicle for personal ambition. One 'rag planter', as Scholefield called those who began newspapers, was an Irish immigrant, Joseph Ives, who between 1868 and 1907 founded 26 papers in New Zealand and five in Australia.[72] Several of his papers provided a comfortable living, but his over-riding motivation was a wish to wield political power, according to Ross Harvey.[73] Seddon's predecessor as premier, John Ballance, turned to journalism and newspaper-owning when his jewellery business lacked customers. He founded the *Wanganui Herald* in 1867, just the second daily evening paper (after the *Evening Post*) in New Zealand. For all his political ambition and later influence, Ballance decreed in the first editorial: 'We are bound to no party and are unbiased in our opinions by such influence.'[74]

The extension of the national telegraph network to Auckland in 1872 coincided with the emergence of newspapers founded on business principles, rather than as a political platform.[75] The *New Zealand Herald*, founded in 1863 and the second of that name, was, according to Scholefield, 'a striking example of a newspaper founded as a business rather than as a political organ'.[76] Its main rival emerged as the *Auckland Star*, founded in 1870. Both papers were innovative and trend-setting. The *Herald* was the first to adopt classification of wanted advertisements and led others in New Zealand with its printing equipment.[77] The *Star* was more innovative and imaginative with its news-gathering. It once photographed a report of a speech by Sir George Grey in Thames, attached the photo to a pigeon which then flew it to Auckland, where the photograph was deciphered through a magnifying glass and the text transcribed.[78] Both papers professed to be interested in 'the people' and causes, rather than politics. 'We shall be ever mindful', the *Herald* said, 'that our duty is to the people and not to any man, or set of men.'[79] The *Star*'s editorial each day (until 1941) was surmounted by the following words:

> For the cause that lacks assistance,
> For the wrong that needs resistance,
> For the future in the distance,
> And the good that we can do.[80]

One of the most dominant personalities of the Auckland newspaper press during the consolidating years of the 1890s and until World War I was Thomson Wilson Leys, an English-born son of a Scot who became editor of the *Star* in 1876 and stayed in the chair for 45 years.[81] He had a chance to move out of it when he was offered a seat in the Legislative Council, but declined because 'a journalist should not accept such a restriction on his freedom to criticise'.[82]

The *Star* under Leys was a notable supporter of the Liberal government and his desire for freedom to criticise did not prevent him
from accepting from Seddon a position on the Royal Commission
on Federation in 1901.[83] The irreverent weekly *Observer* seldom
passed up the chance to poke fun at its daily rival, as in this doggerel
that preceded an Auckland deputation to the Premier, Sir Joseph
Ward:

> The *Star* in glory will be there,
> For folk must all agree
> That Seddon was in power because
> Leys said it had to be.
> And comforting it truly is
> That we can surely know
> That Leys has said he'll act as head
> And brain of poor Sir Joe.[84]

Later the same year, it adapted the children's rhyme and called it
'T. W. Leys':

> Twinkle, twinkle little *Star*,
> Kindly tell us what you are;
> Also, tell us what you mean,
> For, 'tis sometimes hard, we ween
> For your readers to make out
> What on earth you talk about.[85]

While political allegiance was an accepted part of the newspaper
landscape in terms of opinion and did not generally impinge on
news, it did have the unintended effect of depriving New Zealand
readers of direct representation when New Zealand troops joined
Australian, British and French forces in the 1915 landings on the
Gallipoli peninsula. This amphibious invasion came to be seen in
New Zealand and Australia as a defining moment in the nationhood

of both countries, but the news of it was provided, in the first instance, by a British reporter.[86] The official New Zealand reporter, through no fault of his own, did not arrive until two months after the landing because of government indecision brought about by trying to appease pro- and anti-government newspapers.

## *A literature of our own*

The changing role and appearance of newspapers in the second half of the nineteenth century brought about the beginnings of a distinctive New Zealand literature. Scholefield, in his capacity as parliamentary librarian, wrote an article about New Zealand literature for a 32-page supplement on New Zealand published by *The Times* in 1927. In it, he quoted an expatriate New Zealand writer, Constance Clyde,[87] as saying: 'A few genuine poets of limited output, some capable historians and interpreters of the Maori race, one or two prose stylists and the promising beginnings of a body of local fiction. What literature has lost, journalism has gained.' Scholefield then added: 'That would be very evident if somebody cared to print from the Press a selection of the very attractive short stories which have appeared for years past.'[88] Unlike in Britain, where book publishing was established for more than a century before newspapers were produced, in New Zealand the newspapers came first. A former national librarian, Jim Traue, has commented: 'If New Zealand's cultural topsoil was deficient in monographs, it was enriched by the newspaper printing press from the very beginnings of European settlement.'[89]

Enrichment within newspapers indeed came early. Among the contributors to the *Press* in Christchurch from its earliest days was Samuel Butler, the celebrated author of the ironic novel *Erewhon*, said to have been based on Butler's property in the headwaters of the Rangitata. Butler spent the years 1860–64 in New Zealand and was a frequent visitor in the *Press* office and a friend of the paper's founder, James FitzGerald.[90] Editor at the time was George Sale, later the founding professor of classics at the University of Otago, but FitzGerald was 'the real controller of the paper'.[91] Although a suggestion that Butler was on the staff of the *Press* could not be confirmed, it was said that: 'It is certain that Butler was very much an intimate of *The Press* set, who delighted in provocative letters and articles, and often manufactured stories and replies that either commenced or sustained a public debate in print.'[92]

The Butler association with the *Press* continued in later years through another accomplished literary figure, Oscar Thorwald Johan Alpers, better known in New Zealand simply as O. T. J. Alpers. He worked for the *Press* and, when a schoolmaster, continued to write editorials for the paper. Alpers reviewed for the paper a later book by Butler, *Erewhon Revisited*, and received from the author a letter of thanks and a complete set of his seventeen volumes which Alpers donated to the Christchurch Public Library.[93] Other papers could not claim such a luminary, but many contributed to a growing distinctive New Zealand literature, one based on observations and lessons in New Zealand rather than imported knowledge from the Australian colonies or Britain. As Professor J. C. Reid noted: 'Quite early in New Zealand writing, there were stirrings of a more independent attitude, a feeling that the country should be able to produce its own distinctive literature, owing comparatively little to British stereotypes and equally distinct from the literature of Australia.'[94]

Wondering how this national distinctiveness could be made plain while New Zealand remained a cultural province of Britain, Reid quoted the Presbyterian minister and social campaigner the Rev. Rutherford Waddell, as writing in an introduction to one of Thomas Bracken's volumes of verse in 1884: 'Before there can be a national literature, there must be a national character.'[95] Politician and jurist Sir Robert Stout wrote in another volume of Bracken's work in 1890: 'We are forgetting we are English, Irish, Scotch, German or Norse, and we are coming to feel we are New Zealanders. As the years

roll on, there will be still greater solidarity, and that seems needed before a national literature can arise.'[96]
It was newspapers which provided the outlet for the embryonic national distinctiveness in literature. While some periodic publications such as the *New Zealand Illustrated Annual* (1880–81), *Zealandia* (1889–90) and the *New Zealand Illustrated Magazine* (1899–1905) were specifically aimed at creative writing, daily and weekly newspapers contributed. Jessie Mackay, described by bibliophile Pat Lawlor as 'the most inspiring and best loved figure' of the first hundred years of New Zealand literature, regularly contributed to newspapers and spent ten years as 'lady editor' of the *Canterbury Times*.[97] A poem of hers about the funeral of Sir John McKenzie, nominated 'our best occasional poem' by Lawlor, includes the following celebrated verses:

The Clan went down with the pipes before
All the way, all the way;
A wider clan than ever he knew
Followed him home that dowie day.[98]

Another noted regular contributor to newspapers was Thomas Bracken, of whom Lawlor wrote:

Everything of colour and fine memory in our early days is linked with his name. He was praised by Prime Ministers, the hero of early journalism, the well tried mate of gold diggers, an able politician, a jovial hotelkeeper, the coiner of the phrase, "God's own country," composer of *Not Understood* and our own National Song, a handsome figure of a man – half a century dead and his fame is stronger than ever.[99]

Bracken not only wrote for the Dunedin papers he part-owned, the *Saturday Advertiser* and the *Evening Herald*, but he also 'did notable and unselfish service for New Zealand literature in throwing his columns open to writers of prose and verse, novelists and essayists'.[100]

When the first anthology of New Zealand poetry was published in 1906, its editors Fred Alexander (a journalist and editor of the *Evening Star* in Dunedin 1920–1946) and Ernest Currie noted that the greatest number of the 41 poets chosen were journalists, either employed full or part time.[101] Politicians were among frequent contributors to newspapers either as poets or essayists. Two of the most notable were Alfred Domett and William Pember Reeves. Domett, briefly premier in 1862–63, was editor of the *Nelson Examiner and New Zealand Chronicle* where among contributors he gathered around him were other political notables David Monro, Francis Dillon Bell, William Fox and Edward Stafford.[102] But Domett's fame endured more as a poet than as a politician. He was best known for his epic 'Ranolf and Amohia', and for his friendship with Robert Browning.[103] In fact, Domett served as the model for Browning's 'Waring':

What's become of Waring
Since he gave us all the slip,
Chose land-travel or seafaring,
Boots and chest, or staff and scrip,
Rather than pace up and down
Any longer London-town?[104]

Reeves' political fame rests on his contribution to the Liberal administration of the early 1890s and his later role as agent-general in London. The son of a part-owner of the *Lyttelton Times* and himself briefly editor, Reeves' greater fame, however, is as a writer. His *Long White Cloud* was described by Alan Mulgan as the most important book of the nineteenth century in teaching New Zealanders their own story and stimulating interest in it.[105] It was Reeves' distinction, Mulgan wrote, to prove that practice of two arts could be combined: 'The breaking in of a new land and the cultivation of letters in the plough's wake.'[106] From a distant London, Reeves wrote of his native land:

God girt her about with the surges
And winds of the masterless deep;
Whose tumult uprouses and urges,
Quick billows to sparkle and leap;
He fill'd from the life of their motion,
Her nostrils with breath of the sea,
And gave her afar in the ocean, ˙
A citadel free! A citadel free![107]

Another significant journalist-politician and man of letters was
Julius Vogel. He was regarded as a prolific journalist when he first
worked in Dunedin in the early 1860s, but according to biographer
Raewyn Dalziel, hankered to compose something more lasting. This
he did when he wrote a dramatisation of a popular and successful
English novel by Mary Elizabeth Braddon, *Lady Audley's Secret*.[108]
The play was staged in Dunedin's Princess Theatre, and at the end,
to much applause, he rose from his private box to acknowledge his
authorship, although it had only been advertised as having been
dramatised by 'a gentleman resident in Dunedin'.[109] (Prolific and
creative Vogel may have been, but his writing was not always legible
– his handwriting was said to have been so bad that compositors at
the *Otago Daily Times* were paid extra to 'set' his leaders.[110]) Vogel
returned permanently to Britain in 1888 and there wrote his novel
*Anno Domini 2000; or, Woman's Destiny*, a prophetic romance about
a New Zealand woman and the 'emperor of United Britain'.[111] It is
set in the year 2000 when women had achieved equality with men,
air travel was common, the Empire had federated and poverty had
been eliminated.

Alexander and Currie predicted there would be a time when New
Zealand would be noted for more than wool, gold, horses and footballers, but 'that time has not yet arrived . . . nevertheless, there are
first fruits ripe already'. They hoped the country would be helped
by 'the labour of such [poets] towards the deep-breasted fulness
of mature nationality'.[112] Domett wrote wholly from the point of

view of a 'naturalised, not born New Zealander', they thought. He wrote for an overseas public. In the 'ardent patriotism' of the poetry of Arthur Adams, however, 'one recognizes a more filial sound which may be expected to permeate the poetry of Maoriland in the future'.[113] Adams was among journalists who left their literary mark on New Zealand newspapers and moved on. He was born in Lawrence in Central Otago and was a reporter on the *Evening Post* under his uncle the editor, Edward Gillon. Scholefield remembered him as being 'unfitted for the rude manners and tedious routine' of daily journalism and that he 'went with the gannets' across the Tasman.[114] In Sydney he wrote a Māori opera, 'Tapu', and with music by another expatriate New Zealander, Alfred Hill, it was success-fully staged throughout Australia in 1904. After journalism took him to the Boxer Uprising in Peking (Beijing) in 1900, Adams published his first novel, *Tussock Land*, and became associated with the *Bulletin* and was editor of the Sydney *Sun*.[115]

Another who Tasman-hopped was David McKee Wright, who contributed prose and verse, especially about country life, to a range of provincial newspapers, including the following:

> For it's chaps of the town and country,
> And it's mates of the swampy green plain,
> Draw your seats to the fire, and here's your desire,
> A song of the country again –
> A rhyme of New Zealand again –
> Of the toilers with muscle and brain.
> There's no one before us, so join in the chorus,
> We're going a-rhyming again![116]

Significantly in terms of identity, the *Otago Witness* ran that verse beneath a generic, weekly heading: 'Rhymes of our own land'. Wright was briefly parliamentary reporter in Wellington for the *New Zealand Mail*. Unusually for writer-poets, he studied divinity at the University of Otago and worked in Oamaru, Wellington and

Nelson as a cleric, before leaving for Sydney in 1910 where he made a mark with the *Bulletin*, often writing as 'Maori Mac'.[117]

Another journalist and editor, John Kelly, like Adams, tried his hand at poetry and opera. Kelly worked for several New Zealand papers, including for a time as editor and part-owner of the weekly *New Zealand Observer* and also as editor of the *New Zealand Times*. After a trip to the South Pacific islands, he wrote a poem, 'Tahiti', and the libretto of a comic opera, 'Pomare'. His verse was published in a collection, *Heather and Fern*, in 1902.[118]

A writer from a slightly later period who was nurtured on New Zealand newspapers before World War I and found fame, if not fortune, overseas was Hector Bolitho, noted as much for his novels as for his royal biographies. His first steps in newspaper writing were with the *New Zealand Herald* and *Auckland Star*. In what may have been an early case of the tall poppy syndrome, Bolitho's work received complimentary reviews in Britain but was criticised, 'descending almost to downright abuse', at home.[119]

Journalism was not entirely a male world. Stella Henderson (later Allan) and Forrestina ('Bessie') Ross required the permission of a committee in 1898 to become the first women to join the parliamentary press gallery and both had lengthy literary careers. Henderson later moved to Melbourne with her husband, Edwin Allan, and her work for the *Argus* was regarded as unique in an Australian daily newspaper for the time.[120] She was later one of the Australian delegates to the League of Nations in Geneva in 1924.[121] Ross was among the first women to have climbed in the Southern Alps and wrote extensively beyond her parliamentary duties.[122] She was married to climber and journalist Malcolm Ross and there were suggestions he owed something of his ability to his wife. When he was appointed New Zealand's official war correspondent in 1915, *New Zealand Truth* referred to 'the sort of copy Malcolm Ross generally grinds out – without the assistance of Mrs Malcolm Ross'.[123]

In an article exploring if there was such a thing as 'a *Bulletin* school' in New Zealand, Jock Phillips concluded there was not, but observed that New Zealand and New Zealanders shared in the Australian cultural movement of the 1890s.[124] He listed many of the New Zealand writers who contributed to the Australian 'bushman's bible', noted that it was widely read in New Zealand and that two of its best-known contributors, 'Banjo' Paterson and Henry Lawson, wrote pieces with New Zealand themes and settings. Reid recorded that between 1890 and 1900 the *Bulletin* published 400 poems and 150 short stories by New Zealanders.[125]

'*Bulletin* school' or not, New Zealand had its own publications that could rival the Australian weekly for content and popularity. One was the *Observer*, first published in 1888, which touted itself in its masthead as 'smart but not vulgar; fearless but not offensive; independent but not neutral, unsectarian but not irreligious'.[126] Being a weekly, it served a different purpose to daily newspapers or the bi- or tri-weekly publications which catered for specific communities and carried the daily news. It commented on the news rather than reported it. Like the *Bulletin*, it had its irreverent side and regularly published full-page caricatures and cartoons by its part-owner, William Blomfield. It regularly published contributions from poets but short stories were less frequent.

Perhaps even more influential and more of a rival to the *Bulletin* because it eventually claimed to be an 'Australasian' magazine was the monthly *Triad*, founded in Dunedin in 1893 by Melbourne-born Charles Nalder Baeyertz,[127] who proclaimed in the sixteen-page first edition: 'This magazine, in common with all other magazines, is made to sell . . . At the same time we make bold to hope that it may be the means of disseminating a small modicum of musical, artistic and scientific information throughout New Zealand.'[128]

Monte Holcroft wrote that within ten years the *Triad* had become 'an institution' and ran to 52 pages on art paper, its principal contributors being Baeyertz himself – 'outspoken and knowledgeable' – and his associate editor, Frank Morton,[129] 'who shocked, stimulated and entertained' New Zealanders. Baeyertz's ambition and the *Triad*'s circulation grew to encompass Australia where it

The masthead for the *Triad* – 'the National Magazine of Australia and New Zealand', as it touted itself.

competed with the *Bulletin*: the latter was read in shepherds' huts in the South Island, according to Holcroft, and the former was read and quoted in Sydneyside taverns.[130] Like the *Bulletin*, the *Triad* encouraged native-born writers but it 'had no strong flavour of life in the Antipodes' compared with the *Bulletin*, which was 'unmistakably and aggressively Australian'.[131] 'The Death of a Rose' by an unidentified Katherine Mansfield was published in the *Triad* in 1908 and Robin Hyde (Iris Wilkinson) wrote that it published 'stuff you remembered'. She called Baeyertz 'rather excitingly rude to almost everyone'. But it was the *Bulletin* that first paid Hyde for a contribution – a guinea for a poem.[132] The *Triad*, after eventually touting itself on its front cover as 'the National Magazine of Australia & New Zealand', closed down in 1929.[133] As Hyde explained: '[T]he light that was the *Triad* flickered and failed when Frank Morton died [1923], and Bayertz was left abandoned and helpless.'[134]

The place of the weekly newspaper as a platform for a distinctive New Zealand literature should not be underestimated either. Many of these were weekly offshoots of daily publications – the *Otago Witness* (*Otago Daily Times*), the *Weekly Press* (the *Press*), the *Canterbury Times* (*Lyttelton Times*), *Weekly News* (*New Zealand Herald*) – and had their genesis when daily distribution to country areas was either not possible or not reliable. The 'large weekly journals', W. H. Clark told a teachers' conference in 1899, were the 'dusty tombs' of much verse:

The grandeur of newspapers. The *Lyttelton Times* building in Cathedral Square in Christchurch. As the building frontage indicates, it also published the *Canterbury Times* and the *Star*. S11-332c, Hocken Collections Uare Taoka o Hākena, University of Otago

How familiar to us all are the weighty piles of printed sheets . . . which reach us every week and how unlike are they to anything journalistic known in the old country! The big weekly is, however, the necessary product of our social condition and the *Witness*, the *Australasian* and the host of other similar publications admirably fill the place in our social life for which they are designed. In the "Back Blocks" the visit to the neighbouring township is performed but weekly, and the sustenance of the ensuing week both physical and mental is at the weekly visit carefully collected and in the big weekly the back-blocker finds his supply of current news and also his sole supply of food for thought.[135]

## *The value of advertising*

Newspapers were not just about who owned them, ran them and wrote for them, however gifted or influential the individuals may have been. Advertisements have been a vital component of newspapers in New Zealand since they began, though the newspapers themselves have been remarkably reticent in reminiscing about their chief source of revenue. Commemorative editions noted the great news events and how the news was obtained; they contained recollections by long-term employees and recounted other significant passages in the papers' histories, but advertising was notable for its almost total absence.[136] Yet advertising and circulation are the twin revenue-generating departments of a newspaper; editorial departments are not, albeit what they produce is intended to aid circulation. The *Evening Post* in its first edition unashamedly courted advertising (in the verbose style of the day) thus:

> Our cotemporary mothers on the world-renowned Mrs Partington
> the idea that "Sweet are the uses of advertisements;" and we trust
> it will be generally allowed that the *Evening Post*, from the fact of its
> being daily brought before the public eye, possesses incomparable
> advantages which strongly recommend it to the consideration of
> all those who have benefitted by a judicious use of the advertising
> medium; and, as may be seen in another column, our scale of charges
> is framed with a view of placing publicity within the reach of every
> one in the community.[137]

Already, sufficient people had seen the benefits of such 'judicious use' and the front page of the first edition was full of advertising, although shored up by two 'house ads' – one the promised column showing advertising rates ('First insertion, Two Shillings and Six Pence per inch.') and the other touting the advantages of the paper's owner, Blundell Brothers, as general printers.

Advertising in newspapers came to have as much a role in

knowledge transfer and in sense of identity as did the news content. Advertisements were a community service in the sense that readers were informed, not just about what was available for sale, but what was happening in their areas: whether it was a stock sale or a pending political meeting or a gathering of a new club or society. The inter-community link was provided by the frequent and often daily advertising of shipping movements which not only told readers what ships were leaving or arriving, but apprised them of postage deadlines.[138] Country papers which did not have the benefit of shipping news carried instead regular advertisements about train and coach times. Readers of the bi-weekly *Tuapeka Times* of Wednesday 6 December 1876, for example, could learn that a Cobb and Co coach left Lawrence daily at 9.30 a.m. to connect with the Dunedin train at Tokomairiro (Milton); the Wesleyan Church advertised that the noted prohibitionist, Leonard Isitt, would be preaching in Lawrence at 11 a.m. on the following Sunday; the 'American War' last night was on at the town hall; and at 'special request Mr H. Stanley will sing a local song entitled, the forthcoming "Hospital Ball!"' The ball itself was advertised with tickets for a 'Lady and Gentleman' costing ten shillings and sixpence. (What was not advertised was that the first public airing of Thomas Bracken's 'New Zealand National Hymn' was to take place at the ball.) Amid the daily run of stock and land sales, there were also several advertisements for Dunedin hotels and 'accommodation houses'; an announcement that 'Miss Prunty of Melbourne' had taken up dressmaking in the town; and a proud proclamation by the Dunstan Brewery that it had produced 'aromatic tonic bitter wines' with the endorsement of the University of Otago.[139]

The first newspaper in Invercargill in 1861, when the town had 210 houses and 1000 inhabitants, was the *Southern News and Foveaux Straits' Herald*, which two years later became the *Southland News*.[140] For all the paucity of population, it still attracted photographer A. S. Wilson, who advertised himself as being prepared 'to take Portraits and Views of Residences'; the Murihiku Brewery offered draught and bottled ales; and an Edinburgh-trained surgeon, J. J. Martin, declared himself ready for business. A 'Waiopai' farmer, B. W. Muter, had lost a white unbranded bull and offered a liberal reward for its recovery; and someone at the Albion Hotel had found a gold brooch which the owner could have on proof of ownership and payment of expenses.[141] The newspaper was thus both marketplace and information exchange.

In contrast to the ownership and content of newspapers, there has been little analysis of the economic aspects. Circulation figures, when they have been available, and what has been able to be gleaned from company records, have made up a sparse fare. Ross Harvey noted that newspapers tended to publish their circulation figures in the most positive light when they tendered for government advertising – the implication being that the proprietors' figures could not be trusted. Harvey does not include advertising income in his study, presumably because owners regarded the levels of such income as no one's business but the company's.[142] Circulation figures, as unreliable as they may have been, were a partial measure of a newspaper's success but they also reflected increased population. (These figures did not determine readership because it was impossible to know how many people might read a single copy.) A more compelling measure of a newspaper's success was pagination since advertising volume in the increasingly businesslike approach to production generally determined the number of pages in any given edition. But this too could reflect population increases, given that more people meant more potential advertisers. The weekly *Otago Witness* began with six pages in 1851 but by the early to mid-1860s, with the increased population because of the discovery of gold, it was up to an average 20 pages a week. By 1870, it was up to 28; and from 1880 it ran to 32 pages or more.[143] The daily *Evening Post*, by contrast, had less spectacular growth. It started with regular editions of four pages but by 1900 it still averaged only eight pages a day.[144] Such figures cannot take into account other vicissitudes of the newspaper business such as newsprint supply.

Newspapers in general – and the Press Association in particular – clearly had a significant if seldom acknowledged effect on the shaping of a distinctive New Zealand identity. While newspapers during Scholefield's 'horse and buggy days' were primarily outlets for either politicians or for the dissemination of 'Home' news, the advent of the telegraph altered the focus. It led to a preponderance of New Zealand news and, at the same time – with increasing literacy, a burgeoning population and consequential wider commercial base – led to bigger newspapers and forced owners to run them on a sound business basis rather than as a platform for a particular political viewpoint. The sense of a distinctive New Zealand identity was enhanced by the increased coverage in local newspapers of what was happening elsewhere in New Zealand, with a consequential decrease in dependence on clippings from British papers. The Press Association, for its part, determined on a policy of providing news about New Zealand for New Zealanders written when possible by New Zealanders; its policy of sending reporters to overseas assignments was in answer to a perceived demand by people in New Zealand to read more fully about the deeds of their compatriots than a foreign hand could or would supply. Newspapers also provided a proving ground, not to mention a source of income, for writers who, in the absence of a developed book trade, had no other literary outlet; growing within the incubator of newspapers therefore was a distinctive New Zealand literary tradition.

Although the role of newspapers vis-à-vis national identity has gained minimal scholarly attention in New Zealand, the relationship in other places has been subject to some scrutiny. As countries, especially settler colonies, developed and as the machinery of state took shape and relationships with other nation-states evolved, the developing newspaper industries reflected and commented on the changes taking place. In an American study, Joseph M. Torsella concluded: 'By searching for clues in different papers at different times, we can monitor the growth of national consciousness during the eighteenth century.'[145] Looking at a politically mixed assortment of newspapers from Boston, Philadelphia and Virginia over a 40-year period, he traced the gradual evolution from a residual British loyalty to a distinctive American allegiance. While not a perfect mirror of popular thought, said Torsella, newspapers provide 'a rich source of evidence about contemporary sentiment. News and opinion pieces explicitly address many issues of relevance to a study of national identity.'[146]

An important factor in the role of newspapers in the shaping of a New Zealand national identity was presentation of material of increasing relevance to their readers. The more the country developed, the more native-born readers there were, so there was an increasing desire for local news, whether from a parochial or a national source. British issues for the most part became more distant while New Zealand issues gained in relevance and immediacy; newspapers became the only available medium through which New Zealand issues could be discussed and debated, through which communities could communicate with each other and understand each other. This entirely natural outcome was matched not just in other settler colonies, where the new home asserted itself over the old, but even in places like Scotland despite it being a formal part of Great Britain for about 300 years. Scottish interests were (and continue to be) so distinctively different from those of the dominant English that Scottish newspapers continued to thrive because they, unlike the British national newspapers, gave Scots readers what they wanted. Scottish newspapers embrace and enhance a Scottish national identity in a way English-based newspapers did not or could not.[147]

A British study of newspapers reflecting national identity during a specific issue, a European ban on British beef in 1996, concluded that newspapers play a key role in 'the way in which the nation is understood in terms of time and space: newspaper reading constitutes the simultaneous consumption of the same newspapers by a group of individuals defined within finite boundaries'.[148] This applied as much in New Zealand in 1896 as it did in Britain a century later – it was like reading about like. If the increase in New Zealand news developed a sense of national identity subliminally, newspapers were also the vehicle for more overt signs of the growing consciousness that New Zealanders were distinct. Advertisements increasingly featured native flora and fauna, often as advertising devices; a newspaper promoted the idea of a national song and others published the winning entry; the increasing use of cartoons, line blocks and photographs imposed national signs and symbols on newspaper readers. The symbols of 'Godzone' were the road signs to that New Zealandness.

# THREE

# The Symbols
# of 'Godzone'

*Groups of people become nations by*
*identifying with common symbols . . .*[1]

New Zealand is a small country. Nothing is far away; not even the past. In a nation that has had formal government for only about 170 years, it is more possible in New Zealand than in longer-established countries to lift the veil from the past to discover, in Leopold von Ranke's words, *wie es eigentlich gewesen* – what actually happened or, to use the interpretation placed on those words by some historians, 'what essentially happened'.[2] While this approach may be regarded as passé in postmodernist theory, it is reasonable to conclude that the facts of history, as far as they can be established, continue to provide the framework to which theory and differing interpretations can later be applied.

The progression, historically speaking, of New Zealand in a period of about 50 years from an undeveloped land with a sparse indigenous population to a modern nation-state, one even looked upon as a model of enlightened government by some, has been traced many times. The institutions of state on the periphery of the British Empire and how they interacted with the power at the core, the lives and careers of politicians and soldiers and other standard-bearers for country and empire, have been examined, dissected and interpreted. State documents, official correspondence and private letters and diaries have been pored over. The structure of the state has been explored and much has been revealed.

But if government is at the heart of any nation-state, its people make up the arteries, the capillaries and the veins. Quoting a dominant British prime minister of the nineteenth century, Benjamin Disraeli, as saying 'Individuals may form communities, but it is institutions alone that can create a nation', historian Karen Cerulo pointed out that Disraeli, like most politicians, told only part of the story.[3] Defining a nation solely in political or economic terms falls 'far short of fully describing any nation': 'Equally important are a nation's symbols, rituals and traditions. These elements constitute a nation's identity, the image of a nation projected by national leaders both to their constituents and to the world at large. This identity, as much as any institutional factor, defines a nation.'[4]

But an Australian historian who studied symbolism in Ireland and chose to work in New Zealand, Ewan Morris, argued:

Groups of people become nations by identifying with common symbols, and individuals become aware of their membership in the nation as they become conscious that they share their attachment to certain symbols with others. They generally also imagine that these symbols mean the same thing to all members of the nation, but in fact common symbols do not necessarily indicate common beliefs.[5]

'Symbols have become part of the currency of identity', a New Zealand biological scientist, John Andrews, added.[6] And national symbols, 'in particular, national anthems and flags', as Cerulo pointed out, 'provide perhaps the strongest, clearest statement of national identity':

In essence, they serve as modern totems . . . signs that bear a special relationship to the nations they represent, distinguishing them from

The grave in Dunedin of Thomas Bracken, politician and journalist and, among other things, writer of the words of 'God Defend New Zealand'. Author's photograph

one another and reaffirming their national boundaries. Since the inception of nations, national leaders have embraced and adopted national flags and anthems, using them to create bonds, motivate patriotic action, honor the efforts of citizens, and legitimate formal authority.[7]

Certainly, one of New Zealand's most significant and defining distinctions was its geographical position: it shared land borders with no one, there were no external territorial disputes, no arguments about where one country ended and another began, no straight demarcation line drawn on a map to draw arguments from either side. New Zealand's isolation was a key factor in its staying away from federating with Australia and in the gradual emergence of symbols and signs which proclaimed a separate identity. This chapter examines the manifestation of a distinctive New Zealand identity through the use of symbols: identity markers which signalled that New Zealand and New Zealanders were in the process of transformation from being a collection of immigrants from Britain or elsewhere, were not an appendage to the Australian colonies, and not even merely a couple of distant dots in the southern hemisphere coloured red and still firmly belonging to mother Britain.

## Voices from 'Godzone'

In New Zealand, national leaders did eventually 'embrace and adopt' symbols such as anthems and flags, but the impetus did not come from them. Even before the symbols, there was at least one phrase that was held to be peculiarly New Zealand's, although its provenance is elusive. The phrase was 'God's own country', sometimes shortened to 'Godzone', and it was a compelling indication of a growing sense of identity – an indication moreover of a burgeoning pride in where one had settled co-existing and perhaps supplanting the natural tug toward a land of birth. In the words of Thomas Bracken's poem of the same name:

> Give me, give me God's own country! there to live and there to die,
> God's own country! fairest region resting 'neath the southern sky,
> God's own country! framed by Nature in her grandest, noblest mold,
> Land of peace and plenty, land of wool and corn and gold![8]

The phrase was most commonly linked to that supposed arch-imperialist, Richard John Seddon, and sometimes attributed to him. The *New Zealand Observer* reacted in 1907 to a cabled message that quoted an Australian politician as saying Seddon originated the phrase: 'But Mr Seddon never, so far as we are aware, claimed originality for the epigram that he was so fond of using.'[9] The newspaper writer thought Seddon probably borrowed the phrase from the poem written by his friend Thomas Bracken, another who had followed the colonial trail from the British Isles to New Zealand via Australia. But even Bracken did not claim authorship. He gained the inspiration for the poem, the paper said, from a remark made by a New Zealander in Collins Street in Melbourne, who said he was doing well in Melbourne but 'would sooner live on a smaller salary in "God's own country"'. 'And further back than this anonymous New Zealander in Collins Street it seems impossible to trace the apt expression', the *Observer* concluded.[10]

The poem 'God's Own Country' was first published in 1893. Bracken's preface to the poem related the story, repeated by the *Observer*, of two New Zealanders meeting in Melbourne. Although the phrase entered the national lexicon in the year its most enthusiastic user, Seddon, became premier, not all were in agreement. An anonymous rhymester, put out by the break-up of the great pastoral leases, argued New Zealand was more than just natural wonder:

> God's own country, Mr Bracken – maybe so, as you affirm,
> But it's been leased to Nicodemus for a pretty lengthy term,
> And it seems to me, between us, that the latter's little game
> Is to make negotiations for the freehold of the same.[11]

Nevertheless, Bracken's friend and political ally, Robert Stout, had written a descriptive introduction for *Musings in Maoriland*, a collection of Bracken's poetry published in 1890, in which he traced the history of New Zealand and reflected on the gradual development of several strands of New Zealand life, including literature. 'A national feeling is no doubt arising amongst us', he wrote. 'We are forgetting we are English, Irish, Scotch, German or Norse and we are coming to feel that we are New Zealanders.'[12]

Giving force to Stout's sentiment was the inclusion in the collection of Bracken's most enduring and best-known work, 'God Defend New Zealand', although it was given the title 'New Zealand Hymn' by its author.[13] It was first published on 1 July 1876 in the Dunedin newspaper then edited by Bracken, the *Saturday Advertiser*

THE BALL OF THE SEASON,
in aid of the Funds of
The TUAPEKA GOLDFIELDS HOSPITAL,
on
THURSDAY, 7TH DECEMBER, 1876.
In the TOWN HALL.

Ticket to admit Lady and Gentleman, 10s 6d.

Refreshments Provided.

GEO. B. KING,
Secretary.

The advertisement for the hospital ball at Lawrence, at which 'God Defend New Zealand' was first publicly performed. *Tuapeka Times*, 6 December 1876

*and New Zealand Literary Miscellany*, which ran competitions – including one seeking views on the most suitable dress for women – to boost circulation. When the embryonic national anthem was published, the newspaper invited its readers to submit a musical score to complement the words. 'National songs, ballads and hymns have a tendency to elevate the character of a people and keep alive the fires of patriotism in their breasts', the paper said.[14] A panel of Melbourne-based German musicians judged the entries and was unanimous that one submitted by 'Orpheus' was more melodic than the other eleven.

'Orpheus' was soon revealed as a Tasmanian-born schoolteacher in the Central Otago town of Lawrence, John Joseph Woods. The first public performance of the new tune has frequently been stated as being at the Queen's Theatre in Dunedin on Christmas Day 1876 and there remains a plaque on the site where the theatre was proclaiming this belief.[15] But research shows Woods' home town of Lawrence got there first. The song's public debut occurred eighteen days earlier at the annual Lawrence hospital ball on Thursday, 7 December 1876, courtesy of the Lawrence brass band and its leader, D. Corrison. As the Lawrence paper, the *Tuapeka Times*, commented:

Later on in the evening, the band gave the first rendering of the "New Zealand National Hymn" composed by Mr J. J. Woods, and specially

94

arranged for the occasion by Mr Corrison, who had obtained the copy-holder (Mr Bracken's) consent to produce it for the first time. The air is very sweet and the melody one that should survive popularity beyond the ordinary run of modern music.[16]

Twelve days later, the song was performed for a second time in Lawrence, this time by the pupils of the school where Woods taught, St Patrick's. The *Tuapeka Times* reported that the children sang the song under Woods' direction 'in excellent style'.[17] Six days after that, it received its first airing in Dunedin.

If its gestation period from conception to first public performance was relatively brief, the song's infancy was prolonged. Despite public endorsement from the premier at the time, Sir George Grey,[18] who asked Bracken for a copy and arranged for it to be translated into Māori, it had no official status until it was adopted for New Zealand's centennial year of 1940 as the 'national song'.[19] It gained status as a national anthem, along with 'God Save the Queen', only in 1977.[20] The original score was composed by Woods in A flat, but more than a century later this was rearranged at the government's request into G major in the belief it would be more suitable for massed singing.[21]

If the state was slow to apply an official seal of approval to Bracken's work, the people were not. It was being performed throughout New Zealand soon after its first public appearance, despite the lack of means at the time for the mechanical transmission of music. People in Nelson heard it when the new Wakefield Choral Hall was opened in November 1877 and a speaker called it 'a dreary dirge for a national song; however, it will be ready if the Russians come'.[22] The fear of Russians also prompted a rendition at a public meeting at Pleasant Point in 1885 and it received an airing when Roman Catholics celebrated the 70th birthday of the Bishop of Auckland, Archbishop Walter Steins, in 1880. Church of England adherents in rural Waiorongomai in the Thames Valley heard it in 1887 and in 1899 it was described as the New Zealand

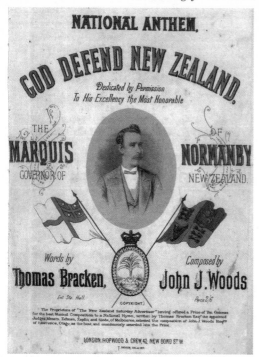

The original edition of the
score for 'God Defend New
Zealand,' published in 1878.

Native Association's national anthem.[23] At the St Patrick's College
prize-giving night in Wellington in 1887, Bracken's work was
described as 'the anthem', and a brass band played both it and 'God
Save the Queen' to close proceedings.[24] The prize-giving night was
noteworthy because the Governor, General Sir William Jervois, was
in attendance; what he thought about a 'native' anthem preceding
the British one was not recorded. Such a brief sampling indicates
that the song/anthem was widely known throughout New Zealand
at a time when the only practical means of its dissemination was by
sheet music.

New Zealand had, therefore, a national hymn or song from 1876,
even if it had no official status. And as James Belich noted, Bracken's
words do not mention Britain or the king or queen once: 'New
Zealand is unmistakably a nation, a "free land" . . . You can find in

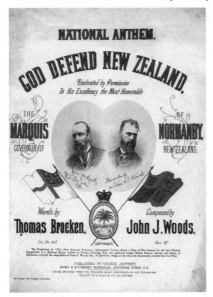

Thomas Bracken and the musical composer, John Joseph Woods, appear on the second edition of the score of 'God Defend New Zealand'.

the words "the predictable and sentimental cliché", or the cloying hyper-piety of the day. But you cannot find cringing colonialism.'[25] An earlier commentary was provided by James Cowan, one of the most prolific chroniclers of taha Māori in the early twentieth century, reacting to news that South Africa had adopted its own home-grown national anthem, 'Die Stem van Suid Africa', and arguing New Zealand should follow suit: 'The best we have to offer . . . is "God Defend New Zealand" which is already a popular song in schools and to some extent at public meetings.' There was a need 'for a chant that shall fitly express the distinctive character of New Zealand, a prayer for the country and the people rather than for the Sovereign', he wrote.[26]

Belich was not alone in his contention that Bracken's lyrics were reflective of the times. As Max Cryer explains, domestic New Zealand nightlife in the late nineteenth century was the piano in the drawing room and many attempted their own nationalistic songs, including another Seddon ally and the man regarded by some as the intellectual architect of New Zealand's ground-breaking social legislation of the 1890s, William Pember Reeves, though he had long been resident in London when he wrote:[27]

God girt her about with the surges
And winds of the masterless deep,
With tumult that rouses and urges
Quick billows to sparkle and leap;
He filled from the life of their motion
Her nostrils with breath of the sea,
And gave her afar in the ocean
A citadel free.[28]

An earlier 'New Zealand Anthem', as it was described, was written by a Christchurch musician, Frederick Leech, and a well-heeled Canterbury farmer from England, Francis Valpy, in 1874. Valpy's words went:

All hail! Zealandia!
Queen of the Southern Isles!
On whose bright destiny
Benignant Nature smiles.
Louder than the cannon's roar
Echo from shore to shore –
All hail! Zealandia!
Zealandia! All Hail![29]

Leech's local paper, the *Star*, enthused: 'The air is pleasing and well adapted to the words, and the chorus is nicely harmonised.'[30] But it never caught the imagination as Bracken's did.

The other white dominions, as they were styled, Australia and Canada, followed remarkably similar paths to New Zealand with both the theme of their anthems and the length of time that elapsed between composition and adoption. 'Advance Australia Fair' was written by Scottish-born Peter Dodds McCormick in 1878 and was declared a national anthem (with 'God Save the Queen') in 1974 and then as Australia's only national anthem ten years later.[31] 'O Canada' was written in 1880 and gained official acceptance exactly a hundred years later.[32] The lyrics of each were redolent of independent thought, an assertion of nation-states blooming far from the imperial motherland.[33] The new anthems therefore, including New Zealand's, reflected pride in country rather than paid obeisance to a distant sovereign. Furthermore, the temporal gap between composition and adoption is indicative of nationalistic feelings being driven by 'the people' rather than by the institutions of state which, for each of those dominions, lagged behind.

## Identity blowing in the wind

Of all the material trappings of national identity, the most recognisable is the national flag. Flags as an identity marker have been in use for thousands of years. Initially, vexilloids, or wooden staffs, were used as a mark of office or a military rallying point. The Chinese developed banners made of silk, which were easier to carry in battle, and the practice spread to Europe, with the purpose of such flags and banners gradually widening. They came to be used as identification for ships and for merchants, the devices reflecting either the identity of the owners or their home ports. From there, it was but a short historical step to flags representing nation-states, with design leaning less to the heraldic and armorial and more to the symbolic.[34] From representing one person such as a monarch or one entity such as a military formation or a company, flags came to represent a collection of people.

The evolution of the New Zealand flag was not straightforward and indeed, when New Zealand troops were dispatched overseas for the first time to South Africa in 1899, there was confusion about which flag New Zealanders were rallying around. One issue of the

*Otago Witness*, the weekly newspaper that served mainly country areas of Otago and Southland, had it both ways. On one page it carried a report of a sermon during which the presiding minister waxed lyrical about what the Union Jack – Britain's flag – represented: 'If you are a fool, you may even talk treason under this flag and it will protect you still. It means, in short, home; secure possession of home, home that is your castle. It means plenty, for no nation is richer.'[35] Twelve pages further on, the newspaper reported that supportive citizens of Wellington had decided to present to the first soldiers to leave for South Africa 'the New Zealand ensign': 'It has been made in blue silk, and is 4½ft [137.1 cm] long and 3ft [91.4 cm] wide, with the stars of the Southern Cross worked in white silk.'[36] The dichotomy thus reflected the tendency for people in New Zealand to still regard Britain as 'home' (more often, 'Home') and an emergent national pride that placed New Zealand allegiance alongside the older imperial loyalty. (The newspaper did not point out, as it could have, that New Zealand at the time did not have its own official flag, although the design described was close to what was eventually adopted.) It may have been this confusion that the Premier, Richard Seddon, had partly in mind when nearly a year later he introduced the New Zealand Ensign and Code Signals Bill into the House of Representatives: 'As the flag with the Southern Cross upon it has been generally recognised as the New Zealand flag, I think we should formally adopt it by general statute; and, in respect to our schools, where the flag is used it ought to be the New Zealand flag.'[37]

The move, which took a further eighteen months before New Zealand had a flag it could call its own, had been more than 60 years in coming. Since 1840, when British sovereignty was proclaimed in New Zealand, a variety of flags had been used to signify either the governing power or the colonial government and these varied whether used on land or at sea. New Zealand also had the unique dimension of Māori to accommodate. In 1835, at the suggestion of the British Resident at the Bay of Islands, James Busby, Māori

The 'Hennessy' flag
(top) and the flag of the
United Tribes of New
Zealand, as it became
known in 1835.

chiefs voted on a flag to be recognised by British authorities as
the national flag of the New Zealand tribes. The chosen design,
endorsed by twelve out of fifteen votes, was for a flag already used
by the Church Missionary Society. It had a red St George's cross
on a white background and in the jack, a red St George's cross on a
blue background pierced with four eight-pointed stars.[38] The British
Union Jack was the official New Zealand flag from 1840 until 1865,
when the British government passed the Colonial Naval Defence
Act, which required colonial government ships to fly the (British)
blue ensign with 'the seal or badge of the colony' in the fly (the
half or edge of a flag farthest away from the pole). Accordingly, the
letters 'NZ' in red with a white border were superimposed. This
was replaced, at the instigation of Governor George Bowen, two
years later by a flag that later formed the basis of what came to be
adopted as the official national flag. It consisted of the four stars of

the Southern Cross in the fly, but also had four stars superimposed on the Union Jack.[39] In 1899, an international code of signals change required the stars on the fly to be contained within a white disc, which prompted some derision in the House of Representatives from a Wellington member, 'Jack' Hutcheson. As *New Zealand Parliamentary Debates* recorded:

He [Hutcheson] took off his hat to the British flag where he saw it, figuratively speaking. But, upon his word, he could not feel the respect he ought to feel for the new design, which reminded him of a Hennessy's brandy-capsule, and all that was wanted to complete it was the word "Hennessy" in the middle, or perhaps two more balls somewhere.[40]

Seddon responded by saying the change to the flag meant 'commercial houses' were insulting it by using it for commercial purposes and this prompted the eventual law formalising the New Zealand ensign:

He would pass an Act making it illegal for the flag to be used for any such purposes. He would, as far as our own flag was concerned, adhere to it, maintain it, and, what was more, he would say to the Boards of Education and to all individuals that when they hoisted the British flag it should have upon it the Southern Cross of New Zealand . . . we should adhere to the grand old British flag, but on every flag there should be in this colony the Southern Cross.[41]

Politicians generally agreed on the principle of a New Zealand flag, but the legislation still did not receive a smooth passage. The Bill, as introduced by Seddon, continued to incorporate the white disc 'for signalling purposes', but this met opposition, most notably from Hutcheson and the member for Waitemata, Richard Monk. 'Let the flag be the same everywhere and always', Hutcheson insisted: 'If it is necessary to make a distinction, let the New Zealand

Vincent Pyke, as depicted by William Blomfield. Detail from *New Zealand Observer and Free Lance*, 12 July 1890, p. 5

owned and registered merchant vessels continue to wear the roast beef of old England – that is the red ensign – without disc or any other blot to sully the flag on which we have looked with pride for so many years.'[42] Monk also argued against the signalling aspect of the flag and quoted from a poem written by an earlier New Zealand politician, Vincent Pyke:

> Three crosses in the Union,
> Three crosses in the Jack,
> And we'll add to it now the Cross of the South,
> And stand to it back to back.[43]

He suggested the stars of the Southern Cross be edged in silver, 'that they might sparkle with the silvery sheen with which we view them in the heavens': 'For it is a glorious badge – something that appeals to our minds, and which the people of New Zealand will become prouder of as the years roll by. It should be exhibited in every school and the children be taught to make it the shrine of their honour, investing it with every manly attribute and the most exalted aspirations.'[44] A South Canterbury member, Richard Meredith, was so impressed with Monk's speech he said he would have it reproduced and distributed to schools at his own cost. Seddon agreed to do so at the government's expense.[45]

During the committee stage, Seddon agreed to drop all references to signals, and the Bill simply became one applying only to the official New Zealand ensign. It was passed in that form, but still there were hurdles. The British Admiralty objected on the grounds that the blue ensign could not be used for 'all purposes', as the preamble to the New Zealand Act said, because the blue ensign was reserved for government ships. This required a change to the New Zealand law restricting the use of the flag to vessels owned by the New Zealand government. The Deputy Governor, Sir Robert Stout, who was acting as governor, also objected to the Bill as passed because he felt a clause reserving the Act for the King's approval impinged on the governor's right to decide what was appropriate. Seddon disagreed and a lengthy correspondence developed between the two, with Stout in the end sending copies of each letter to the Secretary of State for the Colonies in London.[46] Seddon took a new Bill, taking into account the Admiralty's objections, to Parliament in September 1901 and by early November it was agreed to. New Zealand had its official flag.[47] It was approved in March 1902 by King Edward VII and a proclamation by the governor was published in the *New Zealand Gazette* on 12 June.[48]

## Home-grown symbols

Rather than flags and anthems – symbols which require the formal approval of the state if they are to have official status – other signs of national assertiveness and identity emerge organically and take on their own significance. New Zealand gradually acquired its own unique national 'branding' through this method. It was unique because it did not rely on imported symbols or on derivatives from Britain or elsewhere; New Zealand's unofficial symbols came from the country's flora and fauna and from Māori – symbols which were provably distinctive to New Zealand and could not possibly have been confused with anywhere else. As John Andrews noted, 'newer ex-colonial societies' also adopted flora and fauna as identity markers: the kangaroo, koala and gum trees in Australia; the bald eagle and giant redwoods in the United States; the maple leaf in Canada; the springbok in South Africa.[49] Foremost in New Zealand was the flightless bird endemic to the country, the kiwi. It made its first official appearance as a symbol of New Zealand as early as 1866 when the House of Representatives received its first mace, a symbol of parliamentary authority that was once described by Robin Hyde as 'a sort of heavyweight fairy wand affair, with nubbly gold coronets on top'.[50] The official seal appeared on one side of the mace and on the other the arms of Great Britain:

> These are supported by two of our indigenous birds, the kiwi and kakapo; whilst the space between them is filled up with rich foliage in high relief, and trees, amongst which the tree fern and the nikaupalon [nikau palm] are conspicuous; and two groups of stars eight in number, may be supposed to symbolize the islands and provinces of New Zealand.[51]

The kiwi is now, of course, such a pervasive symbol of New Zealand identity that it is a colloquial synonym for the very term 'New Zealander'. Harry Orsman in his *Dictionary of New Zealand English* traced the origins of 'Kiwi' as a nickname for New Zealanders to wartime – from an outline of a kiwi carved into a chalk hill above Sling Camp on the Salisbury Plain in England during World War I – and he noted that 'after 1940 the kiwi became synonymous with New Zealand servicemen overseas'.[52] However, for the name of the bird to acquire such status, it had to have entered the consciousness of New Zealanders as a distinctive symbol much earlier and it did this through the 1890s.

The parliamentary mace on which the kiwi appeared would not have been seen by many people, but advertisements most certainly were. One of the earliest – if not the earliest – pictorial representations of a kiwi was used by the Dunedin drug company, Kempthorne, Prosser and Co, which applied to register an image of a kiwi in 1892 as branding for a veterinary medicine. In its application, it said it had been using the kiwi trademark for fourteen years – that is, from 1878.[53] This was only four years after the Dunedin politician and businessman Alexander Bathgate had written *Colonial Experiences*, in which he referred to 'one of the greatest natural curiosities' of New Zealand as the 'kirvi', reflecting a pronunciation, if not a spelling, evidently common at the time.[54] David (later Sir David) Monro also referred to the 'kivi' in his chronicling of the 1844 survey of the Otago area.[55] For all the political and commercial weight of the southern area of New Zealand at the time, 'kivi' never endured, soon to be supplanted by the now orthodox spelling 'kiwi'.

The kiwi gained an even wider exposure as a unique symbol of New Zealand when it featured on the sixpenny stamp in 1898 in the first New Zealand issue (and one of the first in the world) of pictorial postage stamps.[56] Ewan Morris described stamps (and seals, banknotes and coins) as 'silent ambassadors of national taste' and noted: 'These symbols play an important role as marks of legitimacy: they signal that the objects in question are backed by the authority of the state, and they must therefore achieve widespread recognition if they are to function effectively.'[57] They were certainly recognised by Charles Douglas, a noted South Island explorer in the late nineteenth century who became known as 'Mr Explorer Douglas', who recorded in a monograph on birds: 'From the fact that bank notes, postage stamps and advertisement chromos, generally have a portrait of this unholy looking bird on them, it is evident that the kiwi is the accepted national bird of New Zealand, on this

Samples of early trademarks drawing on New Zealand imagery.

subject I will enter more fully when treating about the Weka.'[58]

True to his word, Douglas returned to the topic and said he thought countries should be careful how they select a national bird or beast. Referring to those adopted by others, such as the beaver in Canada and the kangaroo in Australia, he noted the kiwi had not a single good or bad quality to recommend it. The weka, he thought, would have been a better choice:

> Here is a bird full of good qualities and who's vices lean to virtue's side. Personal valour of a high order. An undying thirst for knowledge – unthinking people give it another name – which causes it to annex everything portable about a hut and carry it into the bush to study at leisure. An affection for its young, that would face the Prince of Darkness in their defence.[59]

Douglas's reaction was not recorded, but he may have noted with approval that by the time he extolled the virtues of the weka, it too had begun appearing in trademark applications, as were the huia, the tūī and the ruru.[60]

There were still reflections of a British past, but representations of a New Zealand present appeared increasingly frequently in the commercial world.[61] The use of names such as 'Maori Chief' butter and 'Wahine' butter and cheese[62] come under the general heading of acculturation or, as Peter Gibbons preferred in his study of the activities of the Danish-born ethnologist and bibliophile Johannes Andersen, 'cultural appropriation'. He defined this as the 'unauthorized utilisation of elements of the signifying systems of the indigenous people by a settler society through incorporation of those elements into the signifying systems of the settler society',[63] and noted that Andersen was one of many Pākehā who incorporated aspects of Māori culture into Pākehā signifying systems in an attempt to develop a sense of identity: 'Andersen chose to emphasize indigenous phenomena, particularly fauna, flora, and the indigenous people – the birds, the bush and "the Maori": these made up what, for him, was distinctively 'New Zealand.'[64] This may have been, for Gibbons and later historians, a valid twentieth/twenty-first century interpretation from a Said-like standpoint, but it seems scarcely credible that a company manager or an advertising copy-writer in the late nineteenth century would have considered such implications.[65] Thoughts then are unlikely to have risen beyond a desire to use a trademark design that was seen as being distinctive to the country in order to sell more of their products.[66]

The kiwi had some opposition from the extinct moa as a national bird. By the late nineteenth century, the moa featured in brands as diverse as oil, clothing and rabbit traps, and New Zealanders were sometimes portrayed by cartoonists as moas.[67] But by early in the twentieth century, the kiwi was well established as a symbol of New Zealand, especially in a sporting sense. After a British rugby team was beaten in 1908, a Wellington writer, Andrew Spence, contributed this to a book about the tour:

> Said Leo: "What's this awful circumstance that's broke my blessed head?"
> It's called out here "The Kiwi" – alluding to N.Z.
> It serves this small Dominion as an emblem for a crest,
> And when you've found out what it means, I'll tell you all the rest.[68]

The pictorial stamp issue of which the sixpenny kiwi formed a part was also reflective of a growing sense of identity – a desire to extol the attractions of New Zealand rather than continue to pay homage to the imperial core (as did previous stamps which carried images of Queen Victoria).[69] The others portrayed either native fauna or natural scenic wonders, including the Pink and White Terraces, which had been destroyed by the eruption of Mt Tarawera in 1886, and a view of Mt Earnslaw from Lake Wakatipu – unfortunately (or perhaps fortunately for some later philatelists), the name of the lake was misspelt 'Wakitipu'. Geographer Eric Pawson saw the link between the postage stamps and national identity: 'That a

The 1896 pictorial issue featured a misspelt Lake 'Wakitipu' on the 2 1/2-penny stamp (top) and the kiwi on the 6d stamp. At right is the 1d stamp issued in 1901 to mark the introduction of universal penny postage.

set of pictorial stamps with a strong alpine theme should be issued at all at the end of the nineteenth century is indicative of early Pākehā pride in such landscapes.'[70]

Charles Rous-Marten, the correspondent in London for several New Zealand newspapers referred to in the previous chapter, saw the stamps in proof form at the office of the Agent-General, William Pember Reeves, and remarked: 'The work has been done exquisitely and no country will be able to boast a finer set of postage stamps than New Zealand.'[71] The pictorials were preceded in 1895 by a letter card (a form of postcard), on the back of which were various scenic views. Within seven months, 363,000 were sold.[72] The Post Office historian, Howard Robinson, confessed he did not know if the success of the cards prompted the decision to issue a pictorial set, but it was evidently a popular one nevertheless: 'They were greeted with much praise as taking a very high rank among the postage stamps of the world.'[73] While they may have served the propaganda purpose of promoting New Zealand overseas and were aesthetically pleasing, they were also profitable. 'Possibly because of their attractive appearance, the sale of stamps sharply increased', Robinson wrote. New Zealanders mailed nearly 30 million letters in 1897, the year before the pictorial issue, and in 1899 the total climbed to 35 million. Thousands of stamps also found their way directly into the albums of collectors.[74]

Another symbol from New Zealand's flora that assumed a lead role in national identity was the fernleaf (*Cyathea dealbata*), most commonly designated as a silver fern because of the silvery underside of its leaves. This has been used and adapted for a great variety of identification purposes but is most associated in the public consciousness with sports teams. It was first used as a representative symbol in 1884 by the first national rugby union team,[75] and its uses and adaptations, and the emergence of black and white as New Zealand's 'national colours', will be explored more thoroughly in chapter 7, which concentrates on the evolution of sport as an identity marker in New Zealand.

On the other hand, a contradiction of the growing trend toward 'New Zealandness' is that the country was remarkably slow in introducing another of the standard 'silent ambassadors' – silent but for the jangle in the pocket or purse. While some businesses introduced their own copper tokens in the nineteenth century, and used local identification marks, the coinage legal tender in New Zealand until the 1930s remained the British, aside from some Australian sovereigns or half-sovereigns. A New Zealand penny was minted in 1879 with the head of Queen Victoria on the obverse and the words 'New Zealand' above a representation of Britannia on the reverse, but only about 20 were produced and it was never in circulation. When eventually New Zealand did mint its own coins (or had its own coins minted in Britain for it), the familiar symbols were represented: a kiwi on the florin, a Māori warrior on the shilling, a huia on the sixpence, two patu on the threepence, a tūī nestling on kōwhai on the penny, and a tiki on the halfpenny.[76]

## Seeing the country

The distinctiveness of New Zealand, and especially its unique flora and fauna unsullied by a land bridge to anywhere, could not just be reproduced on stamps and in commercial trademarks – it needed to be shared. As Monte Holcroft observed: 'After discovery, and re-discovery, and organised settlement, New Zealand was ready for closer inspection.'[77] The first tourists were the wealthy or the celebrated, encompassing New Zealand in an antipodean extension of the 'Grand Tour', eager to write for their audiences, usually British, of the wonders they beheld. Holcroft listed among these early observers 'the most hyphenated person ever to visit these shores', Alice A. Temple-Nugent-Brydges-Chandos-Grenville, Duchess of Buckingham and Chandos, whose book was dismissed by Thomas Hocken, he said, as 'a seven weeks' scamper through New Zealand, chiefly personal gossip'.[78]

A more celebrated and better-known visitor was the English novelist Anthony Trollope, who spent several weeks in New Zealand in 1872 after visiting his son in New South Wales. He commented on the history and government of the country but also presented to his readers descriptions of some its natural wonders, especially the thermal areas around Rotorua and Taupō.[79] He also remarked that while New Zealand could be more John Bullish than John Bull, not all the habits of home were transferred to the new land:

But for men who can and will work with their hands, for women who can cook and be generally useful about a household, for girls who are ready to learn to cook and to be generally useful, these colonies are a paradise. They will find the whole condition of life changed for them. The slight estimation in which labour is held here will be changed for a general respect. The humbleness, the hat-touching, the servility which is still incidental to such work as theirs in the old country, and which is hardly compatible with exalted manhood, has found no footing here. I regard such manhood among the masses of the people as the highest sign of prosperity which a country can give.[80]

As tourism historian Margaret McClure noted, William Fox was one of the first politicians to see the potential of a tourist trade, even though he dreaded 'crowds following in his footsteps'.[81] Fox saw not just the tourist potential of the hot springs district of the North Island, but its therapeutic qualities as well, and wrote a lengthy letter to his successor as premier, Julius Vogel, to tell him so:

At present, the difficulty of travelling in the hot springs country, and the almost entire absence of accommodation for invalids, prevents more than a very small number of persons from visiting it, either for health, recreation or curiosity. Yet it might be, and is probably destined to be, the sanatorium not only of the Australasian Colonies, but of India and other portions of the globe.[82]

McClure said Fox had been to the United States and was impressed with the federal government's protection of the thermal area at Yellowstone 'and to prevent a repetition of the trashy com-mercialism that dominated the Niagara Falls'.[83] Another early tourism visionary was an Auckland merchant, Scottish-born Robert Graham, who gained land in the thermal area, apparently because of a role in peace talks between warring Māori, although his right to the land was disputed. He developed tourist facilities at Huka

Falls, Ohinemutu and Te Wairoa and produced a book, *Graham's Guide to the Hot Lakes*.[84]

With the increasing number of visitors, whether well-known or not, there came an increasing number of guidebooks; some specific, some not. Writers of the calibre of Charles Baeyertz, James Cowan and Malcolm Ross each supplemented their normal occupations and incomes with books extolling the scenic wonders of New Zealand.[85] In Baeyertz's case, he reflected his interests and education, and perhaps that of his anticipated readers, by including classical allusions as well as the occasional sentence in Greek.[86] Yet, alongside the encomiums for the natural beauty of New Zealand ran complaints that it was too inaccessible or too uncomfortable.

Ross, one of a small group of New Zealanders who vowed to be the first to the highest peaks in the country, wrote of a German traveller, Max Herbertz, who thought New Zealand slow to take advantage of what it had to offer: 'The scenery, he admits, is wonderfully fine, but the difficulties and the time occupied in getting there, together with the arrangements encountered when one gets there, are such as to prevent one's going again, or from recommending others to make the journey.'[87] Ross also quoted from a letter to the editor by Richard Tecce, the New Zealand-born, Sydney-based general manager of the AMP Society, which talked about 'our neglect of a most valuable asset'. Complaining of the costs incurred when sightseeing in Rotorua and of how difficult it was to get to Mt Cook and the lack of accommodation at Pukaki, Tecce submitted: 'As a Native of this beautiful colony and a frequent visitor to it, I am actuated only by a desire to see this splendid national asset utilised to the fullest extent.'[88]

William Pember Reeves, before he was posted to London as New Zealand's agent-general, visited Rotorua and told the Minister of Lands and Survey, Robert McNab, that the government should 'centralise, nationalise and systematise' the tourist industry as soon as possible.[89] Sir Joseph Ward, number two in the Liberal government, then stepped in. He had 'seen enough of the world to appreciate the tourist potential in New Zealand's extraordinary scenery', one biographer, Michael Bassett, wrote.[90] Ward was also 'sufficiently attuned' to current health fads 'to know of the growing European craze for thermal pools and spas'.[91] Accordingly, in a speech in 1901 he said a section of the Railways Department would be given the job of setting up and running 'a better and more widely organised tourist department': 'I share with my colleagues the opinion that every pound judiciously spent in making for the comfort of the visitors to the colony, and also for comfort and pleasure of the people who reside amongst us, will be recouped indirectly over and over again.'[92]

So was launched the Department of Tourist and Health Resorts which, according to the architectural magazine *Progress*, 'began its labours in a back room of the New Zealand Parliamentary Buildings with a staff of three officers'.[93] These tentative steps toward state tourism promotion were entrusted to Thomas Edward Donne, a career public servant who at the time was a railways traffic manager in Auckland. It was written of his appointment: 'It would be difficult to find in the length and breadth of New Zealand a more suitable man to fill the new appointment, or one more alert to take advantage of every point in the interest of the departments allotted to him.'[94] Donne at the same time became secretary of the Department of Industries and Commerce – it being rationalised that the primary source of visitor traffic from overseas included those countries providing New Zealand's main markets[95] – and was described as being a close friend of Ward's:

> They had many ideas in common and to them alone the genesis of the separate Department of Tourist and Health Resorts and of the regenerated Department of Industries and Commerce are largely due. These two men, indeed, are the authors, too, of the system of New Zealand official representation overseas – elsewhere than in London, where an Agent-General (later elevated in status to High Commissioner) had already long represented the then colony of New Zealand.[96]

The man entrusted with tourism promotion, Thomas Edward Donne.
A-312-1-189, ATL

Donne's brief was wide: as he noted in his first annual report, one of his first tasks was to make arrangements for a tour of New Zealand by a thousand soldiers (the 'Imperial Representative Military Corps') who had been at the celebrations marking Australia's federation. One of his next was to organise, and accompany, the Duke and Duchess of York (later King George V and Queen Mary) on their tour of New Zealand. These duties were in addition to his primary role as manager of tourism spots in Rotorua; of organising advertising of the country throughout the world; and of ensuring better access to, and accommodation at, other scenic spots throughout the country. He was also responsible for the importation and control of game (for sport shooting) and the appointment (from 43 applicants) of a balneologist to oversee the proper use of the thermal resorts for people seeking remedial or recuperative care.[97] The department's progress under Donne was rapid:

> Probably not even the prescient Minister responsible for its birth had anticipated to the full the remarkable success and phenomenal development of what is now one of the most indispensable of our Government departments. The staff has increased in less than six years from three to one hundred and fifty; and this expansion has been brought about by the multifarious nature of the Department's duties and by the exceedingly valuable nature of its services to the State.[98]

In fact, the department's function was not only to promote tourism, as Donne noted in his report for 1907, the increased promotion and advertising also helped immigration:

> This position has ... been forced on it by virtue of the fact that the great majority of the thousands of letters received from oversea in response to Department's advertisements are from persons in search of new homes – people who desire to emigrate to a land where a freer life, greater possibilities and more healthful conditions obtain.[99]

Donne calculated that New Zealand visitors usually averaged four to every one from overseas (see the following table), and his interest in promoting New Zealand in general and tourism in particular was said to be complemented by a desire to retain as much as possible the natural beauty and attraction of the country:

> Donne was long interested in the preservation of scenery and like natural assets ... He was, for example, a staunch and persistent advocate for the protection of large areas of the Waimarino Forest

adjacent to the route to the Main Trunk railway in the vicinity of Tongariro National Park; he also urged similar protection of natural scenery along various other routes. He deplored the unnecessary and wasteful destruction of native woodlands in many localities and urged the protection of certain storied trees once venerated by the Maori. He appealed against the despoliation of colourful pohutukawa groves around the northern North Island coasts and against the removal of this handsome tree in large numbers from Hauraki Gulf islands and from other offshore islands.[100]

TABLE 3.1 NUMBER OF VISITORS 1903-1907

|  | 1903-04 | 1904-05 | 1905-06 | 1906-07 |
| --- | --- | --- | --- | --- |
| Australia | 2726 | 2892 | 3463 | 5612 |
| United Kingdom | 1795 | 2025 | 2376 | 2394 |
| United States, Canada | 417 | 563 | 652 | 763 |
| European Continent | 102 | 146 | 175 | 260 |
| Africa | 64 | 113 | 137 | 196 |
| India | 61 | 86 | 92 | 85 |
| Other | 68 | 167 | 247 | 374 |
| Totals | 5233 | 5992 | 7142 | 9684 |
| Est. expenditure | £261,000 | £299,000 | £357,000 | £484,000 |

Source: Tourist and Health Resorts Department annual report 1907, *AJHR*, vol. 4, H-2, p. 3.

The development of tourism, gradual at first through individuals and later through sponsorship by the state, aided a sense of New Zealand identity, a sense of belonging to a land that was different and a land that was 'ours' to embrace. This affinity was noted by Holcroft:

In the last decades of the 19th century and the first decades of the 20th, they [New Zealanders] were still exploring, though roads had been made for them, and railways. These islands were young in European occupation; their inhabitants could not really be at home here until they had seen for themselves what lay beyond the mountains and the forest. Perhaps it was not merely curiosity, but a strong impulse, almost an instinct, which in so short a time opened the country for organised travel.[101]

New Zealanders, whether immigrants or native-born, came increasingly to identify with the natural wonders of their land, in a similar way to the reverence and respect accorded by Māori to their natural environment.

## The age of exhibitions

Exposure of New Zealand – a desire by those in the country to show to the rest of the world what they had and how they had developed – also came through international exhibitions, which were increasingly common in the second half of the nineteenth century after the exhibition at the purpose-built Crystal Palace in London showed the way.[102] William Schneider wrote that exhibitions, or expositions or world's fairs, had their origins in the medieval trade fairs in Europe but were given their modern form by London in 1851, 'whose Crystal Palace showed the marvels of the new industrial age'.[103]

> The commercial purpose continued in the fairs which followed in the second half of the nineteenth century, but as different nations competed to outdo their rivals, not only in individual displays but in the overall splendour and size of the fair presented by the host nation, the element of chauvinism and national rivalry was added to the exhibitions.[104]

An earlier scholar, Carroll D. Champlin, remarked: 'An exposition sends the whole world to school, and there is no better teacher than the experience of having visited a world's fair. Immeasurable benefits are derived from this commingling of personalities, ideas,

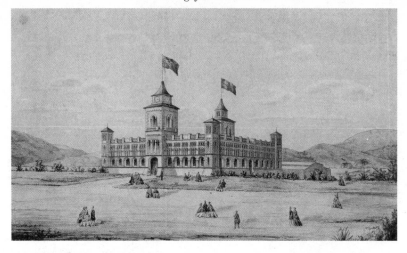

A lithograph by Thomas George of the New Zealand Exhibition in Dunedin in 1865.
Acc. 8,934, Hocken Collections Uare Taoka o Hākena, University of Otago

languages, factory products and the creations of man's mind at its best.'[105]

New Zealand first exhibited at the International Exhibition in London in 1862 but it was not, if the London correspondent of the *New Zealander* was an accurate observer, an outstanding success: 'Internationally we do not shine . . .', he said.[106] Although 'nothing could have been better' than New Zealand's exhibit, the layout of the exhibition space meant one colony was confused with another:

> Persons entering the Queensland department from the New Zealand court supposed they were still in New Zealand till some one or other showed them that they were out in their geography. They had passed through New Zealand, and had scarcely known it, so little has New Zealand shown as compared with other places not heard of in the Exhibition of 1851.[107]

New Zealand mounted its own exhibitions, with the first in Dunedin in 1865. At the official opening, the Otago Superintendent, John Harris, thought 'through this exhibition New Zealand will be brought out from its obscurity into a face-to-face meeting with the outer world'.[108] A series of New Zealand-only exhibitions were staged in Christchurch from 1880 but that city also held the next international exhibition (in 1882) and others followed in Wellington (1885), Dunedin (1889–90), Wellington (1896–97), Auckland (1898–99) and Christchurch again in 1906–07.[109] As David Hall wrote: 'To a young country an exhibition offered the opportunity of showing graphically the stage of development achieved. It also gave expression to the community spirit always so strong at the beginning of a pioneering enterprise and provided an outlet too for a love of spectacle the settlers had few enough occasions to indulge.'[110]

An unidentified writer in the catalogue for the New Zealand and South Seas Exhibition in 1925–26 said such displays were the best means of measuring the industrial progress of a community.

A young country makes a beginning with a modest display, probably of no more than local interest. But as it prospers and develops, growing in population and wealth, its exhibitions grow in size and importance until soon it is able to exhibit with credit in international ones . . . As a young country still in the making, New Zealand had frequently taken stock of its progress in this way.[111]

When Dunedin made known its plans for its 1889–90 exhibition, it won praise from its provincial rivals in Canterbury. 'Their project for holding an exhibition is like an act of faith in their country and its prospects', the *Lyttelton Times* editorialised.[112]

Showing off at home was one thing; New Zealand needed to advertise itself overseas as well and it did so at exhibitions in Paris (1878), Sydney (1879), London (1886), Melbourne (1888) and Brisbane (1897). Although the exhibitions were aimed primarily at increasing trade by promoting a country's wares, they also had the potential effect of stimulating immigration and tourism or simply a greater awareness. As Hall remarked: 'Even if the direct stimulation of trade was not always great, these enterprises did help to make the country better known in a wider world and always included material emphasising New Zealand's unique scenic attractions and scientific interest.'[113]

The exhibitions later came under the aegis of Thomas Donne and he oversaw New Zealand's contribution to the Louisiana Purchase Exhibition at St Louis in 1904–05 which 'earned awards including a special award for a hunting and fishing exhibition'.[114] Donne made an extended tour of the United States after that promoting the Christchurch exhibition of 1906–07. 'Its success in very large measure was due to the personal efforts of this persuasive promoter, organiser and publicist.'[115]

The fairs presented a hegemonic face to the world, extolling the virtues of a nation-state, a way of life and a race. Although, as Meg Armstrong remarked: 'It is well known that ethnological displays of exotic peoples at many world fairs were designed to promote a hierarchy of races that maintained the dominance of white Europeans and Americans.'[116] New Zealand was not immune from such retrospective criticism of its portrayal of Māori at exhibitions. Commenting on the replica of a Māori kāinga at the 1911 London exhibition, Paul Greenhalgh thought a description of it treated 'clinically and lightly the genocide of the Maori's and the desperate struggle for freedom they had fought in their own country, merely in the hope of a right to share it'.[117]

New Zealand also had a permanent exhibition at the Imperial Institute in London but the Agent-General, Sir Westby Perceval, worried that not enough New Zealanders were contributing to it. Unless they did, a newspaper correspondent thought, New Zealand would lag behind the other Australasian colonies:

> The Agent-General would like it, I think, to be clearly understood that the success and genuine utility of the New Zealand Court at the Imperial Institute in the future depends not so much upon himself and Sir Walter Buller as upon the co-operation of the Colony. They have set things going and given the section a capital start, but it

remains for the Colony to fill up important gaps . . . and to keep the court up to date with fresh exhibits of all new industries.[118]

The exhibitions, whether in New Zealand or overseas, were platforms from which the country could show off, an opportunity to proclaim to the world what it had done and what it could still do. They were also a part of the foundation on which national identity was built. As Jock Phillips wrote in an article about the exhibitions and national identity, 'international exhibitions provide an opportunity for governments and people to determine deliberately and consciously how to represent themselves and their countries to the world'.[119] Phillips related how the *Evening Star* in Dunedin put the Christchurch exhibition in 1906–07 on a par with the All Blacks' tour of the United Kingdom and Ireland a year earlier as 'one of the coping stones upon which the edifice of increased reputation and importance of the colony will be erected'.[120]

But the exhibitions were not solely for the wondering and wandering visitors. New Zealanders poured into the exhibition halls to see for themselves what their country could do, as the figures in the following table indicate.

TABLE 3.2 INTERNATIONAL EXHIBITIONS IN NEW ZEALAND 1865–1940

| YEAR | VENUE | HOST CITY POPULATION | NZ POPULATION | ATTENDANCE |
|---|---|---|---|---|
| 1865 | Dunedin | 15,121 | 190,607 | 31,250 |
| 1882 | Christchurch | 15,184 | 517,707 | 226,360 |
| 1889–90 | Dunedin | 45,898 | 625,508 | 625,478 |
| 1906–07 | Christchurch | 67,878 | 956,457 | 1.9 m |
| 1925–26 | Dunedin | 67,544 | 1.4 m | 3.2 m |
| 1940 | Wellington | 162,800 | 1.6 m | 2.6 m |

Based on table in John Mansfield Thomson, ed., *Farewell Colonialism: The New Zealand International Exhibition, Christchurch, 1906–07* (Palmerston North: Dunmore Press, 1998), p. 29.

Attendance well exceeded populations, even in the earlier years when travelling from one centre to another was a journey seldom undertaken on a whim. If New Zealanders took no pride in their country, if they did not identify with their country, would they have bothered?

⤜

Symbols such as anthems, flags and stamps became Eric Hobsbawm's 'signs of club membership'[121] and Ewan Morris's 'silent ambassadors' for the burgeoning New Zealand identity.[122] These were the material symbols, but they were complemented by the unique natural symbols of the country – its flora and fauna, its rivers and mountains, its thermal areas and lakes – which were exposed and promoted to inhabitants and visitors as emblematic of New Zealand. But what enduring use would there be of mountains being 'freedom's ramparts'[123] or having 'Nature in her grandest, noblest mold' if such sights could be seen by just a few? Stirring emotions backed by fine phrases needed to be translated into hard cash. To the emotional was added a commercial value as the government, and its individual members and employees, realised the economic prospects of what New Zealand had and what its own inhabitants and overseas visitors might want to see. This led to promotion not just of the natural wonders but of the country as a whole, boosting both tourist and immigration numbers.

However, while there was doubtless a pragmatic, commercial reason for the exploitation of New Zealand's natural gifts, there had also to be an underlying pride, a sense of a unique land inhabited by a people increasingly aware of their own identity. This fervent 'place attachment' was embodied in Thomas Donne, as described by E. S. Dollimore:[124]

> Though born in an Australian city, he had come to New Zealand at a
> very early age, and had been brought up and educated here and this

was always for him his beloved native land. He was intensely a New Zealand patriot who zealously and unceasingly promoted his country's special attributes, its scenery, marvels and sport, and the high standard of its products; he sought to conserve our natural assets and to build up a prosperous tourist industry.[125]

By the early twentieth century, New Zealanders had their own song to sing (and would eventually), their own flag to fly (and did), and their own stamps to put on letters. Such symbols were theirs; they belonged to no other. This accumulation of symbols proliferated in the last decade of the nineteenth century and coincided with the Liberal era of government, a time in which New Zealand's advanced social legislation was held up as an example to the world, and this in turn enhanced national identity as New Zealanders increasingly saw themselves for what they were, not by comparison with others.

# FOUR

# Was New Zealand Exceptional?

*I knew of the New Zealand of Tasman from reading, but the*
*New Zealand of to-day took me by surprise. – Mark Twain*[1]

New Zealand historian Miles Fairburn has periodically asked: 'Is there a good case for New Zealand exceptionalism?' and answered in the negative while at the same time lamenting the lack of academic debate about it when compared with the level of interest in other countries.[2] The notion of 'exceptionalism' as a national theory is most firmly embedded with the United States which, according to the theory, was unique among developed nations in its historical evolution, political and religious institutions, and origins.[3] The nub of Fairburn's argument in relation to New Zealand was that it had not had a chance to develop what he called an autochthonous culture and was instead dominated by the cultures of Britain, Australia and the United States. 'No one has yet advanced a good case that New Zealand's history diverged in significant respects from that of other comparable societies', he wrote.[4] 'To be regarded as exceptional, a country's history must not only experience a unique or unusual event but also take a divergent path from that of others in consequence. Most significant phenomena that are considered to have made New Zealand's history different are, on close inspection,

not different at all.'[5] In his view, none of the milestones of New
Zealand history such as the Treaty of Waitangi, the reforms of the
Liberal government in the 1890s and the 'man alone' concept as
embodied in New Zealand literature by John Mulgan were unique
in qualifying for New Zealand exceptionalism.[6]

In *Disputed Histories*, Fairburn elaborated that for a country's history to be exceptional, it must satisfy three requirements:

> (i) the country must experience an event or state of affairs that is
> specific to that particular country (or highly unusual); (ii) the event
> or state of affairs must be capable of being composed into a theory
> that can explain or unify many important successor events or states of
> affairs; (iii) these successor events or states of affairs must be unique
> or rare.[7]

He thought New Zealand's lack of so-called autochthonous culture was attributable to 'the structural effects of physical isolation'
and that its remoteness 'led it to be exceptionally exposed to
the global revolution in transport and communication from the
mid-19th century'.[8] But without answering Fairburn's essential
question – 'Is there a good case for New Zealand exceptionalism?' – in a resounding affirmative, it is possible to argue that New
Zealand's remoteness and physical isolation were the very factors
which helped provide an environment in which the country could
meet in all essential respects his criteria for exceptionalism. In so
doing, New Zealand and New Zealanders through the nineteenth
century, and particularly in its last decade or so, found a national
identity that was unique, and was distinctive from the influences
Fairburn argued prevented an autochthonous flowering. As Raewyn
Dalziel remarked: 'A strident Imperialism and the presentation of
New Zealand as a social laboratory for the new century were both
attempts by a settler society to convince themselves and others that
they had secured a home and an identity yet remained part of an
important global community.'[9]

In terms of New Zealand providing a point of difference from other settler colonies, or indeed, from other developed or developing countries at the time, the Liberal reforms of the 1890s attracted most interest. This was the 'social laboratory' theory that gave New Zealand and New Zealanders a reputation as being radical and visionary and helped cement the country's identity as being distinct from those with which it was most closely associated, especially the Australian colonies. As R. P. Davis noted, New Zealand became 'the talk of the world today' and leading Liberals such as John Ballance, Richard John Seddon, John McKenzie and William Pember Reeves became 'left-wing heroes in the English-speaking world' as they produced experimental legislation which appeared more advanced than that attempted elsewhere.[10] New Zealand became a Mecca, in Davis's words, for social writers and theorists of all sorts.

Among those who came to inspect, read, wonder and analyse were the English socialist intellectuals Beatrice and Sidney Webb, the French academics André Siegfried and Albert Métin, the American radical reformer Henry Demarest Lloyd and an English student of the imperial phenomenon, Richard Jebb.[11] Another was an American university professor, James Le Rossignol, who co-wrote *State Socialism in New Zealand* with a Dunedin barrister, author and politician, William Downie Stewart.[12] Less scholarly, but no less observant, were the Irish nationalist Michael Davitt and literary figures such as Mark Twain, Rudyard Kipling and Anthony Trollope. They were among the more prominent of the temporary imports; there were also exports, especially by the government after Sir Joseph Ward established an embryonic tourism and publicity department in 1900 whose aim was partly to tell the New Zealand story often and widely, all the better to attract visitors, immigrants and investment.[13] Ward had willing allies, especially in the United States, where New Zealand was praised as 'the birth place of the 20th Century' and where there was a campaign to 'New Zealandize' America.[14] Peter Coleman wrote that 'the New Zealand fever' entered the American bloodstream 'to reappear in the 1930s with the New Deal. In this way, antipodean Liberalism helped prepare the way for the modern American welfare state."[15]

But for all the breadth and originality, if such it really was, of the Liberals' legislative programme and its promotional impact overseas, this chapter argues that New Zealand held up a collective hand well before then to signal that it was different; that what applied in other countries did not necessarily have to happen in New Zealand; and that the country possessed unique circumstances which did not apply elsewhere. Geographically, New Zealand was a place apart – a few remote islands at the bottom of the globe, so isolated they had their own flora and fauna, their own unique characteristics. New Zealand solutions were found for New Zealand problems and this created the climate for a sense of national identity, a sense of being its own nation while still tied to Britain in particular and the Australian colonies by blood and mentality. This independence of thought and deed was evident from the earliest days of European settlement.

## *Opposition to 'the seed of vice and crime'*

A desire for New Zealand not only to be different from other British colonies, but also to be seen as being different, was apparent early. It was another example of an identity marker. One of the manifestations of this individuality was the desire shown by New Zealand not to be 'tainted' by being a repository for unwanted British criminals, as some of the Australian colonies were. Again, Māori were a point of difference from other settler colonies; they were invoked as both a deterrent for convicts and as being in need of protection from them. New Zealand had been suggested as a penal colony before the First Fleet set sail for Botany Bay in 1788. A proposal written by an unidentified hand sometime between 1783 and 1786 suggesting New South Wales become a penal colony also included New Zealand: 'The same idea might be extended farther by supposing that fifty

men and as many women or any given number of convicts of both
sexes, were sent to any part of New Zealand . . . and there landed
with animals, seeds, implements and other necessaries of life proper
for the climate and country.'[16]

More precisely and more identifiably, the member of Parliament
for Salisbury, William Hussey, suggested in the House of Commons
in 1784 that New Zealand become a penal colony. Convicts were
being kept in ships on the Thames while politicians tried to find an
alternative destination for them since the American colonies ceased
to be an option. Hussey proposed a remedy: 'He would advise
Government to send them to an island, and to give every man a
woman; there was an island where they might be landed, and where
they might establish a useful colony (he was called upon to name
the island) and he said he meant New Zealand, lately discovered in
the South Seas.'[17] As Rüdiger Mack observed, this recommendation
was never followed up and the decision to send convicts to Botany
Bay was made soon after.[18]

The commander of the First Fleet, Arthur Phillip, wrote his views
on the treatment of convicts and remarked that the death penalty
should be reserved for murder and sodomy: 'For either of these
crimes I would wish to confine the criminal till an opportunity
offered of delivering him as a prisoner to the natives of New Zealand
and let them eat him. The dread of this will operate much stronger
than the fear of death.'[19] As the expatriate Australian Robert Hughes
noted, this proposal was never put into practice – 'there were no
spare ships to ferry the "madge culls", "mollies" and "fluters", as
homosexuals were known in Georgian cant, across the Tasman Sea
to enrich the Maori diet'.[20]

The desire by settlers in New Zealand not to become a penal
colony had the early support of the Colonial Secretary, the Marquis
of Normanby, in 1839 when the decision was made to bring New
Zealand under the administrative umbrella of New South Wales.
In a letter to William Hobson, spelling out his duties, Normanby
also wrote of why the British government needed to take action:

The reports which have reached this office within the last few
months establish the facts that about the commencement of the
year 1838, a body of not less than two thousand British subjects
had become permanent inhabitants of New Zealand; that amongst
them were many persons of bad or doubtful character – convicts
who had fled from our penal settlements, or seamen who had
deserted their ships; and that these people, unrestrained by any law,
and amenable to no tribunals, were alternately the authors and the
victims of every species of crime and outrage.[21]

Normanby proposed administration from Sydney, 'whatever may
be the ultimate form of government to which the British settlers
in New Zealand are to be subject', and added: 'The proposed
connection with New South Wales will not, however, involve the
extension to New Zealand of the character of a penal settlement.
Every motive concurs in forbidding this; and it is to be understood
as a fundamental principle of the new colony, that no convict is ever
to be sent thither to undergo his punishment.'[22]

Normanby's words were recalled on two occasions when it
seemed, or some associated with New Zealand thought it seemed,
that such an unequivocal edict might be being breached. The first
period, in the early 1840s, manifested in an aversion to accepting
'Parkhurst boys', youths aged between twelve and eighteen who had
been incarcerated in the Parkhurst Prison on the Isle of Wight and
who, showing sufficient signs of rehabilitation, were deemed suitable for settlement elsewhere. The second period occurred in 1849
when the British Colonial Secretary, Earl Grey, diffidently suggested
that New Zealand accept convicts.

The dispatch of 'Parkhurst boys' could be seen as nothing more
than transportation by another name, as a later report to the Home
Secretary, Sir George Grey, by the prison's governor, George Hall,
made clear: 'The desire to get their liberty by removal to the colonies for good conduct has a very strong influence over the prisoners
here.'[23] The arrival of the boys in New Zealand could not be viewed

'without the most serious alarm', an editorial in the *New Zealand Gazette and Wellington Spectator* proclaimed. While conceding the difference between the 'disposal of these boys and the assignment system of a penal colony', the editorialist said there was still an appearance of evil. The boys should be assisted in the pursuit of an honest livelihood, but:

> [i]t is no less our duty to see that New Zealand is not turned into a bed for the seed of vice and crime. As we value our own interests – the moral welfare of our families – the destiny of the Aborigines – and the character and credit of the colony, we must make an instant and unanimous effort to prevent the introduction of a system that, in no long time, would prove fatal to the prosperity of the colony.[24]

In Auckland, where 92 'Parkhurst boys' were landed from two ships in November in each of 1842 and 1843, the *Southern Cross* argued that New Zealand should not be seen by Britain in the same way as other colonies because land-owning Māori were superior to other indigenous people.[25]

> Let them send their Parkhurst boys, their anticipated convicts, and poor-house inhabitants to New South Wales where they are wanted and where they may be of use in the absence of a native population in reclaiming the wilds and wastes of that country and where they are not, as in this country, under the necessity of first purchasing every inch of land before they can sell to the settlers.[26]

Further indication of the feeling in New Zealand was provided by an Auckland merchant (and later member of the House of Representatives), Walter Brodie, in evidence to a House of Commons select committee on New Zealand. Brodie was asked, 'Did they turn out well?' and responded:

Very badly; there was hardly a day in the police-office but one was
before the police magistrate; I think they have done this colony great
injury; I think they are much worse than sending convicts out, who
would be able men to work on the roads. Many parties that went
to New Zealand were very much deceived after Lord Normanby's
despatch . . . to Captain Hobson where he mentioned that he would
avoid sending out convicts, and that his opposition to sending out
convicts was fixed and unalterable.[27]

Brodie also told the committee that the Parkhurst boys 'made a
great many natives as bad as themselves'. George Clarke, a missionary who could speak Māori and was made Protector of Aborigines
by Hobson, was also concerned about the impact the Parkhurst
boys might have on Māori: 'The introduction of the Parkhurst boys
will have a very injurious effect upon the morals of the natives and
be the means of disseminating vice . . .'.[28] The *New Zealand Journal*,
the London-based publication of the New Zealand Company,
argued that Normanby's promise was being evaded 'in a most
dishonourable manner' by the sending of Parkhurst boys and by
including New Zealand in the conditional pardons of convicts in
Van Diemen's Land (Tasmania).[29]

Two years later, New Zealand alarm was renewed when the
Colonial Secretary, Earl Grey, wrote to the New Zealand Governor,
Sir George Grey, outlining changes in the transportation system.
Grey wrote his letter on 5 August 1848 not just to his namesake in
Auckland, but to all colonial governors,[30] saying convicts should
be given 'tickets of leave' rather than freed in whichever colony
they were sent and that they would eventually have to pay the cost
of their passage and that would accrue to the colonies. In his final
paragraph, he suggested New Zealand might accept convicts under
such conditions.[31] New Zealand would gain a supply of labour, which
Grey noted was a constant source of representations to his office,
as well as funds: 'There is good reason to hope that their presence,
in moderate numbers, will not be found injurious to the general

Sir George Grey,
governor and premier.
1/2-005087-G, ATL

character of the community.' Grey concluded his letter by asking
the Governor to ascertain the opinion in New Zealand about the
country being included in the transportation scheme, stating, 'and
if I should learn from you that the measure would be wished for, I
should be prepared to take the necessary steps for including New
Zealand in the places into which convicts holding tickets of leave
may be introduced'.

The opinion the Colonial Secretary sought was neither long in
coming nor equivocal in nature. Within three weeks of the letter
being published in New Zealand, a concerned group of Aucklanders
drew up a petition in opposition and called for a public meeting.[32]
The petition said they regretted such a measure had been contemplated 'and they at once distinctly and solemnly declare that they

120                      PAPERS RELATIVE TO

NEW ZEALAND. (No. 58.)                    No. 1.
No. 1.
          COPY of a DESPATCH from Governor GREY to Earl GREY.
                        Government House, Auckland, May 8, 1849.
                                        (Received October 26, 1849.)
                              (Answered November 26, 1849—No. 77, p. 126.)

MY LORD,
          I HAVE the honour to acknowledge the receipt of your Lordship's
Despatch, No. 68,* of the 5th August last, upon the subject of the exiles with
tickets of leave whom it was proposed to send to New Zealand if the inhabitants
were willing to receive them.
          2. I have felt it my duty carefully to consider the suggestions made by your
Lordship, with a view to secure, if possible, the assistance of this country for the
promotion of those benevolent objects which are contemplated in the plans of
prison discipline which are at present being carried out under the direction of
Her Majesty's Government. But, after bestowing a lengthened consideration
upon the subject, I have been forced to the conclusion that probably no country is
less adapted than New Zealand for the reception of exiles of the description
alluded to in your Lordship's Despatch of the 5th of August last.
          3. I think that this country would hold out to men of their characters almost
irresistible temptations to retire into the interior of the country, there to live
amongst the native population and to cohabit with their women. In fact, I feel
quite certain that such would be the course adopted by a large proportion of
these exiles, and in adopting this course they would entail evils—even in the
present day—of very great magnitude upon New Zealand, whilst the future
results of such a system must, I think, be in every respect hurtful to all classes
of Her Majesty's subjects in this country.
          4. I find that these views of my own are participated in by almost every person
with whom I have conversed upon the subject, even by those persons who concur
with me in thinking that it is our common duty to assist, in as far as practicable,
not only in giving effect to the principles of prison discipline which Her Majesty's
Government are endeavouring to bring into operation, but also to afford, if
possible, to those unfortunate people who have fallen into crime, an opportunity
of atoning for their past misdeeds, and of entering once more upon a reputable
and virtuous career.
          5. I find also that both the European and native races in this country are very
unwilling, for the reasons I have alluded to, that exiles with tickets of leave
should be sent to this country.
          6. I beg therefore to recommend your Lordship not to include New Zealand
in those places into which convicts holding tickets of leave are to be introduced.
                                                  I have, &c.
The Right Hon. Earl Grey,          (Signed)          G. GREY.
     &c.     &c.     &c.

Sir George Grey's dispatch to Earl Grey opposing the sending of convicts
to New Zealand. *Convict Discipline and Transportation. Further Correspondence,*
31 January 1850, House of Commons Parliamentary Papers

entertain the most decided and insuperable objection to the introduction of convicts under the name of "exiles" . . . .'[33] The petitioners
asserted they had no faith in Grey's hope for reformation because
they drew on the experience of the Parkhurst boys:

> After the arrival of even those juvenile convicts, in whom great
> reformation was supposed to have been made, property became
> much more unsafe and subject to pilfering and loss, than it had previ-
> ously been; and although these young delinquents did not contribute
> one-twentieth to the European population of this Province, yet for

two years after their arrival, the committals for felony were doubled as compared with previous years, and more than one half of such offenders were emigrants from Parkhurst.[34]

The petition eventually gathered 445 signatures and was forwarded to the Queen via the Colonial Secretary by Grey on 7 July. It was accompanied by another signed John Grant Johnson, Interpreter to Civil Secretary, described as 'the letter of the chiefs of New Zealand', which bore 376 signatures. It read, in part: 'O Lady, we shall be perplexed if the convicts are allowed to come here. They would steal the property of the Europeans and the natives would be accused of the thefts and we should be very much displeased. It would be bad; evil would spring up.'[35]

A public meeting was also held in Dunedin, a settlement then barely a year old, and it too noted the effect on Māori. The meeting declared the result of the Parkhurst experiment in Auckland 'had been to the serious injury of that settlement and more especially to the demoralising of the natives who in that neighbourhood are numerous'.[36] A motion put forward by the religious leader of the community, the Rev. Thomas Burns, was carried unanimously. It proclaimed 'that a young colony is the very last which could venture to receive any portion of such a class [of] persons into its bosom'. It also noted that 'without the rigid appliances of a penal settlement it would be impossible to hinder any number of them from going where they pleased and nestling among the natives'.[37]

Edward John Eyre, the lieutenant-governor of New Munster (the South Island) resident in Wellington, sent to Governor Grey various responses to Earl Grey's letter and noted:

The opinions expressed are so uniform, and the feeling of the colo-nists of New Munster so strong and general against the introduction of exiles into New Zealand, that it is unnecessary for me to do more than refer Your Excellency to the accompanying enclosures and to state that I fully concur in the opinion that the introduction of exiles into a colony so peculiarly circumstanced as New Zealand is would be productive of most serious evils and might be the means of materially interfering with the present good understanding subsisting between the two races.[38]

The cries of opposition in New Zealand were echoed by the directors of the New Zealand Company in London who reiterated their 'known repugnance' to transportation and complained about the absence of assurance that 'the Colonial Office does not intend to treat New Zealand as it has treated the Cape Colony'.[39]

Admiration for New Zealand's opposition was expressed in a colony that did receive convicts, Western Australia. In a letter to the editor, J. W. Hardey of Swan wrote that the reaction in New Zealand was 'the brightest and most glorious display of opposition to such a diabolical and debasing system':

> From the conduct of vicious runaway sailors, ticket-of-leave and truant convicts they have taken their standard of judgment as to the probable results of such a fearful speculation. Ye Swanites, theirs is a glorious protest – a heaven inspired prayer, the which proclaims their high tone of moral feeling – their happiness in the enjoyment of christianity – and their satisfaction at the possession and of the enjoyment of civil rights.[40]

Hardey's letter came at a time of increasing opposition in the Australian colonies to transportation. From a colony that did not receive convicts, the *South Australian News* noted: 'The unanimity with which the Australian settlers have opposed the transportation of England's criminals to their shores is one of the most significant facts that can be adduced to prove the impolicy of the system.'[41]

It is possible to read almost a sense of exasperation in Earl Grey's reply to the New Zealand governor. He repeated that his August dispatch of the previous year was sent to all colonial governors (despite it specifically mentioning New Zealand twice) and noted, 'it is scarcely necessary to observe that the object of that Despatch was simply to ascertain whether such a measure would be acceptable to the colonists under the conditions proposed ... I need scarcely add that I should have been most willing to have afforded any assurance necessary to allay the apprehension expressed in the accompanying resolutions, if the parties concerned had thought proper to afford me the opportunity of doing so before giving publicity to their sentiments.'[42]

New Zealand's peripheral role in the whole issue of transportation in the nineteenth century has been little analysed, perhaps because it was never a penal colony. One scholarly examination, however, noted that while New Zealand was steadfastly opposed to the introduction of convicts, 'she was a spectator rather than an active participant in the general anti-transportation movements in Sydney, Melbourne and Hobart Town'.[43] C. C. Blackton also said that 'despite Grey's inclinations', the British government never made very determined efforts 'to plant penal establishments in New Zealand'. Grey's circular letter and the responses from New Zealand were the last steps in any attempt, however benign, to formally introduce a form of transportation to the colony, but concerns continued about freed convicts from the Australian colonies moving to New Zealand for several years.[44] Transportation eventually ended after 1867 when the last shipment of convicts left Britain for Western Australia.[45]

The tone of correspondence, especially the petitions which were prompted by Earl Grey's letter of August 1848, indicated that concern for Māori provided New Zealand with an additional and unique argument against transportation of convicts. This solicitude became evident in the comments about the Parkhurst emigrants earlier in the 1840s and was more pronounced in the letters and petitions which followed Grey's letter. Both Governor Grey and Eyre used the phrase 'peculiarly circumstanced' in relation to New Zealand, clearly showing that they thought Māori provided a significant point of difference between New Zealand

and other British colonies. Such a conviction could be interpreted as yet another indication of an emerging and distinctive New Zealand identity.

## One Māori, one vote

Fairburn argued that the Treaty of Waitangi, signed on annexation in 1840 between the British crown and a representation of Māori leaders, was not a unique agreement between a colonising power and an indigenous people: 'From the eighteenth century, it had become a more or less common practice for European colonising powers to sign treaties with indigenous people, exchanging sovereignty for protection or recognition of property rights.'[46] Keith Sinclair noted that New Zealand endured 'a decade of racial war', during which Māori land was confiscated (and much of it later returned): 'New Zealand seemed a typical settlement colony.'[47] But was it?

Despite the British, their agents and settlers not adhering to aspects of the treaty, despite the nearly ten years of intermittent warfare in the North Island, the musket barrels were still warm when New Zealand politicians in 1867 welcomed Māori into Parliament as colleagues. Not only were Māori parliamentary seats created, but Māori received the right to vote irrespective of any property-owning qualification – a right not extended to Pākehā for another twelve years. As a Parliamentary Library background paper notes: 'From today's perspective, it is perhaps difficult to appreciate how radical a step it was in 1867 to grant voting rights on any other basis than property ownership.'[48] It was too radical for the editor of the *Nelson Examiner and New Zealand Chronicle*, who argued Māori members would not understand the debates or 'have any other idea of the questions discussed'. The move, he thought, was 'a sacrifice of good statesmanship to the imbecility of mere sentiment'.[49] The 'sentiment' outlived the newspaper, which closed down in 1874.

The legislative move was promoted by the member for Napier, Donald McLean (Sir Donald from 1874), of whom Guy Scholefield wrote: 'His mana with both races was very high and he was listened to with great deference in the native debates which dominated Parliament in the sixties.'[50] During the second reading of the Native Representation Bill, McLean explained his attitude to the Māori vote:

> He [McLean] did therefore hope that in the interests of the Native people – a highly interesting race of people, who have fought us in politics and war for seven years – that we should make an endeavour to do for them what has been successfully done for other people and give them a voice in the administration of the Colony and make them feel that they have a voice in the management of public affairs. Let them have the wholesome excitement resulting from freedom of election to replace the excitement of war.[51]

The Bill passed without division in the House and with only three dissenters in the Legislative Council.[52] It was intended as a temporary measure until such time as Māori land was converted to individual title but was extended indefinitely in 1876.[53] It was nevertheless a remarkable concession at a time when indigenous people in other settler colonies were marginalised. Aborigines in Australia, for example, did not have the right to vote in federal elections until 1962 unless they were also enrolled as voters for state elections. The federal parliament waited until 1971 for its first Aboriginal member when Neville Bonner was appointed to fill a vacancy. Remarkably, an Aborigine was not elected to the House of Representatives until 2010. 'Status Indians' in Canada could not vote in federal elections until 1960 and the first elected to the Canadian House of Commons was in 1968.[54]

Some concern was expressed by New Zealand politicians that the distribution of the Māori seats, three in the North Island and one in the South, would alter the balance of geographical representation, a matter of moment at the time because of the commercial value of the South. Members were not aligned to parties and tended to vote along provincial or geographic lines on most issues. A Christchurch member, John Hall, who had advocated better representation for West Coast miners, put the principle ahead of political pragmatism: 'But he [Hall] did not think that consideration was a matter of so much consequence as the greater principle involved, and it was rather as a measure of justice to our brethren of the Native race that he hailed the introduction of this Bill.'[55]

Sinclair noted that there could be 'few wartime parallels to this act of justice'.[56] He argued that unlike South Africa, North America and Australia, New Zealand was settled after the British missionary societies had become powerful and after slavery was abolished by Britain in 1833: 'It was accepted by educated Christians that God had created all nations equal. Of course British settlers felt superior to the Maoris in many ways, especially relating to hygiene and European ideas of industry. But doctrines of "white" racial superiority were never generally accepted in New Zealand.'[57] He acknowledged a perception among settlers that Māori were 'superior' to the indigenous people of North America and Australia and that this 'must have helped to make racial relations less tense in New Zealand than in other similar colonies'.[58]

There were, of course, qualifications to the Pākehā largesse. The white rulers of New Zealand were much less liberal and accommodating to Chinese immigrants when they matched the other settler colonies and some American states with restrictive legislation, but the invitation to Māori to join them in Parliament was nevertheless a move well ahead of its time. It therefore fitted Fairburn's first requirement of 'an event or state of affairs that is specific to that particular country (or highly unusual)'.[59] The provision of the Māori seats was described by James Belich as 'another fruit of collaboration' by some Māori during the Māori wars. 'Humanitarian principles may have been a factor in some Pakeha support, but the need to keep the kupapa on side was probably more important', he wrote.[60] As a direct consequence of the 1867 legislation, Māori have been represented in the New Zealand Parliament continuously since; James Carroll (Sir James from 1911) became the first Māori to be elected in a European constituency (in 1894), the first Māori cabinet minister, and was, for a time, acting prime minister.[61] In terms of a settler colony sharing governance with indigenous people, this may not have qualified as 'exceptionalism', and there were caveats, but it was exceptional.

## From several governments to one

The improved communications and the consequential drawing together of New Zealanders led to the abolition of the provincial governments; in the later context of the Australian federation debate, New Zealand rid itself of its federal system a quarter of a century before it considered and rejected joining Australia's. Under the 1852 New Zealand Constitution Act, the country was governed by a central government comprising an elected House of Representatives and an appointed Legislative Council and by a partial federal system that comprised six provinces: Auckland, New Plymouth, Wellington, Nelson, Canterbury and Otago (with Hawke's Bay, Marlborough, Southland and Westland added later). One rationale for the provincial governments was that 'communications were so bad that it was impossible to set up a Central Parliament to govern them from a distance'.[62] As W. P. Morrell noted: 'The physical configuration of the country had not merely favoured their establishment but imposed formidable obstacles in the way of communication between them.'[63]

Preceding chapters have shown that time (in two senses – the imposition of a standard time and the effluxion of time), the telegraph and improving communications and technology became influential factors in making New Zealand a unitary state. The drawing of New Zealand settlements closer together for administrative purposes had already begun in the 1860s with the transfer of the capital of the colony from Auckland to Wellington, the latter primarily because of its more central location in a country geographically based on a north–south axis.[64] Rapidly improving communication and the resulting interaction between settlements was a process that not only led to a sense of a national identity but also rendered the provincial governments obsolete. Morrell was among those who saw the unifying effect of the telegraph on an emerging New Zealand identity. Writing about the abolition of provincial government, he had this to say: 'When the provincial centres began to hear day by day commercial and political news from all over the colony, it is little wonder that people in the various provinces felt a unity of feeling and interest which they had not felt when interprovincial communication was a matter of difficulty and even danger.'[65]

There were, of course, many reasons beyond improved communications for the abolition of the provinces and just as many arguments by politicians for their retention. The 'centralism' versus 'provincialism' debate was one of the defining issues of New Zealand in the early 1870s and the period has been well covered by historians.[66] It was in essence an argument between parochial and national interests. In the central government debate on the Abolition of Provinces Bill in 1875, a former premier, Edward Stafford, recalled when he first formed a government in June 1856, a government which was in office for five and a half years:

> From that moment, I determined to be a New Zealander. I determined to neither know Auckland nor Nelson nor Wellington nor Otago; and it has been a matter of reproach to me that I have no local sympathy. I have a great deal higher sympathy than that of mere locality. I can claim to have done something towards effecting the prosperity, the unity, and the future greatness of a country which has a natural geographic boundary, which is inhabited by a homogeneous race, and which I say it is a miserable spectacle to see torn by petty local dissensions.[67]

As Stafford's biographer, Edmund Bohan, noted: 'Few others even used the term New Zealander.'[68] He could have added the adverb, 'then'.

Unity was the theme of the debate on the Abolition Bill, which has been called 'outstanding in the annals of parliamentary history'.[69] A later premier, Harry Atkinson, said the people of New Zealand 'are determined that this shall be one united colony'.[70] One of Atkinson's younger brothers, Arthur, watched part of the debate and wrote to his brother-in-law, Christopher Richmond, a politician and jurist:

> The abolition policy seems quite in the ascendant . . . The Opposition headed by Sir George Grey . . . had a caucus today at which it was resolved not to oppose abolition but only to require it should be referred to the country! So I think we may assume that at last, thro' the agency of some occult solvent, those Provincial rocks upon which (since 1861) so many noble vessels have suffered shipwreck . . . have been disintegrated and resolved into the primordial mud – or should I say slime? – out of which they were formed.[71]

With the system of provincial government abolished, the interests of national unity – and therefore a burgeoning feeling of national identity as New Zealanders – gained hegemony.

## Education for all

While overseas attention focused on the legislative programme of the Liberal government in the 1890s and the extension of the franchise to women in 1893 was the law change that historically gained most focus, the Education Act of 1877 is also worthy of note. It was, according to Guy Scholefield, 'perhaps the most potent factor in unifying the provinces, so recently abolished, and developing a national spirit'.[72] New Zealand was not unique in ensuring education for all within its borders and, as John Mackey observed, the development of education in New Zealand was 'typical of nineteenth century concern for the political and social equality, irrespective of creed, and hence for the separation of church and state'.[73]

As typical as it may have been, New Zealand steered its own course toward educating its young and it did this, according to Mackey, because 'the community was essentially a frontier one with a deeply felt need for promoting its sense of communal and national unity'.[74] New Zealand chose the secular principle as the basis for its national system of education, and this was 'the most interesting feature' in Mackey's view:

> In the first place the acceptance of this principle was contrary to the
> development of the administrative structure of primary education
> as it had taken shape in England. In almost every other feature New
> Zealand's education depended upon English educational practice.
> In the second place, the majority of the members and the community
> were not in favour of this principle as the ideal basis for a system of
> education. They accepted it as a compromise between openly violat-
> ing the consciences of those who objected to non-sectarian religious
> instruction, or possibly imperilling the unity of a national system
> of education.[75]

In his view, the New Zealand community was more akin emotionally to new societies such as the United States rather than to England, and 'lower middle class usefulness' was the purpose of the common school and thus would not offend the religious conscience of anyone.[76]

Jeanine Graham lent credence to Scholefield's view that the 1877 Act helped create a national spirit when she wrote that it 'replaced provincial variety with a colony-wide system of primary education', thus reducing if not eliminating regional disparity.[77] But for all its nationalising and unifying effects, the 1877 Act also divided. Roman Catholics in particular resented what they saw as the injustice of paying state taxes which went toward maintaining secular schools while at the same time they financed a separate Catholic school system.[78]

Provincial governments had originally been responsible for education in their own areas, some with success, such as in Otago, and some with less success. While the provinces continued to have their own governments, the central government had already taken a lead role, and with the abolition of provinces in 1876 the take-over was complete. Hereafter, the provision of education for every child was the responsibility ultimately of the elected politicians in Wellington. The first education minister was John Ballance, who never uttered a word in the House while the Bill made its passage through to becoming an Act.[79]

The Education Act, following on from the earlier opposition to transportation and the vote for Māori, came in what noted lexicographer Harry Orsman called a period in New Zealand governance marked by expressions of self-reliance and independence.[80] These included New Zealand talk (but little action) about creating its own South Pacific 'empire', motivated partly by trade and partly by a perceived need for external security.[81] Orsman detected what he called 'another side to this distrust of European nations (including Britain)' in the realisation by Julius Vogel and William Fox that it would be 'neither practicable nor politic for New Zealand to enter into schemes for imperial defence'.[82] This was at the time of the withdrawal of British troops from New Zealand. An even more radical expression of New Zealand's growing assertiveness was talk of the country becoming a colony of the United States:

> This was by no means a fantastic expression of independence
> from Britain and Europe. New Zealand had seen American traders
> and whalers from the earliest days; there was a large American or
> Americanised element among the gold-seekers; the steamship con-
> nections with the west coast of America were quicker, more regular
> and direct than that with Britain, and the Pacific cable was completed

in the Eighties. America would certainly be recognised as a potential Pacific power.[83]

At the same time, there was a 'curious growth of political and national apartness' from the Australian colonies. Orsman noted there was 'no doubt that these were original attempts at accomplishing a desirable independence' even though they had a 'certain air of wildness'.[84]

## Wellington's decision, not London's

In the first period of the Liberal administration elected in 1890 (though John Ballance did not take office as premier until January 1891), New Zealand again asserted itself over the hegemony of Britain. At issue was the government's ability to appoint new members to the Legislative Council. Ballance wanted to appoint twelve new members, the better to ensure government legislation was passed by the upper house. The Governor, the Earl of Onslow, disagreed and his successor in 1892, the Earl of Glasgow, took the same line, arguing that twelve new members would amount to 'swamping' and that he would agree to only eight.[85] Ballance appealed directly to the British Secretary of State for the Colonies, Baron Knutsford, who told Glasgow that Ballance's proposal 'seems to me a reasonable one'.[86] Knutsford's successor later in 1892, the Marquess of Ripon, upheld his predecessor's view and was more specific about why a New Zealand minister should have his way over a British government representative. There was a constitutional aspect whose broad principles should be considered, Ripon wrote, and the governor had the right to discuss with his ministers the desirability of any course of action:

He should frankly state the objections, if any, which may occur to him; but if, after full discussion, Ministers determine to press upon

Richard John Seddon, New Zealand's longest-serving prime minister.
1-2-005255-F, ATL

him the advice which they have already tendered, the Governor should, as a general rule, and when Imperial interests are not affected, accept that advice, bearing in mind that the responsibility rests with the Ministers, who are answerable to the Legislature, and, in the last resort, to the country.[87]

Within a week of Glasgow receiving Ripon's letter, Ballance went ahead and appointed twelve new members to the Legislative Council. The affair was a clear signal of New Zealand autonomy winning out over British dominance. Ballance died the following year and was replaced as premier by Richard John Seddon, ushering in the longest tenure by any political leader as well as the legislative

# Le Petit Journal

5 CENTIMES  SUPPLÉMENT ILLUSTRÉ  5 CENTIMES  ABONNEMENTS

Le Petit Journal

DIMANCHE 17 MAI 1908

L'ACTION FEMINISTE

Les « suffragettes » envahissent une section de vote et s'emparent de l'urne électorale

Following on from New Zealand: Suffragettes in France, 1908.
*Le Petit Journal*, 17 May 1908

programme that elicited so much attention from Australia, Europe and the United States.[88]

The law change that prompted most reaction, both at the time and subsequently, was the extension of voting rights to women, with New Zealand being hailed as the first nation-state in the world to take such a step,[89] and as such, a far-seeing and liberal society which gave 'a very remarkable object lesson to the world'.[90] The extension of the franchise was no rushed-through legislation by a fresh government anxious for change, however. Such a law had first been proposed in 1878 by Seddon's opponent for the Liberal leadership, Robert Stout, and similar Bills extending the vote to women had been introduced and foundered several times between 1878 and 1893.[91] The law change made it through in 1893 despite strong opposition from powerful interests both inside and outside the House (especially brewing interests outside who feared for their profitability), and because of political manoeuvring and miscalculations. 'The enfranchisement of woman has been accomplished by her enemies', was how the *New Zealand Herald* put it. Patricia Grimshaw said the Bill passed by 'the action of the Government's enemies to annoy and anger their adversaries' and noted comparable political chicanery got similar laws through in Wyoming, Western Australia and South Australia.[92]

The last legislative hurdle for the Bill was the third reading in the Legislative Council where it was carried by 20 votes to eighteen. Of the twelve councillors added by Ballance to smooth the path of Liberal legislation, two were absent and the remaining ten were evenly split for and against. Of the four Labour-aligned additions among the twelve, one voted against the Bill and two were in favour.[93] The Bill was also passed despite Seddon's opposition, and 'with consummate impudence' he sent a telegram to the leading campaigner, Kate Sheppard, suggesting that doubts about the government's sincerity must have been removed.[94]

For all the attention the granting of the franchise to women gained both at the time and in later years, there was more to the Electoral Act of 1893 than that. As Tony Ballantyne noted, it was an extensive consolidation of electoral laws, among which was the exclusion of 'aliens' from voting, 'which reflected the investment of the state in both policing its borders and defining the nation's place in the world'.[95] But it was the women who garnered top billing. The Australian writer and poet Henry Lawson, whose mother was a noted campaigner for women's rights, arrived in New Zealand for the first time in November 1893 and observed in a newspaper article

Daniel Hoskyn, a British naval surgeon visiting Auckland, drew this sketch of women going to the poll for the first time in 1893 at Devonport. *The Graphic*, 27 January 1894, p. 92

on the eve of the 1893 general election: 'A variety of reasons gives to-day's ballot unusual significance, but women's franchise is the most revolutionary of them all.'[96] The following month, he broke into verse:

> In the morning of New Zealand we should sing a Marseillaise!
> We should sing a hymn of triumph, we should sing a song of praise!
> For our women are ennobled! The narrow days are o'er,
> And the Fathers of New Zealand shall be famous evermore.
>
> 'Tis the glory of New Zealand that her sons were first to see
> That there never was a free land where the women were not free!
> Time shall hear the nations asking why it was not ever thus,
> For the freedom of our women comes with liberty to us.[97]

A local rhymester, who styled himself David Will M. Burn, had beaten the more illustrious Lawson into rhyme, part of which went:

THE SUMMIT AT LAST.

An unidentified artist sums up the achievement of 1893. *New Zealand Graphic and Ladies' Journal*, 1894, PUBL-0126-1894-01, ATL

"Ye have the vote!" – O God be praised,
Another step is won
On the golden Stair of Progress
That leadeth to the Sun.

New Zealand, O my country,
I thrill with pride this day,
To think where Nations pause and shrink
Again thou lead'st the way![98]

There appears also to have been a redefining of New Zealand's place in the world during what came to be known as the Seddon era. Orsman attributed it to a New Zealand need to resolve its external problems within a framework wider than that of the Pacific 'by attaching herself as an integral part to the British Empire': 'She hoped that by paying outspoken and extreme lip service to a commercial and defensive alliance under the necessary control of Britain she would be able to gain real and practical advantages without great cost to national independence.'[99] The key to this strategy was

NAILING HIS COLOURS TO THE MAST.

Readers of the *New Zealand Graphic* were left in no doubt about how Richard Seddon might have viewed his tenure. This cartoon was published after his last election victory in 1905. *New Zealand Graphic and Ladies' Journal*, 9 December 1905

Seddon. It was he who had to straddle political asymmetrical bars, metaphorically tugging the forelock in the imperial direction while asserting a national identity in the other. As Orsman noted:

> It was fortunate that a man so suited to promoting this policy rose to power at this time. He was an apt politician accustomed to move only when he considered that public opinion supported him. Hence he displays many inconsistencies in his approach to external affairs partly due to this fact and partly from lack of mature perception of the effects of his actions and statements. But nonetheless, Seddon was a pragmatist who (for all his words) had grasped the fact that New Zealand was a very small fish in an ocean dominated by European powers.[100]

Guy Scholefield, journalist and librarian who lived through the Liberal era and who wrote copiously on New Zealand nationalism, also discerned the Seddon balancing act.[101] In a letter to Australian writer and poet Vance Palmer, Scholefield remarked how nationalism in New Zealand was boosted by the Legislative Council imbroglio, then went on to say:

> Seddon himself was a New Zealander then out and out, and I fancy
> he hoodwinked the advanced members of his own party with his true
> blue imperialism. When the [Boer] war was over and Seddon had
> carried his legislation there was not a voice of native nationalism in
> the country. He had skilfully canalised it into closer relations with the
> Mother Country.[102]

## '1882 and all that'

While Scholefield may have underestimated or misread the effect of the Boer War on New Zealand identity, it was clear he could see, like Orsman, that Seddon appreciated the pragmatic path was to follow Britain at the same time as asserting a New Zealand independence of thought and deed. New Zealand was already well embarked on this course of commercial dependence on Britain, emphasised in the most visible of ways by the introduction in 1882 of exports of frozen meat. New Zealand was not first in this field – Australia, the United States and Argentina had already experimented with the process – but New Zealand's first shipment that arrived at the East India Docks on the Thames on 26 May 1882 gained the attention because of the distance travelled and the condition of the meat.[103]

As the company that installed the refrigeration equipment on the sailing ship *Dunedin* noted in a letter to the editor of *The Times*: 'This shipment differs from all other importations of frozen meat, from the fact of having been made in a sailing vessel, which has been 98 days on the passage, during which time the holds of the ship containing the meat have been kept at about 20 degrees below freezing point.'[104] The significance was noted in an editorial in that

paper: 'To-day we have to record such a triumph over physical difficulties as would have been incredible, and even unimaginable, a
very few years ago.'[105] The New Zealand agent-general in London,
Sir Francis Dillon Bell, saw the significance for both the United
Kingdom and New Zealand. In a letter to the editor noting the
volume of American meat imports to Britain, he observed that
'every year you are becoming more and more dependent on other
countries for the food supply of your people'.[106] Promotion was then
combined with promise: 'Is it not better, since you must needs have
so huge a supply, that you should get as much of it as you can from
your own colonies, rather than from foreign countries? We in New
Zealand, at any rate, mean to send you plenty of it, and you must
regard this first shipment as only the harbinger of a great trade.'[107]

An expatriate New Zealander in London, Charles Rooking
Carter, had already perceived the possibilities for New Zealand.
'Frozen meat importing may yet become a great trade in London',
he wrote in a letter to the editor prior to the first shipment from
New Zealand. There may be opposition from trade interests, 'but
the great body of the working classes hail the frozen meat as a
boon and a blessing'.[108] A Wellington law student at Cambridge,
William Barton, put a carcass from the first shipment to the most
practical of tests. He had it examined by the head cook at St John's
College who pronounced it 'excellent' and then sought proof of the
pudding (or of the main course, to be precise): 'On the following
day the greater part was cooked: a joint was sent to the "Fellows"
of the College, whose nicety of taste has descended to them from
those historically epicurean monastics of old, and they declared the
quality of the meat superior to any which was supplied here by the
college butcher.'[109]

James Belich may have indulged in whimsy when he remarked
that the date of the *Dunedin*'s voyage should be as well known in
New Zealand as that of the Battle of Hastings is in England but he
was in no doubt of its significance. It is 'one of the most important of all New Zealand stories' and it was a 'geographic miracle,

The *Dunedin* leaves Port Chalmers in 1882 to begin the trade in frozen farm products.
Detail from an H. L. Mallittee painting

a staggering conquest of distance'.[110] The advent of the frozen meat trade, soon to extend to dairy products, underpinned what Belich called the 'recolonial' period and created an interdependence between New Zealand and the United Kingdom that lasted unconditionally until the latter's joining of what was then known as the European Economic Community in 1971.[111] New Zealand meat and dairy exporting to Britain was 'a classic re-colonial industry', Belich wrote.[112] It helped that the emergence of the frozen meat trade coincided with a decline in English agriculture. In 1881, there were about a hundred thousand fewer farm-labourers than ten years before and England, as opposed to Britain as a whole, increasingly relied on imported food, trusting in its policy of free trade and the strength of the British navy, if the need arose, to ensure delivery.[113]

It was the economic importance of the trade in primary produce that shaped future New Zealand thoughts and deeds. Imperial loyalty engendered through kinship and the colonial ties that bound was gradually overtaken, if not replaced, by the pragmatism of commercial necessity and it was this reality, as writers such as Orsman and Scholefield detected, that partly motivated Seddon's imperialism. The head began to rule the heart. As Belich noted, talk of a formal imperial federation had faded away because the dominions valued their political autonomy – 'from each other as much as from Britain; they were spokes of a wheel whose hub was London'.[114] The links with Britain were tightened not just because of an emotional link with the 'mother country' but because of a need driven *by* New Zealand *for* New Zealand: it was the driving in of another pile supporting New Zealand identity. This connection was made by the French academic and geographer André Siegfried, after his inquiring visit to New Zealand in 1899. The most powerful of interests which retained New Zealand in 'England's orbit' was the economic one:

And is this not the factor, with Anglo-Saxons, on which everything turns? For, although they too are susceptible, like the other races, to fleeting impulses, their return to the clear notions of egoism is quicker than that of others. It is for this reason that a mere sentiment of loyalty would not be enough to explain the fidelity, till now unshaken, of New Zealand. We must find the real cause in the state of economic dependence to which the young Colony is still placed.[115]

## Pragmatic 'humanist' politics

The legislative programme of the Liberal era which was ushered in by Ballance and dominated by Seddon and which drew observers and admirers from Britain, Europe and the United States was described as 'a sort of socialism' by one of its intellectual architects, William Pember Reeves.[116] But to Siegfried and lawyer and politician William Downie Stewart, who wrote the introduction to Siegfried's book, it was more pragmatism than socialism. As Stewart noted:

> They [New Zealanders] are persuaded that the eyes of the world are centred on their country and on their daring experiments in legislation. He [Siegfried] notes also the entire absence in their politicians (with the exception of Mr W. P. Reeves) of any political philosophy – their contempt of political theories, and their practical and empirical opportunism.[117]

This standpoint was also noted by Michael King, who wrote that the Liberals' 'unifying belief' was in a dominant role for central government 'but on pragmatic rather than ideological grounds'.[118] An external view came from Peter Coleman who said that while the Liberal reforms were often labelled 'state socialism' or 'state capitalism' by contemporaries, ideology played little part and politicians mostly thought of themselves as humanists.[119] Sinclair recorded the warm glow of pride New Zealanders felt through the 1890s as they asserted, or were told, that their isolated little country was

How the first Liberal ministry was portrayed for readers of the
*New Zealand Observer. New Zealand Observer*, 2 November 1892

leading the world, but more careful onlookers knew that some of
the reforms had been introduced, or would soon be introduced, in
other places as well, especially the Australian colonies.[120] Reeves did
not hide the fact, hence the title of his 1902 book, *State Experiments
in Australia and New Zealand* – in which not only did he include
Australia in the title, but placed it first.

Reeves also found himself having to answer charges of plagiar-
ism over the wording of one of the landmark pieces of legislation,
the Industrial Conciliation and Arbitration Act. Reeves, by then

agent-general in London, happily conceded that the South Australian premier, Charles Kingston, was the real pioneer. He also said he acknowledged Kingston's role in *State Experiments*.[121] Nevertheless, if some of the Liberal reforms were tried elsewhere before or concurrent with New Zealand, it was their cumulative effect that set New Zealand apart and prompted such comments as: 'Has it ever occurred to you that the truest reflections of our national character and tendencies are to be found in our statute books?'[122]

Providing a thundercloud where almost everyone saw sunshine was V. I. Lenin, who noted while preparing his work on imperialism: 'The country at the end of the world . . . A country of obdurate, provincial, dull, selfish philistines, who exported from England "culture" and lie upon it as a dog on hay. (The natives – Maoris – have been exterminated; by fire and sword; a series of wars) . . . New Zealand – the most "loyal," faithful colony of Great Britain.'[123] Lenin also had comments on Siegfried's work on New Zealand:

> The distinctive feature of imperialism: exclusiveness. The Yellow race is completely barred from entering the country . . . a country of inveterate, backwoods, thick-headed egotistic philistines who have kept their civilisation to themselves and exterminated the Maori . . . Prime Minister Seddon – a representative of Australasian imperialism. An imperialist of the first water . . . the imperialist bourgeoisie is buying the workers by social reforms.[124]

American reformers – who in Coleman's words 'understood New Zealand's determination to prevent the spread of Old World problems to the New' – clearly held an opposite view.[125] While Coleman conceded that most of the New Zealand legislative ideas had been talked about in the English-speaking world for at least a generation: 'All that New Zealand could claim was that it had acted while the rest of the world had talked.'[126] American interest in the New Zealand changes, he recorded, was passive until

An advocate of the New Zealand way, Henry Demarest Lloyd.
Library of Congress

Henry Demarest Lloyd returned home from his visit to New Zealand in 1899. Then, the interest 'changed dramatically to an active campaign to "New Zealandize" America'. Lloyd cloaked his advocacy of New Zealand with objectivity but it was camouflage: 'He encouraged his readers, usually by implication but sometimes explicitly, to equate New Zealand with civilization, the United States with barbarism. The idea of a country with neither tramps nor millionaires, neither strikes nor lockouts, became a symbol for all that was wrong with America.'[127] Lloyd himself wrote:

In all the list of Australasian reforms, there is nothing bizarre, nothing out of line with the evolution in progress, even in monarchical countries; but it was the good fortune of the Australasians, and of us who can see that they are experimenting for the rest of the world, that they could make the history we sigh for, without making the revolutions for fear of which we do nothing but sigh.[128]

Such was the impact of Lloyd's proselytising that a fellow reformer, William E. Smythe, ran for Congress from the San Diego district on what he described as 'the New Zealand ticket'; another politician, Annie L. Diggs, announced plans to run for the Kansas legislature on a platform based on New Zealand reforms; and they and other reformers were in regular correspondence with New Zealand thinkers such as the Labour Secretary, Edward Tregear, and the agent-general in London, William Pember Reeves, the former Minister of Labour.[129] But Seddon was far from overlooked or side-lined. When he died in 1906, reforming publisher Benjamin Orange Flower eulogised him 'as if the progress of world civilization had suffered some irreparable disaster'.[130] Coleman's conclusion after his study of this American turn-of-the-century enthusiasm for New Zealand thought and deed was that antipodean Liberalism helped prepare the way for the modern American welfare state:

> The course of twentieth-century American reform bears a New Zealand imprint, among others. Even if Lloyd's "last best hope" and Parsons' "prophesy for the rest of the world" had little direct legislative impact in the Progressive era itself, the virus of "New Zealand fever" had entered the American bloodstream to reappear in the 1930s with the New Deal.[131]

This marvelling at and about New Zealand was not indulged in an ocean away purely by intellectuals for the edification of other intellectuals. The views of Lloyd, Siegfried and other visitors were widely reported in New Zealand newspapers, as were reports and reviews of their books.[132] Newspapers in New Zealand also reproduced what material they could glean from American papers, such as a report in the *Detroit Free Press* about a Lloyd book, *Newest England*, and a lengthy report of a Lloyd meeting in Plymouth, Massachusetts.[133] New Zealanders, intellectuals and otherwise, were thus informed of how others praised their country and held it up as an example, further confirming for them that New Zealand had carved out its own identity.

At a less scholarly level, other visitors to New Zealand were even more widely reported. Newspapers carried almost daily accounts of the celebratory progress through the country of writers Anthony Trollope, Rudyard Kipling and Mark Twain. Another visitor was the Irish nationalist Michael Davitt – 'my well beloved friend and shipmate', according to Twain – and he too was widely reported, although his published comments were confined to his quest for Irish home rule.[134] Newspapers reported packed halls for their meetings and lectures, and politicians basked in the celebrity. Twain met the Governor, the Earl of Glasgow, and shared a late supper in Wellington with several cabinet ministers; Richard Seddon took the stage in Wellington with Davitt.[135] A Twain comment would have fallen on receptive ears: 'I knew of the New Zealand of Tasman from reading, but the New Zealand of to-day took me by surprise. [New Zealanders contend that their land is] the finest in the world. From the glimpses I have had, I am inclined to believe them.'[136]

Some who thought it the finest in the world would have been those farmers who benefited from the bitter experience and sweet vision of one of Seddon's ablest ministers, Sir John McKenzie. He had seen in his youth from his home in the Highlands the depredations of 'landlordism' and the evil of the clearances and determined that in his new home neither would be possible. If a desire for a better life and conditions, an unswerving determination not to repeat in the New World what was prevalent in the Old, were what motivated immigrants, McKenzie was its apotheosis. It was through his indefatigable efforts and powers of persuasion that large estates in New Zealand were forcibly broken up during the 1890s. A combination of state enterprise under McKenzie and private enterprise led to what Tom Brooking called 'the triumph of the efficient family farm' that underpinned the bedrock export industry.[137] McKenzie was a folk hero: 'In Otago, Canterbury, Marlborough and Hawke's Bay especially, he was viewed as a benevolent giant who slew the monster of oligarchy and unlocked the gates of opportunity for the ordinary people of New Zealand.'[138] Disdainful of the aristocracy's monopoly of fish and game in Scotland (and other parts of Britain), McKenzie also incorporated into the 1892 Land Act a provision

giving all New Zealanders the right to access rivers, lakes, forests and coast to fish or hunt.[139] This too would have made him a
folk hero.

Through a series of governmental moves and actions in the
second half of the nineteenth century, beginning with resistance
to transportation, New Zealand demonstrated an assertion of
independence and innovation, sometimes based on pragmatism,
sometimes on idealism, and sometimes on a determination not to
repeat in the New World the injustices of the Old. Māori provided
a unique dimension to this self-determination and New Zealand,
alone among settler colonies, involved its indigenous people in the
decision-making process while at the same time leading the world
among nation-states in also involving women.

Such ground-breaking moves may not fit Miles Fairburn's exact
interpretation of exceptionalism, but it is worthy of note that
the country for which exceptionalism was originally claimed, the
United States, did neither until much later. The aggregation and
the cumulative effects of decisions by successive governments, and
most notably by the Liberals from 1891, set New Zealand apart as a
state with its own national identity. This conceptual independence
was given practical effect by the decision not to join the other
'Australasian' colonies in the Australian federation.

# FIVE

# 'New Zealand for the New Zealanders'

*Nature has made 1200 impediments to
the inclusion of New Zealand...*[1]

As the clock ticked over and the nineteenth century became the twentieth, New Zealand turned down a chance to become a state of Australia. The six colonies of Australia – New South Wales, Victoria, Queensland, Tasmania, South and Western Australia – decided to join together in a federal system and the plan was for New Zealand to join too. But it did not. The Premier, Richard John Seddon, was against any such notion and so were a great many other people, but such a significant and far-reaching decision for the future of New Zealand was not decided by the people and a royal commission report recommending against federation was not even discussed in Parliament. Seddon promised it would be, but the politicians never got around to it. The former Australasian colleagues, linked together by the Tasman Sea, by birthright and by common concerns, headed into the twentieth century as separate countries.

The comment about nature making 1200 impediments was made by the New Zealand parliamentarian and 1879–82 premier Sir John Hall and came to encapsulate the desultory debate about whether New Zealand should have joined the other Australasian colonies in federation. It was the tyranny of distance, to use Australian historian Geoffrey Blainey's expressive phrase, that more than any other factor was held to have been the reason for New Zealand, neither its politicians nor its people, seriously entertaining the idea of becoming Australians.[2] It is worth putting Hall's comment into context and repeating it in full. The former New South Wales premier and the man regarded as 'the father of federation', Sir Henry Parkes, had said at a Melbourne conference on federation in 1890 that 'Nature had made no impediment to the federation of the Australasian colonies', according to Hall.[3] He then responded: 'Nature has made 1200 impediments to the inclusion of New Zealand in any such federation in the 1200 miles of stormy ocean which lie between us and our brethren in Australia.'[4]

Hall went on to explain what he meant, an explanation that has seldom been attached to the recounting of his portentous sentence. Government, he said, must be for and of the people, but it must also be 'in sight and within hearing of the people', and the government of a federation that included New Zealand would not 'give satisfaction to the people of that colony'.[5] He worried, too, whether New Zealand had men sufficiently able and with the time to commit themselves to a distant government. Reservations were also aired at the conference by the other New Zealand delegate, Captain William Russell. He suggested the word 'Australasia' in Parkes' motion for 'early union under the crown' should be substituted by the word 'Australia': 'It will be a marriage of affection if these colonies come together. But with New Zealand it would simply be a *marriage de convenance* . . .'[6] He then suggested a rider to the motion that 'the remoter Australasian colonies shall be entitled to admission at such times and on such conditions as may hereafter be agreed upon'.[7]

Distance in the geographical sense and distance from decision-making were what concerned Hall and Russell. Wellington was as far from Sydney as Rome was from Moscow, Bucharest from London (and, of course, as Perth was from Melbourne). For all the interconnectedness between New Zealand and Australia, for all the

Premier Richard Seddon and the Opposition leader, Captain William Russell, as portrayed by William Blomfield. Detail from *New Zealand Observer*, 29 December 1894, p. 1

trans-Tasman trafficking in goods, services and people, there was an increasing distance between the two.[8] Despite the commonalities between New Zealand and Australia, the shared past and present, New Zealand's evolving national identity in the late nineteenth century was at the root of its lukewarm feeling for, and eventual rejection of, federation into the Commonwealth of Australia. The two countries were similar and were complementary, but they were not the same. As a weekly newspaper, the *New Zealand Observer*, put it late in the federation debate: 'New Zealand has a destiny before her, just as Australia has, and our destiny is something more than to swell the greatness of Australia. It is to create a new nation which shall grow in wealth and population until it eventually rivals that of Australia, or one of the nations of the old world.'[9] The newspaper aped its Sydney competitor, the *Bulletin*, with its heading on the story: 'New Zealand for the New Zealanders'.[10]

As Keith Sinclair remarked, such a significant subject as whether New Zealand stood alone or joined with Australia has attracted

surprisingly little comment.[11] Since the years leading up to federation were contemporaneous with the legislative social reforms of
the Liberal government, the issue became inseparable from comment on them, and indeed, New Zealand's attitude was shaped in
no small part by them. Certainly, the link was made by the French
academic, André Siegfried: 'Having affirmed her autonomy by
means of daring and original legislation, it was necessary for her
next to define her attitude to the outside world, and especially to
this Commonwealth which was set up by her side.'[12] It was also
made by the travelling observer of imperial affairs Richard Jebb,
who thought New Zealand's 'prosaic preoccupation' with federation was pushed aside by the militaristic rush to colours in the Boer
War.[13]

William Pember Reeves, who had an insider's knowledge of
the Liberals' legislative programme, wrote for a British audience
when he said New Zealand was 'in no sense an offshoot or outlying
province of Australia' and: 'The majority of New Zealanders . . .
seem far from persuaded that it is either their destiny or to their
interest to become an Australian province.'[14] A year later, Reeves
returned to the subject and said New Zealand 'lay a thousand miles
too far away from Sydney to count. She has always been outside
of the Federal circle.'[15] Another expatriate New Zealander living
in London, Guy Scholefield, saw a distinct difference between his
country and Australia:

> The insularity of the country was personified in the independence
> and individualism of the people. On every conceivable subject they
> struck out on their own line . . . New Zealand accepted without
> enthusiasm the invitations of Australia to attend federal conventions
> and conferences. The majority of New Zealanders preferred the idea
> of the separate identity.[16]

Thereafter, federation in a New Zealand context faded from the
pages for nearly another half-century before what Sinclair called

'the first scholarly investigation',[17] by E. J. Tapp of New England University College, appeared in 1952.[18] Scholars' pens lay fallow again for more than 20 years until an Australian professor working in New Zealand, Frederick Wood, produced a provocative take on the issue, which prompted a brief flurry of responses.[19] Almost another two decades went by before the publication of *Tasman Relations: New Zealand and Australia, 1788–1988* which included Sinclair's essay on federation. Among the contributors was Blainey.[20] A view from afar came in 2001 from Ged Martin.[21]

In the meantime, a contribution of a different type appeared when an Australian Federal Court judge, Michael Kirby, argued that 'Australia should consider an act of generosity' and admit New Zealand as two states.[22] He returned to the theme 20 years later when in a public presentation in Auckland he asked 'whether we should explore our options with a little more attention and care than we have in the recent past'.[23] Other public figures periodically renewed talk about New Zealand joining Australia – the Australian Prime Minister, Andrew Fisher, in 1912 and a prominent Wellington businessman, Sir Charles Norwood, in 1940.[24]

The centenary of federation prompted several publications in Australia, but very little in New Zealand.[25] Philippa Mein Smith contributed the New Zealand section to Helen Irving's *Centenary Companion to Australian Federation* and in 2003 wrote an account of the visit to Australia in 1901 by the members of the New Zealand Royal Commission on Federation.[26] The federation issue also became a part, if a small one, of *Remaking the Tasman World* in 2008, as it had been in Denis McLean's *The Prickly Pair* in 2003.[27] Both these books looked at the enduring relationships between New Zealand and Australia as a whole, rather than simply during the federation era. A contrary view to most opinion was published in 2007 when art historian Hamish Keith argued 'we had no good reason not to federate with Australia. We just didn't want to.'[28]

A rare Australian scholarly examination of why New Zealand did not become part of Australia appeared in 2009.[29] It mounted the familiar 'distance argument' and contended that the federation decision demonstrated an emerging concept of what a nation was – it was not a region and, quoting Tapp, 'it was common to view the ocean as a barrier and land as a link in defining "the nation"'.[30] Ultimately, New Zealand's decision not to bridge those '1200 miles of stormy ocean' in federation with the other antipodean colonies was, in the words of William Parker Morrell, 'another milestone on the road to national self-consciousness'.[31]


## 'For the common good'

Federation had been a word in the back of the Tasman mind from the 1840s when it was, according to Manning Clark, a matter of convenience for a unified approach to services such as postal, health, quarantine and railways.[32] In South Australia, there was a plea to 'put an end to the bickerings and jealousies which have hitherto too unhappily prevailed, and . . . unite now in one general confederacy for the common good'.[33] *The Times* in London, ever watchful of the interests of Empire, traced the beginnings of federation to proposals by the British Secretary of State for the Colonies, Earl Grey, to separate Victoria from New South Wales and it quoted Grey as once saying: 'For the first time in the world's history, there will be a continent for a nation and a nation for a continent.'[34] Indeed, the British legislation granting autonomy to Victoria contained federal provisions – including the appointment of a governor-general – but these clauses were omitted by the House of Lords, Grey saying that as they stood they would have been a 'dead letter' and it was therefore decided to omit clauses which would have been inoperative.[35] A Victorian government select committee report in 1857 worried about the colonies' vulnerability to foreign aggression and argued that while there were various opinions on federation, 'we are unanimous in believing that it is not too soon to invite a mutual understanding on the subject throughout the Colonies'.[36]

The 'father of federation', Sir
Henry Parkes. State Library of
New South Wales

In New Zealand, politicians seemed always to have an ear cocked
for changes in the South Pacific winds. The future of the colonies
across the Tasman became a part of the wider interests beyond their
borders with which they concerned themselves: encroachment by
other countries, especially Germany; hopeful and unfulfilled prospects about South Pacific trade; concerns about violence against
natives and whether intervention was warranted. All of these things
and more were the subject of New Zealand submissions to the
imperial masters in London, as Angus Ross noted in his detailed
study, *New Zealand Aspirations in the Pacific in the Nineteenth Century*.[37]

Federation continued as an occasional theme. Intercolonial conferences in the 1880s established a Federal Council but it proved to
be moribund when the New South Wales Premier, Henry Parkes,
withdrew his colony on the grounds that it would delay federation
rather than enhance its prospects.[38] New Zealand had also decided
not to join. The final impetus toward federation – when a nibble

became a bite, according to Clark – came with a speech by Parkes at Tenterfield on the New South Wales–Queensland border on 24 October 1889: 'The great question for you to consider is whether the time has not now arisen for the creation on this Australian continent of an Australian parliament as distinct from a local government. The thing will have to be done, and to put it off will only make the difficulties greater which stand in the way.'[39]

Parkes put the case more eloquently the following year: 'The crimson thread of kinship runs through us all.'[40] Parkes' Tenterfield Oration, as it came to be known, was not contextually isolated. It followed (by three weeks) a report by a British army officer, Major-General Bevan Edwards, questioning the colonies' ability to defend themselves:

> If the Australian Colonies had to rely at any time solely on their own resources, they would offer such a rich and tempting prize that they would certainly be called upon to fight for their independence, and isolated as Australia would be, without a proper supply of arms and ammunition . . . its position would be one of great danger.[41]

Within four months of Tenterfield, the seven Australasian colonies met at the conference on federation in Melbourne, with Parkes opening proceedings by declaring: 'The best interests and the present and future prospects of the Australasian colonies will be promoted by an early union under the Crown . . .'[42] Parkes gained initial success and the colonies agreed to meet in Sydney in 1891 where they approved a constitution that had been drafted by the Queensland Premier, Sir Samuel Griffith. But for all Parkes' own enthusiasm for federation, the scheme collapsed in the face of New South Wales opposition.

Two years later, federation gained renewed impetus under what the Australian historian, John Hirst, called a much broader federal movement.[43] This was based on popular, as opposed to political, support; and the formation of bodies such as the Australasian

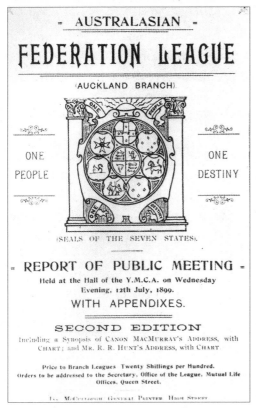

A report of the Australasian Federation League, one of the few bodies in support of a new constitution 'for the common good'.

Federation League and the Australian Natives Association (that is, white people – mainly men – born in Australia) drove the adoption of a new constitution that was eventually accepted by each of the colonies, apart from New Zealand, and ultimately accepted by the British Parliament in 1900 to come into force on 1 January 1901.

The leading Victorian advocate of federation, Alfred Deakin, said its 'actual accomplishment must always appear to have been secured by a series of miracles'.[44] Another Australian historian, Stuart Macintyre, gave secular reasons, rather than the intervention of any divine hand, for the six becoming one. 'The Australian nation', he wrote, 'was shaped by the fear of invasion and concern for the purity of the race.'[45] This was both the defence and the racist argument rolled into one – a continental fear of invaders from the north dispossessing the white Australians, and the drive before and after federation to keep Australia white (or as white as the whites could make it). Acceptance of Macintyre's argument, and there is much evidence to commend it, leads axiomatically to the view that a prime reason for federation was a quest for a distinctive identity as Australians. This was spelt out by Parkes at the 1890 conference in Melbourne: 'And there is, highest of all, the object of national honour. Why should not the name of an Australian be equal to that of a Briton?'[46] It was also fostered by the *Bulletin*, which shamelessly promoted the distinctive 'bush imagery' of Australia and carried on its masthead the epigraph 'Australia for the Australians'. Ironically, it was not just Australians who played significant roles in the image-shaping at the *Bulletin*. A New Zealand journalist, Arthur Adams, appeared in verse on 17 June 1899 to greet the new nation:

So, toward undreamt-of destinies
He slouches down the centuries.[47]

Adams was later the editor of the magazine's monthly publication *The Lone Hand*. A more noted New Zealander, David Low, was a cartoonist at the *Bulletin* from 1911 until 1919.[48]

Neither country operated from within a silo. As noted, there had been constant trans-Tasman traffic since before the British annexation of New Zealand in 1840.[49] Seddon had arrived in New Zealand from Lancashire via the Victorian goldfields, as had many other adoptive New Zealanders. One example of the traffic in people was the president of the Australian Natives Association, James Newton Haxton Hume Cook, most commonly known as 'Hume' Cook. Though the pro-federation ANA was established by and for native-born Australians, Cook was a New Zealander, born in south Waikato, who moved to Melbourne with his parents when he was fifteen.[50] Another New Zealander in an influential Australian position was Thomas Bavin, a Kaiapoi-born lawyer who worked in chambers with the first federal prime minister, Edmund Barton, from 1897 and became private secretary to both Barton and the second prime minister, Alfred Deakin. According to one biographer, Bavin 'campaigned vigorously' in the cause of federation and wrote many of Barton's speeches.[51] Barton himself was no stranger to New Zealanders beyond the political level at which he operated. He was the founding vice-president of the Southern (later New South Wales) Rugby Football Union and hosted the welcome and farewell dinners for the first New Zealand rugby team to go to Sydney, in 1884.[52] Chris Watson, who was prominent in the New South Wales Labor movement and who argued against the proposed Commonwealth constitution, was born in Chile but raised in New Zealand. In 1904, he became Labor's first Australian prime minister.[53]

While politicians and federalists focused on the mechanics of federation and while historians have since concentrated on what the politicians did or did not say or do, other Australians had gone ahead with surrogate federalism anyway. For instance, by the time the Commonwealth became a twentieth-century fact, a representative Australian cricket team had already played more than 50 test matches against England and an Australian rugby union team had played four test matches against Great Britain.[54] A Melbourne accountant, Edwin Flack, had won two gold medals at the first of the modern Olympic Games, in Athens in 1896; he was listed as Australian rather than Victorian.[55] Separate colonies the six may have been politically and officially, but their inhabitants were already forging ahead with de facto nationalism. Issues such as defence, immigration and trade (New South Wales operated a protectionist policy; Victoria was for free trade) were all uppermost during the various federation debates, but they were the detail behind the overall guiding principle that federation was both desirable and, in a nationalistic context, inevitable.

The Australian Natives Association was formed in Melbourne in 1871 and during the 1880s and 1890s it was one of the foremost advocates of federation and promoted 26 January as a national day holiday (26 January 1888 was when Captain Arthur Phillip entered Port Jackson and first raised the British flag).[56] New Zealand followed suit, if not to the same extent, but it was clear from a founding meeting in Auckland in 1894 that a national identity was a driving motivation: 'The object of this association is to promote social intercourse and a feeling of comradeship among the young men of the community, native born, to make the society mutually helpful to members, to create a feeling of patriotism and nationality; in fact, to form a young New Zealand party in its widest and best sense.'[57] Five years earlier, 'J. W. K.' had written a letter to the editor of the *Evening Post* in Wellington and urged the formation of a natives' association. New Zealand's jubilee in 1890 would be 'a most fitting time' for its inception: 'If my countrymen will but realise the importance, the necessity of standing shoulder to shoulder now, they may receive from their children and their children's children that gratitude and admiration which we now feel toward those whose unity and perseverance built up our native land.'[58]

An association was operating in Wellington by at least 1896 'to foster in the breasts of the New Zealand born a sincere love for their native land and fellow-countrymen'.[59] It was apparent there was also a rising quest for identity but there is little evidence that many people in New Zealand wished that identity to be shared with Australia. One advocate, a schoolteacher, H. J. del Monte Mahon, lamented New Zealand politicians' 'apathetic indifference'.[60] There was a similar lament from the only daily newspaper that campaigned for federation, the *Evening Post* in Wellington, which said in an editorial that New Zealand may 'without any real sacrifice of independence, greatly gain in prosperity and power as a federated state rather than by remaining an isolated colony'.[61] Keith's view more than a century later was provocatively succinct: 'We neither knew where we were, nor where we were going, and we had disowned where we had been.'[62]

But the advocates of New Zealand joining the Commonwealth were but a whisper compared with the clamour to be separate. As Sinclair noted: 'Most of the newspapers in the main towns were indifferent or hostile. There was no public campaign for Federation until the last moment. There was no organisation fighting for Federation.'[63] George Hargreaves, a visiting British observer who was in New Zealand and Australia to study what was described as 'the Chinese question', thought the two countries were drifting apart. He was quoted as saying there were 'striking indications of a growing jealousy and estrangement between Australia and New Zealand'.[64]

As in Australia, the federation debate simmered along in New Zealand for several years and only came to the boil late in the century. The official New Zealand attitude was not always ambivalent or negative. The Victorian Premier, James Service, said during an 1883 intercolonial conference that 'no one has gone more heartily than the delegates of New Zealand to form a united Australasia'.[65] One of the delegates, Harry Atkinson, later admitted, however, that the idea was not received in New Zealand with much favour and the House of Representatives did not support New Zealand joining the Federal Council.[66] The delegates at the 1890 Melbourne conference were unequivocal, as already noted. Hall's use of the '1200 impediments' analogy was not the first time that distance had been argued for the case against. A New Zealand Legislative Council member, the Hon. Captain Thomas Fraser, during the debate on the Federal Council in 1884 said, with some geographical confusion: 'I do not see what we have to do with an island 2100 miles away from New Zealand.'[67] Russell, the other delegate to Melbourne in 1890 with Hall, likewise used the distance argument when he addressed the House of Representatives. 'Here we are twelve hundred miles from any other land except islands of the most insignificant description.'[68] He then added the nationalist argument to that of distance. 'A remarkable individuality must spring up in this country, and . . . I think we should endeavour to form a distinct race for ourselves in the colony of New Zealand, rather than amalgamate with other colonies and have our characteristics probably very materially changed by so doing.'[69]

## The quiescent years

Then came what, for federation and New Zealand, were the quiescent years. The report on military preparedness in the Australian colonies by Major-General Bevan Edwards was one of the triggers for Parkes' Tenterfield speech. A similar report by the same British general in New Zealand raised barely a murmur, yet it carried a foretaste of Anzac along with the provocative comment: 'Combined action between New Zealand and Australia would lead to economy and efficiency; and it is a question for consideration, whether the forces of New Zealand should not eventually be federated with those of the Australasian colonies, so that they may be prepared to mutually assist each other.'[70] New Zealand was at the federation convention in 1891 that was designed to draw up a federal constitution, but not represented thereafter. The issue for New Zealand arose again only in June of 1899 when New South Wales, at the second time of asking, delivered the required 80 per cent majority on the federation referendum.[71]

Seddon played a key role in New Zealand deciding against federation. He, the Wellington-based Australian historian Wood believed, was 'incapable of high level intellectual activity' but was 'extremely successful in sensing the way the wind was blowing'.[72] Wood concluded that Seddon 'knew in his heart he could not count on outdistancing men of the calibre of Deakin and Barton, and preferred to settle for the secure domination of his own small backyard'.[73] New Zealand historian Miles Fairburn disagreed with that harsh indictment, arguing that it was not Seddon but a set of circumstances unique to New Zealand that made the country more disinclined to federate than the Australian colonies.[74] These

New Zealanders attended a federation convention for the last time in Sydney in 1891.
In this sketch by Sydney artist A. H. Fullwood, Sir George Grey is depicted at front on
the left; Harry Atkinson is second from the right in the middle; and William Russell is
second from the back on the left. The 'father of federation', Sir Henry Parkes, dominates
in the centre front. *The Graphic*, 13 June 1891, p. 677

circumstances, including the state of the New Zealand economy
compared with those in the Australian colonies, were clearly in
evidence before Seddon became premier.[75]

Seddon was far from indecisive in other directions, however, and instead of supporting federation he chose to advocate
instead an imperial federation scheme, with the central government based in London, at the same time proposing New Zealand
annexation of various South Pacific islands into a 'Dominion of
Oceania'.[76] In the event, New Zealand annexed only the Cook
Islands in 1900 and gained Western Samoa by default in 1914
when at Britain's request it wrested it from Germany. The various ideas for some form of South Pacific federation had occupied
New Zealand political minds for nearly 60 years, as Angus Ross
noted.[77] They seemed rooted in fear of 'foreign' domination
(France, Germany) or concerns about Asian imperialism, or
more practically, the desire to expand trade horizons and, later
in the century, as a counterbalance against the perceived power
of a federated Australia. These aspirations toward the end of the
nineteenth century also coincided with American imperialism
and commercial ambition as manifested in the Spanish–American
War and the annexation of Hawaii.[78] Imperial federation or

Cartoonist Ashley Hunter characterised Premier Richard Seddon's attitude to federation in this sketch that was labelled 'Aut Caesar aut nullus' ('Caesar or nothing'). The caption read: 'Chorus of federalists: "Don't you want to come aboard our ship?" Seddon: "What? Give up my position as skipper of this 'ere little craft to be a bosun's mate along of you? No thanks."' *New Zealand Graphic*, 8 July 1899, J-040-007, ATL

Oceanic federation 'lurked inconsolable in the New Zealand mind', according to Scholefield.[79]

Premier Frederick Whitaker had spoken in favour of federation as part of imperial federation when in Sydney but found few receptive ears in New Zealand. As the *Waikato Times* put it: 'Those twelve hundred miles of sea which separate our islanders from other lands, disconnect also and cut off our interests from those of other colonists. There can be no real community of interest between us and New South Wales and Queensland.'[80] Another newspaper, the *Wanganui Herald*, said in an editorial that 'public sentiment runs strongly against the idea of an Australasian federation so far as New Zealand is concerned'.[81] This was not just an idle view of a local

Wellington cartoonist Ecildoune Frederick Hiscocks gives his view of federation in the *Free Lance* at a time when Premier Richard Seddon harboured thoughts of imperial federation. The newspaper carried the caption: 'Handy Man Dick: Good morning ladies. Just pulled across to tell ye as how your sister New Zealand wishes you a real good time and is sorry she can't join you in your Commonwealth trip. Ye see she's busy with a little picnic of her own. But she hopes to be with you and the rest of the family at the Imperial Federation Ball.' *Free Lance*, 5 January 1901, p. 7

newspaper. The *Herald* was owned by John Ballance, the future premier and leader of the Liberal Party, and he wrote most of the editorials.[82] Ballance later told Parliament that if New Zealand 'surrendered' to any federal power, 'the people will become discontented, just as has happened in the case of Ireland'.[83]

While public interest in federation was not noticeably intense, it still exercised some New Zealand minds which were not in positions of political or commercial influence. As an example, the Gore Young Men's Society at a weekly meeting in July 1899 had a debate on its programme: 'Should New Zealand federate with Australia?' The majority, it was reported, favoured the affirmative. Before interpreting that outcome as indicating a groundswell of public opinion for New Zealand joining, two factors should be borne in mind: the debating skills of the society members and the fact that 'inclement weather' restricted attendance to about a dozen.[84] Morrell noted

Members of the 1901 Royal Commission on Federation. Back row, from left: Thomson Wilson Leys, William Russell Russell, John Mackintosh Roberts, Charles Christopher Bowen. Middle row: Harold Beauchamp, Walter Scott Reid, Albert Pitt, John Andrew Millar, William Jukes Steward. Front row: Morris Fox (secretary), Charles Manley Luke, William Henry Russell (reporter). Wellington Chamber of Commerce Collection, PAColl-5676-02-03, ATL

that supporters of federation 'entirely failed to rouse the general public from its apathy'.[85]

Toward the end of the 1890s, Seddon showed he was in no rush toward finality on the issue of New Zealand and federation. He was asked in Parliament if a referendum could be put to voters at the time of the general election in 1899 and was at his most disingenuous best when he replied that voters' minds would be so concentrated on the election he questioned if a referendum would do the issue justice.[86] He made a similar reply three weeks later and, the election out of the way, told Parliament six months afterward the issue was not one that could be rushed.[87] Seddon was questioned again in August 1900, when he said it was 'too soon' to appoint a commission to inquire into the merits or otherwise of federation.[88] Eventually, in October, when the House of Commons had passed the enabling

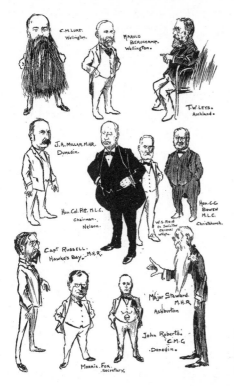

How the *Free Lance* depicted members of the Royal Commission on Federation. *Free Lance*, 9 March 1901

Act authorising the Australian colonies to federate, Seddon was ready. He told the House he was setting up a royal commission: 'We want to have the fullest information before this country and before this Parliament declares for or against federation.'[89] By the end of the year, on the very eve of Australia marking its federal birth, the composition of the commission was finally known.

Seddon had promised 'no selection of those biased against or for federation', but was the promise kept?[90] Malcolm Ross, a parliamentary correspondent for several newspapers including *The Times* in London, thought not: 'It is essentially Ministerialist in its composition and distinctly anti-federal in its opinions. Six of its members are staunch followers of Mr Seddon, three are Oppositionists, and one – the late Solicitor-General, who has just retired on a pension – may be considered as Independent.'[91] Ross believed there could be little doubt what the commission would decide. Although he worked mainly for the *Press* and the *Otago Daily Times*, papers which were opposed to Seddon, it did not necessarily mean either they or he favoured federation because Seddon did not. Dunedin-born of Scottish parents, Ross was a member of the Wellington branch of the New Zealand Natives Association and his personal view of federation may be surmised from the following remarks: 'We are an island race dowered with advantages unpossessed by our brother colonists on the great continent across the Tasman Sea. The climate, the resources, and the physical characteristics of our land will tend to breed a sturdier race than that which is now being evolved in Australia.'[92]

## Royal commission hearings

The commission, which was chaired by Albert Pitt, the recently retired attorney-general, met for the first time in Wellington on 17 January 1901 and began hearing submissions in Invercargill on 5 February.[93] Between then and mid-May, the commissioners met in twelve towns (five in New Zealand and seven in Australia), and received 260 submissions (six of which were written). The commissioners adduced evidence in two ways – by commanding to appear those people they wanted to hear; and by welcoming others who wished to appear (in Australia, the 'command' was more likely couched as a request). It seems reasonable to assume that the large majority of those who appeared for one reason or other had a personal interest in federation or a vested interest; many represented interest groups such as growers, farmers or trade unions.[94] Of the 186 New Zealand submissions, 114 were against, 49 were in favour and 23 were non-committal.[95] The commissioners in Auckland were evidently so concerned about the weight of opposition they were hearing they made a special effort to seek people in favour.[96] A further 73 submissions were heard in Australia and only four were against New Zealand joining the other colonies in the Commonwealth. Thirty-nine witnesses, however, either were not asked directly if they were for or against, or said they had no view either way. Many of these were public servants, and while they were happy to help the commissioners on trade statistics or with opinions on defence, they felt constrained because of their positions from giving a personal view.[97]

Whether the contention by Malcolm Ross that the commission's view was predictable from the outset was valid or not, the weight of the evidence was against New Zealand joining. As Keith Sinclair noted: 'From the evidence, considered as a whole, it seems reasonable to conclude that most New Zealanders did not want to become Australians.'[98] By that, of course, Sinclair meant most New Zealanders whose views were heard. The silent majority was a sizeable one – 186 witnesses before the commission represented just 0.002 per cent of New Zealand's population of 768,278 at the end of December 1900.[99] Even allowing for people under 21 within that population, and also allowing that some witnesses spoke on behalf of organisations (trade unions, chambers of commerce, and so forth), a collective view as expressed before the commission would still amount to a tiny percentage of the whole. The views of women were either not sought or not offered because, as far as could be determined, the witnesses in New Zealand were wholly males.[100]

Ged Martin pointed out that basic to any assessment of the evidence was the point with which the commissioners began their report: 'The question has been but little considered by the people of New Zealand.'[101] Martin also noted: 'The low level of public interest enabled groups determined to block change to play a disproportionate role as lobbyists.'[102] This was also noticed by one of the early witnesses to give his views to the commission, Mark Cohen, the editor of the pro-Liberal *Evening Star* in Dunedin and therefore someone in the business of trying to gauge public opinion:[103] 'There is no public opinion on this question in New Zealand.'[104]

Nor should it be overlooked that by the time the commission began hearing evidence, the federation horse had well and truly bolted from the trans-Tasman stable. Federation had become a fact on 1 January 1901 and the commission hearings began more than a year after a last-minute attempt in London by William Pember Reeves, acting for Seddon, to have the Australian constitution amended to allow New Zealand later admission on the same basis as if it were an original member and to make other changes to the Commonwealth Bill. This was rebuffed by the colonial premiers.[105] As Reeves sadly remarked in a letter to Seddon: 'I am sorry that we have not got the "open door" but in face of the opposition from the Australian premiers, I did not expect to succeed.'[106]

A recurring theme in testimony before the commission was that New Zealand was a separate and distinct nation, a pointer to the argument that New Zealanders had by then a well-developed sense of national identity and that it was not an admixture of the Australian, as the following sampling indicates:

The Rev. William Curzon-Siggers, vicar of St Matthew's, Dunedin: ". . . Australia has its own line of tendency, New Zealand has its. They are different people, themselves fashioned a great deal by the countries they dwell in respectively."[107]

Donald Reid, farmer and politician, Dunedin: "We have here a country peopled by a grand race of settlers for developing a young country – a people having a common history, identity of interest and united by national sympathies . . ."[108]

"Scobie" Mackenzie, politician, Dunedin: "The imagination of the members of this Commission may be more vivid than mine, but I am unable to conceive of any New-Zealander outside of a lunatic asylum saying to his neighbour, 'We must abandon our right of self-government; we will get a better price for our oats.'"[109]

James Izett, journalist and "old Australian", Wellington: "There is a difference in character between the people of Victoria and the people of New South Wales and, I venture to think, a greater difference still between the people of New Zealand and the people of Australia."[110]

David Robertson, engineer, Wellington: "I think we have everything to lose and nothing to gain – we have too good a country to give away to them."[111]

Pierce Freeth, journalist, Wellington: "My observation is that the Australians differ from us in character, disposition and sympathies . . . the Australian is not the same robust, moral, vigorous type as the New Zealander."[112]

Richard Laishley, barrister and solicitor, Auckland: "I think the arguments against Australian federation as for New Zealand are overwhelming . . . [one] factor is the ignoble surrender of our independence."[113]

Samuel Vaile, land agent, Auckland: "I think that to join the Federation would have the effect of entirely destroying our national life . . ."[114]

John McLachlan, retired businessman, Auckland: "New Zealand is unique as regards its insular position, its climate and scenery, and its productiveness."[115]

The commissioners completed their hearings in Brisbane on 24 April and met eight times on their return to Wellington, although it was at the third of those meetings, on 11 May, that they decided 'it is not desirable that New Zealand should federate with the Commonwealth and become a State under the Commonwealth of Australia Constitution Act'.[116] They delivered their report, including transcripts of all the evidence and 31 exhibits (appendices), to the Governor, the Early of Ranfurly, on 30 May 1901, five months

THE NEW ZEALAND

OBSERVER

AN ILLUSTRATED JOURNAL OF INTERESTING AND
AMUSING LITERATURE.

*Smart, but not vulgar; fearless, but not offensive; independent, but not neutral; unsectarian, but not irreligious.*

EDITED BY W. J. GEDDIS    ESTABLISHED 1880.    ILLUSTRATED BY W. BLOMFIELD

VOL. XXI.—No 1153.    SATURDAY, FEBRUARY 2, 1901.    THREEPENCE

NEW ZEALAND A FAR-OFF COUNTRY.

RICHARD SEDDON: Ahem! This is pure. We're a far-off country, and people in Australia are not interested in MY people. This decides the Federation idea. What chance would New Zealand have, mixed up with that lot?"

This William Blomfield cartoon on federation was captioned: 'New Zealand a far-off country.' It carried the caption: 'Richard Seddon: Ahem! This is pure. We're a far-off country, and people in Australia are not interested in MY people. This decides the Federation idea. What chance would New Zealand have, mixed up with that lot?'
*New Zealand Observer*,
2 February 1901, p. 1

after Australia without New Zealand had become a federated Commonwealth and three weeks after the Duke of Cornwall and York (the later King George V) had opened the first federal parliament in Melbourne.[117]

When the report was made public, Malcolm Ross commented in *The Times* that it 'will seal the fate of this colony in respect to Australian Federation for many years to come'.[118] In the House of Representatives, Seddon said the commission 'had come to a decision in accordance with the views of the majority of the people'.[119] He was responding to a question from an opposition member and future prime minister, William Massey, who asked if the House would have an opportunity to debate the report. Seddon said it would but he wished members 'to read, mark, learn and inwardly digest' the report first and it could be debated in perhaps a year. It never was.

A British view of the issue was published in New Zealand at about this time. The correspondent in London for several New Zealand newspapers, Charles Rous-Marten, mailed a précis of a story in the *Morning Post* which addressed itself to New Zealand's attitude to federation and what it called its love of independence: 'New Zealand is so far from Australia and possesses so many features of unlikeness that its people have always been proudly persistent in asserting their individuality. Nothing offends them more than to confuse them with Australians, or to regard their lovely and well-watered country as a mere Australian island.'[120] The author of the *Morning Post* article was not identified, but whoever it was seemed to have a better understanding of the New Zealand–Australia relationship than was common in the United Kingdom. As the *Graphic* remarked in a review of Reeves' book, *The Long White Cloud: Ao Tea Roa*: 'The English public, as a whole, are woefully ignorant about New Zealand; the usual idea is that it is very much to Australia what the Isle of Wight is to England.'[121]

At least that vigilant imperial observer Rudyard Kipling showed he knew his antipodean geography if not its politics when he wrote a poem celebrating federation. 'The Young Queen', Australia, gained the blessing of 'the old queen', Britain:

And she came to the old Queen's presence, in the Hall of Our Thousand Years –
In the Hall of the Five Free Nations that are peers among their peers:
Royal she gave the greeting, loyal she bowed the head,
Crying: – 'Crown me, my Mother!' . . .

Kipling, who visited New Zealand and Australia in 1891, traversed west to east in his versifying in the name of the old queen:

How can I crown thee further? I know whose standard flies
Where the clean surge takes the Leeuwin or the notched Kaikouras
rise . . .

Kipling's inclusion of the Kaikouras, and thus an implied belief
that New Zealand was a part of the new federation, appeared in
*The Times* on Australia's first day as a federated Commonwealth.[122]
Later reprintings of the poem, however, left no trace of the
Kaikouras and Kipling's eastern extremity had retracted to the
Queensland coast.[123]

## The Māori difference

As in other spheres of New Zealand life, Māori were a point of
difference and how Māori would be affected if New Zealand
were federated was raised several times before the commission.
The Australian weekly magazine the *Bulletin* put its characteristic
slant on the issue and linked it with the unrequited New Zealand
dreams of a South Pacific federation:

> When Seddon discovered his famous mare's nest – that the Maoris
> would have no vote under the Commonwealth – he was moved almost
> to tears at the thought of the prospective injustice to that stalwart
> race. He is now, however, doing his best to consummate a Federation
> with 100,000 niggers, none of whom have, or are intended to ever
> have, a vote.[124]

Seddon himself was quoted as saying that had New Zealand inter-
fered when the Commonwealth Bill was being drafted, it would have
been considered unwarrantable. But he took exception to the clause
that dealt with voting for members of the federal parliament. To
place Māori 'on the same footing as aliens or the blacks of Victoria
would be penalising a noble race and he would not permit that to

be done'.[125] One passage in the Bill which concerned Seddon and other New Zealanders was clause 25, which determined that people of any race disqualified from voting in a state would not be counted among the population. The other was clause 127 which stated: 'In reckoning the number of the people of the Commonwealth, or of a state or other part of the Commonwealth, aboriginal natives shall not be counted.'[126]

The place of Māori had been raised long before the commission was contemplated. William Russell in his speech to the convention in 1890 had expressed concerns about an elective body, 'mostly Australians, that cares nothing and knows nothing about native administration':[127] 'The advance of civilization would be enormously delayed if the regulation of this question affecting New Zealand was handed over to a body of gentlemen who knew nothing whatever of the traditions of the past.'[128] The legal standing of Māori and women, especially in relation to the franchise, was occasionally raised in evidence before the commission and both issues were put to Edmund Barton. He was cautious in his reply on Māori, less cautious about women:

> We understand that this question operates only in New Zealand and with a diminishing race, and that it is part of a solemn covenant you have entered into; and in the settlement of that question, if a demand were made that the Maoris should be counted as integers of the population, that demand would certainly have to be taken into account.[129]

Asked by commission member Harold Beauchamp about the probability of early enfranchisement for women, Barton replied: 'The intention of the Government is to endeavour to pass an Act for that purpose before a second appeal to the people. We cannot have it now. . . . the endeavour would be to pass it before another general election should come on.'[130] As Philippa Mein Smith remarked, women in New Zealand opposed federation because they worried about 'a subsequent loss of political influence' in an enlarged Commonwealth: 'If the New Woman were to shape a new nation, then it was better for New Zealand to stay apart.'[131]

Nevertheless, New Zealand and Australia had similar views on race and Māori were seen as being in a different category to Australian Aboriginals or Chinese or others less welcome in Australia. As Barton told the commission: 'If one may judge from the conversations I have had with Mr Seddon, I should think that our objections to alien races and New Zealand's objections are practically the same, and that we have the same desire to preserve the "European" and "white" character of the race.'[132] The federal treasurer, Sir George Turner, put what seemed to be the prevailing view: 'I do not regard the Maoris as being on anything like the same grounds as our aboriginals.'[133] Sir John Forrest, the Western Australian premier for ten years and the new federal defence minister, had a similar opinion and said he did not think the 127th section of the constitution was ever intended to apply to Māori.[134] The commission in its final report noted that New Zealand would be deprived of one member in the federal House of Representatives if Māori were not included in the count. But it was not just, in the commission's view, a matter of representation. Exclusion of Māori would be a great injustice.[135] As Mein Smith noted, the disparity between Māori and Aboriginal became 'a pivotal feature of New Zealand identity'.[136] While she was talking in relation to the federation debate, Māori had already set New Zealand apart on the road to identity in other ways and would continue to do so, in the arenas of war and sport.

## The influence of geography

Concomitant with the distance argument was a belief that climate and geography combined to create different types of people. This sentiment was enunciated in 1890 by Captain Russell who informed the federal convention in Melbourne that 'with every distinct physical environment there comes a distinct national type':

> With a population of 700,000 people in New Zealand, dwelling in an island where the climate is dissimilar to a very great extent from that of Australia, which has been colonized in an entirely different manner, and speaking colloquially, having had a very much rougher time than the colonies of Australia, we are likely to develop a very complete individuality – a distinct national type.[137]

He returned to the theme when the convention was discussed in the House of Representatives later in the year. New Zealand was in an 'altogether unique' position geographically and that must materially affect 'the whole future of the country in ages to come'. Talking of isolation and winds whistling through Cook Strait, he prognosticated:

> It shows that in due course a remarkable individuality must spring up in this country and, as such, I hold, must almost inevitably be the case, I think we should endeavour to form a distinct race for ourselves in the colony of New Zealand, rather than amalgamate with other colonies and have our characteristics probably very materially changed by so doing.[138]

A decade later, Seddon made Russell one of the members of the Royal Commission on Federation.

Factors such as geography, climate and distance were mentioned in the commission's recommendation against federating. Geoffrey Blainey, in his essay in *Tasman Relations: New Zealand and Australia, 1788–1988*, quoted the director of the Auckland Art Gallery, Peter Tomory, as writing: 'In all cultures and civilizations the land has held a dominant position in myth and legend.'[139] Blainey noted how the physical environment shaped emotions and aesthetic attitudes and he underlined the geographical contrasts between New Zealand and

Australia – water being just one example: 'Water, whether in snow or running streams or lakes or bays, is almost a characteristic of New Zealand. It is strikingly so to Australian eyes.'[140] He went on to say: 'In Australian nationalism the creative writers and painters have had an emotional and myth-making influence which far exceeds that of New Zealand artists on their own land. But they would not have become so influential so early if the settled parts of Australia had possessed New Zealand's climate, land-shapes and vegetation.'[141]

This linkage between environment and identity, between landscape and culture, was also acknowledged by Richard Waterhouse in an Australian context in his analysis of Russel Ward's version of the Australian bush legend.[142] It was also a bond favoured by Australia's pre-eminent chronicler of World War I, Charles Bean: 'The bush still sets the standard of personal efficiency even in the Australian cities.'[143] The climate and the country's flora and fauna constituted New Zealand as 'a place', and as John Andrews argued: 'Sense of place is embedded in the concept of identity.'[144]

In Australia, there seemed a sense of inevitability about federation, even given the initial entrenched positions on trade by New South Wales and Victoria, and despite various other issues and problems which had to be surmounted along the way. Henry Parkes' 'crimson thread of kinship' proved to be the tie that bound the colonies together – eventually. Alfred Deakin could speak of 'miracles' but there was much that was practical and pragmatic in the decision to move from colony to state, from separate colonies to one Commonwealth. Given the enormity of the task, and given that other federations had been created only after wars or insurrections, the transition in Australia was almost seamless. In some ways, it could be argued that Australian nationalism created the climate for federation rather than being a product of it. As Australian historian Helen Irving observed: 'Before a nation can be formed, a group of separate populations must imagine themselves part of a larger national community."[145]

In New Zealand, however, there was no sense of belonging to Australia – Australasia perhaps, but not Australia. Some politicians, from time to time, favoured federation, but not enough and not at the right times. Public interest in federation appeared to be muted to the point of silence. The federation debate in New Zealand, such as it was, served more to convince New Zealanders of their uniqueness – of their own national identity – than it did to persuade them to cross the Tasman divide. This sense of establishing their own nation rather than being an appendage of another that was an ocean away was articulated domestically. It was New Zealanders telling other New Zealanders and, to a limited extent, Australians, that they were happy to forge ahead on their own and continue to create their own distinctive state.

At the same time, New Zealand sent troops to a foreign war for the first time, and the dispatch of troopers to South Africa became an external manifestation of the assertion of New Zealand independence. While imperial loyalty remained an overlay, New Zealanders went to South Africa and in effect said: 'Look, this is what and who we are and we are different from Australians.' The Boer War, far from establishing a national identity, would simply confirm and affirm what already existed.

Richard Hutton, English-born and an Auckland surveyor, one of the senior
New Zealand commanders during the Boer War.

# SIX

# For God, for Queen and for (Which?) Country

*Then New Zealand shall be there,*
*In the van.*
*Young New Zealand shall be there, –*
*Her rifles from the mountain and her horsemen from the plain,*
*When the foeman's ranks are reeling o'er the slain.*[1]

When their country called, men came running and riding. At least, that was how it seemed in the early summer of 1899 when New Zealand's politicians, aided and abetted by enthusiastic public figures, decided troops would be sent to South Africa to stand by Britain in its hour of need. New Zealand dispatched troops to fight beyond its shores for the first time and the country's involvement in the Boer War was seen as both a mark of solidarity with mother Britain and the efflorescence of a distinct New Zealand identity.[2] That peripatetic observer of imperial affairs, Richard Jebb, combined his honeymoon with a fact-finding trip through New Zealand in 1899 and concluded that the 'accident of war' was the really decisive factor that determined the national destiny of New Zealand.[3] The dispatch of troops created an excitement, he believed, with which the 'prosaic preoccupation' with the possibility of federation with Australia could not compete. But the war fervour was no accident, as Jebb surely knew, because he saw how the premier, Richard Seddon, adroitly swung the majority of public opinion behind his enthusiasm to nail New Zealand's colours to the imperial mast: '[T]he novelty of the imperial situation was exploited to distract attention from the inconvenient perplexity of the nearer domestic problem.'[4]

While remarkably forthright for a man just 25 years of age and in New Zealand for the first time, Jebb may have overstated the significance of the concurrent federation debate. Had he been in the country longer, he may have realised that a burgeoning sense of national identity existed already, war or no war. Jebb's views are important because of the weight given them by Keith Sinclair and his agreement that the Boer War provided a major stimulus for New Zealand nationalism.[5] But what the war really did was exhibit the New Zealanders' growing sense of self on a wider stage and provide comparisons for New Zealanders – with Britain most importantly, but also with other settler colonies, especially Australia and Canada. Thanks to the war, New Zealand's distinctive identity – distinctive when compared with the British or Australian – was exported on a grand scale for the first time.

To argue that the war came along in the nick of time to push the prospect of federation with Australia into the background was also to misread the mood in New Zealand. While it is true that some New Zealanders – and more Australians – wanted New Zealand to follow the six colonies into the Commonwealth of Australia, an overwhelming majority either did not, or simply did not think about it one way or another. As an issue in 1899, federation barely registered. Jebb wrote of the war: 'Suddenly, the people of the colony had seized the idea that they were indeed an island race apart, to their future glory rather than to their present misfortune; no longer "Britons of the South," nor Australasians, but Maorilanders first.'[6] Yet, there was no 'suddenly' about it. The distinctiveness had been coming for some time; the war merely emphasised and exposed it to a wider gaze.

The South African war was certainly a time of national and imperial fervour – a time of, in the vernacular of the day, 'jingoism'.[7] While Seddon's request in the House of Representatives to support his motion to dispatch mounted troops to South Africa was suitably solemn – 'on no previous occasion have I risen in this House with a greater sense of . . . responsibility' – New Zealand was infected with enthusiasm for the war, with the willing public subscriptions to send soldiers away just one manifestation of that enthusiasm. Not all was as it seemed, then or later, however. While the imperial enthusiasm for the war held sway on the public platforms, private voices could hold a different view. One of the five members of Parliament who opposed the war motion in the House, John Hutcheson, was the highest-polling candidate in Wellington in the general election just over two months later. His anti-war views were well known but he gained more popular support than any other candidate.[8] Generally, though, it was a time of almost breathless rush to send young men and their horses away to support the Empire in a fight whose origins probably escaped most people. It was sufficient to know that Britain wanted help and New Zealand was ready, willing and able to rally round the British flag. Prominent Wellington journalist Malcolm Ross, a parliamentary correspondent for several newspapers, wrote: 'It is a glorious page in our history. The whole nation is aroused and the Imperial spirit has taken firm hold.'[9]

Newspapers from the early part of the war leave an overwhelming impression of the imperial rhetoric, of New Zealanders proudly eager to display their martial mettle. There was opposition, but it was never at a level to persuade a reversal of New Zealand policy and attitude and, in recording it, care must be taken to avoid an undue emphasis. The infectious enthusiasm for the war that was evident in the first few months waned, however. Newspapers increasingly reflected a dawning realisation that there was more to war than merely dispatching fit young men and their horses with a wave of a flag, a few bellicose speeches and a chorus or two of 'Soldiers of the Queen'. It was these additional factors, as much if not more so than the dispatch of the soldiers or the actual fighting, which helped solidify the sense of national identity: a sense that while the imperial motivation was strong, if it came to a choice – New Zealand or Britain – New Zealand must come first.

This mood became evident in a number of ways. One was in the manner of the opposition to the war which, in some cases, was motivated as much by New Zealand interests as was the martial urge itself. Another was the level of disagreement with the imperial overlords, particularly over such issues as the place of Māori in the war, the refusal by imperial authorities to maintain distinct New Zealand formations in the field, and different views in Wellington and London about the dispatch and use of nurses. Another significant difference – one that became more apparent as time and the war wore on – was that the soldiers from the settler colonies, and especially New Zealand, callow troopers though they may have been, were more adept at, and more adaptable to, the particular conditions in which the war was fought. The practical experience of war confirmed there was a distinct difference between the make-up and attitude of 'colonials' and those from whence they came.

### Fragmented historiography

In his 1986 book, *A Destiny Apart: New Zealand's Search for National Identity*, Keith Sinclair largely traversed events during the Boer War and reactions in New Zealand, concluding that Jebb was right – that the war was the decisive factor in determining New Zealand's national identity – and also that the effect of the war upon New Zealand opinion has been underestimated and obscured by the greater influence of World War I.[10] A year later, Jock Phillips' hypothesis on New Zealand as a masculine society was published and he too saw an awakening of New Zealand nationalism at the turn of the twentieth century as well as an enthusiasm for war which he found intriguing but difficult to explain.[11] Noting the absence of a 'good book' about the war – 'it is said because their [soldiers'] letters, diaries and other documents, collected in Wellington, were destroyed in a fire"[12] – Sinclair was dismissive of the only official account, one that was published nearly 50 years afterward.[13] The centenary of the war brought another spurt in publications, with a series of works by a private researcher, Richard Stowers, the most detailed.[14]

If the Boer War was so influential in the shaping of New Zealand opinion and self-esteem, why was it that so little had been written about it, especially compared with the volumes of literature, fact and fiction, about the two world wars?[15] The answer lies partly with a defence establishment that was not happy with various writers either hired or suggested for the task, and the fact that two completed manuscripts lay fallow, one of which is still available in the Alexander Turnbull Library and the other of which was lost – or at least, all attempts to find it have been defeated. Plans for an official New Zealand history of the Boer War were confused and contradictory from the outset and involved five different potential authors in a complexity of editorial musical chairs.

The first earmarked for chronicling New Zealand activities in the war was an officer with the Second Contingent, Captain Norman Smith. According to one of the later writers, Frank Beamish: 'He circularised all contingent officers with very small result and the work was never completed.'[16] Smith's transfer to the King's Own Scottish Borderers at the end of 1900 would not have been conducive to compiling a New Zealand history. A sub-editor with the *Lyttelton Times*, William Campbell, appears to have been appointed to the task in April 1902, but in February the following year, the commandant of New Zealand forces, Major-General James Babbington (later Lieutenant-General Sir James), told a senior cabinet minister, William Hall-Jones, that another journalist, Robert Loughnan, had been approached.[17] Later in 1903, Seddon (who was also Minister of Defence) told Babbington that Captain John Russell MacDonald, who lived in Victoria, would do the job, but MacDonald later

withdrew and was asked to refund the £50 advance he was paid.[18]
The Army Department file does not make clear what happened to
either Campbell or Loughnan (though the latter was a well-known
journalist and wrote a biography of Seddon's successor, Sir Joseph
Ward).

After MacDonald's withdrawal, Beamish, who served with the
Sixth Contingent, entered the lists. He had Seddon's support: 'Mr
Beamish is the only applicant for this work and so far as I can see
is the most fitted officer that I know of to undertake such a duty.'[19]
Beamish, tucked away in an office in Parliament, worked for the
next five years on his history, but government enthusiasm for it
seemed to have waned after Seddon's death in 1906. 'The succeeding defence minister and the (then) chief clerk were anything but
sympathetic', Beamish wrote to the Defence Minister, Sir Joseph
Ward, in 1909.[20] Though a Defence Department minute sheet
shows Beamish was asked several times when the work would be finished, it turned out that time was hardly a pressing factor. When the
Defence Minister during World War I, Sir James Allen, asked Alfred
Robin – who commanded the First Contingent in South Africa and
by 1919 was Major-General Sir Alfred Robin and commandant of
forces in New Zealand – what had become of the Beamish history,
Robin replied:

> The history in draft form has been on file for years. I have had it
> out and glanced over it in places. The real reason why it was not
> printed is because it seems to require editing or revising either by
> some experienced literary expert or by a small committee to make it
> a History . . . From a rough glance, I consider it should be revised in
> some way as opinions, criticisms and copies of irresponsible letters
> and newspapers do not constitute a History worthy of issue by a
> Government.[21]

A year later, Robin's successor as commandant, Major-General Sir
Edward Chaytor, was of a similar view and described the manuscript

as 'merely a mass of information which has not been edited and would be of little use as an official history'.[22] A letter from the new Defence Minister, Sir Robert Heaton Rhodes, carried a margin note: 'Manuscript filed in Central Registry.'[23] The South African War Veterans' Association pleaded ten years later for the history to be published but the matter seemed at an end when the next commander of New Zealand Military Forces, Major-General Sir Robert Young, told the association that no action would be taken because of the cost involved.

A new author then appeared on the scene. The South African veterans turned their attention from Defence to the Department of Internal Affairs and the Cabinet agreed that another journalist, James Shand, who had been in South Africa as a war correspondent, should be paid to write the long-delayed history. Shand was quicker than Beamish – and may have had the use of Beamish's typescript – and the finished work was presented to the Minister of Defence, John Cobbe, who wrote a foreword: 'I am gratified that recognition – tardy though it may be – has been made of the splendid response made by NZ to the call of the Motherland and to the courage, efficiency and endurance of our soldiers during the campaign.'[24] But Shand fared no better than Beamish. The Cabinet decided in May 1936 that publication would be deferred.[25] It was only after the establishment of the War History Branch of the Department of Internal Affairs in 1945 to co-ordinate and publish the official histories of World War II that a Boer War history finally found its way into bookstores.[26] Unimpressed by Shand's manuscript (by this time, Beamish's could not be found), the editor-in-chief, Major-General Sir Howard Kippenberger, instructed a journalist employed by the branch, David Hall, to write the history and it was this that was eventually published in 1949.[27]

The passing of the years, which included two world wars in which New Zealand's turn-of-the-century enemies became allies, was reflected in Hall's introduction: 'Many men of British stock have today an uneasy conscience about the South African War.'

While Hall may have been correct that the war of 50 years before troubled the consciences of some (though produced no supporting evidence), his was a retrospective view and did not reflect the mood of the times the history purported to cover. In a review of New Zealand war history, literary commentator Alan Mulgan practically dismissed Hall's work by calling it a 'booklet'. 'Journalists and historians were handicapped when they wished to deal with that war, and public interest in history suffered', he noted.[28]

Boer War veterans complained in 1940 at the start of World War II when the 'Special Force' was renamed the 2nd New Zealand Expeditionary Force to provide a continuum from the 1st NZEF of World War I, that it properly should have been called the 3rd NZEF.[29] Their complaints were conveyed to the government but without apparent success – certainly the force was not renamed. New Zealanders' knowledge of the war, and the cementing role it played in the creation of national identity, was thus not aided by the fragmented historiography. It became almost the forgotten war in the nation's history.[30]

## A unique dimension

Māori, as in so many aspects of New Zealand life, provided a significant point of difference from both Britain and the other settler colonies in the Boer War and an appreciation of this factor is critical to the belief that the war consolidated rather than created a national identity. While other settler colonies subjugated or tried to ignore their indigenous populations, encouraged by the Victorian belief in white Anglo-Saxon superiority, New Zealand's was absorbed and embraced.

With the ready agreement, even encouragement, of their enemies, the British declared the war to be 'a white man's war' and there seemed joint abhorrence at the prospect of natives fighting against the whites (whether Briton or Boer). 'Disarm your blacks and thereby act the part of a white man in a white man's war', the Boer general, Piet Cronje, was quoted as saying in a message to Colonel Robert Baden-Powell during the siege of Mafeking.[31] An under-secretary at the War Office, George Wyndham, made Britain's official attitude plain when he was asked in the House of Commons in the first month of the war if 'native races' would be encouraged to take up arms: 'I can hardly find words in which to repudiate the suggestion of the Hon Member. The first duty of the paramount power in South Africa is to act as a guardian against the possibility of any such horrors.'[32] Yet, the determination that it would be a white man's war did not appear to extend to the menial tasks of digging trenches, mucking out stables and other such labours. The war's foremost historian, Thomas Pakenham, reckoned that at least 40,000 non-whites served on each side, some of them armed, some not.[33]

The British intended that a stricture against 'native' combatants also applied to New Zealand. Ian McGibbon thought this was 'in the nature of a tacit understanding' between London and Wellington, but it was more than that.[34] The Secretary of State for the Colonies, Joseph Chamberlain, was quite specific when he replied to a request from the Governor, Lord Ranfurly, that Māori be included in contingents. 'Natives most eager', Ranfurly cabled.[35] But Chamberlain was adamant: 'They [the British government] would have been glad to afford an opportunity of active service for the Queen to the Maoris who have so often proved their soldierly qualities and courage, but political considerations peculiar to South Africa render it impossible.'[36] Chamberlain observed in a handwritten postscript that he was sorry Māori could not be given a chance, but then added: 'If they had sent them without asking and mixed up with others, no one would have known the difference.'[37]

Chamberlain's nod and a wink was taken literally, whether he knew about it or not. Many Māori served in the war, including at least two, Walter John Callaway and William Tutepuaki Pitt, in the First Contingent. Callaway was mentioned in dispatches for rescuing some Queenslanders under heavy fire and Pitt later joined the permanent army and was a captain in the Māori Contingent on Gallipoli in World War I.[38] Callaway served with two other contingents and it was 'the opinion of returned troopers that for courage on the field of battle . . . he was unsurpassed at the front'.[39] Another celebrated (and decorated) Māori soldier was 'Tip' Broughton, who falsified his age to enlist in the Ninth Contingent. He was later an officer in the Māori (Pioneer) Battalion during World War I and again falsified his age in 1940 to enlist in the Australian Imperial Force.[40] Henry Te Reiwhati Vercoe, who died in 1962 as the leader of the Arawa, was mentioned in dispatches for his courage when serving with the Seventh Contingent. He also served in World War I, where he was again mentioned in dispatches and awarded a Distinguished Service Order, his military career ending during World War II when he was commandant of the Matata Military Camp.[41] While it is not possible to be definitive about exactly how many Māori served, partly because some concealed the fact, among them were Christchurch brothers Ahere te Koari Hohepa and Ohere Hohepa, who went with the Third Contingent as Arthur and Arthur Henry Joseph.[42]

Māori did not go only as troopers. A Māori Medical Corps comprising up to 20 men and women, some of them medically trained, served in South Africa for a year from mid-1900 under the aegis of the United Tribes of New Zealand.[43] They, too, adopted European names (presumably to avoid official detection). Commanded by a Captain Murray (Maremare Kunaiti of Ngāti Kāhungunu) and a head nurse, 'Hannah Goodnight' (Hāna Kunaiti also of Ngāti Kāhungunu), they made their own way to South Africa and were attached to Queen Alexandra's Imperial Military Nursing Service.[44]

Perhaps fortunately for New Zealand–British relations – and in particular the regard some Māori had for Britain or at least for the monarch – certain British comments about Māori involvement were not published at the time. In a series of inter-ministry notes about

a suggestion Māori troops could be sent to other British possessions and thus free troops for service in South Africa, Chamberlain
remarked: 'Maoris would be useless and very costly for garrison duty
and unless there is actual fighting going on somewhere in which
they could be utilised, it would be absurd to accept this offer.' An
indecipherable hand suggested 'softening the refusal' by inviting a
Māori Contingent to King Edward VII's coronation. 'This means
a haka at London, but I don't object!' someone wrote. 'They are
merely children and though they might fight as well as any coloured
troops officered by English men, they would soon become a great
trouble in a garrison.'[45] This Anglocentric view was not echoed in
New Zealand.

## Opposition to the war

The level of opposition to the war could also be interpreted as
indicative of national, as opposed to imperial, feeling; that it was
in New Zealand's interests not to fight rather than in Britain's or
the Empire's to do so. This attitude was evident both within the
first weeks of the war and, for different reasons, again later when
the war entered its second phase, the irregular or guerrilla phase.
Among the most outspoken opponents from the outset was one of
the three members of Parliament representing Wellington, John
Hutcheson.[46] His argument against Seddon's motion that a force
be sent was predicated on a belief that there may come a time when
New Zealanders were required to fight for the Empire, but the time
was not now:[47]

> When the time arrives for a proof of New Zealand's loyalty, even to
> her very heart's blood, I feel certain she will not fail. But I regret, even
> in the face of the warlike and inspiriting sentiments uttered both by
> the leader of the Government and the leader of the Opposition, that
> I cannot give my voice to commit this young and peaceful country to

participation, however small, in a war beyond our confines and which, moreover, whatever else it may be, is not a defensive war.[48]

Hutcheson was one of five members who voted against Seddon's proposal (54 were in favour). *Hansard* recorded that after the motion was agreed to, members 'then rose and fervently sang the [British] National Anthem and, on the call of the Premier, gave three hearty cheers for Her Majesty the Queen'.[49] It did not record if the five 'noes' were among the fervent choristers.

Just over two months later, New Zealanders went to the polls and, as mentioned earlier, despite the supposed prevailing jingoism and a greatly increased majority for the Liberals, Hutcheson was the highest-polling candidate in Wellington. Another opponent of Seddon's, Arthur Richmond Atkinson, gained the second-greatest number of Wellington votes and was elected for the first time after two previous attempts.[50] Another of the war opponents in the House, Michael Gilfedder, was re-elected to the Southland seat of Wallace by a slightly reduced majority. While none of the three retained their seats in the following election, held in 1902, their election in 1899, given their widely publicised views opposing the war, suggests that the influence of jingoism was perhaps not as great as has been commonly supposed. It is possible that women voters who opposed the war were significant in the 1899 support for Hutcheson, Atkinson and Gilfedder, but this is not possible to quantify because votes within electorates or for individual candidates could not be broken down by gender. The National Council of Women and other similar groups opposed to the war were active and well publicised and women certainly exercised their franchise – in Gilfedder's electorate of Wallace, 77 per cent of women eligible to vote did so, and nationally the figure was 73 per cent.[51]

There were opponents on religious grounds too. The Roman Catholic weekly published in Dunedin, the *New Zealand Tablet*, was remarkably prescient when it described the war as 'one of those big little wars which will cost the Empire a vast expenditure in blood

and treasure' and predicted that it would be followed by 'a green
and vigorous outgrowth of racial hate that can bode no good for
the future of the land of promise that lies between the Zambesi
and Cape Town'.[52] The newspaper was then edited by an Irish-
born priest, Henry William Cleary, described as a moderate in the
church at a time of agitation over Irish nationalism (and therefore,
opposition to most things English).[53] Speaking of the supposed
root cause of the war, the refusal by the Transvaal government to
grant franchise to foreigners ('uitlanders'), the *Tablet* (presumably
Cleary) asked why Britain 'should fling away thousands of useful
lives and millions of good money over the difference between the
tweedle-dum of a seven years', and the tweedle-dee of a five years',
franchise'.[54]

Another public opponent was a Presbyterian cleric, Rutherford
Waddell, who was known nationally for his successful campaign
against 'sweating' (the practice of long hours and low pay) in
clothing factories. A social reformer, he was a member of an 1890
royal commission into sweating that led to a Factory and Shops
Act and other laws aimed at improving conditions for workers,
especially women and the young.[55] He was the first editor of the
weekly Presbyterian newspaper, the *Outlook*, and in an editorial
on 21 October 1899 expressed his horror at the war. He borrowed
from Shakespeare for the heading, 'Cry havoc and let slip the dogs
of war', but looked to no one for his comment: 'We have not hesi-
tated all along to aver our disbelief in Mr Chamberlain and we are
more than ever convinced that he has jockeyed the nation into an
unnecessary war.'[56] Although Waddell was mild in his criticism and
described men who volunteered as gallant, a week later he returned
to the theme: 'Hoping against hope that war might be averted in the
Transvaal has come to an end. We are face to face with hostilities
which threaten not only to be sanguinary but protracted. It irks us
terribly to say that we can see no good or sufficient reason for the
disastrous step that has been taken.'[57] By the next issue, Waddell
felt compelled to proffer an explanation:

The Presbyterian cleric
opposed to the war,
Rutherford Waddell.
J. Collie, ed., *Rutherford
Waddell: Memoirs and Addresses*
(Dunedin: A. H. Reed, 1932),
frontispiece

Our position in regard to this war seems to be misunderstood. It can
be stated in a sentence. We disapprove of the war. With such information as we have, we thought, and still think, that war might have been
avoided. But we applaud the patriotism of the colonies in sending
help to the mother country . . . We cannot consciously agree that this
was the best way out of the difficulty; but it is the only way left to us
now.[58]

Waddell's views were not matched by the church as a whole,
but at the Presbyterian synod a fortnight later an attempt to cen-
sure him failed. Instead, the synod favoured a resolution that it
'expresses its appreciation of the independence of opinion on public
questions'.[59] The church later dispatched a minister, Daniel Dutton,
to serve as chaplain with New Zealand troops and he presided at
the peace service in 1902.[60]

Seddon, who showed himself to be less tolerant than the Presbyterian synod about the independence of opinion on public questions, was partly to blame for opposition to the war gaining a level of publicity disproportionate to its impact because of his relentless pursuit of one of the opponents, James Grattan Grey. Grey was an Irish-born journalist who worked on several New Zealand papers and, from 1875, on the staff of *Hansard*, the formal record of parliamentary debates.[61] Since Parliament sat for only a few months of the year, Grey had approval to supplement his income by continuing to write for newspapers. There was no caveat in his agreement that he should write only stories approved by the government. However, for Seddon, Grey went too far when he gave readers of the *New York Times* his critical views of New Zealand's support of Britain in South Africa:

> To outside nations it will appear not a little odd that self-governing colonies 7000 miles away from the scene of strife should send off bodies of men to do battle against people they have had no quarrel with, or that they should think it necessary to assist in the subjugation of a people who claim the right of self-government the same as they do; but the jingoistic spirit at the Antipodes is too inflamed just now to care anything about the rights or wrongs of the question.[62]

He returned to the theme a few weeks later after Britain and the United States agreed to Germany taking over control of what became Western Samoa: 'The outbreak of the Transvaal war has brought with it a tidal wave of imperialism all over the colonies of Australasia, and the feeling is so intense that for the moment the colonists generally are blind to the danger of having a great European power like Germany brought into such close proximity to their shores.'[63]

Extracts from the first *New York Times* article found their way into the Dunedin *Evening Star*, a paper that was an avid Seddon supporter.[64] The *Star*'s unidentified writer described Grey's writing

Hansard reporters, 1896. J. Grattan Grey is seated, third from the right.
J. E. Martin, *The House: New Zealand's House of Representatives 1854–2004*, (Palmerston North: Dunmore Press, 2004), p. 119

in the *New York Times* as being in a 'sneering form of language most offensive in its assumption of knowledge as well as inaccurate in its knowledge of facts'. More serious than the 'self-evident insolence', the *Star* writer went on, was the fact Grey's comments were published in a 'if anything, pro-Boer journal of large circulation'.[65] Grey, who saw an accusing hand at the *Star* in collusion with that of the premier, felt he was assailed 'in the coarsest and most vindictive terms', but in a pamphlet he published did not name his accuser.[66] While Seddon may have enlisted the aid of the paper in 'exposing' Grey, he also took direct personal action and wrote to the reporter asking him to confirm he was indeed the author of the offending article. After an exchange of letters, Grey agreed he was and said he believed he lived in a free and enlightened country: 'Is it possible that I have been under a delusion all the best years of my life, and that I am now to realise that freedom of thought and speech in New Zealand – that boasted palladium of individual and collective liberty – is nothing but a myth after all?'[67]

Required to appear before a parliamentary committee, Grey reaffirmed his authorship of the articles and that he did not retract a word. For all his protestations, and the acknowledgement he had agreement to write for newspapers when his *Hansard* duties permitted, he was dismissed. He did not lack support for his principle, if not the detail of what he wrote. The House of Representatives debated his case from half past seven one night, and when a decision was needed at two o'clock in the morning, 47 members voted against him and 11 for.[68] The debate was led by Seddon, who argued that Grey's actions by writing the first *New York Times* article were exacerbated by his second article about the governance of Samoa and subsequently by his widely circulated pamphlet.

But there were other supporters beyond the eleven members of Parliament who opposed Grey's dismissal and who thought the government went too far in denying one man's freedom of speech. In an editorial, the Wellington-based weekly *New Zealand Free Lance* called the dismissal a satire on New Zealand's boast that it was the most advanced democratic country in the world. Although begging to differ with Grey's sentiments about the war: 'We nevertheless hold that to callously deprive him of his living because he dared to disagree with the sentiments of the multitude is simply to establish a parallel with the unreasoning brutality of a French mob in the days of Robespierre or to resort to the malignant methods of hidebound Toryism in the past history of Great Britain.'[69]

Even the government's representative in London, William Pember Reeves, became caught up in controversy about the war. He reported to Seddon in February of 1900 his estimates of the numbers of Boer forces, numbers which he calculated from a variety of sources, and some opinions on the progress of the war. While Reeves' comments were intended only for the premier, Seddon made them public, and the tone of the public reaction was that New Zealand's agent-general in London was at best pessimistic. One writer of a letter to the editor of the *Evening Post*, identified only as 'Loyalist', accused Reeves of a 'gross libel' on New Zealand.[70] Underlying the objections, it seemed, was that Reeves in his cables to Seddon was not reflecting the jingoistic patriotism of his premier, or indeed, of a great many other people. Reeves wrote a lengthy reply to Seddon in which he justified the figures and opinions he gave and noted, with some literary aloofness, that he would not bother to comment on charges of disloyalty, adding:

An official who is sending cable messages to his Government at 3s 11d a word is not likely to indulge in flowers of sentiment, or in spread-eagle descriptions of picturesque and interesting episodes. Nor is he called upon to consider what effect his messages will have upon enthusiastic readers imperfectly informed upon the incidents of the war. It is his business to tell his Government the driest facts in the briefest and plainest words. This is what I honestly endeavoured to do.[71]

## Changing views

Perceived positions at the outset of the war could change, another indication of identity as a New Zealander taking precedence. The imperialist ardour did not always last and some people who were assumed to be stridently anti-war at the beginning were not always what they seemed. Some early advocates had their enthusiasm curbed as the war progressed. One such case concerned a Wellington trooper, Charles Borland Tasker, a member of the Sixth Contingent who was court-martialled for sleeping while on guard duty and sentenced to three years' imprisonment in England. The term was reduced to one year by the commander-in-chief of British forces in South Africa, Lord Kitchener.

Tasker, while on board ship to England, was apparently locked below the waterline in a guardroom where the heat was intense. He told his parents in a letter that he lost so much weight a ring his mother gave him fell off his finger and was not recovered. On landing in Southampton, he and other prisoners were handcuffed in pairs and marched to the railway station. 'I would like to know what he had done to be tortured and subjected to such indignities as that?' his mother asked.[72] His parents were not without influence. His father was John Tasker, who was chief clerk in the Police Commissioner's Department, and his mother was Marianne Allen Tasker, who formed and headed the Women's Democratic Union whose aims were to improve the lot of women in society through law reform and education. She was the union's delegate to the National Council of Women and organised the 1898 Wellington conference of the council, at which she and a better-known campaigner for the cause, Kate Sheppard, gave the opening addresses.[73]

But neither parent was named when Tasker's case eventually found its way into the newspapers in November, four months after his dereliction of duty, and they remained publicly unnamed in the succeeding weeks as a campaign to secure their son's release was mounted. Marianne Tasker even wrote a letter to the editor of the *Evening Post* in Wellington, but signed it only as 'Trooper Tasker's Mother'.[74] In the letter, she made it clear she would in future be less keen to support the Empire's cause than she was when she farewelled her son: 'Leaving the individual out of the question, England, with all her boasted civilisation, wants the "man with the muckrake" to uncover some of her foulest spots. The day has now arrived when her soldiers should be treated like human beings, not like machines.'[75] Her view was that New Zealand lent troops for a specific purpose in a specific place; the military authorities exceeded their jurisdiction in sending a native-born New Zealander to the United Kingdom.

Marianne Tasker appealed to Seddon and he cabled the agent-general in London, Reeves, to lobby British government officials. She also sent a petition to the premier, who passed it on to the Governor, Lord Ranfurly, with an accompanying letter urging clemency. Ranfurly passed the letter and petition on to Joseph Chamberlain, adding he was unable to make a recommendation.[76] The petition was not published in New Zealand, then or later, but another indication that the Taskers were using the *Evening Post* while maintaining their anonymity was that the newspaper was able to publish details of Tasker's offence in wording at times identical to that in the petition.[77] The *Post* concluded its summation with the sentence: 'The colonial volunteer, it is becoming increasingly evident, is out of place as a part of the British Army.' The petition pleaded Tasker's youth – he was eighteen when he left New Zealand – and his ignorance of military discipline and said his 'confinement with criminal prisoners in a Military Gaol will be likely to ruin his future life'.[78] After submissions from Reeves and a Wellington solicitor, Edwin Jellicoe, Tasker was released on 21 December 1901 and returned to New Zealand.

In addition to not publicly making the connection between Tasker and his mother, newspapers also seemed loath to recall that Marianne Tasker was a prominent peace campaigner who had seconded a motion proposed by the feminist and peace advocate Wilhelmina Bain at a meeting the year before of the National Council of Women in Dunedin. Scottish-born Bain was one of the war's most outspoken critics. The motion deplored 'the militarism which is extending its ravages over the world, increasing the burdens of every people, fomenting national and international jealousies and inciting virulent racial hatreds'.[79] Marianne Tasker also read a paper, which she said was written by a member of her Women's Democratic Union, which 'strongly protested against war and all its attendant horrors'.[80] Tasker, like Bain, was clearly opposed to the war. But she and her husband created an entirely different impression in their petition to Seddon, the penultimate paragraph of which read: 'That your petitioners have always actively interested themselves in formation and departure of Contingents to South Africa and gave their Son to assist in the Empire's service.'[81]

The Tasker case, similar to the more serious and more publicised Wilmansrust case for the Australians, raised a question in the minds of colonials whether their volunteer effort was as appreciated as it should have been by the British and whether professional British army commanders paid due regard to the callow military experience, and to the separate national identities, of the colonial men under their command – whether, in fact, the colonial expenditure was worth the price.[82] In an editorial, the *Evening Post* linked the two cases and remarked that Tasker's cause became the cause of every New Zealand trooper. If Tasker was ill-treated on the voyage to England, as his mother suggested, 'we for our part will not be so ardent upon the side of more contingents when they are asked for'.[83]

## *Second thoughts*

The nationalist feeling, the assertion of a colony's will in the cause of the Empire, that was used to send troops to South Africa could equally be invoked to bring them home again, or at least to stop more being sent. Before the war was a year old, second thoughts were being expressed. 'Our first duty as colonists is to ourselves', an unidentified writer in the *New Zealand Observer* remarked. Complaining that troopers were being lost to bullets and disease, as well as to openings in British units, the South African police and commercial opportunities, 'it is coming home to us very forcibly that this contingent business is working out to our positive disadvantage', the writer said.[84]

This was about a month after Seddon, at a social function in Wellington, had said he was thinking about sending New Zealand troops to support the British in the Boxer Uprising in China.[85] The *Evening Post*, whose editorial policy opposed Seddon, ridiculed the suggestion as 'rampant and senseless jingoism' and said his vanity could not resist appeal to the imperial gallery.[86] Its invective was based on nationalistic concerns, however, maintaining that the more urgent need while troops were in South Africa was the organisation of a citizen army for self-defence. Another newspaper that could not usually be counted an ally, the *Otago Witness*, commented in an editorial that Seddon's ability to interpret the feelings of the people had on this occasion failed him: 'Even the

A William Blomfield cartoon that reflected on the number of New Zealanders joining other units during the war. The caption read: 'Right Honourable R Seddon: "Who the dickens are you, anyhow, and what do you want here, you scarecrow?" No 163: "I'm the remains of the First, Second, Third, Fourth and Fifth Contingents, Sir. The rest, alas, are policemen in South Africa, or have joined the British Army. They say even the promise of a medal, with a bust of yourself, will not bring them back."' *New Zealand Observer*, 4 August 1900, p. 1

most loyal and Imperialistic spirits here have received the proposal very coldly.'[87] The Wellington-based *New Zealand Free Lance* reduced Seddon's motivation to the venal: 'If the Premier's proposal to send a contingent to China will have the effect of stirring Her Majesty up to a recognition of Mr Seddon's claims to an earldom, then we frankly admit that the end may justify the means used to achieve it. But, if there is to be no earldom, there certainly ought to be no contingent for China.'[88]

It was not just newspaper talk. Ranfurly noted Seddon's offer in his quarterly report to Chamberlain and commented: 'But the other members of the Cabinet did not consider there was sufficient cause to justify such an act when all the European powers were combined against China.'[89] Little more was heard of the idea and in the event no New Zealand troops were sent.[90]

In a similar vein, in a leading article in May 1901 the *Evening Post* questioned whether Seddon accurately represented the feelings of the people by continuing to offer troops for South Africa. 'We are sadly in want of our young men at home', it said, 'as the country settlers are finding to their cost.'[91] Following suit, the *Observer* later the same year noted: 'It is difficult to view with complacency and unconcern the withdrawal of 1000 of our finest young men from agricultural and manufacturing pursuits. War is not our destiny so much as the walks of industry and peace.'[92]

## The hands of friends

It was not just fit young men who could ride, shoot and live off the land who were sent to South Africa. So, too, were New Zealand nurses, and while it is possible to only generalise and speculate about their motivations, it seems clear that a sense of national identity, a desire to serve New Zealand and New Zealanders, was present. A self-described 'Old Soldier' expressed why New Zealand nurses had to be in South Africa:

> Think what it would be to "our boys" to see about them in the hospital tent in that far-off strange land the cheery faces of nurses they have known in Dunedin – friends of their families – instead of strangers, however clever, however kind ... think what it would mean to the mothers in Dunedin to know their sons are in the hands of friends.[93]

More than two years later, 'A Parent' wrote a like letter to the editor of the *Evening Post*:

We have nurses who are quite willing to pay their own fare to go to South African hospitals to nurse their brothers, friends and kinsmen; and how pleased our boys are to have some nurses who know their friends and country, to share their troubles and sufferings alike, and make the dreary stay in hospital less dreary by their presence and assistance.[94]

Rudyard Kipling did not overlook the nurses in his poetic comments on the war either:

Who recalls the noontide and the funerals through the market,
(Blanket-hidden bodies, flagless, followed by the flies?)
And the footsore firing party, and the dust and stench and staleness,
And the faces of the Sisters and the glory in their eyes?[95]

Despite an initial reluctance by the government, about 35 nurses from New Zealand were among the estimated 1700 military and civilian nurses, laywomen and volunteers who went to tend the wounded and sick.[96] Seddon was not averse to the sending of New Zealand nurses; his reluctance was born of a concern that money spent on their dispatch might better be spent on sending more men.[97] After meeting a group of women in Dunedin who were anxious for nurses to go, he said the issue was really one for the imperial authorities, and in any case, there were no doubt many qualified nurses in South Africa able to be called upon.[98] Undaunted by the premier's seeming indifference, committees were set up in several cities to raise money to send nurses and pay their wages. The committee set up in Dunedin to raise funds to send the Fourth Contingent also busied itself with raising money for nurses. One of the committee members, John Fraser, a barrister and sometime crown solicitor in Dunedin, proffered this opinion: 'That in view of the fact that there would soon be 1200 fighting men from New Zealand in South Africa, it was our bounden duty to send our women there to look after them if they were wounded.'[99] Fraser's use of the

A group of Otago nurses sent to South Africa by public subscription. Back row, from left: Dora Louisa Harris, Dora Peiper, Elizabeth ('Bessie') Rennie Hay. Front row: Nellie Monson, Sister Janet Williamson, Sarah Jane Ross, Isabella Campbell. Sister Williamson received the Royal Red Cross, the first New Zealand nurse to be so honoured and the first New Zealand woman recipient of any royal honour. *The Volunteers: The Journal of the New Zealand Military Historical Society*, vol. 25, no. 2 (Boer War commemorative issue), p. 68

collective pronoun made it clear he saw a difference between New Zealand and British – for him, identity was distinctive.

Whatever the merits of ill or wounded New Zealand soldiers being tended and treated by compatriots, there was clearly a feeling of shared identity and camaraderie between New Zealand nurses and troopers. One of the nurses, Dora Harris, wrote in her diary of meeting two New Zealanders while she was having coffee in Cape Town:

So they asked us to see them off. Mr P took us to the train. Cap. Smith was there and I spoke to Donald MacDonald. Some of them gave us badges, NZMR [New Zealand Mounted Rifles]. When we left they gave the Maori War Cry and 3 cheers for Mr Pilcher . . . It was a strange evening and we felt very excited.[100]

Moreover, the nurses and troopers soon discovered that the greatest danger in South Africa was not Boer bullets, but disease. Of the estimated 230 deaths of men serving in New Zealand contingents, 57 per cent were from what was called at the time enteric, now more commonly known as typhoid fever.[101] Typhoid was described as 'the scourge of 19th and early 20th century armies' and it killed more soldiers in the Spanish–American War (1898) and in the Boer War than did bullets or other more intended agencies of death.[102] Seddon also revealed his nationalistic side in a report he tabled in Parliament showing a return of New Zealand troops with enteric:

> The number of deaths, the number invalided and the number lying ill in South Africa point to something wrong ... Our men are sent there to fight the battles of the country and it is the duty of those in charge to see that proper hospital accommodation and attendance are provided. It may be difficult to avoid insanitary conditions, but when our men are stricken down they should have the necessary hospital accommodation.[103]

While the prevalence of disease was rarely mentioned so boldly by politicians and military commanders, nurses were not so reticent. Sister Bessie Hay of Dunedin, in a letter written from a hospital in Bloemfontein, said she had never been busier – or (she added in an incongruous note) happier. Some of her patients went insane after recovering from fever, she wrote: 'One did today. It is all fever – no wounds. We see funerals by the score every day passing. Several of the sisters have died.'[104] Sister Emily Peter, who led the contingent of six Christchurch nurses, was interviewed in January 1901 when she returned home. She was not complimentary. 'As for the Army Medical system', the story went, 'Sister Peter is very outspoken as to the crying need for reform, root and branch.'[105] Another New Zealand nurse, Elizabeth Teape, was attached to the Imperial Army Nursing Reserve and sent to Bloemfontein: 'On arrival I found the place a hotbed of fever – enteric raged everywhere. It was no wonder. There were no sanitary arrangements and dead animals lay everywhere.'[106]

Nurses could look beyond the disease, beyond the war even, in a manner which the men involved perhaps could not. A nurse identified only as 'a Colonial' wrote of a long day of duty tending the wounded and the dying and reflected at its close:

> The last drink is given, the last dressing applied, and the orderlies come on duty for the night. Weary and footsore I stumble down the winding path . . . As a sad memento of the war I carry with me a Mauser bullet, and a piece of shell, for, as the giver says, with tears in his eyes, "My poor wife will never want to look at the bullet that hurt me." And being a woman, I feel that I want to cry, for it does not fall to my lot to see the "glory of war" – it is mine only to look upon the maimed limbs, the ghastly wounds, the suffering, the sad deaths, the after-results of an engagement, be it a victory or a defeat. And, being a woman, I feel that I want to cry, too, for the Dutch women, on the lonely farm on the veldt, whose grey-haired husband and youngest son, scarce strong enough to fire the rifle, died together in the trenches yesterday morning. For Rachel is weeping for her children on "both sides of the sea."'[107]

Joan Rattray in her history of New Zealand nursing noted that while monuments were erected for soldiers: 'Little was heard of the women who also served.'[108] That was not quite correct. Four years after the war, the *Observer* recalled: 'It was not only the "boys" of New Zealand who distinguished themselves in the South African War. New Zealand "girls" in considerable number did valuable service on the army nursing staff and at least one has risen to distinguished position in consequence.'[109] It singled out Rose Shappere from Timaru who 'won such a name for devotion to her work that . . . some of the best positions in her profession were at her disposal'.[110] It could also have acknowledged, but did not, Sister Janet Williamson from Dunedin, who served in Bloemfontein for seventeen months and later on a hospital ship. She was mentioned in dispatches and became the first New Zealand recipient of the Royal Red Cross. As such, she was also the first New Zealand woman to receive a royal honour of any type.[111]

## Motivation and reputation

The war was the first opportunity for New Zealand as a whole to display its distinctive identity outside the country. There were two integral elements to this exposition: one was what prompted young men to enlist to fight in a far-distant war; and the other was the manner in which they fought and which established the reputation of the New Zealand soldier. New Zealanders played a full part in the war from almost the beginning until the end. But were the young men of New Zealand motivated by a need to rush to the aid of the Empire? Not everyone thought so. An unidentified columnist in the *New Zealand Observer* considered it more likely men were in search of adventure and travel in strange lands:[112]

> It is safe to assert that only a man here and there understands the cause of the war, and the majority don't care as long as they get a share of the fighting. The jingo idea sounds all right, but it has no foundation in fact. New Zealanders excel in fighting as they do in football. They don't play football for the Empire, but only for the personal honour success wins.

The Australian bush poet and lawyer 'Banjo' Paterson, who was in South Africa as a war correspondent, could have been speaking for New Zealanders as well as Australians when he wrote:

> The English flag – it is ours in sooth
> We stand by it wrong or right.
> But deep in our hearts is the honest truth
> We fought for the sake of a fight.[113]

The Second Contingent church parade at its camp in Karori, Wellington, shortly before departure. M. Ross, *A Souvenir of New Zealand's Response to the Empire's Call* (Wellington: McKee & Co., 1899)

New Zealand sent ten contingents of mounted troopers between 1899 and 1902, the first two of which were paid for by the government, the third and fourth by local subscription mainly in Canterbury for the third and Otago and Southland for the fourth, and the British government paid for the remainder. In total, more than 6000 New Zealanders served in the war, although a precise number cannot be arrived at because of the many who served in more than one contingent, some re-enlisting in South Africa and others returning home only to go again. Several hundred New Zealanders are also known to have served with the forces of other countries, notably the Australian colonies and Britain. Conversely, it has been estimated that slightly more than 200 Australians served with New Zealand contingents.[114]

Artist F. J. Waugh's impression of an encounter between First Contingent company commander Captain William Madocks and a Boer 'leader' on what came to be known as New Zealand Hill. From H. W. Wilson, *With the Flag to Pretoria – A History of the Boer War of 1899–1900* (London: Harmsworth Brothers, 1900), vol. 4, p. 333

Nationality was a portable label, however. One of the most celebrated 'New Zealand' soldiers was a First Contingent company commander, Captain William Madocks, who led New Zealanders in their first significant action, on 14 January 1900. But to describe Madocks as a New Zealander is to draw a long bow. He was posted to Wellington in 1896 as staff officer with the New Zealand Permanent Force and soon after the action in South Africa he returned to the British Army.[115] Madocks, paradoxically, was central to the case argued by Jock Phillips about a New Zealand male mythology.[116] Phillips wrote of Madocks responding 'quickly and imaginatively to the Boer attack' (at New Zealand Hill, as it came to be known), comparing that with the Yorkshire regiment the New Zealanders aided 'who, left leaderless, lacked all initiative'. 'The contrast between the

An artist's interpretation of the fighting on New Zealand Hill.
From Wilson, *With the Flag to Pretoria*, p. 331

disciplined but passive Tommy Atkins and the adaptable colonials was often made', Phillips wrote.[117] Yet Madocks was more Tommy Atkins, if a middle-class one, than he ever was colonial.

Whether native-born, second-generation New Zealanders or just temporary visitors, men responded enthusiastically to the call for volunteers to go to South Africa. While a collective memory may see the New Zealand contingents as comprising mainly rural workers who were adept at riding, shooting and general bushcraft, the reality was that they comprised a cross-section of society or, as Colin McGeorge put it, 'a remarkably representative sample, socially and geographically, of the male population'.[118] However, McGeorge's analysis confirmed Phillips' estimate that there were considerable class (or wealth) differences between officers and men. The latter calculated that 31.5 per cent of commissioned officers had professional civilian occupations as opposed to only 3 per cent of the men. 'Similarly, no officers had formerly been labourers whereas, except for the 1st and 2nd Contingents, over 15 per cent of their men were so described. There was also a considerable difference of age and experience between the ranks.'[119]

The definition of rural was not necessarily what would be considered rural more than 100 years later either. People living on the edges of cities and towns lived as much a rural lifestyle as any on farms in the hinterlands and would have been as familiar with riding horses, which were still widely used for conveyance as well as work. One of the first volunteers in Dunedin and one who passed all the necessary riding and shooting tests was James Moore, whose address was given as Stafford Street in central Dunedin.[120] He remarked on the diversity of those who presented themselves for selection in the Fourth Contingent: 'There were those among them who had roughed it in the backblocks since childhood . . . and many who had held good positions in the city and had never known what it was to sleep out of a feather bed or to miss their regular meals.'[121]

The intense patriotism felt by the troopers while they readied for war, including, as Moore noted, being treated like heroes, was replaced on departure by a mix of emotions as the reality set in: 'How many of them would be spared to return to the little island colony, time alone would tell.'[122] One of the privates in the First Contingent, Alexander Wilkie, showed it was New Zealand rather than Britain or its empire in the minds of men when they left these shores: 'In the afternoon the hills were getting smaller and smaller and all hands, sick and strong, mustered on deck to catch the last view of New Zealand, showing what a great love the men had for their home.'[123]

Much of the New Zealanders' time in the guerrilla phase of the war was spent in the pursuit of forces led by General Christiaan de Wet, and it was in an effort to ensnare them that New Zealand lost the most men in a single battle. De Wet's commando – the name coined during the war for the Boer units – drove a herd of cattle ahead of them to take the hill being held by the New Zealand Seventh Contingent in company with the 3rd New South

Wales Rifles. 'Driving up cattle as a screen, they . . . fought their way through the Seventh Contingent posts, annihilating each in turn', according to Hall in his history. The action, variously known as Langverwacht (the name of the hill) or Bothasberg, cost the New Zealanders 24 killed and 41 wounded of the total complement of eighty. Although de Wet and the president of the Orange Free State, Marthinus Steyn, were among the 600 Boers who broke through the British lines, several hundred more retreated and were later captured. As Hall remarked: 'This was the most severe action fought by any of the contingents, and for the numbers engaged, one of the most severe ever fought by New Zealand troops. In view of the large numbers of Boers who failed to pass the gap created, at the cost of so much blood, the action cannot be described as a defeat.'[124]

Given that de Wet and Steyn broke through and escaped, along with several hundred other Boers, and that Boer casualties were only 14 dead and 20 wounded, later observers may wonder what else it could be described as but defeat. It was a gallant action, however, by the New Zealanders and others against considerable odds and, as Sarah Hawdon recorded, the overall British commander, Lord Kitchener, wasted little time in saying what he thought and, significantly, singling the men out as New Zealanders rather than as merely a 'British' unit.

> I rode these weary miles today to tell you that I am proud of you. The large capture of . . . Boers and also of many thousands of sheep and cattle is entirely due to the gallantry displayed by the New Zealanders, who are all an honour to the little country from which you come. I am glad to think that the Boers happened to strike against you . . .[125]

This was music to the ears of the men who survived. A Christchurch schoolteacher, Sergeant Hastings Andrews, wrote home that Kitchener's speech was all the men talked about that night:

The Boer War Memorial in Oamaru that bears the name of Lieutenant James Parker, Lord Kitchener's nephew. It is known locally as 'Trooper Jack' because the 2.74-metre figure atop the memorial was modelled on Trooper David Mickle Jack of the Fourth Contingent. Author's photograph

He said the manner in which we held our posts was an example to the whole British army and not even the oldest hand out here can remember another occasion when he left headquarters and praised in person a column's action. On all former occasions he sent messages, always complimentary, but on this occasion he passed some score of columns operating conjointly with us, asked specially for New Zealanders only, and delivered his speech.[126]

Reports of the New Zealanders in the action featuring Madocks began a series of encomiums which continued throughout – and after – the war. Some were exaggerated, especially some written by troopers themselves, but some also were heartfelt expressions of genuine regard for the fighting qualities of New Zealanders (speaking generally and taking the men en masse, regardless of whether some, such as Madocks, may not have been New Zealanders at all). Whatever the motivation and whatever even the truth, such comments about the New Zealanders set them further apart from their allies, especially the Australians with whom they were most closely associated in the public mind, and laid the foundations for a reputation that would be enhanced and embellished over two world wars.

The more detached an observer, the more valued his (or her, because Sarah Hawdon had no shortage of praise for her compatriots) comments. One with no vested interest in the reputation of New Zealanders was the Australian, Paterson. After fighting at Arundel in Cape Colony in December 1899, he wrote there was no doubt 'that the New Zealanders are as fine a body of men as there are on the field'.[127] The following February, he noted the arrival of the First Contingent at an Orange River camp: 'The New Zealanders arrived yesterday, dusty and travel-worn, but carrying themselves with all the swing of a regiment that has earned distinction and means to earn more.'[128]

The gradual emergence of New Zealanders (and Australians) as distinct types was also noticed by another writer of diverse talents, Arthur Conan Doyle. Trained as a medical doctor and with a reputation founded on the Sherlock Holmes detective stories, Conan Doyle was in South Africa as a surgeon and part-time war correspondent. He noted the separate identity of the colonial contingents: 'Be it said, however, once and for all, that throughout the whole African army there was nothing but the utmost admiration for the dash and spirit of the hard-riding, straight-shooting sons of Australia and New Zealand. In a host which held many brave men there were none braver than they.'[129] Conan Doyle also wrote of the Seventh Contingent's role at Langverwacht and remarked that the troopers 'proved themselves to be worthy comrades to their six gallant predecessors'.[130] In like vein, Charles Lowe wrote in the English illustrated news magazine the *Graphic*, after fighting in 1900, of the 'exceptional bravery throughout the day' of the New Zealanders.[131]

Even more relevant to an acknowledgement of a separate and distinctive New Zealand identity was comparisons made by Australians. One view had Australians rating themselves as below the New Zealanders, if spuriously drawing on the Māori land wars as a reason for New Zealand excellence, overlooking perhaps that Australians also fought in those battles: 'Australians refined their sense of themselves by looking at their colonial cousins. New Zealanders, when seen as different at all, were suspected of being abler soldiers, perhaps a legacy of their "own bloody wars" with the Maori.'[132]

The commander-in-chief of the British Army, Field Marshal Lord Wolseley, said of New Zealanders at the British royal commission into the conduct of the war, 'if you compare them with our troops I should say they were better than any troops that I know of in Europe, not only of our own'.[133] One oft-quoted tribute to the worth of the New Zealanders appeared in the seven-volume *The Times History of the War in South Africa* written by Leo Amery, a noted imperialist: 'Of the service of the New Zealanders in the field it would hardly be an exaggeration to say that after they had a little experience they were by general consent regarded as the best mounted troops in South Africa.'[134] One of the British officers associated with the New Zealanders in South Africa, and who later had an even closer association as the commanding officer of the Gallipoli campaign in 1915, was General Sir Ian Hamilton. He had this to say: 'I have soldiered a long time now, but I have never in my life met men I would sooner soldier with than the New Zealanders. I feel the greatest affection for them and I shall never forget the work they did in South Africa.'[135] And according to a special edition of the *Illustrated London News* in 1900 about the war, the New Zealanders were distinguished by their initiative, their eye for the country, their hardiness and endurance and their boyish delight in getting even with the Boer: 'For gallantry and

'Farewell to the Australians and New Zealanders.' From Wilson, *With the Flag to Pretoria*, p. 911

steady courage, they are not beaten by any of the soldiers in the Queen's Army.'[136]

Naturally enough, perhaps, the troopers by and large seemed to lap up such praise and this solidified the growing 'New Zealandness' of the men as distinct from other 'Australasians'. Constance Barnicoat, the 'lady correspondent' of the Christchurch *Press* in London, seized upon this point when she interviewed a war correspondent from the *Daily News*, Arthur ('Smiler') Hales, who had just returned from the war. Hales said he could not speak too highly of 'them', meaning New Zealanders, though he seemed a little confused. 'I meant Australia to include New Zealand of course', he said, to which Barnicoat responded: 'Oh, you must not do that. Male may include female, but Australian cannot possibly include New Zealander. We love our trans-Pacific cousins immensely, but we are not going to be muddled up with them for all that.'[137]

While some of the praise was undoubtedly genuinely won and sincerely expressed, some objective beholders thought enough was enough. The *New Zealand Observer* in its unsigned 'Free Lancings' column in March 1901 railed against 'atrocious nonsense' being written from the front, saying it detested the tone taken by the press and some returned soldiers 'whose achievements have principally been in getting sick as soon as possible': 'The reputation of the New Zealand troops has been well won, but the men who have honestly held up their end are sickened with the frightful twaddle sent home from the front glorifying generally the writer.'[138] This view was emphatically supported by one of the soldiers, Captain Norman Smith, a staff officer who served with the Second Contingent and with the King's Own Scottish Borderers.[139] On his return, he told the *Press* in Christchurch he had an undisguised loathing for the news sent by war correspondents and others to newspapers and said some of the correspondents were 100 miles from the scenes they described:

> While recognising that the correspondents of the New Zealand papers were expected to emphasise the doings of our own contingents and consequently that this matter was frequently out of perspective, Captain Smith considers they might have been more accurate in their statements and less fulsome in their references to the doughty deeds of valour performed by the members of the contingents.[140]

Smith nevertheless acknowledged that the New Zealanders 'undoubtedly' were the best colonial troops in South Africa but others should not be belittled by comparison.

James Belich wrote that the New Zealanders' performance against the Boers was obscured 'by New Zealand martial mythology, which modern research has yet to fully penetrate'.[141] The lack of penetration is most likely due to the widely scattered duties of the New Zealand forces and their attachment to British columns, as well as the lack of a thorough, complete history of New Zealand's role in the war. Among the New Zealanders who served with units from other countries was 24-year-old Lionel Phillips Russell, a son of the New Zealand opposition leader, Captain Sir William Russell. Although sent to England to be educated and commissioned, Russell's pride in identifying himself as a New Zealander was evident in letters he wrote to his parents. A lieutenant with the York and Stafford Mounted Infantry in South Africa, he wrote of meeting some New Zealanders at 'some long-named station':

> I only had two or three minutes to talk to them but soon found a Hastings man I knew called Horne and told him to let the family know that he had met me. The band of some English regiment was playing them off and a good crowd were very enthusiastic about them, the New Zealanders having made themselves very popular out here; they are spoken very well of by all and greatly preferred to the Australians as they have some small amount of discipline, whereas the Australians have none and are tremendous rascals.[142]

A few days later, writing about food the troopers had with them, he mentioned tins of Australian butter, 'which is splendid, although it annoys me greatly to eat Australian butter when New Zealand could be supplying it'.[143] He had suggestions for his father about where 'mealie' (maize) could be planted on his Hawke's Bay farm and wrote of his intention to return to New Zealand with his horse which he felt may not be suitable for polo.[144] Russell was killed in a surprise encounter with Boers on 19 December 1901.[145]

Concomitant with the growing reputation of the New Zealand soldier, either real or imagined, was a belief that the New Zealander, like the Australian, could play hard off the field of battle as well as on it; that the colonials were not kindly disposed to the niceties of British military discipline and that they did not readily acknowledge any difference between officers and 'men'. The numerous examples of tributes to their fighting qualities, both by their compatriots and by the British, far outweighed the publicity given to their

235

off-field antics. Soldiers of the Sixth Contingent went on strike in 1901 over the poor quality of their clothing and an apparent refusal by British authorities to issue them with new gear. One sergeant was court-martialled and given five years' imprisonment, but this was remitted by Kitchener.[146] Later in 1901, the same regiment threatened to strike over a delay with pay.[147] One trooper, William Bunten, expressed what he thought of the war: 'I suppose you are sorry you are not with us but you can take my word for it most of us wish it was over. War and suffering is not the game it is cracked up to be, especially in this god-forsaken country.'[148] Another trooper, unidentified, wrote home from Pretoria in January 1901 that he and his comrades were 'heartily sick and tired of the whole thing, and are anxious to return home. Mr Seddon would have a rough time if we could get hold of him for telling Lord Kitchener he could keep us for as long as he liked.'[149] Yet another, Trooper William Brown of Dunedin, made his views equally plain:

> We have been digging trenches and throwing up breastworks for the last four days. The boys do not like it either. They say they can get pick and shovel work in New Zealand without coming here for it. I hear that there is a sixth contingent coming over. Is it true, or is it only a bush telegram? If they knew as much as we do they would stop in New Zealand.[150]

There was a sense among men of the Fourth Contingent that they were being used by the British authorities and, when their usefulness was at an end, were not well treated. James Moore wrote that when the contingent was heading for Cape Town and home, the troopers were not allowed off the train on to station platforms, which were reserved for officers and civilians.

> As may be imagined, this did not serve to improve our already sorely-tried tempers and – well, we were too full for words. What had we done, we asked ourselves, that we should be treated like so many

niggers. We had fought and bled and starved on the veldt for months. We had suffered all manner of indignities at the hands of men who were superior to us only in rank . . . now that our regiment had gone out of commission, and we were of no further use to the British Army, we were dumped into trucks like a mob of cattle, hunted from the platforms of railway stations, and placed on a level with the scum of South Africa. Twelve months of active service had convinced us that there is no sentiment in warfare, and that no such thing as patriotism exists; but surely we deserved better treatment than was meted out to us by the authorities.[151]

Members of the Fifth Contingent took matters into their own hands when they felt they were being unfairly treated. They were posted to Worcester north of Cape Town prior to embarking for home and, according to Frank Perham, their commander was 'something of a martinet' and restricted the men to normal military duties in camp, some distance from the town. The men, Perham wrote, felt they were entitled to some leisure and relaxation after a year of strenuous campaigning but they were banned from town because 'it was reeking with typhoid'. The commander himself lived in the town, so:

One day four hundred men donned their "glory rags" and marched to the Town in a body; and quite enjoyed themselves too! The fat was then in the fire, they were "dam rabble," "mutineers," and everything but soldiers. To quiet things Colonel [Richard] Davies made a special trip from Capetown. He talked quietly to us and possibly without our knowledge to the Officers as well. At any rate things improved after his visit.[152]

New Zealanders were not above looting Boer farmhouses, however, even though the practice was forbidden. A trooper, William Macpherson, wrote home: 'Any houses we have looted have been splendidly furnished. I got a silver watch and gold chain, and a large bundle of love letters in a house last Sunday and a 10gal jar of fig jam on Monday. The letters are most interesting. The girl appears to have been engaged to no less than three men."[153] The same trooper overheard General John French (later Field Marshal the Earl of Ypres) talking about the New Zealanders thus: 'I spoke to them once about so much chattering and swearing at each other in their ranks. They take no notice; it still goes on yet they never lose their places in the ranks and take good care that they are not left behind. As for gallopers, damn me, if I ever saw anyone like them."[154]

As the war dragged on and as the reputation of the New Zealanders was consolidated, there was increased agitation for them to be kept together and not hived off, a company here, a company there, with different columns. In short, a national unit in the field was sought. The agitation came from the top. At the end of 1901 when New Zealand agreed to an Eighth Contingent, Ranfurly cabled Chamberlain that the government wanted the men kept together:

> [It] should not unless absolutely necessary be subdivided but be
> kept in one column and with it sixth and seventh contingents now
> in South Africa placed in same column. By so doing, twofold object
> would be gained New Zealand would maintain its own identity and
> lend strength and field efficiency tending to encourage large number
> of officers and men and sixth and seventh whose time soon expires to
> remain and volunteer for extended service.[155]

Ranfurly added there was grievance in the past that the contingents had been split up and that the men were strongly objecting. He received a reply ten days later saying that New Zealand's wish would be carried out 'as far as possible'. In the event, it did not happen. As Ian McGibbon noted: 'Behind this growing willingness to assert colonial wishes lay a belief that Imperial officers did not understand colonial officers or men, whose morale had suffered as a result of the detachments."[156] An unidentified writer for the monthly *New Zealand Illustrated Magazine* thought the New Zealanders' efficiency had suffered: 'It is true that by dividing the contingents already sent, and not allowing them to have a free hand and work together, much of their efficacy was wasted in the past. Whenever they were allowed their heads, free of restriction, they rendered excellent account of themselves . . .'[157]

For all the imperial rhetoric of the debating chamber and the public platform, the Boer War confirmed and consolidated a feeling of national identity for New Zealanders. It showed in their ability as soldiers, especially the free-ranging mounted roles they were given, and in their disdain for the ingrained English class distinctions between officers and men. It showed, too, in their independence of spirit and their desire for 'a fair go'. Their uniqueness as New Zealanders, on show for the first time beyond its shores, also grew more readily apparent alongside Australians. This individuality became evident not only with what they said and wrote themselves, but also with what others wrote and said about them.

The distinctive New Zealand identity that had been coalescing for thirty or more years was given full rein on the veld of South Africa. War was one way in which this identity was put on display to the rest of the world. Another was sport, a prime outward expression of what distinguishes one country from another.

INTERNATIONAL WALKING CONTEST

JOSEPH SCOTT

# SEVEN

# Forging a National Identity
# Through Sport

*An identity is to be found in the embodied habits of social life.*[1]

About 10,000 people crammed into the Caledonian Ground in Dunedin on the first day of 1889 not just for the Caledonian Society's annual sports, but also to welcome home one of their own. As a precocious thirteen-year-old, slight of build but strong of will, Joe Scott had competed in a two-mile walking race at the same sports and was disqualified for breaking into a run (or so the judges said – race walking has always been a contentious event). But Scott's courage and readiness to compete against grown men twice his size gained him the support of the crowd, as well as of Dunedin's most distinguished visitor at the time, the Governor, Sir James Fergusson.[2] According to a report many years later, Queen Victoria's man in New Zealand patted young Joe on the head and said: 'Bravo little man, well walked indeed; some day you will be champion of the world.'[3]

On the equivalent day of the equivalent sports fourteen years later, Joe Scott entered the arena clad in his competition uniform of tights and singlet and wearing the silver champion's belt he had been awarded in London the previous May for the prodigious feat of walking 363 miles and six laps in the Agricultural Hall in London over a period of six days.[4] The feat earned him the title of world champion, the first such crown to be won by a New Zealander.[5] The president of the Caledonian Society, James Barron, greeted Scott and made an impromptu speech, telling the crowd that Scott by his unparalleled deeds 'had done honour not only to himself, but also to the colony at large'. Scott was led around the running track on a spontaneous lap of honour by the Ordnance Band – a mixture of pipes and brass, it appears – playing Handel's 'See the Conquering Hero Comes'.

This was not just a local event and an exhibition of parochialism. Scott's career was widely and extensively covered by newspapers as he developed as a race walker and competed against the best New Zealand had to offer, then Australia and then Britain. In the words of the *Lyttelton Times*: 'Joe Scott returns to New Zealand full of honours. His tour has, from first to last, been a great success . . .'[6] For 20 years from the late 1870s, Scott was the celebrated New Zealand athlete of his day. He was a professional pedestrian in an era of increasing amateurism and when the fad for race-walking long distances was on the wane; such factors should not detract from his standing in sport, however. A twentieth-century sports broadcaster and writer, Wallie Ingram, once asked a veteran athletics official and a former competitor, Dorrie Leslie, who was the greatest track athlete he had seen in New Zealand. 'Without hesitation, he informed me that the palm should go to Joe Scott', Ingram wrote.[7] This was in 1935 when Jack Lovelock was certainly known but his greatest achievement was still to come; Leslie's compass would have included some early champions such as sprinter Jack Hempton, hurdlers George Smith and Arthur Holder, and sprinter Arthur Porritt, who was the only New Zealander to win a sprint medal at an Olympic Games.[8]

The tale of Joe Scott demonstrates how avidly New Zealanders followed the deeds of their compatriots on the sporting field, taking both pleasure and a vicarious pride in their achievements. Scott was the first in a long line of athletes of varying descriptions who scaled the heights they set themselves and helped establish sport as a central part of New Zealand culture, a part of who and what we are. The role of sport in shaping national identity in the late nineteenth and early twentieth century has been frequently debated by historians and writers.[9] Sport, as with other facets of life, was layered: there was the suburban bonding as manifested in club competitions; provincial loyalty through national sport; and national identity through the following of the endeavours of New Zealanders testing their skills against competitors from other countries. Sport in New Zealand, as elsewhere, became the vehicle for what Michael Billig called 'banal nationalism'[10] – routine signs through which the sense of nation is daily communicated, as Jeffrey Hill put it.[11]

The role of sport in shaping national identity gains an added significance because it was driven by its participants and followers rather than imposed by a ruling clique; it is 'bottom up' history rather than 'top down'. Governments, in New Zealand and elsewhere, could and did capitalise on the growth and popularity of sport for their own purposes, but in New Zealand, at least, politicians followed sport rather than led it.[12] As Scott Crawford observed: 'For New Zealanders, the image of themselves as belonging to a country devoted to sport has been an important foundation for the development of national identity.'[13] Allied to that personal attachment to sport was the gradual adoption of symbols and colours which became significant markers of identity – the silver fern of New Zealand or the wattle of Australia.[14]

Indeed, such has been its significance in New Zealand that the country should be, according to James Belich, a world capital of the historical study of sport.[15] It is not and could never claim to be: New Zealand is more a small village than a world capital when it comes to the historiography of its own sport,[16] as Charlotte Macdonald recognised: 'For all the observations that New Zealand has been a "sports-mad society", very little attention has been paid to the subject in existing general histories.'[17] Notwithstanding a number of recent efforts,[18] the scholarly examination of New Zealand sport history remains lean: there is no academic history of sport as a whole – although one is in preparation – and no general history of the sport that is most often credited with contributing to New Zealand identity, rugby union (the development and evolution of which into the New Zealand 'national game' and as a prime marker of identity is examined in the following chapter).[19] If New Zealand is indeed 'sports-mad', as Macdonald asserts, the affliction is not one shared by her academic colleagues, at least in terms of published output.[20]

## The beginnings of a 'games revolution'

Sport was recognised early as a marker of national identity; indeed, it preceded the so-called 'games revolution' that was partly caused by the industrial revolution in Europe, and especially Britain, in the mid-nineteenth century. One of the earliest British sports historians, Peter McIntosh, pointed out that the Swiss-born French philosopher of the eighteenth century Jean Jacques Rousseau proposed that 'sport could and should be used for political and nationalistic ends'.[21] Giving advice to a reconstituted Polish government in 1773, Rousseau talked of the value of education in inculcating patriotism but added that sport had a special role to play in the production of patriots: games were to make children's 'hearts glow and create a deep love for the fatherland and its laws'.[22] Although the advice was tendered to Poland it was, according to McIntosh, taken and acted upon in Sweden, Denmark, Germany and the United States. The philosophy crossed the Channel into Britain in the nineteenth century where sport came to 'promote solidarity and patriotism'.[23] Sport itself, in its multiple rudimentary folk guises, had in fact made the crossing earlier.[24] However, few modern sports had been developed or formalised before the beginning of the nineteenth century.[25] By the beginning of the twentieth, most had, and even modern sports such as triathlon or

BMX can trace their origins not to California but to nineteenth-century Britain.

Traditionally, sports had been the preserve of the British (usually English) aristocracy: horse racing, hunting, cricket, yachting, real or royal tennis, fist-fighting and fencing. Factors such as increased leisure time for the majority of the population, urbanisation and the railways brought about the 'games revolution'. The playing of games ceased to be the preserve of the upper class and came to be associated with the middle class, especially at the public schools and the two great universities, Oxford and Cambridge. Football (before there was a distinction between its various forms) moved from the villages, where it had been a game of few rules and much violence, onto the more controlled, and controllable, spaces of village greens and purpose-built grounds at the schools and universities. Adherents set about establishing rules for their games. In the case of football, rules were associated with particular schools or universities – hence, rugby union stemmed from the rules at Rugby School and association football (or soccer) came from 'Cambridge rules football'. In effect, as McIntosh also noted, the pupils and students took the games of the masses, redefined and codified them, then gave them back again.[26] They also gave them to Britain's sprawling empire.

The received wisdom is that as games were developed and codified in Britain, especially at the public schools in southern England, they were infused with a wider Victorian ideology that included an assumption of moral and ethnic superiority and the notion of muscular Christianity which was expressed as *mens sana in corpore sano* (a healthy mind in a healthy body).[27] The newly regimented games were then distributed through the British Empire, along with language, parliamentary democracy and literature, by enthusiastic proselytisers, especially missionaries, soldiers and well-educated members of the upper middle class, all intent on establishing their forever England in some corner of a foreign field.[28] As Sir Charles Tennyson remarked: 'One achievement of Victorian England has,

George Selwyn, an example
of muscular Christianity in
New Zealand. From an original
published in the *Derbyshire
Times*, May 1878

I think, not been adequately appreciated. She was the world's
games-master.'[29]

But the English manner of sport was not transferred *in toto* to
its far-flung possessions, much less to those countries which it did
not possess. Crawford noted: 'The characteristics of recreation and
sport undergo considerable changes in situations which are inevita-
bly different from those in which they were initially developed.'[30]
Cricket, for example, one of the earliest of sports to develop on
an organised basis in England, did not become a significant sport
in North America; soccer as an evolved form of football did not
take hold in the Empire's most populous country, India.[31] Fox hunting, a preserve of the upper middle class in England, found little
popularity in many areas of the Empire if only because of a lack of
foxes, although it did gain fleeting renown on one occasion in the
Wellington area when, in lieu of a fox, a sheepskin soaked in kero-
sene was dragged over the course. Men and women followed the

THE GRAPHIC
*AN ILLUSTRATED WEEKLY NEWSPAPER*

No. 1,144 — Vol. XLIV. ] EDITION
Registered as a Newspaper] DE LUXE     SATURDAY, OCTOBER 31, 1891     WITH EXTRA SUPPLEMENT [ PRICE SIXPENCE
                                                                                       By Post 9½d.

FOLLOWING THE HOUNDS BY TRAIN—A SCENE IN NEW ZEALAND
DRAWN BY JOHN CHARLTON

Following the hounds.
An English view of an
English sport in New
Zealand – when a train
was part of the hunt.
*The Graphic*, 31 October
1891, p. 1

hounds in the traditional manner on horseback, but some watched
the action from horse-drawn carriages and a few even from railway
carriages.[32]

While cricket was played early in New Zealand in European
terms and horse racing was a popular form of recreation with the
earliest settlers, at least until 1860 in towns and for longer in rural
areas, 'the Protestant work ethic moulded the prevailing lifestyle'.[33]
It was clear the imperial sporting template did not fit all of Britain's
colonies. By the 1860s in New Zealand, missionaries were less active
than they had been and the presence of British soldiers did not
last beyond 1870 and, in any case, they had been confined to the

North Island. A contributing factor, and one that is not considered in Anglocentric histories which recount Britain as the centre of a ripple effect that enveloped the Empire, was the gold strikes in the Coromandel area of the North Island and in Nelson, Otago and the West Coast in the South. The population boosts which these areas received because of the gold brought not sporting proselytisers from Britain, but miners with hope in their hearts from Victoria and California. In a sporting sense, they blended with immigrants from Britain to create a sporting environment that came to be markedly different from that for which the well-educated British may have hoped. This was best reflected in the evolution of football in New Zealand: various forms of 'folk' football led to the adoption of 'Rugby rules' throughout the country from 1870, and while the administrators of the game may have been imperial-minded and imbued with the Corinthian ethic of the elite of southern England, not all the players were.[34] A different attitude to sport between the imperial core and its periphery was noted by a New Zealand journalist working in London, Guy Scholefield, who said he found in sport 'some of the strongest discords between English and colonial ideals'.[35]

> The one great factor underlying our difference is, on the one hand, the innate conservatism of the English – the natural objection to innovation of an historically old race – and on the other the eager inventiveness and desire for change of the colonials ... whereas in the colonies all sports are democratic, in England most of them are class activities.

While the observation that the Protestant work ethic held sway in the settlement days of the new colony is probably an accurate one, there would also have been practical factors inhibiting the playing of sport, such as a lack of cleared land and a dearth of facilities and equipment. It was not all work and no play, though. One of the first sports to be pursued was horse racing, a preserve of the aristocracy in England, but its advent in New Zealand did not merely mirror the circumstances of 'Home'. Edward Jerningham Wakefield, who arrived among the first settlers in Wellington as secretary to his uncle, Colonel William Wakefield, recalled the organisation of an 'anniversary fête' to mark the first year of the Wellington settlement: 'The prosperous state of the working-classes did not fail to show itself by their very obstinate, but inoffensive, determination to have a share in the arrangement of the forthcoming festival. The democracy and aristocracy of the place could not manage to agree about the persons to be appointed as a Committee of Management.'[36] Already, the circumstances of fledgling New Zealand proved to be different from what the settlers had left behind.

A compromise was found 'after many days' good-humoured dispute' and it was decided to hold two fêtes, one 'popular' and one 'select'. The latter consisted of only a ball after bad weather stopped any outside activity and on the following day a rowing match took place on the harbour but a proposed sailing match was cancelled. The activities organised by the 'Populars' proved to be more successful and included a race between four whaleboats, a sailing match, a rifle-shooting competition, and what would now be described as 'picnic sports' such as jumping in sacks, climbing a greasy pole and wheeling wheelbarrows blindfolded. Another event organised by the 'Populars' was a horse race, which proved to be the first to be run in New Zealand, and it brought the 'Populars' and the 'Selects' together because it was won by Henry William Petre, a director of the New Zealand Company and the son of a peer, riding a horse he had brought to New Zealand with him, Calmuck Tartar.[37] Māori were not forgotten either, competing in a canoe race, much to the horror of a Wesleyan missionary who 'taught them to look upon our gifts with suspicion and upon our invitation to them to be joyful with us as forbidden and of no good'.[38] Whatever the misgivings of the missionary, the two extremes of society, separated by birth, breeding and wealth in Britain, in New Zealand were coalescing in the field of play.

It was early horse races such as this that laid the groundwork for the popularity of horse racing throughout New Zealand, itself a marker of national identity. As Miriam Macgregor Redwood, one of the few horse-racing historians, noted: 'The success of the event set the fashion for Auckland and Nelson to hold race-meetings on anniversary days and, as they became settled, Canterbury, Otago and other places followed suit.'[39] Greg Ryan recorded that racing clubs were established in Wellington in 1848, Auckland in 1849 and Christchurch in 1854.[40] A club had also been established in Nelson and, by 1848, one of its stewards was Henry Redwood, who later gained the sobriquet of 'Father of the New Zealand Turf'. He established the first stud in New Zealand and began importing breeding stock from the early 1850s. One shipment of 33 horses in 1852 included a leading New South Wales sire, Sir Hercules, and Redwood's role was duly praised: 'The breeders of horses, and the public generally, are greatly indebted to Mr Redwood for this valuable importation; for, if ever horses are to pay to export from New Zealand, it will only be by breeding the best of their kind.'[41]

## The origin of the cricket species

Another distinct English pastime that formed part of the baggage of settlers was cricket, and it is 'possible' the game was played soon after the arrival of missionaries in northern New Zealand in 1814.[42] It is equally possible it was played even before then among Europeans who had made their way from New South Wales, but it fell to one of the missionaries, Henry Williams, to chronicle the first appearance of the game which, like horse racing, began as the preserve of English aristocrats. Williams supervised a match on 20 December 1832 at Paihia but the game in a New Zealand context gained a wider publicity three years later when Charles Darwin, during the seminal *Beagle* voyage, saw young Māori engaged in a game at Waimate in the Bay of Islands: 'These young men and boys

Charles Darwin's journal entry in which he remarked about 'young men and boys' playing cricket at Waimate in Northland. C. Darwin, *The Journal of a Voyage in H.M.S.* Beagle (Guildford: Genesis Publications in association with Australian and New Zealand Book Company, 1979), p. 671

appeared very merry and good-humoured; in the evening I saw a party of them playing at cricket; when I thought of the austerity of which the Missionaries have been accused, I was amused at seeing one of their sons taking an active part in the game.'[43]

Organised cricket – that is, matches between teams assembled for the purpose – is generally held to have begun in Wellington in 1841.[44] It could even have been a year earlier, because the *New Zealand Gazette and Wellington Spectator* in May 1840 recorded 'eleven gentlemen at Thorndon are desirous of making arrangements to play a side from Britannia'.[45] The newspaper did not record if the match was played but, given its notice was in May, perhaps Wellington's winter intervened. A young British soldier, Abel Dottin William Best, more often recorded in New Zealand history as simply 'Ensign Best', wrote in his diary that he played cricket in Wellington in January 1841.[46] It may have been one of the games to which the *Wellington Spectator* referred:

> We have great pleasure in recording that a cricket club has been established at Wellington, by a number of young men, who are anxious that so manly an exercise should not be forgotten in the Antipodes. Several games have been played in the last fortnight on Thorndon Flat for the purpose of practice; and some excellent science displayed. We hope to see this club prosper. New Zealand is admirably adapted for the game, as the climate will permit its being played throughout the year.[47]

Early cricket organisation may have reflected class divisions prevalent in Britain, but if so, they did not survive. A Wellington Cricket Club which included among its members so-called leading colonists, including officials of the New Zealand Company, did not last beyond 1843 and another club, Albion, which included artisans and labourers, lasted little longer. Cricket as it developed in Wellington and elsewhere in New Zealand came to reflect the social environment in which it was played and not the one from whence the players came. British soldiers stationed in New Zealand played as regimental sides but matches between teams of 'Married' and 'Single' or 'Civilians' and 'Military' were common; and in Christchurch, the Christchurch Cricket Club, presided over by John Robert Godley, the leader of the Church of England Association that founded the city, played the Working Men's Club in a first anniversary match.[48] Whether working men or 'gentry', players were dispersed among teams according to ability and in the interests of even competition.[49]

Intended as entertainment, the visit to the South Island of an All-England Eleven in 1864 also marked the beginning of international sport. The weekly *Otago Witness* marked the team's arrival with a rare front-page illustration. *Otago Witness*, 6 February 1864, p. 1

It was a natural progression from interclub to interprovincial matches, and the first of these took place in Wellington in March 1860 against Auckland. The pitting of one province against another solidified a provincial identity and laid the groundwork for a continuing interprovincial rivalry, long after the provincial governments ceased to exist in 1876. The next logical progression was for international matches, and the first of the overseas teams to visit New Zealand was a purely commercial venture. A Dunedin merchant and hotelier, Shadrach Jones, brought George Parr's All England XI from Australia, where it had been touring, for matches against Otago and Canterbury, as well as one against a combination of the two.[50] Teams such as the English were not formally representative, but were more a travelling troupe of professional cricketers. Otago was able to call on cricketers among miners and settlers from the goldfields in Central Otago, including William Gilbert Rees, the first runholder at Lake Wakatipu and a cousin of the renowned cricketing Grace family from Gloucestershire.[51] Parr's team brought with them one of the leading cricketers in Victoria, Tom Wills, and he bolstered the provincial teams.[52]

Similar incoming tours followed for the rest of the nineteenth century and the Canterbury provincial team blazed its own pioneering trail in the summer of 1878–79 when it went to Victoria and Tasmania. The standard of New Zealand cricket was reflected in the fact that the English teams frequently played 'against the odds' – that is, they fielded the regular eleven but against teams made up of eighteen players. Such tours were designed to make money for their promoters, provide sport for participants and spectators alike, and to entertain. But the tours had another, if unintended, result. They raised the level of awareness of the colonies they visited or, in the case of colonial teams going to Britain, promoted the colonies in a way that few other activities at the time could. This aspect was remarked upon by G. K. Wakelin in a letter to the editor of the *Evening Post* in Wellington in 1889, and while he was writing of Australian cricket and after visits by a British rugby team to New Zealand and of the New Zealand Natives rugby team to Britain, his point encompassed all such tours.

> The fact is self-evident that the visits of the Australian cricketers [to England] have caused a considerable amount more attention to be directed to Australia than would have been the case if these cricket contests had not taken place. Now, with regard to the Native team of footballers who are at Home, everyone, I think, will agree that they will be able to give more truthful and practical information over a wider area than has been done by paid agents, who have, in many instances, spoilt their cause by making extravagant statements.[53]

As for the British rugby team that toured New Zealand, Wakelin said its 'more observant members will no doubt have gained more practical information about the geography and resources of the colonies than highly educated men in England, who have only read about them'.

As 'scratch' teams evolved into club teams which then made the progression to provincial teams, the next logical step was national teams, and it can be seen that as sport developed there were several factors at play. There was a desire to promote a sport throughout a colony or to other colonies; there was the perfectly natural sporting desire to test skills against a team from another colony or country; and there was the opportunity to promote the colony itself. But sometimes, a sporting venture was purely about the promotion of the sport. This was evident in the case of two American baseball teams which played in Auckland in 1888 with the express purpose of hoping the game would prove popular – and boost sales for balls, bats and gloves made by its promoter, A. G. Spalding – as well as affirm its primacy in American eyes.[54] Spalding brought with him the Chicago White Stockings and a team called American All-Stars and they played an exhibition match at Potter's Paddock in Epsom but the game was not a conspicuous success. The baseballers had with them a balloonist, 'Professor Bartholomew', who, the advertisements said, would 'parachute leap' from the balloon at a height of 4000 feet. The *Observer* noted that the crowd of between 1000 and 1500 seemed more interested in balloons than bases and many 'began to yawn and consult their watches after half an hour'. When Bartholomew said his attempt was cancelled because of the weather, the crowd drifted off.[55] Baseball was also played in Wellington in 1888, but with less serious purpose. A visiting entertainment troupe, the American Hicks-Sawyer Minstrels, took a break from vaudeville to show their prowess on the diamond and they beat a Wellington team of novices 51–10.[56]

Other sports which were regarded as having been developed and codified in Britain took root in New Zealand in the last 30 years of the nineteenth century, but it was only in the twentieth that they progressed, as athletics and rugby had done, as international standard-bearers for New Zealand identity. Sports such as golf, bowls, tennis, croquet, swimming and gymnastics were essentially recreational pursuits in the nineteenth century, and rowing made its first tentative steps on the journey that would produce three New Zealand holders of the world professional single sculls title in the first quarter of the twentieth century.[57]

## Early New Zealand competitors overseas

Among the first individual New Zealanders to compete overseas was a Māori boxer, Herbert Slade.[58] He was 'discovered' by a British boxing promoter, Jem Mace, who travelled the outlying empire in search of fights, money and boxers he could take to the United States or Europe and thereby make more money.[59] One fighter he found in Timaru was English-born Bob Fitzsimmons, who under Mace's tutelage went on to become the first to win world titles at three different weights and was one of the celebrated identities of American sport in the 1890s and early in the twentieth century. Although he was variously described as a Cornishman, an Englishman, a New Zealander or an Australian, he came to be regarded in New Zealand as one of its own.[60] Slade, who preceded Fitzsimmons, was shamelessly promoted by Mace as 'the Maori giant' to whip up enthusiasm in the United States. It must have worked because before a fight in New York against John L. Sullivan of Boston, touted as the heavyweight champion of the world, it was reported that 'sporting men have been pouring into the City from all quarters of the country to witness the great match'.[61]

A New York boxing promoter, Harry Hill, was quoted before the fight as saying: 'If that Maori goes in with his pluck up instead of with his heart in his throat he's going to do something. If he can stand up for two rounds before Sullivan it's my opinion that he'll

New Zealand's first world sports champion, Joe Scott, is remembered in the Northern Cemetery in Dunedin. Author's photograph

stand up all through it.'[62] Hill was proved wrong. Slade did 'stand up' for two rounds, but was knocked out in the third. As the *New York Times* remarked, 'it is now a historical fact that Sullivan has proved himself a better man than Slade'.[63] In those days, however, boxing was as much showmanship as it was sport, and Sullivan and Slade afterward combined in a troupe that toured the United States, sometimes fighting each other (in those states in which boxing was allowed), sometimes fighting challengers, and, on at least one occasion, just fighting.[64]

The walker Joe Scott was another who plied his sporting talents overseas. The practice of walking great distances either against other competitors or against the clock had its heyday in the mid-eighteenth century, especially in Britain. Like boxing, it had its unseemly side, and Scott Crawford observed that 'the incidence of chicanery, match-fixing and unethical practices reached alarming proportions'.[65] In a history of gambling in New Zealand, David Grant remarked of the walking races: 'Pedestrianism, like other individual-based sports, flourished as long as it offered gambling possibilities. It engendered a colour and glamour among enthusiastic spectators who relished the chance to make money in the unregulated environment.'[66] Apparently, the 1881 Gaming and Lotteries Act, which banned public betting on sports contests, was honoured more in the breach.[67] Open gambling was rife at all sports meetings, even at Otago's Caledonian Games: 'Notably absent was the concept of the amateur, the gentleman who played merely for the sake of the game.'[68]

If Scott indulged in such practices to boost his income, he was singularly unsuccessful, because he was declared bankrupt soon after the trip to Britain in 1888 on which he gained his world title, sold his trophies and ended his days in Dunedin as a cobbler.[69] His trainer, Alfred Austin, like a boxing promoter, arranged races for his charge, agreed to terms or stakes, and touted for bets, as this advertisement in *Sporting Life* showed:

> The backer of Scott . . . wishes it publicly known that he is willing to wager £500 that his representative beats the six days (twelve hours a day record). If any gentleman is desirous of accepting the offer, Mr Alfred Austin . . . will be prepared any time today (Friday) to deposit £500 or £100 with the referee.[70]

This was the race at the Agricultural Hall in London in which he walked a record 363 miles over 72 hours and was declared the world champion. He beat his nearest competitor by 26 miles. Scott's races in Britain were widely reported in New Zealand months later, allowing for the arrival of ships carrying newspapers with the news. Reports were also published in Australian newspapers, gleaned from British publications. Scott's efforts, and the resulting publicity, were an early indication of the power of sporting performance in establishing and confirming national identity. He preceded by a few weeks the Native rugby team in Britain which provided even more publicity for the colony and yet another example of sporting prowess being allied with a burgeoning sense of national identity.

## New Zealand makes a mark

Charlotte Macdonald noted five broad phases in her general survey of New Zealand sport. The first was from 1840 to the 1860s when sports were mostly informal events. The second was from about the 1870s to World War I when there was 'a more organised set of competitions, from which the first national representatives emerged to win acclaim'.[71] Foremost among these, aside from rugby, was the emergent sport of athletics, and it was the next after rugby to send a national team overseas. A New Zealand team went to Sydney in 1890 and then, far more adventurously, to the United Kingdom and France two years later. Both trips had long-term consequences for New Zealand sport and for the assumption of a national identity. A central figure was a Christchurch insurance agent, Leonard Cuff, who in 1887 had founded the New Zealand Amateur Athletic Association and helped stage (and compete in) the first national championships.[72] The team gained conspicuous success when competing at the New South Wales championships in Sydney in 1890, winning seven of the twelve events in which they were entered and gaining five seconds and two thirds. The *Observer* was among those newspapers quick to see the national significance of the success: 'Their chain of victories will do more towards bringing New Zealand into prominence than most people imagine, and in future [we] hope to see New Zealand receive due credit when she turns out athletes prepared to hold their own against allcomers and not hear them spoken of as Australians.'[73] The writer went on to indulge in what was known at the time as 'blowing' when he remarked that New Zealand already supplied Australia with the 'pick of horseflesh' and was superior 'at the old Rugby game of football'.

The New Zealand athletics team that competed in the New South Wales championships in Sydney in May 1890. Leonard Cuff, the founder of the New Zealand Amateur Athletic Association and the first International Olympic Committee member in New Zealand, is on the extreme right. *Illustrated Sporting and Dramatic News*, 8 November 1890, p. 260

In terms of national identity, perhaps more significant than the results was the fact that the athletes competed wearing black singlets bearing a silver fern emblem and black shorts with a white stripe down the sides. The silver fern had first appeared as a national sporting emblem on the blue jerseys in the privately organised rugby tour of New South Wales in 1884 and again on the black jerseys of the Native team in 1888–89. It may be that the athletes, and most probably Cuff, saw the rugby jerseys with their silver ferns as an embryonic expression of national sporting identity and decided to follow suit. But athletics already had championship caps which were awarded to the winners of national titles and they were 'of black velvet with silver piping cord'.[74] Two years later, when a different team of athletes (but still including Cuff) was preparing to go to Britain, the *Observer*

1ʳᵉ Année. — N° 1.                                                      Juillet 1894

# BULLETIN DU COMITÉ INTERNATIONAL

DES

# JEUX OLYMPIQUES

PARIS, 229, Rue Saint-Honoré          *Citius — Fortius — Altius*          Rue Saint-Honoré, 229, PARIS

## LE CONGRÈS DE PARIS

The front page of the first edition of the International Olympic Committee's *Olympic Bulletin*, which listed the founding IOC members, including Leonard Cuff of New Zealand. *Bulletin du Comité International des Jeux Olympiques*, no. 1 (1 July 1894), p. 1

remarked: 'Our New Zealand representatives will, it is antici-pated, compete (while at Home) in the New Zealand costume – black and silver, with silver fern worked on the left breast of the jersey – used when the New Zealand team competed in the New South Wales Championship.'[75] The writer's anticipation was fulfilled. Photographs were still a rarity in newspapers then and artists were used for illustrations. At least one sketch of the athletes in action in Britain showed the Invercargill sprinter Jack Hempton decked out all in black with what could be interpreted as a passable image of the silver fern on the left breast.[76] However, the Anglo-French tour was not noted for its sporting success – in a lengthy interview on his return, Cuff said his men had suffered bad luck with injuries and struck English athletes in a 'hot' year.[77]

261

There has been a recurring view that colonial sportsmen went to Britain to show 'Mother' how well the 'offspring' had adapted to its games. If that was the case for the athletes of 1892, it was a miserable exhibition.

Along with the prosaic motivations of a trip overseas at someone else's expense, the satisfaction of representing a new, young country in a sporting endeavour, or simply a fulfilment of wanderlust, the athletes also had much more pragmatic goals. One was the desire to compete against the best available competition and that competition happened to be in Britain.[78] Another was that their performances on the sometimes indifferent grass tracks in New Zealand or Australia were frequently questioned on the basis of inefficient timing or measurement or, even worse, 'local' timing – that is, New Zealand officials deliberately giving their compatriots inflated times. The only way to gain legitimate and unquestioned recognition was to compete in front of neutral officials or officials in Britain who may have regarded themselves as being more competent than their colonial counterparts. Allied to the timing issue in those days of a lack of uniformity in regulations was that some tracks were the later to be standard 400 metres, but others were of odd distances and shapes. In the case of George Smith, an all-round athlete for whom a world record was claimed in Auckland in 1902, there were questions about the height and rigidity of the hurdles (different from Britain's) and whether the race in which the record was claimed was a legitimate competition. It was partly to confirm his ability to sceptics elsewhere that the public later that year subscribed to send Smith to Britain where he won the (English) Amateur Athletic Association 120 yards hurdles title.[79] One later athletics historian believed New Zealand officials were in fact harder on their own athletes than officials elsewhere:

There were five watches. One timed Smith at 15.0s and four at 15.2s. So the NZAAA granted him a record of 15.4s! Why the change, I can't say. But I can say, for anyone who might doubt the accuracy of old-time records, that it proves New Zealand officials have always taken a more cynical view of timing than the rest of the world.[80]

The significance of the 1892 tour was not in its results, but in the long-term consequences of the athletes competing in Paris where Cuff met Pierre de Coubertin, who was then formulating his plans to revive the ancient Olympics. A year later, Coubertin wrote to Cuff, inviting him to the *Congrès International de Paris pour la rétablissement des Jeux Olympiques*. Cuff apologised for not being able to attend, and after the congress (which agreed the first of the modern Olympic Games would be staged in Athens in 1896) Coubertin again wrote to Cuff, asking him to be the member in New Zealand of the newly formed International Olympic Committee. Cuff responded:

> After all your hard work it must indeed have been gratifying to yourself and co-workers, as it must have been to all those who take an interest in amateur sport, to see the revival of the Olympic Games settled . . . I can quite understand the success of the congress as no nation can compare with the French in the amount of energy and enthusiasm it puts into any undertaking of this description.[81]

Listed as one of the original thirteen members of the International Olympic Committee,[82] Cuff was named the member in Australasia – that is, the colonies of New Zealand, New South Wales, Victoria, South Australia, Queensland, Western Australia and Tasmania.[83] New Zealand, through Cuff, was thus in on the ground floor of what would become the biggest sporting event in the world. His task was to educate sports followers in the other colonies about the Olympic Games and encourage participation, although he pointed out at an early stage the difficulties imposed by distance. The *Olympic Bulletin* noted Cuff supported all the decisions made at the congress in Paris, but talked of 'l'enorme distance' to 'du grand continent océanien'.[84] It was the distance (and its associated costs) that contributed to sparse representation by New Zealand or Australia at early Olympic Games and the fielding of a joint team at the games in London in 1908 and in Stockholm in 1912. Individual Australians competed at earlier games (1896, 1900 and 1904) but New Zealanders did not.[85]


## *Federation when it suits*

An increase in competitive sport, particularly international, coincided with the federation debate in New Zealand and Australia, and it may seem contradictory that while on the one hand distinct national identity was being cemented through sport, on the other the two countries were combining. But as Greg Ryan noted, the combinations were largely for pragmatic reasons.[86] In tennis, for example, New Zealand and Australia combined in the early years of the twentieth century mainly because each country had a player of outstanding merit – Anthony Wilding in New Zealand and Norman Brookes in Australia. Leonard Cuff and an Australian who equalled Cuff's enthusiasm for sport, Richard Coombes, together began a joint annual athletics championship that survived until the late 1920s.[87] Other sports such as swimming also combined in championships for a time and the first rugby league teams from each country borrowed players from the other. But the dominant sports in each, rugby union in New Zealand and cricket in Australia, showed no such inclination.[88]

There seems no suggestion that the unions which did exist between some sports would continue indefinitely as some sort of physical federation when New Zealand in the wider sphere had made it plain it wanted no part of the political and constitutional federation. A writer in the *New Zealand Times* asked, in relation to the Australasian Athletic Union, why should New Zealand 'be so foolish as to enter into an agreement which is quite unnecessary and absolutely opposed to its interests?'.[89] Three years later, the same writer said, 'New Zealand cannot afford to be dragged at the

tail of Australia much longer'.[90] When talk surfaced about a possible Empire team to take part in the Olympic Games, an *Otago
Witness* editorial protested: 'We have as good all-round material as
Australia. New Zealand is not Australia and it is unfair that they
should combine to compete against any other country . . . if any
honour is to be gained, it should be credited to the country with
which it belongs.'[91]

Talk of an Empire team for the Olympic Games in Stockholm in
1912 was raised by Coombes and by people in England at the time
of a 'Festival of Empire' to mark the coronation of King George V
in 1911. It met with little enthusiasm in New Zealand or Australia,
just as a similar suggestion nearly 20 years before met with no
practical response. Loyalty to the Empire there undoubtedly still
was in the layers of allegiance, but it clearly did not extend to sub-
jugating national identity. John Astley Cooper, an Adelaide-born
son of an Anglican clergyman, wrote in various British publications
in the early 1890s of his vision for a 'Pan-Britannic' festival as a
means 'of increasing the good will and the good understanding of
the Empire'.[92] It was not to be just a sporting occasion; it should
also cover industry and culture. Neither would it comprise just the
Empire; he proposed to include the United States, 'with the hope of
drawing closer the family bonds'. Cooper elaborated on the scheme
two years later by suggesting the festival be held every four years,
and in the intervening years, 'social, athletic and military festivals'
would be held in Empire countries; Canada was suggested for 1895,
Australia for 1896 and South Africa for 1897.[93] Aside from the wide
publicity Cooper's writings gained, there was no response in the
sense of any practical organisation and, with the emergence of
Coubertin's plans for an Olympic Games, the Pan-Britannic Festival
of this 'imperialist dreamer' faded from public view.[94]

Through his administrative and sporting ability, Cuff, on the
other hand, did not just organise the sport of athletics in New
Zealand; he also took it – and the silver fern emblem – to Australia
and Europe. The athletes, like other national sports teams, did not

operate in a vacuum. They were extensively covered in newspapers and, indeed, gained as much publicity in Australia during the 1890s as they did in New Zealand. Much of the Australian publicity was generated by Cuff's colleague, Coombes, who was editor and athletics columnist for the Sydney *Referee*. The athletes, and especially the prowess of sprinter Jack Hempton at the start of the decade and hurdler George Smith from the end of it, played a central role in the affirmation of the country's national identity through sport.

## Claiming the high ground of identity

A much more exclusive, though no less competitive, group also laid claim to an assertion of New Zealand identity while at the same time showing what they thought of British class-consciousness. These were the small number of enthusiasts who pioneered mountain climbing in New Zealand.[95] They did not benefit, as did their counterparts in Europe, from well-used routes or from alpine guides and porters. The pioneering work of New Zealanders in the high mountains was characterised by their finding their own methods and their own routes and carrying their own gear.[96] A link to national identity was emphasised, Graham Langton felt, 'by an awareness that their activity in New Zealand was a little different from that elsewhere in the world'.[97] Their independence led to some accusations that the New Zealanders did not show enough caution, to which one of them, Malcolm Ross, responded: 'My answer to that will be that we were always, or nearly always, doing pioneer work and so had to discover the dangers as well as the routes.'[98] Ross was not unhappy that the New Zealanders adopted different methods to Europeans: 'I have had to be my own guide and also my own porter – I feel pleased that this is a guideless colony. I have often wished though that it was not as "porterless".'[99] Another of the pioneers in New Zealand, Arthur Harper, had experience of climbing in Switzerland in 1888, and was equally scornful of European practices:

While climbing with guides, a mountaineer has nothing to do but follow and keep steady, and if he can't follow he is helped over the difficulty, doing his climb from start to finish in a most luxurious manner ... if an able bodied man, who has never seen a mountain before, wishes to climb, and can afford it, he can be taken up every peak in Switzerland, and, as is often the case, know very little more of the art of mountaineering than when he began.[100]

In climbing, as in other activities, it seems, English sports travelled but attitudes did not: 'The English concepts of elite and common, of amateur and professional, were at odds with the colonial ethos of greater egalitarianism.'[101]

Increased European interest in conquering the high peaks of the Southern Alps and especially the greatest prize, Mt Cook (now formally known as Aoraki/Mt Cook although Ross said he and his fellow climbers preferred to refer to it as Aorangi), fired the nationalistic instincts of the New Zealand climbers. The desire to be first to climb their own mountains, as Ross explained, was a recurring theme: 'There were several determined, if possible, to win for New Zealand the honour of the first ascent of New Zealand's highest mountain.'[102] Another of the pioneers, Marmaduke Dixon, quipped: 'Or perhaps, it is that there is quite a number of kindred spirits in New Zealand who would like to have the honour of being the first on the top [of Mt Cook], placed to their credit – but they will have to hurry up or else, from what I have recently seen, the enterprising rabbit will be there first ...'[103]

In the early days, Ross declared, the high alps of New Zealand were 'shrouded in mystery and regarded with awe'. The spell was broken in 1882 when an Anglo-Irish cleric, William Spotswood Green, arrived with a guide experienced in the Swiss Alps, Ulrich Kaufmann, and a Swiss hotelier with mountaineering experience, Emil Boss, with the intention of being the first to the summit of Mt Cook: he came, he saw, but did not quite conquer, although it was widely reported he had.[104] Green was fêted in Christchurch and regretted in Timaru. The *Timaru Herald* in an editorial remarked it was disappointed with Mt Cook: 'We thought we possessed an Alpine height which conferred credit on the country it belonged to by being practically well nigh inaccessible by mortal foot.'[105] The feat even inspired an unidentified rhymester:

> Climb of the unforgotten brave,
> Green ever will thy laurels wave,
> And all exclaim who read thy book –
> Most cooks do greens; this Green's done Cook.[106]

But, as later became clear, weather and ice conditions conspired to halt the Green party tantalisingly short of the summit. In his defence, Green did not pretend he had achieved something he had failed to do. There seemed semantic differences of the interpretation of the word 'ascent'. Some, especially the newspapers, took it to mean all the way to the top; Green merely meant he and his guides had climbed further than anyone had gone before: 'It may be said that I have claimed the ascent of Mount Cook, without having set foot on the actual summit. Be it so – I shall willingly relinquish any such claims to the man who passes the point where we turned.'[107]

Ross was editor of the *New Zealand Alpine Journal* and noted in 1894 that he had received letters saying an English climber, Edward FitzGerald, would be in New Zealand for the 1894–95 climbing season but 'the writers emphasise the point that the last intention of Mr FitzGerald is to rob any local men of the honour of first ascents'.[108] Ross recalled that when he first attempted Mt Cook, ten expeditions had tried and failed: 'There are quite a number of hardy Maorilanders who covet the honour of being the first to set foot on the actual summit of the highest mountain of their native land.'[109] The news of FitzGerald's pending visit spurred on another local effort – 'a solemn compact was entered into' – which culminated in the first ascent of Cook on Christmas Day 1894 by a trio of New Zealanders, George Graham, Tom Fyfe and Jack Clarke.[110]

The jacket of the first issue of the *New Zealand Alpine Journal* in 1892. The 'R' in the bottom left corner of the illustration suggests it was by Malcolm Ross, journalist and author, who was one of the Alpine Club's founders. Author's collection

'Thus was the conquering of Aorangi, after many heroic struggles, accomplished by the pluck, endurance and initiative of the young New Zealanders, who, in a far country, had taught themselves the craft of mountaineering.'[111]

Early in the twentieth century, another English climber, Samuel Turner, arrived on a climbing expedition sponsored by the New Zealand government. An at times difficult person who liked to boast of his own achievements,[112] Turner was described as probably 'the most disliked climber ever' by a distant and dispassionate observer, Sally Irwin, the biographer of Freda du Faur, the Australian who in 1911 became the first woman to reach the summit of Aoraki/Mt Cook.[113] While Turner had nothing but praise for the resourcefulness of the New Zealanders, he brought his English class-consciousness with him and often complained, further underlining the difference in attitude to climbing, as in other competitive pursuits, between the British and the trailblazing 'colonials'.

Charlotte Macdonald's division of sports organisation into phases could be extrapolated to mean that the first phase was when sports brought from Britain were practised and when English attitudes continued to largely prevail, although even then there was evidence of mixing classes in a decidedly non-English way. The second phase was when New Zealand individuals or organisations, given more leisure time, a more developed country and more effective communication, began to make their own distinctive way in sport. While individuals such as the boxers Bob Fitzsimmons and Herbert Slade, and the walker Joe Scott, made their marks and gained prominence in New Zealand and overseas, it was team sports which had the most impact. The athletes who went to Sydney and then to London and Paris led to the country's involvement in the Olympic Games but, perhaps more significantly for national identity, took the silver fern as an emblem of New Zealand to a new and wider audience. It was rugby union, however, which New Zealand took to more enthusiastically and thoroughly than any other colony, that did most to establish a sense of identity through sport: both within New Zealand and wherever the New Zealanders played.

# EIGHT

# In Thrall
to the Oval Ball

*Oh some talk of cricket and some of lacrosse*
*Some long for the Huntsman's loud call,*
*But where can be found such a musical sound,*
*As the old Rugby cry, "On the Ball"* [1]

When members of the 1905–06 New Zealand rugby union team were given a civic reception in Wellington after their tour of the British Isles, France and North America, the city's mayor, Thomas Hislop, told the hundreds of people present they were there for 'a great national occasion'. The performance of the team 'was of national importance', he said.[2] Much of New Zealand seemed to agree. Thousands evidently greeted the team when it arrived in Auckland from California, including the Premier, Richard Seddon, who was dubbed the 'Minister of Football' by his newspaper bête noire, the *Evening Post*.[3] For the civic reception in Wellington for those team members travelling south, the concert hall had been chosen as the venue. 'But by the time fixed for the function the hall was crowded and hundreds were struggling for admittance.' Hislop therefore arranged for the reception to be transferred to the adjacent 'big hall and soon a crowd of over two thousand people was comfortably seated'.[4] When the player with the most distance to travel home, Billy Stead, arrived at the Invercargill railway station: 'Though heavy rain was falling, the station platform was crowded with waiting friends and at the entrance a large number of enthusiasts congregated.'[5] Within weeks, the first book about the tour, written by the manager, was published; and within months, a second book, by the captain, David Gallaher, and Stead, who was the vice-captain, was also available. So too was a book published in Britain.[6]

The footballers won 34 of their 35 matches – losing only to Wales – and scored 976 points against just 59 by their opponents. Encomiums for the team, effusive at times, came on different levels. There was praise for the players for purely sporting success, there was gratitude for their demeanour both on and off the field, and there was acknowledgement for what they had achieved in New Zealand's name. The Auckland newspaper, the *Observer*, encapsulated a prevailing national view: 'Their tour and its splendid achievements have not only added to the prestige of New Zealand football, which had already achieved fame in the world of sport, but have also advertised this country in a way that a score of immigrant agents and half-a-dozen Tourist Departments could not have done.'[7]

In Auckland, Seddon told the welcoming reception: 'The names of all members of the team would live in the history of football and the colony would always look upon their achievements with the feelings of the greatest pride.'[8] The names of some members of the team do indeed 'live on in the history of football' – as examples, New Zealand and France since 2000 have played for the Gallaher Cup named for the 1905–06 captain, and Stead's newspaper columns during the tour were republished in 2005, as were several books commemorating the tour.[9] The name of the player who thought he scored against Wales and would thus have tied the scores and given the team an unbeaten record, Bob Deans, lives on through his own deeds and those of his rugby-playing great-nephews, Bruce and Robbie Deans (the latter becoming coach of Australia in 2008).

The tour has assumed significance beyond the merely sporting because of its impact on New Zealand identity. It has frequently

been relived through the keyboards of more than just sports reporters or other enthusiastic chroniclers of the game. Keith Sinclair
called the defeat against Wales 'the game's Gallipoli' and wrote that
what occurred in terms of the supposed try that was denied Deans
'is famous in the New Zealand secular religion of nationalism'.[10]
'If there was any doubt before', he declared, 'there was none after
1905 that rugby football had become the national game.'[11] The tour,
according to Jock Phillips, led to rugby becoming 'a defining element of national consciousness' and the game 'a barometer of the
nation's health'.[12] Charlotte Macdonald concurred that 'the tour
came to be seen as the defining moment in both rugby and the wider
national history'.[13] An unidentified writer in the weekly newspaper,
*New Zealand Truth*, remarked in 1924 on the eve of the All Blacks'
next visit to Britain that the names of rugby players were better
known than those of politicians and added: 'Even for Scotsmen,
there is only one Wm Wallace . . . rugby in New Zealand is more
than a game. It is a great medium of thought.'[14]

Central to the foundation role that the tour played in the nation's
sense of identity are two suppositions: one that rugby somehow
blossomed as 'the national game' as the direct result of the tour; and
the other that the team left Wellington in September 1905 as 'New
Zealand' but returned in March 1906 as 'the All Blacks' – acquiring
a British-imposed nickname along the way. The veracity of both
suppositions is examined in this chapter and found wanting.


*A crude beginning*


Rugby, by most published accounts, was introduced to New Zealand
in 1870 by Charles John Monro, a son of the Speaker of the House
of Representatives, Sir David Monro, who had been sent to Christ's
College in London to be educated. Christ's was one of the schools
that had embraced the 'Rugby rules' of football as formulated at
Rugby School in Warwickshire, and Monro when he returned home

persuaded his friends in Nelson to play the 'new' game.[15] There have been reports of rugby matches earlier elsewhere, although proving what type of crude football was played would be challenging. For example, the founder of the New Zealand Rugby Football Union, Ernest Hoben, wrote in 1895 that three well-known men in Wellington – among them William Rees, a cousin of England cricketer W. G. Grace – constituted themselves a football club 'in the 60s'. 'Only a round ball could be procured at first, but a Rugby ball was ultimately obtained from Melbourne.'[16] (Rees at the time would have been 32 or 33 years old and while there is evidence he procured a rugby ball, none has been found that he organised or played in a game. A kick-about with friends is more likely.)

However it began, rugby soon supplanted other forms of football in New Zealand affections, aided no doubt by an influx to the country of 'men of the same public school mould as those who had shaped the game in Britain', as Greg Ryan put it.[17] But as Ryan and Geoffrey Vincent have observed, it was not merely an assertion of will and skill by well-bred and well-educated men from southern England that transformed a mélange of football into the single shape of rugby.[18] While men such as George Sale, a former pupil of Rugby School who was first editor of the *Press* in Christchurch and later the first Professor of English and Classics at the University of Otago, were influential, it was 'ordinary' men who played and spread the game.[19] Alfred Drew was a watchmaker and jeweller in his father's business in Nelson when he played in the first games recorded by the rugby statistician Arthur Swan; he moved to Wanganui where he went into partnership with a brother and helped introduce rugby there in 1872; and in 1874 he set up his own business in New Plymouth and played in the first recorded game of rugby there.[20] Another in the first Nelson game, Robert Tennant, worked in a bank and continued his rugby proselytising when he was transferred to Taranaki. Some of those with an English public school background were admired not for their breeding, education or assumed 'class', but because of their ability at the game. One of those mentioned by

Football at Rugby School in England as pictured by the founder of the magazine the *Graphic*, William Luson Thomas. This was published in 1870, the year in which rugby was first played in Nelson. *The Graphic*, 8 January 1870

Phillips was Alfred St George Hamersley, who had been educated at Marlborough College in England.[21] Hamersley was credited with establishing the South Canterbury Rugby Football Union. He had played for England in what came to be recognised as the first rugby international, against Scotland in 1871, and he later captained England before moving to New Zealand.[22] As one of the Dunedin players, Samuel Sleigh, remarked: 'The Timaru men were captained by Mr Hammersley [Hamersley] and we have only to mention that this gentleman captained the English team against Scotland in 1874 to show that the Timaru Club had an advantage that no other club in New Zealand could boast of.'[23] Hamersley thus impressed himself upon New Zealand minds because of his ability as a player rather than because of any perceived 'superiority' emanating from birth or education.[24]

Phillips wrote that one of rugby's attractions was its physical appeal among rural workers, while in the towns, men in sedentary occupations 'felt a special urgency to prove their virility'.[25] Leaving aside the difficulty of neatly dividing nineteenth-century New Zealand into 'rural' and 'town' without overlapping areas as well as attempting to determine the motives of men who left nothing to posterity but their names, it seems much more likely that men (or boys) played the game for entirely pragmatic reasons: because their friends did and because they enjoyed it and because they could find a team to play against.[26] The opposite must also hold true. The Victorian rules game as developed in Melbourne had adherents in New Zealand through the 1860s and beyond, but as rugby developed, so the Australian game faded. The gold strikes in Otago and on the West Coast provided the heyday for the Australian game. Australian historian Geoffrey Blainey recorded: 'Early football games in most towns of [the] South Island – except perhaps Christchurch – were as likely to have been played accordingly to "Victorian Rules" as English rules.'[27] In fact, it would have been surprising had the game not made headway there:

> Many Victorian footballers went to New Zealand in the 1860s in search of gold or as clerks, bank tellers and merchants. The South Island of New Zealand was in commerce almost a province of Melbourne and any journalist who chanced to tour its goldfields would have found Victorian shopkeepers, publicans, teachers, mine manager and labourers in every town worthy of the name.[28]

It is important to note that the introduction of rugby did not automatically mean an end to other forms of football. Some teams played a mixture of rules, often within the same game, for several years, while specific rugby clubs sometimes played 'association rules' against each other. Nevertheless, rugby developed throughout New Zealand remarkably quickly given limited communications between areas. The first time an Auckland team ventured south to play, in 1875, only seventeen players were able to make the trip and their ship was stuck fast overnight on the Manukau bar, which meant the opening match in New Plymouth had to be delayed. They eventually made it to Dunedin where, on 22 September – six days after leaving Auckland – they played a team made up of players from the Dunedin and Union clubs, both of which had converted to rugby rules from a mixture of association (soccer) and Victorian rules earlier in the year. The game thus came to be recorded as the first interprovincial fixture.[29] By 1880, a decade after the first game, the first provincial unions (Canterbury and Wellington) had been formed and another in Otago (1881) was pending.[30] 'The years 1875–1879 were remarkable for the growth of Rugby in New Zealand', Swan remarked. 'Wherever there was settlement, there were players.'[31]

There was also opposition. Rules were not uniform and, it seems, in some cases more noted for their absence. This was in a period when the game was noted for its roughness and when law changes in England such as the abolition of hacking (the deliberate kicking of shins) took a while to find their way to New Zealand. The Bank of New Zealand in Auckland in 1878 ruled that if any of its employees could not attend work because of football injuries, they would be instantly dismissed. The *Otago Daily Times* thought the bank's senior people no doubt appreciated the value of legitimate athletic exercise but not 'a brutal, savage game' that was 'a disgrace to civilisation'.[32] Disdain for the game at a different level came from Annabella McLean, the youngest sister of a politician and influential Native Minister, Sir Donald McLean, writing from Wellington to her brother in Napier: 'Football has commenced. I wish it would pour of rain every Saturday for it is a rough game.'[33]

Rugby nevertheless had taken a hold and it began to be written about as 'the national game' at least as early as 1882. A writer in the *Otago Witness* identified only as 'Place-Kick' referred to a report in the *Australasian* newspaper in Melbourne 'that the Victorian game is played by fully half the clubs in N.Z.'[34] He responded that from Cape Reinga to the Bluff, 'there is not a solitary club that plays Victorian rules': 'There are now four Rugby Unions in New

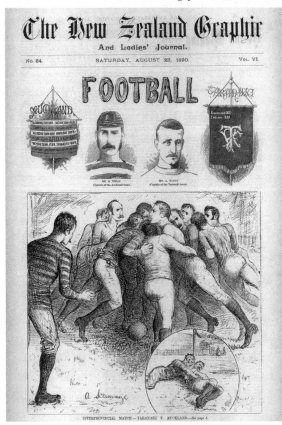

An early example of rugby's prominence. This 1890 front page marked merely an interprovincial match between Auckland and Taranaki. *New Zealand Graphic and Ladies' Journal*, 23 August 1890, p. 1

Zealand, and I hope the day is not far distant when we shall see a New Zealand Rugby Union formed. I don't think I am far out in saying that the Rugby Union game will be the national game in New Zealand.'[35]

Nine days later, the day was proved not far distant at all. In a report of a match between Greymouth and Hokitika, the *Grey River Argus* said: 'The above-named clubs met for the first time on the Camp Reserve to try their skill and strength in the national game of football.'[36] The report showed the game was not just for a male elite either, with class and gender neatly incorporated in the second sentence: 'The Mayor, at the request of the leading tradesmen of this town, having kindly complied to proclaim Saturday afternoon a half-holiday, a number of both sexes availed themselves of the opportunity of enjoying the afternoon's outing, not fewer than four hundred people witnessing the contest.'

Rugby in New South Wales and Queensland was also developing and, as in New Zealand, slowly supplanted 'the Victorian game' as the game of choice.[37] Influential figures in Sydney were the Arnold brothers, William ('Monty') and Richard, relatives of Thomas Arnold, who had encouraged the game at Rugby School as ideal for young boys preparing for life.[38] They founded the Wallaroos club in Sydney and were prominent in the early days of the Southern Rugby Union (later the New South Wales union), as were a Sydney solicitor who made his mark with the University club, 'Toby' Barton, and his close friend, Fred Lea.[39] Together, they organised a first intercolonial match against Queensland in August 1882 on condition that only rugby rules be entertained. Around the same time as the Queensland match was being organised, 'Monty' Arnold wrote to the secretary of the Wellington union, Arthur Bate, suggesting a New Zealand team play in Sydney. 'As might have been expected, the difficulties in the way were too formidable and the proposal fell to the ground.'[40] If the New Zealand Mohammed could not come to the mountain of New South Wales, the mountain would come to Mohammed. And it did in September 1882, a bare minimum of sixteen players paying £5 each to go, with their host unions covering other expenses. Auckland offered £100 and half the proceeds; Canterbury offered two-thirds; Otago offered to pay all costs and keep whatever profits there may be; and Wellington, which co-ordinated the trip, offered £50 and half the proceeds.[41] The New South Welshmen, wearing olive-green jerseys bearing the stars of the Southern Cross in gold, played seven matches and won four, losing twice to Auckland Combined Clubs and once to Otago.[42]

Though the New South Welshmen did not play a composite national team, the tour lit the fuse for a national identity as expressed through football. Early the following year, 1883, the provinces discussed how best to make a return visit across the Tasman; and at the same time, the initial 1882 tour was noticed in London. 'It will be strange if Macaulay's New Zealander should be realised in the shape of a footballer', the London *Sporting Life* remarked.[43] The unidentified writer, whose comments were reproduced in the *Otago Witness*, noted the New South Wales players 'had a jovial time of it' and generally met with success, but 'at Otago they found their match and they were easily beaten by a goal and three tries'. A 'young Maori named Taiaroa' was singled out for a 'fine game at half'. This was a reference to Teone Kerei (otherwise known as John Grey) Taiaroa, who was 20 at the time of the game and in his last year at Otago Boys' High School.[44] Another Māori, Joseph Astbury Warbrick, played for Auckland against New South Wales, evidence that the developing 'national' game was both interesting and embracing Māori.[45]

Both Taiaroa and Warbrick were included in the first New Zealand team that was chosen from the provinces of Otago, Canterbury, Wellington and Auckland in 1884 to tour Australia. Another step toward rugby as an identity marker came, as well as the national aspect of the team, with the uniform chosen: 'The uniform will consist of navy blue jersey, with a gold fernleaf on breast, and knickerbockers and stockings of same colour', the *Otago Witness* noted.[46] For the first time, the 'silver' fern was being used as a national symbol of New Zealand beyond the country's shores. Evidence about why blue was chosen for the jersey remains elusive but a clue may be found in the fact the organiser and manager of the tour was a Dunedin merchant, Samuel Sleigh, whose club, Dunedin, and province, Otago, both wore blue.[47]

The New Zealanders won all nine of their matches, beating New South Wales three times, causing the Sydney *Telegraph* to lament:

"No glorious uncertainty" appears to attach to the series of football matches now being played between the local clubs and the visiting team from New Zealand. By universal consent the championship

The first national rugby team in a studio photograph during the 1884 tour of New South Wales. The organiser and underwriter, Samuel Sleigh, is on the extreme right. The captain, William Millton, holds the ball, and a later influential figure, Joe Warbrick, is in front of him in the centre of the three sitting cross-legged. Jack Taiaroa is seated extreme left in the middle row. Author's collection

belongs to the strangers. The New South Wales players are not much more than "muffs" by comparison with the genial fellows who are teaching them how to play the game. But the humiliation of defeat after defeat is somewhat softened by the recollection that Rugby football is the game of New Zealand as cricket is the game of Australia.[48]

Taiaroa was described by Sleigh as brilliant, and in an early indication of the power of sports marketing, Sydney newspapers advertised the final match against New South Wales with the line: 'Last great match – final appearance of TAIAROA'.[49] The nineteen players who went to Australia were a cross-section of society rather than representative of a particular 'class' or social status; they were also overwhelmingly native-born. Only three were born overseas – one in India, one in England and one in Ireland. A variety of occupations were represented, too, including solicitors, farmers, clerks, a printer, a tinsmith, a policeman, a timber worker and a telegraph operator among them.[50]

The 1884 tour also raised the prospect of New Zealanders proving their rugby worth against the English, not because of the notion of the 'son' showing the 'mother' how well he had grown, but because with New South Wales beaten, the British were the next sporting challenge.[51] As Sleigh wrote: 'Having shown that New Zealand footballers need not fear to be measured by a standard outside their own islands, I venture to express a hope that we shall ere long see an English team coming round the world to try their manhood against ours in the football arena.'[52] Not only was Sleigh's hope fulfilled 'ere long', he gained more than he bargained for. Shortly after returning from Sydney, he noted that the *Otago Daily Times* in an editorial recommended the sending of a team to England but he thought 'the matter would as yet be too great an undertaking'.[53] But within four years, teams travelled in both directions – beginning with a private venture Great Britain team organised by cricketers Arthur Shaw and Arthur Shrewsbury which toured New Zealand for nineteen matches, winning thirteen of them. The team also went to Australia where it played both rugby and Victorian rules matches.[54]

Such contact with other countries was important because rugby in New Zealand developed in a cocoon, players interpreting the written laws of the game without knowing the interpretations of players in other countries. Emergence from the cocoon was the great value of these early contacts, especially with the British team. As Tāmati Rangiwahia ('Tom') Ellison, one of the early influential players remarked, back play in New Zealand before the British tour of 1888 was almost non-existent because of New Zealanders' strict interpretation of the offside law. The process of heeling the ball back from a scrum and allowing the backs to move the ball was considered to be illegal because the forwards were in front of the play and therefore offside:

> After, however, the visit of the English team that year [1888] who
> were allowed to heel back, notwithstanding the law, we immediately
> developed back passing, by imitating them in disregarding the off-side

Most of the members of the 1888 Natives team are in this photograph published in Britain. From the Rev. Frank Marshall, *Football: The Rugby Union Game* (London: Cassell, 1892), p. 505

rule as regards forwards in the scrum and using, in a systematic way, the rear of the scrum as the starting point of the passing game.[55]

In other respects, Ellison was content with the way the New Zealand game had developed in its antipodean isolation: 'I challenge anyone to tell me what else they taught us.'[56]

It was a significant lesson, however, and its fruits did not take long to ripen. Even before the arrival of the British, some New Zealanders decided they would take a team to Britain. This was not the brainchild of an educated elite, of well-off men who had been educated at Rugby or any of the other select English schools which had applied 'Rugby rules' to their form of football, but of indigenous New Zealanders. Foremost among them was Joe Warbrick, son of an English father and a Ngāti Rangitihi mother, who had played for Sleigh's original New Zealand team in 1884 and who was 'a player of interprovincial and intercolonial fame'.[57] Warbrick, who was then working on a farm in Hawke's Bay, had the idea of forming an all-Māori team to tour New Zealand, to play the visiting British team if possible, and to tour Britain.[58] Efforts to play against the British team came to nothing – 'the Englishmen were not disposed to play' – but Warbrick nevertheless went ahead with the organisation and his team left New Zealand in August. It was supplemented by four Pākehā to fill positions in which the Māori were perceived to be weak, especially after Warbrick broke an ankle in a pre-tour match against Auckland:

It certainly is a great pity that palefaces have to be included in the team, but after Warbrick's accident at Auckland the promoters had hardly any alternative. The team seem to be greatly dependent upon Joe Warbrick, they will do anything for him without grumbling, and his presence on the field behind the scrum urging them on in their native tongue is now greatly missed.[59]

Their tour, in a purely rugby sense, was both arduous and successful – they played either 107 or 108 matches and won 78 of them, including a victory against Ireland.[60] But it had an impact beyond mere fleeting sporting success. The press in Britain adopted a tone of wonder when the team first arrived with comments such as: 'We have been invaded and the Maori is upon us', but the paper responsible for that remark then went on to sketch a rudimentary background of Māori history, made what seemed at the time to be an almost obligatory reference to Macaulay's prophesy, and assured its readers the Māori came in peace.[61] Also mentioning Macaulay, the satirical magazine *Punch* noted the serious underlying purpose of the footballers after their opening matches:

You've come then, brother Maoris
At us to have a shy
And if we'd guard our glories,
We'll have to mind our eye.

Our camp you seem to flurry,
And stir its calm content;
You've flabbergasted Surrey,
And scrumplicated Kent.

Your kicking, brother Maoris,
Has given us the kick;
You're well matched all, well "on the ball,"
And strong and straight and quick.
By jove, this is a rum age,
When a New Zealand team
Licks Bull at goal and scrummage!
It beats Macaulay's dream.[62]

Tour manager Thomas Eyton noted what appeared to be a British expectation to see what he called 'blackfellows' but said most of his players were only 'badly sunburned' and 'it looked almost like a fraud to expect the British public to believe such as the Warbricks and the Wynyards to be typical of the Maori race':[63] 'In order to try and keep faith with the British public the team on one occasion . . . purchased some black masks and they were paraded by some of our jokers wearing them, and looking out of the railway carriage windows at the expectant crowd.'[64] Ellison was more concerned with the quality of his own team's play and with his assessments of British rugby than he was with such frivolous diversions:

I was not very deeply impressed with the play of the Britishers;
for, with all the players they had available, I saw no one to compare
with Jack Taiaroa, J. Warbrick, Whiteside, Keogh and Co., except
Lockwood, Stoddart [who had taken over the captaincy of the British
team in New Zealand], Valentine, Bonsor and a very few others.
Their play generally was of the one style and description, from start
to finish – hooking, heeling out, and passing all day long, whether
successful at it or not.[65]

The comments about the 1905–06 team in the United Kingdom – Phillips' 'barometer of a the nation's health', Sinclair's about rugby becoming the 'national game', Macdonald's on that tour coming to be seen as 'the defining moment in both rugby and the wider national history' – could all have been applied with equal legitimacy to the tour by the much less publicised Native team seventeen years earlier. As one of the Native players, Billy ('Mother') Elliott, remarked many years afterward: 'The Britishers learned a lot from us, I reckon. We widened rugby's scope everywhere.'[66]

## The Natives set the precedents

Aside from the concept of the grand tour itself, the first of its kind, the Natives introduced elements which came to be more associated with later national teams. Two factors indelibly associated with the later All Blacks – the black jersey and the haka before a game – were both introduced by the Natives. Quite why Joe Warbrick or others chose black as their team's jersey colour has never been explained and probably now never can be, given that footballers generally did not follow the practice of politicians and colonial officials of recording their deeds in diaries or otherwise leaving archival records. It may be that the reason was as prosaic as black being available and that Warbrick knew it would not clash with the white of England, the green of Ireland or the scarlet of Wales. It could equally be true that black was adopted because there was black in the colours of Hawke's Bay (Warbrick's province) and Wellington (Ellison's province). It may also be that Warbrick or Ellison or someone else in the team knew that the New Zealand Amateur Athletic Association had already adopted black and silver for its national champion's cap.[67] As for the adoption of the silver fern on the breast of the jersey, Warbrick was a member of the team in 1884 that adopted that emblem first, though it was embroidered in gold on the jerseys and caps rather than in silver.

There is a little more surety about the introduction of the haka. One version has it that it was Ellison who in 1888 began the practice of the Natives' haka before matches which has become 'the most celebrated and visible sign of the Māori contribution to rugby union in New Zealand'.[68] The founder of the New Zealand Rugby Football Union, Ernest Hoben, had a different version of events. The tour occurred four years before the NZRFU was formed and Hoben at the time was secretary of the Hawke's Bay union, in which position he would have been well acquainted with Warbrick and other members of the Native team.[69] Hoben recalled Warbrick 'considering a war cry for the Maori team for England'[70] and said he told him of how Rewi Manga of Ngāti Maniapoto was supposed to have said, 'Ake, ake, kia kaha' in response to a call for surrender from the British general, Duncan Cameron, at Ōrākau in 1864, and this was wrongly interpreted by a reporter at the time as meaning, 'We will fight on for ever and ever'. Hoben recorded that what in fact Rewi said was: 'Ka whawhai tonu, ake, ake, ake' ('We will fight only, for ever and ever'). He said Warbrick was considering 'kia maia' ('be brave'), 'haere tonu' (go forward only) and other Māori expressions:

"Why not," I suggested, "link Orakau with the first Maori invasion of England. Take ake, ake. Add kia kaha and make it declaration and adjuration." And so, "Ake ake, kia kaha" ("Be strong, forever and ever") came into being as the war cry of the first Maori football team to go abroad. It rang to victory on many a British field. When the New Zealand Rugby Union was formed I had it again made the war cry of its teams and as such it was used in Australia and Britain.[71]

While Hoben was no doubt sincere in his recall of events, 'kia kaha' was earlier associated with the first team in 1884, as Sleigh wrote: 'And future teams of Maorilanders, be they footballers, cricketers or athletes, will not do amiss in endeavouring to warm the cockles of their hearts by adopting the war-cry of the 1884 team of Rugby footballers – 'Kea Kaha!'[72]

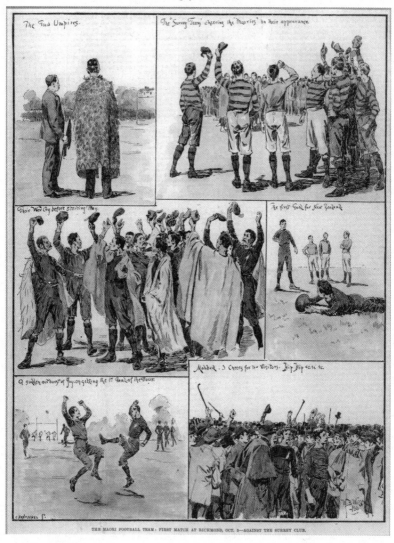

How *Illustrated London News* artist Carl Hentschell depicted the Natives football team during its opening match against Surrey. *Illustrated London News*, 13 October 1888, p. 417

The *Illustrated London News* ran a full page of sketches of the Natives' first match, against Surrey, and one of them was of the players uttering their 'war cry'. Ryan noted that the haka seemed to serve the dual purpose of cultural significance and commercial opportunism. 'This intimidates the other side and attracts huge piles of gate money', the Sydney *Bulletin* said, foreshadowing Anglo-Australian criticisms of the haka through to the twenty-first century. Frank Marshall, an English cleric who wrote prolifically about rugby, saw the haka as a gimmick whose usefulness was overtaken by the quality of the Natives' rugby:

> In the early matches of the tour, the New Zealanders appeared on the field in their native mats and headdresses and uttered their well known cry of "Ake, ake, kia kaha". . . . and undoubtedly curiosity had much to do with the attendance at the games. Later, when the real merit of their play was recognised, they discarded these advertising spectacles and depended upon their genuine exhibition of football to attract spectators.[73]

The *Sporting Life* described the haka as a 'whoop in the vernacular'.[74] The Natives were in Britain at the time of a dispute between England's ruling body, the Rugby Football Union, and the three-year-old International Rugby Football Board over a difference in law interpretations.[75] While Ireland, Scotland and Wales still played international matches over the 1888–89 northern hemisphere winter, the Natives provided the only international games in England, filling the gap nicely it appears. 'With the New Zealand team over here the loss of England's Rugby fixtures was not so keenly felt', one newspaper remarked.[76] It recorded how the Natives 'got through an extraordinarily heavy programme with much credit'. The Natives also, unlike the 1905–06 team, played against the strong clubs of Yorkshire and Lancashire, which split from the amateur Rugby Football Union in 1895 because of a difference over compensating players for time lost from work while on rugby duty. These clubs formed what was initially known as the Northern union and later came to be known as rugby league.[77] Consequently, in Ryan's assessment: 'Only the Native team – and neither of the two All Black teams [1905–06 and 1924–25] can claim to have encountered the full weight of British rugby strength during the period in which they played.'[78]

They followed their British tour with matches in Australia – including some according to Victorian rules – and finished with games in New Zealand. Yet their tour was not without controversy – something that became a recurring theme for New Zealand rugby tours of the United Kingdom – when they were criticised after some players walked off the field in the match against England because they felt the referee, George Rowland Hill (who was also the secretary of the English union), unfairly awarded a try to England. And toward the end of the tour in Australia and New Zealand, four players were stood down after allegations of match-fixing in Queensland. An Otago Rugby Football Union investigation found 'no facts before them justifying the accusations'.[79]

One of the features of the 1905–06 team's tactical appreciation was that the forwards had designated positions rather than the prevailing system in Britain of 'first up, first down' – that is, forwards taking positions in scrums according to their order of arrival. The All Blacks played in set positions and a scrum was not formed until all the players were in those specified positions.[80] But this refined approach originated with the Natives, not with the All Blacks, as most accounts would have it:

> In the scrum we invariably beat the English packs, not through
> having better men, but through our more scientific system of packing
> the scrum and having specialists in each position instead of merely
> fine all-round men; the result being, that our two front-rankers, for
> instance, simply buried the two Jacks-of-all-Trades who happened to
> be pitted against them in the different scrums.[81]

Ryan contended that the Native team 'deserves a position of honour' on the landscape of sport in New Zealand and Britain.[82] Swan called the tour 'the greatest of all'.[83] The publicity that the 1905–06 team gained, both at the time and later, overwhelmed the Natives in the public memory – but the 1888–89 team did as much, if not more, in establishing rugby as an identity marker for New Zealand, both internally and externally. A particular cachet was that it was a team largely of Māori, organised by Māori, playing a supposedly elite English game that had been introduced to New Zealand less than 20 years earlier. The success of the Natives led to calls for a truly representative New Zealand team to go to Britain, and to do that, a national body was needed. The Natives thus were a prime mover in the formation in 1892 of the New Zealand Rugby Football Union and in the tour by 'the Originals' in 1905–06, although the Natives could lay a greater claim to that soubriquet. The development of international rugby in New Zealand, which laid the basis for national identity through identification with sporting success in the name of New Zealand, thus owed as much if not more to indigenes as it did to an Anglo-Saxon elite.

It is worth noting, too, that Māori had an influential role in the development of rugby at a time when indigenous people in other settler colonies were generally ignored or marginalised. Outside of New Zealand, rugby was almost exclusively a white man's game. England fielded a player of Caribbean extraction, Jimmy Peters, in 1906 but did not pick him again when the South Africans objected; the next non-white to play for England was not until Chris Oti in 1988. The first to play for Wales was Glen Webbe in 1987; and for Scotland, Joe Ansbro in 2010. The first Aborigine to play rugby for Australia was Lloyd McDermott in 1962; and South Africa, infamously, did not include any non-whites until Errol Tobias in 1981.

The Natives also had unforeseen moral benefits, at least for a young boy in Southland. James Herries Beattie, a great collector and chronicler, was eight years old when the Natives played in Gore.[84]

He recalled watching 'goggle-eyed while strong men bowled one another over in the arena'.

> The incident that is indelibly inscribed on my mind was when a Gore player . . . punched a big Maori forward on the nose. The Maori just laughed and leaned forward and let the blood run. I tugged my father's hand and exclaimed, "O look, Father, that black man has blood the same colour as a white man." Thus early in life I [was] brought to know the truth of the Apostle Paul's statement to the Athenians, "God hath made of one blood all nations of men."[85]

## A home-made nickname

Contrary to the generally believed theories that the name 'All Blacks', a prime signpost of New Zealand identity, emerged with the 1905–06 team, the Natives can lay considerable claim to that distinction as well. Rather than the name being imposed on the later team while it was in Britain – yet another influence by the English on the colonials, and forelock-tugging on the part of the colonials in return – research shows that the name in fact preceded 1905 and that all the subsequent tour did was give it a wider circulation and a greater popularity (thanks to the greater number and competitiveness of British newspapers). The tour did not bring about the neologism: the name had its origins more than fifteen years earlier and was greatly influenced by Māori.[86]

The most often repeated version of the origin of the name came from one of the star players of the 1905 team, Billy Wallace, who at a reunion of the team in 1955 was reported as saying the London *Daily Mail* referred to the team after the eighth match of the tour, against Hartlepool, as 'all backs' because the forwards could run and pass just as effectively as the backs.[87] Apparently a sub-editor or printer inserted a rogue 'l' and so the name was born, at least according to

Wallace. This assertion went unchallenged and, because Wallace proved to be the longest-lived of that team, his version of events came to be accepted as fact.[88] It even gained an authoritative endorsement when it appeared in the official *Encyclopedia of New Zealand* in 1966 and it continues to be repeated as the definitive version, even years after publication of contrary evidence.[89] Why, however, if Wallace set such store by his 'all backs' belief, did he not mention it when he wrote his memoirs for a Wellington sports weekly, the *New Zealand Sportsman*, in 1932? His only reference to the origin of the name in those reminiscences was the recollection of seeing a poster when the team arrived in Taunton in Somerset that exhorted people to 'come and see the wonderful All Blacks play': 'The name "All Blacks" had now stuck to us. It is the name with which we were christened by the *Daily Mail* and it caught on with the general public, though quite a number were misled into thinking we were a team of black fellows.'[90]

And how come Wallace's 'all backs' version is not supported by the *Daily Mail* itself? The *Northern Daily Mail* in its report of the Hartlepool match traversed fourteen paragraphs before it listed the players' vital statistics and said: 'A glance at the undermentioned weights of the invincible "all blacks" will convey some idea of the calibre of the team ...' The *Northern Daily Mail*'s parent paper, the London-based *Daily Mail*, repeated the name the next morning when it reported the New Zealanders' 63–0 win: 'This is a record in the tour, which is yet barely a month old, exceeding as it does by eight points the 55 points the "All Blacks", as the Colonials are dubbed, piled up against Devon.'[91] In neither paper was there any reference to the ability of the team to play as 'all backs'. Rather, the first reference to the New Zealanders being known as the 'All Blacks' had come several weeks earlier, after their first game, against Devon, when the local paper, the *Express and Echo*, reported in the body of its story on the team's 55–4 win: 'The "All Blacks," as they are styled by reason of their sable and unrelieved costume, were under the guidance of their captain (Mr

Gallaher) and their physique favourably impressed the specta-tors.'[92] The paper's wording, 'as they are styled', implied that the name had been used before.

Journalist and author Terry McLean, whose rugby writing career spanned 60 years, attempted an explanation.[93] In the final book he wrote, he told how two newspapermen were on the tender that greeted the All Blacks' ship when it arrived off Plymouth at the start of the tour.[94] McLean's version of events is that one of the reporters asked a player about the team's uniform: its jersey, its shorts, its socks. To each question, the player answered with one word: 'black'. 'The conversation ended', McLean reported, 'when the player, in a burst of eloquence, remarked, "We are all black."' McLean, with liberal journalistic licence, then wrote of the reporter heading for his office and hugging his secret to himself 'until the triumphant moment when he lays before his sports editor the item which leads off by proclaiming that "the All Blacks have arrived"'. It is curious that McLean, author of about thirty books and long-time writer for the *New Zealand Herald* whose first rugby touring experience was in 1930, had not reported this incident earlier.

Ryan repeats the Wallace version of the naming, but dismisses it by quoting the team's vice-captain, Billy Stead, from a column he wrote for the *Southland Times* which shows the 'all backs' theory was a complete reversal of how it was perpetuated.[95] About the time the team was in Scotland for its first test, Stead reflected on the tour thus far. He wrote about the All Blacks' unbeaten record to that point and how British writers were trying to work out why the team was so good: 'The nearest guess to the secret of our success was by a well known army officer who suggested the altering of the name All Blacks to "all backs" for, he said, the moment the ball is secured or lost in the scrum then the whole fifteen "sweeps" seem to be backs.' There was a similar reference to 'all backs', this one in a *Daily Chronicle* report by 'Linesman' (otherwise unidentified) of the match against Oxford University which looked toward the match against Cambridge University:

I see that Cambridge are to employ the device of five threequarters and seven forwards in tomorrow's match and this seems to be a move in the right direction for the scrummage is the merest detail in New Zealand football. At the same time, even five threequarters, plus the two halves, cannot be regarded as possessed of the capacity to cope with a team who, ignoring all the traditional theories, convert themselves into all backs.[96]

Phillips does not specifically address the origin of the All Black name but the implication is plain when he writes: 'In the 1905 tour English descriptions of the games were widely reprinted, and the Gordon & Gotch volume *Why the All Blacks Triumphed* consisted largely of the *Daily Mail* reports. New Zealanders, in other words, conceived a stereotype about their males partly through the eyes of upper class Englishmen.'[97] English reports of the tour were indeed widely distributed in New Zealand but there is nothing remarkable in that. As noted, it was commonplace at the time for English newspaper reports of a whole range of activities to be either telegraphed to New Zealand or for English newspapers, when they became available on ships arriving in New Zealand, to be clipped and articles reproduced. Indeed, the Anglocentricity of overseas news sources for New Zealand continues into the twenty-first century. While it is true that *Why the All Blacks Triumphed!* was available for sale in New Zealand, so too were accounts of the tour by the manager, George Dixon, soon after the team returned home and, later in 1906, by the captain, Gallaher, and the vice-captain, Stead. Throughout the tour, overseas reports were supplemented by local comments, sometimes by reporters and sometimes by columnists. Newspapers also regularly ran reports from Britain filed not by English reporters but by New Zealanders with the team, including a regular column in the *Southland Times* by Stead.[98]

New Zealanders' views of the tour would have been formed from the newspaper reports (both the imported stories and the local comments) and from the words of the New Zealanders themselves. To suggest, therefore, that the 'eyes of upper class Englishmen' were influential is an overstating of the case since few, if any, rugby writers, then or now, could genuinely lay claim of belonging to what is regarded as the British upper class. Phillips also overlooks the fact that *Why the All Blacks Triumphed!* featured an article by Gallaher, which was promoted on the front cover: '"Secret of our success", by the New Zealand captain'. If British opinion did influence the thinking of New Zealanders, it was at least matched by the quantity of New Zealand opinion on the tour.

As was clearly implied by the Devon paper's phrase, 'as they are styled', the name 'All Blacks' had a prior use. The real genesis of the appellation lies not with the national team at all, but with the Wellington provincial team and the Native team. Wellington initially played in black jerseys, black shorts and black socks, and while they were most often referred to as 'the Blacks', they were also on occasion 'the All Blacks', such as in this passage from the *Evening Post* previewing a match against Auckland in August of 1889: 'Many people are of opinion the boys will have their hardest struggle with Wellington, and although an old Wellingtonian myself, I think the "all blacks" should be pleased if they can obtain a draw against the "blue and whites".'[99]

The Wellington provincial union, formed in 1879, had adopted the colours of its first club, Wellington, which had been playing football under rugby rules since 1871. The Wellington club had been formed by a Crimean War veteran, Captain James Clarendon Ramsbottom Isherwood, who apparently chose for the club the colours of his old British Army regiment, the 69th (South Lincolnshire) Regiment of Foot.[100] Wellington was not always black, though. The Natives played Wellington before leaving on their tour and because the Natives had their black jersey bearing the silver fern, Wellington obligingly changed to blue and white stripes similar to Auckland's colours, and match reports of that game, and of others, referred to the Natives as 'the Blacks'.[101]

Tāmati Rangiwahia ('Tom')
Ellison, one of the most
influential men in nineteenth-
century rugby. E6628/37a,
Hocken Collections Uare
Taoka o Hākena, University
of Otago

Tom Ellison provided a link between Wellington, the Natives
and the All Blacks. Born and raised in the Ngāi Tahu settlement
of Otākou on the Otago Peninsula, he first played the game there
in 1881 when introduced to it by a cousin, Jack Taiaroa, and his
'real introduction' took place a year later when he went to Te Aute
College in Hawke's Bay.[102] He later moved to Wellington, where he
played for the Pōneke club and was instrumental in refining the
wing forward position – the defining characteristic of New Zealand
rugby until the position was outlawed by the International Rugby
Board in 1931. In addition to playing for Pōneke and Wellington,
Ellison was one of the most influential members of the Natives
team. He was described thus by the tour organiser, Eyton: 'Ellison's
prowess in the football arena [is] well known in Wellington. When
on Tour he played as a forward and was second to none other in the

297

Native team. His knowledge of the finer points of the game; his weight, strength and activity rendered his services invaluable.'[103]

Ellison became an administrator while still a player and represented both Otago and Wellington at meetings of the New Zealand Rugby Football Union. At the union's first annual meeting in 1893, Ellison successfully moved that the national team's uniform comprise a black jersey with a silver fern.[104] Fittingly, he captained the first national team under the auspices of the NZRFU on a tour of Australia in 1893. It was common practice for newspapers to refer to teams by their jersey colours. It seems reasonable to conclude that newspaper reporters (or columnists writing under pseudonyms) did not operate in a vacuum and that identification by colours was also a part of everyday conversation. Manager Dixon used the descriptor 'the Blacks' in his 1905–06 private diary, but it was not of his making.[105] The name was applied to the first 1893 team when it played Wellington before going to Australia. The Wellington Rugby Football Union *Annual* of 1894, in a reference to the match, said: 'The Blacks (ie, the New Zealand representatives) won . . .' – the parentheses were the *Annual* editor's. Later in the same report, the writer said: 'The Blacks now played up with great determination . . .'[106] The weekly Auckland newspaper *New Zealand Observer and Free Lance* took the name a step further when the team was in Australia, previewing a second match against New South Wales in these words:

> Next Saturday, the deciding match against New South Wales takes place, and with this last success fresh on their memories, they should require nothing more to urge them on, and despite the gruelling they got at last meeting, I expect to see the all blacks come out on top with a substantial majority.[107]

The *Observer* had run a full-page cartoon a fortnight earlier depicting the players before, during and after their loss to New South Wales. They were not all black at all. Cartoonist William Blomfield

Again New Zealand reps. have met Queensland, and again they have administered a decided defeat. The score of 35 points to nil is certainly a monstrous one, and when we think of the hollow victory of Canterbury reps. against Auckland last season and consider that they only scored 23 points, one can easily imagine the runaway victory the New Zealand boys had last week. Next Saturday, the deciding match against New South Wales takes place, and with this last success fresh on their memories, they should require nothing more to urge them on, and despite the gruelling they got at last meeting, I expect to see the all blacks come out on top with a substantial majority.

The first known reference to the national rugby team as 'all blacks'. *New Zealand Observer*, 29 July 1893, p. 5

showed them accurately in black jerseys with a silver fern and white knickerbockers – precisely the uniform Ellison had persuaded the New Zealand union to adopt at its first annual meeting earlier that year.[108]

The new name for the national team continued beyond Ellison's playing career. When a British team played in Australia before continuing on to New Zealand in 1904, the Sydney correspondent of the *Evening Post* in Wellington previewed its imminent arrival. Assessing New Zealand's prospects in what would be the first international played between New Zealand and Great Britain, the correspondent wrote: 'If the New Zealand forward team is as good as it ought to be, I think the chances favour the "all blacks".'[109] It therefore becomes abundantly clear that the name All Blacks preceded the 1905 team and was of New Zealand manufacture, though it gained a wider acceptance during that tour, largely through the agency of the multiplicity of British newspapers. The name crossed the Atlantic with the team, and by the time the players were on their way home in early 1906, New Zealand newspapers habitually referred to the footballers as the All Blacks.

Clearly, Ellison, who died before the name gained wide usage, was a pivotal figure. He played for Wellington when they were 'all

BEFORE THE BATTLE—STALE, VERY STALE

THE BATTLE—THE STALENESS MAKING ITSELF FELT

AFTER THE BATTLE—CRUSHED, OH, HOW CRUSHED

OUR BOYS IN SYDNEY.

How William Blomfield saw the first official New Zealand team in 1893 after being beaten by New South Wales. The new uniform of black jersey with silver fern and white knickerbockers, agreed to in April, was pictured in the press for the first time. *New Zealand Observer*, 15 July 1893, p. 17

black', he was one of the leading members of the Natives team that wore all black, and it was he who transferred the Natives' jersey to the shoulders of all who played for New Zealand, and then captained the first New Zealand team to be known, if only briefly, as All Blacks, in 1893. If the word 'myth' can be associated with the naming of the All Blacks, the myth is that the neologism was British, or more specifically English, and gratefully seized upon by imperial-minded New Zealanders. The reality is that the name was coined in New Zealand for a national sports team that, more than any other in sport, came to be associated with what defined New Zealand. It would also serve as the base source for a wide variety of other sports teams' nicknames.[110]

Tom Ellison also applied his active mind to an issue that character-ised rugby for more than a hundred years: the staunchly amateur ethic of the game that led to northern English clubs forming their own game and consequently to rancour between the New Zealand and the Scottish and English unions.[111] Ellison argued that New Zealand players going to Britain should receive some financial allowance beyond having their hotel and travelling expenses paid. The rigid rules about professionalism applying in Britain were the 'only difficulty' standing in the way of a New Zealand team touring Britain, he wrote, well before the 1905–06 tour: 'Personally, I think that these laws were never intended to apply to extended tours abroad. Such tours were never contemplated at the time the rules were framed. However, if I am wrong in this view, I think that the law should be under certain circumstances relaxed.'[112]

In other words, while the games themselves may have reached all points of the Empire, the conditions under which they were codi-fied did not. Rugby may have been developed in southern England for a particular type of Englishman, but in its exportation to the rest of the world the conditions where it was played were different and its organisation was met with a colonial pragmatism. Rugby in general, and the All Blacks in particular, came to reflect a national identity that was born in New Zealand conditions and not those of the game's origins.

## THE UN-LICKED CUB.

[The New Zealanders have met several of our best Rugby teams, and easily defeated them.]

One of the last cartoons depicting New Zealand as a cub of the British lion. This was from the English *Punch*, which appeared not to have caught up with the growing number of depictions of New Zealanders as first, moa, and then, kiwi. *Punch*, 11 October 1905

# Conclusion

Winston Churchill never visited New Zealand, but he had good reason to regard the country with fondness. His biographer, Martin Gilbert, related how Churchill, just turned sixteen, prepared for an army entrance examination while at Harrow in 1890. He knew that in geography, he would have to answer questions about a particular country, but none of the boys knew which. The night before the examination, Churchill wrote out on scraps of paper the names of 25 countries he considered possible and put them in a hat. He closed his eyes and drew one out. 'New Zealand was the one', he wrote to his mother, 'and New Zealand was the first question on the paper.'[1] With such luck buttressing hard work, Churchill passed. Many years later, Churchill again had cause to remember New Zealand. Writing in the final volume of his *A History of the English-Speaking Peoples*, he talked of the rapid political development of the country and recalled how New Zealand 'faced and mastered all the problems of federal government thirty years before Australia did'.[2] 'Indeed', Churchill wrote, 'her political vitality is no less astonishing than her economic vigour. The tradition and prejudices of the past weighed less heavily than in older countries.' He noted that when the British Liberal government in 1906 introduced what were regarded as extreme innovations, they were nothing more than what had been accepted in New Zealand over the previous decade. These reforms, he thought, testified 'to the survival and fertility even in the remote and unfamiliar islands of the Pacific, of the British political genius'.

But by then, as the preceding chapters have endeavoured to show, the political genius was not so much British as defined as being of Great Britain, but a New Zealand political genius with British antecedents. New Zealand had well and truly been taken over by the New Zealanders – justifying the proclamation in 1899 by the *Observer* newspaper in Auckland: 'New Zealand for the New Zealanders'.[3] Rather than this apotheosis occurring because of the national identity signposts erected by earlier historians – the war in South Africa or the 1905–06 rugby tour of Britain – it happened well before such events. National identity was established in New Zealand in the final third of the nineteenth century, rather than at the dawn of the twentieth, and its beginnings were apparent even as early as the 1840s when formal government had barely been established. As much as the concept of national identity may be deprecated by some postmodernist historians, it cannot be denied: people were born in a country, they lived in a country, they were of that country for good or ill. The more people born in New Zealand, the more New Zealanders there were – the number of native-born as a percentage of population passed the 50 per cent mark in the early 1880s.

National identity – the process of identifying oneself with a nation-state in the sense of belonging and allegiance – is not a complex issue, but it can give rise to apparent conundrums, such as: How could people in the nineteenth century on the periphery of the British Empire call themselves New Zealanders when the metropolitan power of the United Kingdom held sway? How could national identity be asserted in New Zealand's name when the British flag fluttered at the top of the mast and when a likeness of its monarch featured – and still does – on banknotes and coins and stamps? How could there be such a thing as a unified national identity in a society dominated by white males? How could those ruling white males consider themselves New Zealanders when they rose to their feet and fervently sang the British national anthem? And how could New Zealanders proclaim a national identity when their economic wellbeing was almost wholly dependent on Britain? There were contradictions, there were imperfections, there were faults. Whether in the colonisation period of New Zealand's history or what James Belich characterised as the 'recolonisation' period – after the development of refrigeration in shipping and an increased economic dependence on Britain – a national identity in New Zealand gradually evolved nonetheless.[4] Immigrants – men or women – came to see themselves as New Zealanders, to identify themselves as New Zealanders, and the ever-increasing number of the native-born *were* New Zealanders. The relationship of New Zealand to Britain, the periphery to the core, was not as monolithic as it sometimes appeared – economic dependence, yes, but there were enough assertions of New Zealand's will to demonstrate a firm independence of thought and deed. British in name, perhaps, and 'Greater Britain' in imagination, New Zealand had a devolving political autonomy and an evolving independence all the same.

The wars and tours of the early twentieth century were an affirmation of the gradual, evolutionary emergence of a national identity rather than its genesis. National identity was already well founded when the mounted troopers rushed to Britain's colours at the turn of the century or when the rugby players went 'Home' to show 'Mother' how well her 'son' had adapted to one of England's games (if that indeed was the players' motivation, which is problematic). Those events signalled not the awakening of a national identity at all, but were rather the first significant manifestations of one to an overseas audience. For the first time, New Zealand's national identity had been exported and exposed internationally, but it had been cultivated in its own backyard for many years.

As for the argument that national identity is a wholly white male construct and therefore flawed because it excluded women and Māori, or at least was not framed for the whole of the population – while it is true that a male hegemony applied in New Zealand in the nineteenth century as much as it did elsewhere in the world (leaving aside the fact British imperialists were presided over by, and paid homage to, a woman, Queen Victoria, for all of the second half of the century), the changes wrought by the evolution of a national identity did not exclude women. Some aspects of nineteenth-century New Zealand that led to a heightened sense of national identity – most notably universal suffrage, introduced by the Liberal administration of the 1890s – were primarily intended for the benefit of women. And while there has been an understandable and justifiable focus by historians on the confiscation of Māori land and the consequential fighting over it, Māori also contributed in no small measure to the manner in which New Zealand's national identity developed.

National identity has been a problematic issue for historians, wherever their focus may have turned. There have been differing interpretations and assumptions of when a country's national identity emerged and there have been questions about the appropriateness of even attempting to define a national identity. But historians disagree on a great many aspects of the study of the past. Some of the differences can be in detail or emphasis; others can be more fundamental. Some can simply be exposed through a fresh look at something already studied, ascribing significance to elements of the past which other historians have either overlooked or considered less significant. But as British historian Arthur Marwick said: 'To concentrate on the differences of interpretation . . . is to miss the main purpose of historical study: deepened understanding of the past.'[5]

In New Zealand, there were early signs that those who settled here wanted their new country to be different from that whence they came and different too from other colonies. One such sign was the determination to resist any attempts from London to turn New Zealand into another penal colony like New South Wales or Van Diemen's Land, as Tasmania then was. The available evidence indicates that London may not have been all that serious about such an endeavour and the suggestions were tentative in the extreme, but those in Auckland, Wellington and Dunedin who led the opposition left no room for doubt. They wanted their new land unsullied and one of the reasons given was the deleterious effect imported convicts could have on Māori. This set New Zealand apart from the start and Māori continued to provide a point of difference that made this country unique. Far from the indigenous people being a missing factor in the evolution of a national identity, they were in fact a major contributor.

Some of the developments in New Zealand which led to a sense of national identity were common to other developing countries, especially the Australian colonies with which it can best be compared: each country developed railways and telegraph networks and other methods of communication which brought communities together, and each extolled characteristics of the land and took pride in burgeoning national symbols, whether it was the silver fern in New Zealand or the wattle in Australia. It was the aggregation of such developments that led to a particular sense of identity in each country; the means were similar, but the end was different.

It was comparison with others that helped shape national identity. As Linda Colley, an expert on the complexities of British national identities, put it: 'Quite simply, we usually decide who we are by reference to who and what we are not.'[6] In New Zealand's case, the 'other' was the Australian colonies or, from 1901, the Australian Commonwealth. New Zealanders, by refusing to join that Commonwealth, decided they were not Australians. It was not a decision made by New Zealanders in any formal sense: a recommendation against federating was made by the royal commission appointed by Richard John Seddon and he, with his customary fine-tuned understanding of what the general populace wanted, sensed there was no desire to be conjoined with colonies the Tasman Sea away. New Zealanders already knew, as Seddon clearly sensed, that they were different from Australians; they knew the country in which they had settled or were born in was different, however similar it may also have been, from New South Wales or Victoria or any of the other Australian colonies that became states. It was those very similarities which caused the differences to be accentuated. New Zealand's sense of national identity existed long before the desultory federation debate.

There was no fixed starting point to the evolution of national identity; no portentous date memorialised as the beginning; no one event like Bastille Day or the Fourth of July looming in a receding historical background. Rather, it formed through an accumulation of events, a process of osmosis. Many factors contributed – some on a national scale that affected most of the population, but others at a purely personal level. For some of the early settlers, it would have come as a form of commitment to life in a new land. This affiliation was given national expression by an early premier, Edward Stafford, when he declared in Parliament that he was 'a New Zealander'. By saying what he was, he was also implying what he was not. He was not an Englishman – or a Scot, or an Irishman – who just happened to be living somewhere else at the time.[7] But equally the sense of identity with New Zealand could have been felt by anyone forgotten by history, anyone whose name never appeared in newspapers, anyone who left nothing behind, anyone whose name may now be known only to genealogists as a twig of a branch of a family tree. The feeling of belonging could have come from reading in newspapers not of what was happening in Britain but of what was going on elsewhere in New Zealand. National identity was not imposed by government decree; it was not something forced upon the people from on high.

Man disposed of the provincial governments – New Zealand's own form of federalism – and made the country administratively whole, but science provided the links between north and south, east and west. The stringing of telegraph lines throughout the land brought New Zealanders closer together and provided a cohesion that hitherto had been missing or, because of reliance on sailing ships, been dangerous, unreliable and slow. With the telegraph came more news about New Zealand in newspapers; for the first time, people in the north could read practically on the same day or soon afterward what people in the south were thinking and doing. Importantly, they could also read what New Zealanders were thinking and doing by comparison with what occurred in other countries: they could compare their country with others. They were also thinking and doing at the same time because it was the telegraph that was the catalyst for New Zealand adopting at an early stage by world standards one uniform time for the whole country. No longer did Wellington operate on one time and Christchurch or Auckland on another; no longer could people say there was 'no time in Hokitika';[8] the same seconds ticked by for all. When southern Africa adopted a uniform time in 1903 – a quarter of a century after New Zealand – one commentator remarked that it was 'a momentous step towards unity'.[9] So it had been in New Zealand, but much earlier.

With the telegraph, the railways and improved shipping, especially after the advent of the home-grown Union Steam Ship Company, contact between centres became more practical, more affordable, and more frequent. The interaction between centres helped cement the feeling of a national identity and this was given more force from the early 1870s by the gradual development of sporting contests. Province could now compete against province, and it was a natural evolutionary step that, once they did, the best of the provincial teams could combine in a national team. They did this most noticeably in rugby football, and by 1882 a New South Wales team had come to New Zealand and a New Zealand team had reciprocated two years later: embroidered on its dark blue jerseys was a gold fernleaf – the emblem, if not the colours, which would come to be recognised as distinctively New Zealand's. But it was not just rugby. A national athletics association adopted black with silver piping for its championship caps in 1887, and these colours were used when Māori took rugby's most significant early step and formed their own team to tour Australia and Britain. The team, known as the Natives, had a white fern on their black jerseys, and it was one of the players, Tāmati Rangiwahia ('Tom') Ellison, who successfully proposed at the first annual general meeting of the New

Zealand Rugby Football Union that the same jersey be adopted for the national team.

Later the same year, 1893, Ellison captained the first truly national team and it was referred to for the first time as the All Blacks. While the tour of the United Kingdom and North America by the national team in 1905–06 has been seen as a significant marker of national identity, and mistakenly believed to have given the national team a new, British-imposed nickname, it was Māori who were the real progenitors of what the All Blacks came to mean in New Zealand's national psyche. A national athletics team toured Britain and France in 1892 and it too competed in black with a silver fern on the chest. These were indications of national identity being established from the bottom up; the rugby players and athletes were not an educated elite – although there were some that could be described as such, they were a cross-section of New Zealand society: an admixture of rural and urban, inherited wealth and weekly wage, posh school and no schooling at all.

At the same time, national identity was being aided from the top down by the socially advanced legislation emanating from the Liberal administration in Wellington. While the extension of suffrage to women was the most notable of such advances, it should not be forgotten that the franchise had been granted to Māori from as early as 1867. Women, widows, workers, children – all benefited from the range of humanist policies introduced by Seddon's government and which made New Zealand the 'talk of the world today', as one commentator put it.[10] New Zealand's reforms were even said to have laid the groundwork for those introduced by United States President Franklin Roosevelt in his New Deal of the 1930s. Influential commentators came to New Zealand to see and write, and what they wrote found its way back to New Zealand newspapers, thereby creating a sense of satisfaction and pride in the country that underlined the sense of national identity.

New Zealand's geography – both its remoteness from neighbours and its physical characteristics – was also a factor in the formation of national identity. This became most evident in the arguments against federation, with Sir John Hall's comment about '1200 impediments to the inclusion of New Zealand' serving almost as a leitmotif of its independence and identity. But self-recognition was not just the preserve of politicians. Guy Scholefield, who wrote about federation for a British audience, said the 'insularity of the country was personified in the independence and individualism of the people'.[11] Another journalist, Malcolm Ross, put it this way: 'We are an island race dowered with advantages unpossessed by our brother colonists on the great continent across the Tasman Sea. The climate, the resources, and the physical characteristics of our land will tend to breed a sturdier race than that which is now being evolved in Australia.'[12]

The physical characteristics featured beyond the political commentary. Mountains and lakes were chosen to feature on the first set of New Zealand pictorial stamps, and flora and fauna became day-to-day items through their use as trademarks and in numerous other ways, including the silver fern as a national sporting emblem. In newspaper cartoons, New Zealanders or their achievements were frequently portrayed via a moa, although in the first few years of the twentieth century it was replaced by the kiwi, which also featured among the pictorial stamps. It was New Zealanders who adopted the native birds as symbols; in at least one English cartoon in 1905, the New Zealander was still depicted as a cub of the British lion.[13]

The national 'hymn' that was later adopted as the national anthem was written in 1876 and it too extolled the natural features of New Zealand. By the mid-1890s, New Zealand's natural scenery was also recognised by the government for its potential to attract visitors and immigrants and an intensive publicity campaign was embarked on, especially in Europe and the United States. Images of the country's natural beauty were increasingly reproduced as newspaper technology developed. Historian Erik Olssen encapsulated the transformation from vassal state to national pride: 'People took pride in the symbols and images of New Zealand, but loved their local landscapes best. And not all had worshipped Seddon. Some dismissed him as a vulgar windbag . . . yet his dominance . . . had created a pervasive sense of New Zealand's identity and destiny."[14]

By the time of the talk about federating with Australia, which reached its apogee in 1899–1900, and of the concurrent Boer War, which began in October 1899, New Zealand's national identity was well established. It was an expression of that identity that lay behind the lack of any serious attempt to join the Australian colonies in federation (or to send a combined Australasian force to South Africa). The Boer War, far from establishing the identity, became an expression of it – an outward manifestation for the first time beyond sport. Public oratory dwelt much on support for Britain and its empire, but there was enough evidence to show that, for New Zealanders, loyalty to their own country came ahead of that to Britain in their layered allegiance. There was imperial rhetoric – New Zealanders did fight under a British flag and British command – but they were New Zealanders first. There was no inherent contradiction in the duality.[15]

The role of the Boer War, the 1905–06 rugby tour, being given dominion status in 1907, and New Zealand's role in the Gallipoli landings – all affirmed rather than established New Zealand's national identity. Instead it was laid down gradually in manifold ways almost from the arrival of the first European colonisers. Those landmark events commonly credited with forging a national identity were significant in the young country and their role should not be downplayed, but in terms of the making of New Zealanders, they simply thrust New Zealand in front of the eyes of a wider world and showed it to be both different and distinctive. New Zealanders already knew.

## Introduction

1 Anthony Trollope, *The New Zealander* (Oxford: Clarendon Press, 1972), pp. 43–44. Trollope wrote his social commentary in 1855 but the manuscript was lost and it was not published until 1972. In the editor's introduction, a reader for the proposed 1855 publisher, Longman, is quoted as saying: 'The object of the work is to show how England may be saved from the ruin that now threatens her!! And how the realisation of Macaulay's famous prophecy of the "New Zealander standing on the ruins of London Bridge" may be indefinitely postponed.'

2 *Auckland Star*, 17 October 1877, p. 2.

3 E. H. McCormick, 'Thomas Arnold and the Land of Hope. An Incident in New Zealand Colonization', paper delivered to ANZAAS congress, Canberra, 1964; quoted in J. S. Ryan, ed., *Charles Dickens and New Zealand* (Wellington: A. H. & A. W. Reed for the Dunedin Public Library, 1965), p. 14.

4 Ryan, *Charles Dickens and New Zealand*, p. 14.

5 Thomas Babington (Lord) Macaulay's review of Leopold von Ranke's *The Ecclesiastical and Political History of the Popes During the Sixteenth and Seventeenth Centuries [Die römische Papste]*, trans. S. Austin, 3 vols, *Edinburgh Review*, vol. 72 (October 1840), pp. 227–58; quoted in David Skilton, 'Tourists at the Ruins of London: The Metropolis and the Struggle for Empire', *Cercles*, no. 17 (2007), pp. 93–119.

6 Macaulay's 1840 passage was not the first use by him of such imagery, although it was his first mention of a traveller from New Zealand. For discussion on other imagery, and whether Macaulay borrowed the idea from Shelley, see Skilton, 'Tourists at the Ruins of London', and 'Shelley and Macaulay', letter to the editor, *The Times*, 13 September 1860. An unidentified writer in the *Philadelphia Times*, reprinted in the *New York Times*, also traversed the origins of the observation, citing Horace Walpole writing about 'some curious traveller from Lima'. The writer concluded: 'The interesting thing is not who said a thing first, but who said it last – who said it, that is, in the form in which it is remembered. Walpole's traveller from Lima failed to strike the popular imagination; but when Macaulay brought him from New Zealand he became at once a national figure.' *New York Times*, 17 August 1901, p. BR13.

7 *Westminster Gazette*, quoted in *Evening Post*, 18 September 1897, p. 2.

8 Ibid.

9 *New Zealand Parliamentary Debates* (hereafter *NZPD*), vol. 110, p. 96; the hyphen in 'New-Zealander' is indicative of how little used the expression was in the nineteenth century.

10 *Sporting Life*, quoted in *Otago Witness*, 12 May 1883, p. 21.

11 *Athletic News*, quoted in *Otago Witness*, 14 February 1906, p. 56.

12 See David Goodman, 'Eureka Stockade', in Graeme Davison, John Hirst and Stuart Macintyre, eds, *The Oxford Companion to Australian History*, revised edn (Melbourne: Oxford University Press, 2001), pp. 229–31.

13 Alan Mulgan, *The Making of a New Zealander* (Wellington: A. H. & A. W. Reed, 1958), p. 73.

14 W. P. Morrell and D. O. W. Hall, *A History of New Zealand Life* (Wellington: Whitcombe & Tombs, 1957), p. 212.

15 See, for example, Keith Sinclair, *A Destiny Apart: New Zealand's Search for National Identity* (hereafter *Destiny Apart*) (Wellington: Unwin Paperbacks in association with the Port Nicholson Press, 1986), pp. 170–71; Sinclair, 'Towards 1990: Nation & Identity' (hereafter 'Nation & Identity'), Hocken Lecture, 1988 (Dunedin: Hocken Library, 1990), pp. 8–9. Christopher Pugsley wrote: 'Every man who served on Gallipoli endured, and established a reputation and a sense of identity that is important to us today.' Pugsley, *Gallipoli: The New Zealand Story* (Auckland: Hodder & Stoughton, 1984), p. 27. See also O. E. Burton, *The Silent Division* (Sydney: Angus & Robertson, 1935), pp. 121–23; Roberto Rabel, 'New Zealand's Wars', in Giselle Byrnes, ed., *The New Oxford History of New Zealand* (hereafter *New Oxford History*) (Melbourne: Oxford University Press, 2009), pp. 245–67. More recent scholarship questions the link between Gallipoli and identity. 'National identity is not irrelevant', George Davis wrote, 'but . . . it may be missing a larger point' – the point being universal respect for

sacrifice rather than recognition of national identity. George Frederick Davis, 'Anzac Day meanings and memories: New Zealand, Australian and Turkish perspectives on a day of commemoration in the twentieth century', PhD thesis, University of Otago, 2008, p. 308.

16  Official Record of the Proceedings and Debates of the Australasian Federation Conference, Melbourne, 1890, <http://setis. library.usyd.edu.au>, p. 83.

17  *NZPD*, vol. 69, 15 August–17 September 1890, p. 586.

18  For comprehensive background on the fixing of New Zealand time, see Thomas King, 'On New Zealand Mean Time, and on the Longitude of the Colonial Observatory, Wellington; with a note on the Universal Time Question', *Transactions and Proceedings of the Royal Society of New Zealand 1868–1961*, vol. 35, 1902 <http://natlib.govt.nz/volume. rsnz_35>.

19  *Evening Post*, 5 October 1868, p. 2.

20  A complete analysis of the background and implementation of the laws is found in William Pember Reeves, *State Experiments in Australia and New Zealand*, 2 vols (London: George Allen & Unwin, 1902).

21  Patricia Grimshaw, 'Tasman Sisters: Lives of the "Second Sex"', in Keith Sinclair, *Tasman Relations: New Zealand and Australia, 1788–1988* (Auckland: Auckland University Press, 1987), p. 236.

22  See Nigel Murphy, *A Guide to Laws and Policies Relating to the Chinese in New Zealand* (New Zealand Chinese Association, 1997); Brian Moloughney and John Stenhouse, 'Drug-Besotten, Sin-Begotten Fiends of Filth', *New Zealand Journal of History* (hereafter *NZJH*), vol. 33, no. 1 (April 1999), pp. 43–64.

23  W. P. Morrell, *New Zealand* (London: Ernest Benn, 1935), p. 86.

24  Linda Colley, 'Britishness and Otherness: An Argument' (hereafter 'Britishness and Otherness'), *The Journal of British Studies*, vol. 31, no. 4 (October 1992), p. 311.

25  A fact not acknowledged by Rabel. See *New Oxford History*, p. 249.

26  Greg Ryan, *Forerunners of the All Blacks: The 1888–89 New Zealand Native Football Team in Britain, Australia and New Zealand* (Christchurch: Canterbury University Press, 1993).

27  *New Zealand Observer and Free Lance*, 29 July 1893, p. 5.

28  Sinclair, *Destiny Apart*, p. 147.

29  Scott A. G. M. Crawford, 'A Sporting Image: The Emergence of a National Identity in a Colonial Setting, 1862–1906', *Victorian*

*Periodicals Review*, vol. 21, no. 2 (Summer 1988), p. 56.

30  Matti Goksøyr, 'Nationalism', in S. W. Pope and John Nauright, eds, *Routledge Companion to Sports History* (Oxford: Routledge, 2010), p. 275.

31  Benedict Anderson, *Imagined Communities: Reflections on the Origins and Spread of Nationalism* (London: Verso Books, 2006; first published 1983), p. 2.

32  Sinclair, 'Nation & Identity', p. 4.

33  J. C. Beaglehole, 'The Development of New Zealand Nationality', *Journal of World History*, vol. II, no. 1 (1954), p. 107.

34  Various interpretations and explanations of 'nationalism' have been offered by scholars, the variety itself underlining the difficulty of defining something that is 'felt' by individuals rather than prescribed. One expert in the field, Anthony W. Marx, embraced the word as meaning 'a collective sentiment or identity, bounding and binding together those individuals who share a sense of large-scale political solidarity aimed at creating, legitimating or challenging states'. Marx, *Faith in Nation – Exclusionary Origins of Nationalism* (Oxford: Oxford University Press, 2003), p. 6.

35  Byrnes, 'Introduction: Reframing New Zealand History,' *New Oxford History*, p. 10.

36  Katie Pickles, 'Colonisation, Empire and Gender', in *New Oxford History*, p. 221.

37  Ibid., p. 222.

38  Ibid., p. 222–23.

39  See W. H. Oliver, 'New Zealand About 1890', the Macmillan Brown Lectures, 1972, pp. 10–11.

40  Colley, 'Britishness and Otherness', p. 315.

41  Linda Colley, *Britons: Forging the Nation 1707–1837* (New Haven: Yale University Press, 2005), p. 6. This concept is also examined by James Belich in *Replenishing the Earth: The Settler Revolution and the Rise of the Anglo-World, 1783–1939* (hereafter *Replenishing the Earth*) (Oxford: Oxford University Press, 2009), pp. 461–65.

42  Ann Curthoys and John Docker, *Is History Fiction?* (Sydney: University of New South Wales Press, 2006), p. 234.

43  Morrell, *New Zealand*, p. 337.

44  Alice Brittan, 'Australasia', in John McLeod, ed., *The Routledge Companion to Postcolonial Studies* (Milton Park, Oxfordshire: Routledge, 2001), p. 81.

45  Peter Hempenstall, 'Getting Inside the Tasman World: A Case for Remembering Local Histories in New Zealand, Australia and the Southwest Pacific', the Jim Gardner Lecture, Canterbury History Foundation, 2009, p. 4.

One *From Many to One: Linking the*
*'Fishing Villages'*

1   *Evening Post*, 21 January 1890, p. 2.
2   N. E. Coad, *New Zealand from Tasman to*
    *Massey* (Wellington: Harry H. Tombs Ltd,
    1934), p. 170.
3   William Fox, *The Six Colonies of New Zealand*
    (London: John W. Parker and Son, 1851;
    facsimile edn, Hocken Library, 1971), p. 17.
4   Geoffrey Blainey, *The Tyranny of Distance:*
    *How Distance Shaped Australia's History*
    (Sydney: Pan Macmillan, 2001).
5   Sir Frederick Chapman, 'The Interest
    and Value of New Zealand History',
    inaugural lecture, New Zealand Historical
    Association (Otago branch), 21 June 1928
    (Dunedin: Otago Daily Times and Witness
    Newspapers, 1928), p. 4.
6   Fox, *The Six Colonies of New Zealand*,
    pp. 139–40.
7   Sinclair, 'Nation & Identity', p. 7.
8   Niall Ferguson, *Empire: How Britain Made*
    *the Modern World* (London: Penguin Books,
    2008), pp. 168–69.
9   *Otago Witness*, 5 July 1862, p. 8.
10  A. C. Wilson, *Wire & Wireless: A History of*
    *Telecommunications in New Zealand 1890–1987*
    (Palmerston North: Dunmore Press, 1994),
    p. 25.
11  A. S. Helm, 'The Early History of South
    Island Telegraphs', MA thesis, Victoria
    University of Wellington, 1951, quoted in
    Patrick Day, 'Julius Vogel and the Press',
    *Turnbull Library Record*, vol. 19, no. 2
    (October 1986), p. 107.
12  James Belich acknowledged the significance
    of the telegraph but incorrectly stated
    the first line was in Dunedin in 1861. See
    Belich, *Making Peoples: A History of the New*
    *Zealanders From Polynesian Settlement to the*
    *End of the Nineteenth Century* (Auckland:
    Penguin Books, 2007), p. 442.
13  *Press*, 19 July 1862, p. 4.
14  Two men, Harry Jones and George Barton,
    were charged with 'making an affray . . . to
    the terror and disturbance of Her Majesty's
    subjects'. The bout was evidently in a ring
    constructed specifically for the purpose
    and several hundred spectators, including
    some notable Christchurch citizens, were
    present. The two fighters were acquitted
    of 'causing an affray', but were found guilty
    of common assault. Each was sentenced
    to a month's imprisonment. See *Press*,
    19 July 1862, pp. 2 and 4; 2 August 1868, p. 6;
    6 September 1868, p. 5; also *Sports Digest*,
    August 1962, pp. 42–45.
15  *Otago Witness*, 27 December 1862, p. 7.
16  Edward Dobson, 'On the present state
    of Applied Science in the Canterbury
    Province', address to the annual meet-
    ing of the Philosophical Institute of
    Canterbury, 5 November 1866, *Transactions*
    *and Proceedings of the Royal Society of New*
    *Zealand 1868–1961*, vol. 1, 1868 <http://natlib.
    govt.nz/volume.rsnz_1>; 'Middle Island'
    was a common nickname for the South
    Island until late in the nineteenth century,
    sandwiched as it was between the North
    Island and Stewart Island.
17  *Evening Post*, 27 August 1866, p. 2.
18  Holy Bible, Numbers 23:23 ('. . . according
    to this time, it shall be said of Jacob and of
    Israel, "What hath God wrought!"').
19  *Evening Post*, 28 August 1866, p. 2.
20  Ibid.
21  Wilson, *Wire & Wireless*, p. 47.
22  Ibid.
23  Howard Robinson, *A History of the Post Office*
    *in New Zealand* (Wellington: R. E. Owen,
    Government Printer, 1964), p. 156.
24  For Murray's early years in Auckland and
    Sydney, see *New Zealand Free Lance*, 30 April
    1904, p. 3. His invention of 'typewriter-
    style' telegraph transmission was the subject
    of a full-page article in the *New York Times*,
    25 January 1914, p. 48. Murray, who worked
    for the *Sydney Morning Herald* in Sydney, was
    a son of John Murray (1835–1915), a one-time
    general manager and director of the Bank
    of New Zealand who, after his retirement,
    was largely responsible for devising the
    government's rescue plan for the bank in
    1894. See *Observer*, 27 September 1902,
    p. 4; G. H. Scholefield, *A Dictionary of*
    *New Zealand Biography*, vol. 2 (Wellington:
    Department of Internal Affairs, 1940),
    pp. 110–11.
25  *Observer*, 11 August 1906, p. 4.
26  For a full explanation of Gell's invention,
    see *Hawera and Normanby Star*, 20 February
    1904, p. 2. See also Wilson, *Wire & Wireless*,
    pp. 55–56; *Observer*, 19 March 1904, p. 5;
    *Evening Post*, 18 August 1905, p. 5.
27  *Progress*, 1 December 1905, p. 41.
28  *West Coast Times*, 7 February 1866, p. 2.
    For details of telegraph charges, see
    G. H. Scholefield, *Newspapers in New*
    *Zealand* (Wellington: A. H. & A. W. Reed,
    1958), p. 14.
29  *West Coast Times*, ibid.
30  *Press*, 25 November 1864, p. 2.
31  Ibid.
32  Eric Pawson, 'Local times and standard
    time in New Zealand', *Journal of Historical*
    *Geography*, vol. 18, no. 3 (1992), p. 279.
33  For comprehensive background on the
    fixing of New Zealand time, see Thomas
    King, 'On New Zealand Mean Time,

and on the Longitude of the Colonial Observatory, Wellington; with a note on the Universal Time Question', *Transactions and Proceedings of the Royal Society of New Zealand 1868–1961*, vol. 35, 1902 <http://natlib.govt.nz/volume.rsnz_35>.

34  *Evening Post*, 5 October 1868, p. 2.

35  For the significance of social change wrought by the telegraph and railways, see Wolfgang Schivelbusch, *The Railway Journey: The Industrialization of Time and Space in the 19th Century* (Berkeley and Los Angeles: The University of California Press, 1986).

36  *Press*, 25 November 1864, p. 2.

37  For a layman's guide to the development of reliability in the fixing of longitudes, see Dava Sobel, *Longitude: The True Story of a Lone Genius Who Solved the Greatest Scientific Problem of His Time* (London: Harper Perennial, 2007).

38  *Evening Post*, 6 August 1868, p. 2.

39  *Otago Daily Times*, 12 March 1868, p. 4.

40  *Evening Post*, 6 August 1868, p. 2.

41  *Otago Daily Times*, 20 March 1868, p. 5.

42  *NZPD*, vol. 3, 2 September 1868, p. 106.

43  Ibid., p. 108. Ironically, although separated on this issue, Reynolds and Macandrew were otherwise close. The pair immigrated to New Zealand together eighteen years before, had been business partners, and Macandrew married Reynolds' sister. See *Otago Witness*, 6 April 1899, p. 15.

44  R. K. Dell, 'Hector, James, 1834–1907', *Dictionary of New Zealand Biography*, vol. 1 (Wellington: Allen & Unwin/Department of Internal Affairs, 1990), pp. 183–84. See also Simon Nathan and Mary Varnham, eds, *The Amazing World of James Hector* (Wellington: Awa Press, 2008).

45  James Hector, 'On New Zealand Mean Time', *Transactions and Proceedings of the Royal Society of New Zealand 1868–1961*, vol. 1, 1868 <http://natlib.govt.nz/volume. rsnz_35>.

46  *New Zealand Gazette*, 31 October 1868, p. 507.

47  Ibid.

48  King, 'On New Zealand Mean Time', p. 431.

49  See *The Journals, Detailed Reports, and Observations relative to the Exploration by Captain Palliser of that portion of British North America which, in latitude, lies between the British Boundary Line and the height of land or watershed of the Northern or Frozen Ocean respectively, and, in longitude, between the western shore of Lake Superior and the Pacific Ocean During the Years 1857, 1858, 1859 and 1860, presented to both Houses of Parliament*

*1863*, House of Commons Parliamentary Papers (Paper 3164) <http://parlipapers. chadwyck.co.uk>.

50  King, 'On New Zealand Mean Time', p. 431.

51  See H. C. Ballon, M.D., 'Sir James Hector, M.D., 1834–1907', in Canadian Medical Association *Journal*, vol. 87 (14 July 1962), pp. 66–73; Ross Mitchell, M.D., 'Sir James Hector', Canadian Medical Association *Journal*, vol. 66 (May 1952), pp. 497–99.

52  Alan Mason, 'Hector, Sir James (1834–1907)', *Oxford Dictionary of National Biography* <www.oxforddnb.com>; see also A. G. Hocken, 'The early life of James Hector, 1834 to 1865: the first Otago Provincial Geologist', PhD thesis, University of Otago, 2007.

53  Sir James Hector, 'Extracts and notes on life of James Hector', MS-0445-1/09, Hocken Library.

54  See, for example, *Nelson Examiner and New Zealand Chronicle*, 3 November 1868, p. 2; *Taranaki Herald*, 24 October 1868, p. 2.

55  *Evening Post*, 5 October 1868, p. 2.

56  *Otago Witness*, 14 November 1868, p. 12.

57  *Evening Post*, 31 October 1868, p. 2. The correspondent was the Rev. Arthur Stock, the vicar of St Peter's in Wellington and a keen astronomer and keeper of the time ball. See Scholefield, *A Dictionary of New Zealand Biography*, vol. 2, p. 336. The time changes were published by Hector in *Transactions and Proceedings of the Royal Society of New Zealand*, vol. 1, 1868 and, slightly amended, vol. 3, 1870.

58  King, 'On New Zealand Mean Time', p. 431. See also *Evening Post*, 15 April 1903, p. 7.

59  Wilson, *Wire & Wireless*, p. 44.

60  Scholefield, *A Dictionary of New Zealand Biography*, vol. 2, pp. 227–28.

61  *Otago Witness*, 6 April 1899, p. 15.

62  Graeme Davison, *The Unforgiving Minute: How Australia Learned to Tell the Time* (Melbourne: Oxford University Press, 1993), p. 63. See also Davison, 'Punctuality and progress: The foundations of Australian standard time', *Australian Historical Studies*, vol. 25, issue 99 (1992), pp. 169–91.

63  'Report of the Intercolonial Conference of Surveyors', *The Surveyor*, Journal of the Institute of Surveyors, New South Wales, vol. 5, no. 12, 12 December 1892.

64  *Report of the Postal and Telegraph Conference held in Brisbane in March 1893, including Reports of Proceedings, Report of Permanent Heads of Departments and Papers laid before conference, Appendix to the Journals of the*

*House of Representatives* (hereafter *AJHR*), 1893, F-4.

65 Davison, *The Unforgiving Minute*, pp. 70–71.

66 Schivelbusch, *The Railway Journey*, p. 44. An international meridian conference held in Washington in October 1884, attended by 41 delegates from 25 countries, determined it was desirable for a single world meridian to replace numerous ones then in existence and that Greenwich be adopted as the 'initial meridian'. See *New York Times*, 15 October 1884, p. 5; *Science*, vol. 4, no. 89 (17 October 1884), pp. 376–78, vol. 4, no. 90 (24 October 1884), p. 406, and vol. 4, no. 91 (31 October 1884), p. 421. Countries gradually adopted the Greenwich meridian although with inconsistent application for several years. For examples, see John Milne, 'Civil Time', *Geographical Journal*, vol. 13, no. 2 (February 1899), pp. 173–94.

67 C. A. Bayly, *The Birth of the Modern World 1780–1914* (Oxford: Blackwell Publishing, 2004), pp. 17, 51.

68 Pawson, 'Local times and standard time in New Zealand', p. 278.

69 Rollo Arnold, *New Zealand's Burning: The Settlers' World in the Mid 1880s* (Wellington: Victoria University Press, 1994), p. 123.

70 David Harvey, 'Between Space and Time: Reflections on the Geographical Imagination', *Annals of the Association of American Geographers*, vol. 80, no. 3 (September 1990), p. 427.

71 Ibid.

72 J. C. Beaglehole, 'The Development of New Zealand Nationality', *Journal of World History*, vol. II, no. 1 (1954), p. 107.

73 *NZPD*, vol. 5, 1869, p. 522.

74 Neill Atkinson, *Trainland: How Railways Made New Zealand* (Auckland: Random House, 2007), p. 22.

75 William Pember Reeves, *The Long White Cloud (Ao Tea Roa)* (London: George Allen & Unwin, 3rd edn, 1934), p. 239.

76 *Evening Star*, 24 December 1873, p. 2. The newspaper became the *Auckland Evening Star* in 1879 and the *Auckland Star* in 1887.

77 *Otago Daily Times*, 7 September 1878, p. 2.

78 Atkinson, *Trainland*, p. 11.

79 Ian Hunter, *Age of Enterprise: Rediscovering the New Zealand entrepreneur 1880–1910* (Auckland: Auckland University Press, 2007).

80 *Union Steam Ship Company of New Zealand Ltd 1875–1925* (Wellington: published by the company, 1925), p. 11.

81 Sydney D. Waters, *Union Line: A Short History of the Union Steam Ship Company of New Zealand Ltd 1875–1951* (Wellington: author, 1951), p. 7.

82 Gavin McLean, *The Southern Octopus: The rise of a shipping empire* (Wellington: New Zealand Ship and Marine Society and the Wellington Harbour Board Maritime Museum, 1990), p. 12.

83 *Graphic*, 19 November 1887, p. 561.

84 By the Reserve Bank inflation calculator, £18 in 1887 was worth about $3,500 in 2011.

85 *Evening Post*, 24 January 1936, p. 11.

86 For an overview of the development phase of telephones, see Wilson, *Wire & Wireless*, pp. 58–61.

87 Ibid., pp. 61–62.

88 See, for example, *Evening Post*, 4 February 1878, p. 2, 11 February 1878, p. 2; *Timaru Herald*, 12 February 1878, p. 4; *Tuapeka Times*, 20 February 1878, p. 3; *Nelson Evening Mail*, 20 March 1878, p. 2; *West Coast Times*, 25 March 1878, p. 2; *Marlborough Express*, 6 April 1878, p. 5.

89 That is, lines to the equivalent of 170 km were laid out in the one building. For Lemon's biography, see Scholefield, *A Dictionary of New Zealand Biography*, vol. 1, p. 493.

90 *Evening Post*, 23 April 1878, p. 2.

91 *NZPD*, vol. 36, 21 July 1880, p. 389.

92 Ibid.

93 Ibid., vol. 43, 28 August 1882, p. 583.

94 *AJHR*, 1882, F-1, p. ix.

95 Ibid.

96 Ibid.

97 *AJHR*, 1903, F-1, p. xxi.

98 *New Zealand Herald*, 17 March 1925, p. 3.

99 Ibid., 18 March 1925, p. 10.

## Two  The Press Stirred into New Life

1 Arnold, *New Zealand's Burning*, p. 220.

2 Ibid.

3 Ibid.

4 Scholefield, *Newspapers in New Zealand*, p. 10.

5 Scholefield, *A Dictionary of New Zealand Biography*, vol. 2, p. 381. A. S. Thomson, *The Story of New Zealand*, vol. III, part II (London: John Murray, 1859), p. 68.

6 Hutchison, James, 1867–1946, Reminiscences, MS-Papers-5341, Alexander Turnbull Library, p. 18.

7 D. R. Harvey, 'The Power of the Press in Colonial New Zealand: More Imagined than Real?', *BSANZ Bulletin*, vol. 20, no. 2 (second quarter 1996), pp. 132–33.

8 Ibid.

9 Arnold, *New Zealand's Burning*, pp. 233–34.

10 Scholefield, *Newspapers in New Zealand*, p. 6.

11   *New Zealand Official Year-Book 1905*
     (Wellington: Government Printer, 1905),
     p. 82.
12   C. F. Hursthouse, *An Account of the Settlement
     of New Plymouth in New Zealand, from
     personal observation, during a residence there
     of five years* (London: Smith, Elder & Co,
     1849), quoted in *Evening Post*, 9 June 1928,
     p. 8; see also Hursthouse obituary, *Evening
     Post*, 23 November 1876, p. 2.
13   Karl du Fresne, *The Right to Know: News
     media freedom in New Zealand* (Wellington:
     Newspaper Publishers' Association, 2005),
     p. 9.
14   Scholefield, unpublished autobiography,
     MS-Copy-Micro-0468, Alexander Turnbull
     Library, p. 55.
15   Ibid., p. 57.
16   Patrick Day, *The Making of the New Zealand
     Press 1840–1880: A Study of the Organizational
     and Political Concerns of New Zealand
     Newspaper Controllers* (Wellington: Victoria
     University Press, 1990), p. 111.
17   Ian Hunter, *Age of Enterprise: Rediscovering
     the New Zealand Entrepreneur 1880–1910*
     (Auckland: Auckland University Press,
     2007), p. 55.
18   Ibid., p. 34.
19   Raewyn Dalziel, *Julius Vogel: Business
     Politician* (Auckland: Auckland University
     Press/Oxford University Press, 1986), p. 13;
     Scholefield, *Newspapers in New Zealand*,
     p. 173.
20   Scholefield, *Newspapers in New Zealand*,
     pp. 170–71.
21   For Cutten biographical details, see
     Scholefield, *A Dictionary of New Zealand
     Biography*, vol. 1, p. 188.
22   The Most Rev. Francis Redwood, SM,
     *Reminiscences of Early Days in New Zealand*
     (Wellington: author, 1922), p. 9.
23   David Burn (1805–1875) diary, quoted in
     D. R. Harvey, 'Editors and Compositors:
     Contemporary Accounts of the
     Nineteenth-Century New Zealand Press',
     BSANZ *Bulletin*, vol. 14, no. 3 (April 1991),
     p. 109. Burn, a former British naval officer
     who came to New Zealand via Tasmania,
     worked on the *Southern Cross*, the *New-
     Zealander*, the *Auckland Register* and the *New
     Zealand Herald*. See Scholefield, *Newspapers
     in New Zealand*, pp. 77, 81, 83, 258.
24   '100 Years of News, 1863–1963', *New Zealand
     Herald* magazine, 13 November 1963, p. 4.
25   *Evening Star* Centenary Edition, 1 May 1963,
     p. 10.
26   *Evening Post*, 8 February 1915, p. 14.
27   Scholefield, *Newspapers in New Zealand*,
     p. 11.
28   R. B. O'Neill, *The Press 1861–1961*
     (Christchurch: Christchurch Press
     Company, 1963), p. 65.
29   Ibid., pp. 66–67. The cost of press telegrams
     initially varied according to distance.
     In 1866, telegrams between Nelson and
     Picton were four shillings for each hundred
     words, but for telegrams between Nelson
     and Bluff the cost was 12s 6d (twelve shil-
     lings and sixpence) for each hundred words.
     A universal rate of 1s 6d for the first ten
     words and 6d for each additional ten was
     adopted in 1869. The basic rate was reduced
     to 6d for ten words in 1870 and to 6d for 25
     words in 1872. By 1890, a night rate of 6d for
     each hundred words had been introduced
     and evening papers were allowed a limited
     volume at that rate during the day. Overseas
     news was distributed at 6d for each hundred
     words. Scholefield, *Newspapers in New
     Zealand*, p. 13.
30   Day, *Making of the New Zealand Press*,
     pp. 192–93.
31   James Sanders, *Dateline-NZPA: The New
     Zealand Press Association 1880–1980*
     (Auckland: Wilson & Horton, 1980), p. 2.
32   Day, *Making of the New Zealand Press*, p. 211.
33   *Otago Daily Times*, 3 October 1870, p. 2.
34   Australian-born lawyer George Burnett
     Barton was the elder brother of the first
     Australian federal prime minister, Edmund
     Barton. See John M. Ward, 'Barton,
     George Burnett (1836–1901)', *Australian
     Dictionary of Biography* <www.adb.online.
     anu.edu.au>.
35   *Otago Witness*, 15 October 1870, p. 1.
36   Dalziel, *Julius Vogel*, p. 87.
37   R. M. Burdon, *The Life and Times of Sir Julius
     Vogel* (Christchurch: The Caxton Press,
     1948), p. 69.
38   A condensed version of evidence given at
     both hearings, plus speeches and other
     material related to the case, including the
     original articles appearing in the *Otago Daily
     Times* and the *Independent*, was published by
     Barton as *The Telegraph Libel Case. Report of
     Proceedings in the Resident Magistrate's Court,
     Dunedin, on the hearing of the charges of libel
     brought by the General Government of New
     Zealand against Mr George Burnett Barton
     in the case of Regina v. Barton* (Dunedin:
     published by the compiler, 1871).
39   *Evening Post*, 23 May 1871, p. 2.
40   Day, *Making of the New Zealand Press*, p. 210.
41   Ibid.
42   John Davies Ormond to Sir Donald
     McLean, 29 February 1872, Papers of Sir
     Donald McLean, MS-Papers-0032-0485,
     Alexander Turnbull Library. McLean was
     Minister of Native Affairs and Ormond his
     successor as superintendent of Hawke's Bay.

See Scholefield, *A Dictionary of New Zealand Biography*, vol. 2, pp. 33–35, 137.

43  *Cyclopedia of New Zealand (Otago and Southland provincial districts)* (Christchurch: The Cyclopedia Company, 1905), pp. 228–29.

44  Sanders, *Dateline-NZPA*, pp. 4–5.

45  Ibid.

46  O'Neill, *The Press 1861–1961*, p. 71.

47  Telegraph Department Annual Report, *AJHR*, 1873, vol. 2, F-7.

48  O'Neill, *The Press 1861–1961*, pp. 72–73. See also *Memorandum of Association and Articles of Association of New Zealand Press Association Ltd* (Wellington: NZPA, 1960), pp. 3–5.

49  Sanders, *Dateline-NZPA*, pp. 129–57.

50  Scholefield, *Newspapers in New Zealand*, p. 15. The NZPA was a co-operative venture owned by daily newspapers. The consolidation of newspaper ownership which culminated in two main groups led to the NZPA's closure in 2011.

51  Arnold, *New Zealand's Burning*, p. 226.

52  O'Neill, *The Press 1861–1961*, p. 110.

53  Scholefield, *A Dictionary of New Zealand Biography*, vol. 2, p. 260.

54  Scholefield, unpublished autobiography, p. 142.

55  Ibid., p. 147.

56  Ibid. Barnicoat was also an accomplished climber with experience in the Southern Alps. See Sally Irwin, *Between Heaven and Earth: The Life of a Mountaineer, Freda du Faur* (Melbourne: White Crane Press, 2000), p. 98.

57  Scholefield, *Newspapers in New Zealand*, p. 233.

58  *Timaru Herald*, 15 July 1865, pp. 3, 4.

59  Ibid., 15 July 1895, pp. 3, 4.

60  *Evening Post*, 8 February 1915, p. 13.

61  *Press*, 25 May 1861, p. 1.

62  Leslie Verry, *Seven Days a Week: The Story of Independent Newspapers Ltd* (Wellington: INL Print, 1985), p. 18.

63  Scholefield, unpublished autobiography, p. 118.

64  Ibid., p. 117.

65  Ibid. For J. T. Paul details, see G. H. Scholefield, ed., *Who's Who in New Zealand and the Western Pacific* (Wellington: Rangatira Press, 1932), p. 281; for Robert Hogg, see Scholefield, *Newspapers in New Zealand*, pp. 41, 43; for Lane, see Gavin Souter, 'Lane, William (1861–1917)', *Australian Dictionary of Biography* <www.adb.online.anu.edu.au>; see also Ed Wright, *Lost and Found in History: Ghost Colonies – Failed utopias, forgotten exiles and abandoned outposts of empire* (Sydney: Pier 9, 2009).

66  Verry, *Seven Days a Week*, p. 17. Verry was

no mere hired chronicler of the history of the Independent Newspapers Ltd stable. He worked for the NZPA from 1940 until 1979, was its managing editor from 1964 until 1975, and general manager from 1975 to 1979. See Sanders, *Dateline-NZPA*, p. 201.

67  Verry, *Seven Days a Week*, p. 18.

68  Hutchison, Reminiscences, pp. 48–49.

69  G. H. Scholefield, *The Richmond–Atkinson Papers*, vol. 2 (Wellington: R. E. Owen, Government Printer, 1960), p. 571.

70  Scholefield, *Newspapers in New Zealand*, p. 38.

71  Ibid., pp. 38–39. The paper later dropped its political affiliation, and its chairman, Sir Donald McGavin, told the annual meeting in 1951 it had no need 'to follow the sometimes vacillating course pursued by modern politicians'. See Scholefield, *Newspapers in New Zealand*, p. 40.

72  Ibid., p. 17.

73  Ross Harvey, 'Ives, Joseph, 1844–1919', *Dictionary of New Zealand Biography*, vol. 2 (Wellington: Bridget Williams Books and Department of Internal Affairs, 1993), pp. 240–41.

74  Scholefield, *Newspapers in New Zealand*, pp. 49–50; Timothy McIvor, *The Rainmaker: A Biography of John Ballance, Journalist and Politician 1839–1893* (Auckland: Heinemann Reed, 1989), pp. 20–22.

75  Wilson, *Wire & Wireless*, p. 46.

76  Scholefield, *Newspapers in New Zealand*, p. 83.

77  Ibid., pp. 85–86.

78  Ibid., p. 89.

79  Ibid., p. 84.

80  This was a slight adaptation of a poem, 'What I Live For', by Isabella Banks (née Varley) (sometimes known as Mrs G. Linnaeus Banks), published in 1844. See Isabella Varley, *Ivy Leaves: A Collection of Poems* (London: Simpkin Marshall, 1844); see also Florence S. Boos, 'The Poetics of the Working Classes', *Victorian Poetry*, vol. 39, no. 2 (Summer 2001), pp. 103–109. The only change the *Star* made to Varley's words was to use the collective pronoun in the last line instead of the personal.

81  Scholefield, *A Dictionary of New Zealand Biography*, vol. 1, pp. 496–97.

82  Ibid., p. 497.

83  'Report of the Royal Commission on Federation, together with Minutes of Proceedings and Evidence, and Appendices', *AJHR*, 1902, A-4.

84  *Observer*, 28 July 1906, p. 18.

85  Ibid., 15 December 1906, p. 25.

86  Numerous books, articles and theses cover the 'birth of a nation' aspect of Gallipoli.

See, in particular, Christopher Pugsley, *Gallipoli: The New Zealand Story* (Auckland: Hodder & Stoughton, 1984) and *The Anzac Experience: New Zealand, Australia and Empire in the First World War* (Auckland: Reed, 2004); John F. Williams, *Anzacs, the Media and the Great War* (Sydney: University of New South Wales Press, 1999); C. E. W. Bean, *The Story of Anzac: The Official History of Australia in the War of 1914–1918*, vol. 1 (St Lucia, Queensland: University of Queensland Press in association with the Australian War Memorial, 1981); Jenny Macleod, *Reconsidering Gallipoli* (Manchester: Manchester University Press, 2004); George Frederick Davis, 'Anzac Day meanings and memories: New Zealand, Australian and Turkish perspectives on a day of commemoration in the twentieth century', PhD thesis, University of Otago, 2008; Ron Palenski, 'Malcolm Ross: a forgotten casualty of the Great War', MA thesis, University of Otago, 2007.

87   Constance Clyde was the pen-name for Glasgow-born Constance McAdam, who began in journalism with the *Otago Daily Times*, then worked for the *Bulletin* in Sydney and the *Evening News* in London. She wrote one novel, *A Pagan's Love* (London: T. Fisher Unwin, 1905) and collaborated with Alan Mulgan in *New Zealand, Country and People* (Auckland: Whitcombe & Tombs, 1925). See A. G. Bagnall, *New Zealand National Bibliography*, vol. 3 (Wellington: Government Printer, 1972), p. 116; George Griffiths, *Southern Writers in Disguise: A miscellany of journalistic and literary pseudonyms* (Dunedin: Otago Heritage Books, 1998), p. 31; Heather Roberts, *Where Did She Come From? New Zealand Women Novelists 1862–1987* (Wellington: Allen & Unwin/Port Nicholson Press, 1989), p. 10.

88   *The Times*, 22 February 1927, p. xxii.

89   J. E. Traue, *New Zealand Studies: A Guide to Bibliographic Resources* (Wellington: Victoria University Press, 1985), p. 12. See also D. R. Harvey, who quotes Traue, 'Newspapers', in Keith Maslen, ed., *Book & Print in New Zealand: A Guide to Print Culture in Aotearoa* (Wellington: Victoria University Press, 1997) <www.nzetc.org/tm/scholarly/tei-GriBook.html>.

90   O'Neill, *The Press 1861–1961*, pp. 46–50.

91   Ibid., p. 16.

92   Ibid., p. 49.

93   O. T. J. Alpers, *Cheerful Yesterdays* (London: John Murray, 1928), pp. 84–100, 102.

94   J. C. Reid, 'A False Literary Dawn', *New Zealand's Heritage*, vol. 4, part 57 (Wellington: Paul Hamlyn, 1972), p. 1593.

95   Ibid.

96   Sir Robert Stout, 'The Rise and Progress of New Zealand', in Thomas Bracken, *Musings in Maoriland: A Jubilee Volume* (Dunedin: Arthur T. Keirle, 1890), p. 19.

97   P. A. Lawlor, *Books and Bookmen* (Wellington: Whitcombe & Tombs, 1954), p. 161.

98   Jessie Mackay, 'The Burial of Sir John McKenzie', quoted in Lawlor, *Books and Bookmen*, p. 163.

99   Lawlor, *Books and Bookmen*, p. 171.

100   Scholefield, *A Dictionary of New Zealand Biography*, vol. 1, p. 85.

101   W. F. Alexander and A. E. Currie, *New Zealand Verse* (London: Walter Scott Publishing, 1906); Scholefield, *Newspapers in New Zealand*, p. 40.

102   Scholefield, *A Dictionary of New Zealand Biography*, vol. 1, pp. 214–16; Edmund Bohan, *Edward Stafford: New Zealand's First Statesman* (Christchurch: Hazard Press, 1994), p. 37.

103   Scholefield, *Newspapers in New Zealand*, p. 157; E. A. Horsman, ed., *The Diary of Alfred Domett 1872–1885* (London: Oxford University Press, 1953); Jane Stafford, 'Alfred Domett, Robert Browning and a Dream of Two Lives', *Journal of New Zealand Literature*, no. 21 (2003), pp. 32–53.

104   John Woolford and David Karlin, *The Poems of Browning*, vol. II (London: Longman, 1991), pp. 143–54.

105   Reeves, *The Long White Cloud (Ao Tea Roa)*; Alan Mulgan, *Great Days in New Zealand Writing* (Wellington: A. H. & A. W. Reed, 1962), p. 33.

106   Mulgan, *Great Days in New Zealand Writing*, p. 40.

107   *Otago Witness*, 27 August 1902, p. 56.

108   Dalziel, *Julius Vogel*, p. 39. Braddon was a sister of Edward ('Ned') Braddon, who became premier of Tasmania; Ned Braddon's son Henry spent some time working in Invercargill and played rugby for New Zealand before returning to Australia. Both father and son were knighted.

109   Griffiths, *Southern Writers in Disguise*, p. 48.

110   Ibid., p. 124.

111   Sir Julius Vogel, *Anno Domini; or, Woman's Destiny* (London: Hutchinson & Co, 1889).

112   Alexander and Currie, *New Zealand Verse*, p. xv.

113   Ibid., pp. xxiv–xxv.

114   Scholefield, unpublished autobiography, p. 99.

115   B. G. Andrew and Ann-Mari Jordens, 'Adams, Arthur Henry (1872–1936)', *Australian Dictionary of Biography* <www.adb.online.anu.edu.au>.

116   David McKee Wright, 'We're Going

A Rhyming Again', *Otago Witness*, 13 July 1899, p. 63.

117 Michael Sharkey, 'Wright, David McKee (1869–1928)', *Australian Dictionary of Biography* <www.adb.online.anu.edu. au>; Sharkey, 'David McKee Wright, Maorilander', *Journal of New Zealand Literature*, no. 10 (1992), pp. 35–55.

118 Scholefield, *A Dictionary of New Zealand Biography*, vol. 1, pp. 454–55.

119 Lawlor, *Confessions of a Journalist*, pp. 180–82. See also Michael Thornton, 'Bolitho, (Henry) Hector (1897–1974)', *Oxford Dictionary of National Biography* <www. oxforddnb.com>.

120 Patricia Keep, 'Allan, Stella May (1871–1962)', *Australian Dictionary of Biography* <www.adb.online.anu.edu.au>.

121 Ibid. Allan's sister, Elizabeth McCombs, became the first woman member of the New Zealand House of Representatives in 1933.

122 Ross was once described as 'talented and vivacious'. *New Zealand Truth*, 17 March 1927, p. 6.

123 Ibid., 10 April 1915, p. 3. See also Mrs Malcolm Ross, *Round the World With a Fountain Pen: The Log of a Lady Journalist* (Wellington: Blundell Brothers, 1913); *Mixed Grill* (Wellington: Whitcombe & Tombs, 1934). Forrestina Ross contributed a poem to her husband's book about the Duke of York's visit to New Zealand in 1901. See Malcolm Ross, *The Duke in Southern Isles: New Zealand's Loyal Welcome* (Wellington: McKee & Co, 1901).

124 J. O. C. Phillips, 'Musings in Maoriland – or was there a *Bulletin* school in New Zealand?', *Australian Historical Studies*, vol. 20, no. 81 (October 1983), pp. 520–35. For the emergence of art as a reflection of New Zealand identity, see Francis Pound, *The Invention of New Zealand: Art and National Identity 1930–1970* (Auckland: Auckland University Press, 2009). Although this work concentrates on the 1930s and beyond, see pp. 4–5 for 'earlier nationalisms'.

125 Reid, 'A False Literary Dawn', p. 1595. Even allowing for the difficulty in determining precisely who qualified as New Zealanders and who did not, the total nevertheless makes the point that the *Bulletin* was as much a 'bible' for New Zealanders as it was for Australians.

126 *Observer*, 1 February 1890, p. 1.

127 G. A. K. Baughen, 'Baeyertz, Charles Nalder, 1866–1943', *Dictionary of New Zealand Biography*, vol. 2 (Wellington: Bridget Williams Books and the Department of Internal Affairs, 1993), p. 19. Scholefield's *Dictionary* had no entry for Baeyertz.

128 M. H. Holcroft, 'Baeyertz of the *Triad*', *New Zealand's Heritage*, vol. 5, part 69 (1972), p. 1924.

129 Dennis McEldowney, 'Morton, Frank, 1869–1923', *Dictionary of New Zealand Biography*, vol. 3 (Wellington: Auckland University Press with Bridget Williams Books and the Department of Internal Affairs, 1996), p. 351.

130 Holcroft, 'Baeyertz of the *Triad*', p. 1925.

131 Ibid., pp. 1927–28.

132 Robin Hyde, *Journalese* (Auckland: National Printing Company, 1934), pp. 21–22.

133 Holcroft, 'Baeyertz of the *Triad*', p. 1928.

134 Hyde, *Journalese*, p. 11.

135 *Otago Witness*, 20 July 1899, p. 61.

136 *Evening Post*, 8 February 1915, pp. 13–23; '100 Years of News, 1863–1963', *New Zealand Herald* magazine, 13 November 1963; 'Daily for 100 Years', *Evening Star* (Dunedin), 1 May 1963; Karl du Fresne, *The Dom 1907–2007: A Century of News* (Wellington: Dominion Post, 2007).

137 *Evening Post*, 8 February 1865, p. 2. Read 'mothers on Mrs Partington' as 'blathers on [like] Mrs Partington' and the first sentence makes more sense to the modern ear. 'Mrs Partington' was an American version of the English error-prone Mrs Malaprop: Benjamin Shillaber, *Life and Sayings of Mrs Partington and Others of the Family* (New York: J. C. Derby, 1854).

138 See Arnold, *New Zealand's Burning*, p. 220.

139 *Tuapeka Times*, 6 December 1876, pp. 1, 2.

140 Scholefield, *Newspapers in New Zealand*, p. 203.

141 *Southern News and Foveaux Straits' Herald*, 16 February 1861, p. 1.

142 D. R. Harvey, 'Economic Aspects of Nineteenth-Century New Zealand Newspapers', *BSANZ Bulletin*, vol. 17, no. 2 (second quarter 1993), pp. 55–78.

143 *Otago Witness*, 8 February 1851, 23 December 1865, 24 December 1870, 18 December 1880.

144 *Evening Post*, 8 February 1865, 23 December 1870, 24 December 1890, 24 December 1900.

145 Joseph M. Torsella, 'American National Identity, 1750–1790: Samples from the Popular Press', *The Pennsylvania Magazine of History and Biography*, vol. 112, no. 2 (April 1988), p. 169.

146 Ibid., pp. 168–69.

147 See I. G. C. Hutchison, 'Scottish Newspapers and Scottish National Identity in the Nineteenth and Twentieth Centuries', address to International

Federation of Library Associations and Institutions, Glasgow, August 2002.

148 Rod Brookes, 'Newspapers and national identity: the BSE/CJD crisis and the British press', *Media, Culture and Society*, vol. 21 (1999), p. 249.

*Three The Symbols of 'Godzone'*

1 Ewan Morris, *Our Own Devices: National Symbols and Political Conflict in Twentieth-Century Ireland* (Dublin: Irish Academic Press, 2005), p. 4.

2 John Tosh, *The Pursuit of History* (London: Pearson Education, 2006), pp. 176–78; Fritz Stern, *The Varieties of History from Voltaire to the Present* (London: Meridian Books, 1957), pp. 57–58; Marnie Hughes-Warrington, *Fifty Key Thinkers on History* (London: Routledge, 2008), pp. 293–300.

3 Karen A. Cerulo, 'Symbols and the World System: National Anthems and Flags', *Sociological Forum*, vol. 8, no. 2 (June 1993), p. 243. Disraeli was speaking at a meeting in Manchester in 1866 and may have used the word 'individualities' rather than 'individuals'. See Emily Morison Beck, ed., *Bartlett's Familiar Quotations: A collection of passages, phrases and proverbs traced to their sources in ancient and modern literature* (Boston: Little, Brown, 125th anniversary edn, 1980), p. 502.

4 Cerulo, 'Symbols and the World System', pp. 243–44.

5 Morris, *Our Own Devices*, p. 4.

6 John Andrews, *No Other Home Than This: A History of European New Zealanders* (Nelson: Craig Potton Publishing, 2009), p. 242.

7 Cerulo, 'Symbols and the World System', p. 244.

8 Thomas Bracken, *God's Own Country and Other Poems* (Wellington: Brown, Thomas & Co, 1893). The phrase was used about California in the 1860s apparently, but never stuck.

9 *Observer*, 23 February 1907, p. 5.

10 Ibid. It may be possible, however, to nail the phrase down a little more closely. An unidentified writer from Dunedin who in 1888 undertook the Union Steam Ship Company's 'Round Trip' from Wellington to Bluff via North Island east coast ports, Auckland, Sydney and Melbourne wrote about his travels for the *Otago Witness* and reported meeting a Dunedin acquaintance in Sydney rather than Melbourne. 'Ah old man', the acquaintance was quoted as saying, 'this is the place to make money in; but for a place to enjoy life, give me God's

own country – New Zealand'. *Otago Witness*, 30 March 1888, p. 16.

11 *Auckland Star*, 15 June 1892, originally in the *Ohinemuri Gazette*, reprinted in Rona Bailey and Herbert Roth, eds, *Shanties by the way: A selection of New Zealand popular songs and ballads* (Christchurch: Whitcombe & Tombs, 1967), pp. 82–83. Nicodemus was a secret disciple of Christ's who provided his tomb.

12 Bracken, *Musings in Maoriland: A Jubilee Volume*, p. 19.

13 Ibid., p. 194.

14 *Saturday Advertiser and New Zealand Literary Miscellany*, 1 July 1876, quoted in George Griffiths, *The National Anthem* (Dunedin: Granville Books, 1977).

15 Griffiths, *The National Anthem*, p. 2; Max Cryer, *Hear Our Voices We Entreat: The Extraordinary Story of New Zealand's National Anthems* (Auckland: Exisle Publishing, 2004), p. 42; press statement by the Minister of Internal Affairs, Allan Highet, 21 November 1977.

16 *Tuapeka Times*, 9 December 1876, p. 3.

17 Ibid., 23 December 1876, p. 3.

18 Grey had heard the anthem sung by schoolchildren in Lawrence and cabled Bracken: 'I have just heard for the first time by 600 children at Lawrence your New Zealand anthem. I admire it exceedingly.' Quoted in *Otago Daily Times*, 12 March 1878, clipping in Woods, John Joseph, Papers re musical composition 'God Defend New Zealand', MS-Papers-0355, Alexander Turnbull Library.

19 Most reports say the song was adopted in 1940, but approval came earlier than that. A report on the New Zealand centennial in the Department of Internal Affairs annual report to the year ended 31 March 1939 recorded that a meeting of the National Centennial Council on 8 December 1938 recommended the adoption. The report noted the recommendation was approved by the government. 'New Zealand Centennial 1940', Department of Internal Affairs annual report, *AJHR*, 1939, vol. 3, H-22, p. 2.

20 See Griffiths, *The National Anthem*; Cryer, *Hear Our Voices*; Supplement to *New Zealand Listener*, 21 June 1940; *Supplement to the New Zealand Gazette*, 17 November 1977; Highet, press statement.

21 *Supplement to the New Zealand Gazette*, 31 May 1979; it became common practice after 1977 for 'God Save the Queen' to be played only at functions specifically involving the monarch or her representative in New Zealand, the governor-general. Although

'God Defend New Zealand' did not gain the status of national anthem until 1977, it was played at New Zealand victory ceremonies at the Olympic Games in 1952, 1972 and 1976. Strangely, both the British and New Zealand anthems were played when Yvette Williams won New Zealand's only gold medal at the Olympic Games in Helsinki in 1952. See Yvette Corlett, letter to author, 1 January 2002, Yvette Williams box, New Zealand Sports Hall of Fame. The Empire (now Commonwealth) Games were quicker off the mark with the New Zealand anthem. At the first games in 1930, New Zealanders were serenaded with the English 'Land of Hope and Glory'; at the second in 1934 it was the British national anthem; but in Sydney in 1938, 'God Defend New Zealand' was played. See entry 22 August 1930, diary of Jack MacDonald, author's collection; Allan Thomas, 'Centennial Music', in William Renwick, ed., *Creating a National Spirit: Celebrating New Zealand's Centennial* (Wellington: Victoria University Press, 2004), p. 237 (Thomas related which music was played at the 1934 and 1938 games though wrongly sited the latter in Glasgow).

22 *Nelson Evening Mail*, 10 November 1877, p. 2.

23 *Timaru Herald*, 27 May 1885, p. 2; *New Zealand Tablet*, 23 July 1880, p. 17; *Te Aroha News*, 12 November 1887, p. 2; *Taranaki Herald*, 9 December 1899, p. 2.

24 *Evening Post*, 9 December 1887, p. 2.

25 James Belich, *Paradise Reforged: A History of the New Zealanders from the 1880s to the Year 2000* (hereafter *Paradise Reforged*) (Auckland: Allen Lane, the Penguin Press, 2001), p. 331.

26 *Auckland Star Weekend Pictorial*, 9 April 1938, p. 2.

27 Cryer, *Hear Our Voices*, pp. 20–28.

28 William Pember Reeves, 'New Zealand', in *The Long White Cloud (Ao Tea Roa)*, p. 21.

29 *Otago Daily Times*, 12 February 1874, p. 5.

30 *Star*, 26 February 1874, p. 2.

31 Jim Fletcher, 'McCormick, Peter Dodds (1834?–1916)', *Australian Dictionary of Biography* <www.adb.online.anu.edu.au>.

32 Gilles Potvin, 'Lavallée, Calixa', *Dictionary of Canadian Biography* <www.biographi.ca>.

33 Such thoughts were not exclusive to the periphery of the Empire, though, as the Welsh hymn, 'Hen Wlad fy Nhadau' – written by a father and son, Evan and James James, in 1856 – similarly praised what was distinctive about the country rather than what was imposed from outside. See David Smith and Gareth Williams, *Fields of Praise* (Cardiff: University of Wales Press, 1980), pp. 153–54.

34 For background on the development of flags, see Alfred Znamierowski, *The World Enyclopedia of Flags: The definitive guide to international flags, banners, standards and ensigns* (London: Hermes House, 2002), pp. 8–23.

35 *Otago Witness*, 26 October 1899, p. 11.

36 Ibid., p. 23.

37 *NZPD*, vol. 114, p. 57.

38 For background on the various flags used in New Zealand, see A. H. McLintock, ed., *An Encyclopaedia of New Zealand*, vol. 1 (Wellington: R. E. Owen, Government Printer, 1966), pp. 693–703; W. A. Glue, *New Zealand Ensign* (Wellington: Government Printer, 1965); 'New Zealand Flag', Ministry for Culture and Heritage website <www.mch.govt.nz/nzflag/>; Henare Broughton, 'Te Hakituatahi o Aotearoa – 1835 (First Flag of New Zealand)', *New Zealand Official Yearbook 2002* (Auckland: David Bateman, 2002), p. 60.

39 McLintock, *An Encyclopaedia of New Zealand*, p. 696.

40 *NZPD*, vol. 111, pp. 321–22. The Hennessy reference was presumably to a labelling device used by the French–Irish cognac-producing company.

41 Ibid., p. 322.

42 *NZPD*, vol. 114, p. 58.

43 *Otago Witness*, 21 October 1899, p. 5.

44 *NZPD*, vol. 114, pp. 60–61.

45 *Otago Witness*, 26 September 1900, p. 24; *New Zealand Observer*, 29 September 1900, p. 1.

46 *AJHR*, 1901, vol. 1, A-1, pp. 17–20. It is not possible to know how much the enmity between the two men influenced this disagreement. See R. M. Burdon, *King Dick: A biography of Richard John Seddon* (Wellington: Whitcombe & Tombs, 1955), p. 165.

47 *NZPD*, vol. 119, pp. 1163–64.

48 The following year, on 28 February 1903, the King approved the similar Australian flag. Its Southern Cross stars are white and the six-pointed 'federation star' sits under the Union Jack. See Geoff Hocking, *The Australian Flag* (Melbourne: Five Mile Press, 2002), p. 6. Each of the Australian states retains the Union Jack in the canton of their flags, as do three of the Canadian provinces; the United States flag was originally based on the Union Jack and nine former British-governed states retain the Union Jack in the canton of their national flags. See Znamierowski, *The World Enyclopedia of Flags*, pp. 130–214.

49 Andrews, *No Other Home Than This*, p. 242.

50 *Dominion*, 15 July 1925, p. 10.

51 *Wellington Independent*, 4 October 1866,

p. 4. The 1866 mace, presented by the first Speaker, Sir Charles Clifford, was destroyed in the parliamentary fire in 1907 and was replaced in 1909 by the mace still in use. See John E. Martin, *The House: New Zealand's House of Representatives 1854–2004* (Palmerston North: Dunmore Press, 2004), pp. 15, 136.

52 H. W. Orsman, ed., *Dictionary of New Zealand English* (Auckland: Oxford University Press, 1997), p. 413. See also Ernest McKinlay, *Ways and By-Ways of a Singing Kiwi: With the N.Z. Divisional Entertainers in France, Belgium, Germany, 1916–1919* (Dunedin: David M. Lister, 1939).

53 *New Zealand Gazette*, 23 June 1892, p. 881.

54 Alexander Bathgate, *Colonial Experiences* (Glasgow: John Machlehose, 1874; reprint Capper Press, Christchurch, 1974), p. 83. This was a pronunciation favoured by Māori south of the Waitaki, especially Ngāti Māmoe, Waitaha and Rāpuwai. Anecdotal evidence is that the area of Invercargill known as Waikiwi was pronounced 'Waikivi' by Māori and Pākehā alike until relatively recent years.

55 'Notes of a Journey Through a Part of the Middle Island of New Zealand', *Nelson Examiner and New Zealand Chronicle*, 5 October 1844, p. 3. See also Sheila Natusch, *Southward Ho! The Deborah in Quest of a New Edinburgh 1844* (Invercargill: Craig Printing and Southland Frozen Meat, 1985).

56 *Otago Witness*, 19 May 1898, p. 53.

57 Morris, *Our Own Devices*, p. 70.

58 Douglas, *Birds* manuscript, quoted in John Pascoe, ed., *Mr. Explorer Douglas* (Wellington: A. H. & A. W. Reed, 1957), p. 225.

59 Ibid., p. 229.

60 *New Zealand Gazette*, 18 August 1892, p. 1209 (huia); 28 September 1893, p. 1415 (weka); 13 September 1894, p. 1444 (tūī); 27 September 1894, p. 1498 (ruru).

61 See Richard Wolfe, *Well Made New Zealand: A Century of Trademarks* (Auckland: Reed Methuen, 1987).

62 *New Zealand Gazette*, 2 February 1893, p. 175; 10 May 1894, p. 739.

63 Peter Gibbons, '"Going Native": A case study of cultural appropriation in a settler society, with particular reference to the activities of Johannes Andersen in New Zealand during the first half of the twentieth century', PhD thesis, University of Waikato, 1992. See also Gibbons, 'Cultural Colonization and National Identity', *NZJH*, vol. 36, no. 1 (2002), pp. 5–17. For the influence of Pākehā interpretations

on Māori lore, see M. P. K. Sorrenson, *Maori Origins and Migrations – the Genesis of Some Pakeha Myths and Legends* (Auckland: Auckland University Press/Oxford University Press, 1979).

64 Gibbons, '"Going Native"', p. 663.

65 Edward W. Said, *Orientalism* (London: Penguin, 2003).

66 For a similar argument to Gibbons', see Terry Goldie, *Fear and Temptation: The image of the Indigene in Canadian, Australian, and New Zealand Literatures* (Montreal: McGill-Queen's University Press, 1989), especially pp. 222–23, in which Goldie argues that a separation between 'native' and 'native New Zealander' will not be erased 'but will become a palimpsest of many meanings'.

67 Wolfe, *Well Made New Zealand*, p. 33. The first portrayal of New Zealanders as kiwis is held to have been in a 1905 cartoon by Trevor Lloyd after the New Zealand rugby team beat England. This may be so, but sometimes it is difficult to discern a difference between cartoonists' kiwis and moas. See John F. Perry, 'Lloyd, Trevor 1863–1937, Artist, illustrator, cartoonist', *Dictionary of New Zealand Biography* (Wellington: Auckland University Press and Department of Internal Affairs, 1996), pp. 277–78.

68 Andrew Spence, 'What "Kiwi" Means', in R. A. Barr, *With the British Rugby Team in Maoriland* (Dunedin: Otago Daily Times and Witness Newspapers, 1908), pp. 54–55.

69 For the value of postage stamps to historians, see Donald M. Reid, 'The Symbolism of Postage Stamps: A Source for the Historian', *Journal of Contemporary History*, vol. 19, no. 2 (April 1984), pp. 223–49. Stamps provide evidence on at least three levels, Reid argues: as physical objects; as proof of postal service; and as 'bearers of symbols, as part of a system of communications'.

70 Eric Pawson, 'The Meanings of Mountains', in Pawson and Tom Brooking, eds, *Environmental Histories of New Zealand* (Melbourne: Oxford University Press, 2002), p. 136.

71 *Evening Post*, 4 January 1898, p. 2.

72 Howard Robinson, *A History of the Post Office in New Zealand* (Wellington: R. E. Owen, Government Printer, 1964), p. 166.

73 Ibid., p. 167.

74 Ibid.

75 S. E. Sleigh, ed., *The New Zealand Rugby Football Annual for 1885* (Dunedin: Otago Daily Times, 1885), p. 4.

76 See 'History of New Zealand Coinage', Reserve Bank of New Zealand website

<http://www.rbnz.govt.nz/currency/money/index.html>; McLintock, *An Encyclopaedia of New Zealand*, pp. 373–74. Imperial acknowledgement continued to be made with the sovereign's head on one side.

77  M. H. Holcroft, 'Mud Pools and Mountain Views', *New Zealand's Heritage: The making of a nation*, vol. 5, part 67 (Wellington: Paul Hamlyn, 1972), p. 1868.

78  Ibid. She was Alice Montgomery before she married the multi-named duke. See E. J. Feuchtwanger, 'Grenville, Richard Plantagenet Campbell Temple-Nugent-Brydges-Chandos-Grenville, third duke of Buckingham and Chandos (1823–1889)', *Oxford Dictionary of National Biography* <www.oxforddnb.com>.

79  Anthony Trollope, *Australia and New Zealand*, vol. II (London: Chapman & Hall, 1873), pp. 469–88.

80  Ibid., pp. 499–500.

81  Margaret McClure, *The Wonder Country: Making New Zealand Tourism* (Auckland: Auckland University Press in association with the New Zealand Tourism Board and the Ministry of Culture and Heritage, 2004), p. 13. See also Ian Rockel, *Taking the Waters: Early Spas in New Zealand* (Wellington: Government Printing Office Publishing, 1986).

82  'Hot Springs District of the North Island', Letter from the Hon. W. Fox to the Hon. the Premier, 1 August 1874, *AJHR*, 1874, vol. 2, H-26, pp. 1–5.

83  McClure, *The Wonder Country*, p. 13.

84  Ibid., pp. 13–14; Douglas Graham, 'Graham, Robert, 1820–1883', *Dictionary of New Zealand Biography*, vol. 1 (Wellington: Allen & Unwin/Department of Internal Affairs, 1990), pp. 156–57.

85  Charles Baeyertz, *Guide to New Zealand, the most wonderful scenic paradise in the world* (Dunedin: Mills, Dick & Co, 1902); for example, James Cowan, *The tourist resorts of New Zealand, Lake Wakatipu and its environs* (Wellington: Department of Tourist and Health Resorts, 1907) and *The Dominion of New Zealand; its characteristics, resources and scenery* (Wellington: Government Printer, 1911); Malcolm Ross, *Aorangi; or, The Heart of the Southern Alps, New Zealand* (Wellington: Government Printer, 1892), *Tourists Guide Book to the Lakes District of Otago* (Dunedin: New Zealand and South Seas Exhibition, 1889).

86  Holcroft, 'Mud Pools and Mountain Views', p. 1871.

87  *Otago Witness*, 13 February 1901, p. 9.

88  Ibid.

89  McClure, *The Wonder Country*, p. 25; while

Reeves' meaning was clear, it is doubtful he used the actual words quoted.

90  Michael Bassett, *Sir Joseph Ward: A Political Biography* (Auckland: Auckland University Press, 1993), p. 118.

91  Ibid.

92  *New Zealand Herald*, 8 January 1901, p. 5.

93  *Progress*, 2 January 1906, p. 64.

94  *New Zealand Illustrated Magazine*, March 1901, p. 426. For biographical details of Donne, see the *Dominion*, 20 February 1945, p. 4.

95  E. S. Dollimore, biographical essay of T. E. Donne, in Dennis, Lawrence Samuel (1915–2000) Papers, MS-Papers-7261-10, Alexander Turnbull Library, p. 7. Dennis was deputy general manager of what was then the Tourist and Publicity Department in 1972, when Dollimore's essay was written.

96  Ibid., p. 6.

97  First Annual Report, Department of Tourist and Health Resorts, *AJHR*, 1902, vol. 3, H-2.

98  *Progress*, 2 January 1906, p. 64.

99  Sixth Annual Report, Tourist and Health Resorts Department, *AJHR*, 1907, vol. 4, H-2, p. 2.

100  Dollimore, biographical essay of T. E. Donne, p. 9.

101  Holcroft, 'Mud Pools and Mountain Views', p. 1872.

102  For background on the exhibition age, see Paul Greenhalgh, *Ephemeral Vistas: The Expositions Universelles, Great Exhibitions and World's Fairs, 1851–1939* (Manchester: Manchester University Press, 1988); Robert W. Rydell, *All the World's A Fair: Visions of Empire at American International Expositions, 1876–1916* (Chicago: University of Chicago Press, 1984). See also John M. MacKenzie, 'Empire and Metropolitan Cultures', in Andrew Porter, ed., *The Oxford History of the British Empire, vol. III, The Nineteenth Century* (Oxford: Oxford University Press, 1999), pp. 282–90.

103  William Schneider, 'Colonies at the 1900 World Fair', *History Today*, vol. 31, issue 5 (May 1981), p. 32.

104  Ibid.

105  Carroll D. Champlin, 'The Cultural Contribution of International Expositions', *Phi Delta Kappan*, vol. 20, no. 4 (December 1937), p. 117.

106  *Otago Witness*, 20 September 1862, p. 7.

107  Ibid.

108  Ibid., 14 January 1865, p. 9.

109  David Hall, 'The age of exhibitions', *New Zealand's Heritage*, vol. 4, part 47, pp. 1313–16.

110  Ibid., p. 1313.

111 Official Catalogue, New Zealand and South Seas International Exhibition, Dunedin 1925–26 (Dunedin: New Zealand and South Seas Exhibition Co, 1925), p. 23.

112 *Lyttelton Times*, 31 October 1888, p. 4.

113 Hall, 'The age of exhibitions', p. 1315.

114 Dollimore, biographical essay of T. E. Donne, p. 11.

115 Ibid.

116 Meg Armstrong, '"A Jumble of Foreignness": The Sublime Musayums of Nineteenth-Century Fairs and Expositions', *Cultural Critique*, no. 23 (Winter 1992–1993), p. 201.

117 Greenhalgh, *Ephemeral Vistas*, p. 94. Schneider also noted that the 1900 World Fair in Paris created a French view of its colonies that continued for years afterward. See Schneider, 'Colonies at the 1900 World Fair', p. 36. Rydell also noted the part exhibitions played in portraying to a home audience a not always accurate view of indigenous people elsewhere; he wrote of the 'comprehensive anthropological exhibition' at the St Louis fair in 1904, which also featured 'anthropological days' at the Olympic Games which coincided with the fair. He quoted a local newspaper as saying: 'The meeting was a grand success from every point of view and served as a good example of what the brown men are capable of doing with training.' See Rydell, *All the World's A Fair*, pp. 154–83.

118 *Star*, 15 August 1893, p. 1.

119 Jock Phillips, 'Exhibiting Ourselves: The Exhibition and National Identity', in John Mansfield Thomson, ed., *Farewell Colonialism: The New Zealand International Exhibition, Christchurch, 1906–07* (Palmerston North: Dunmore Press, 1998), p. 17.

120 Ibid., p. 18.

121 Morris quoted Eric Hobsbawm as saying the crucial element in developing social solidarity 'seems to have been the invention of emotionally and symbolically charged signs of club membership rather than the statutes and objects of the club'. Morris, *Our Own Devices*, p. 5.

122 Ibid., p. 70.

123 Cowan thought the best lines were contained in the last verse of Bracken's anthem: 'May our mountains ever be / Freedom's ramparts on the sea / Make us faithful unto thee – / God defend our free land.' 'There is a touch of Welsh mountain symbolism in those lines', he wrote. *Auckland Star Weekend Pictorial*, 9 April 1938, p. 2.

124 Of the 54 mountains in Colorado that are 14,000 feet (4267 metres) or more above sea level, Kevin S. Blake wrote how they are 'increasingly popular as environmental icons in place attachment at national, regional, state and local scales'. They influence, he thought, how Americans identify with nature. Blake, 'Colorado Fourteeners and the Nature of Place Identity', *The Geographical Review*, vol. 92, no. 2 (April 2002), p. 155.

125 Phillips, 'Exhibiting Ourselves', p. 18. By sport, Dollimore meant 'field sports' as opposed to athletics sports; sports such as hunting and fishing.

*Four  Was New Zealand Exceptional?*

1 Coleman O. Parsons, 'Mark Twain in New Zealand', *South Atlantic Quarterly* (Winter 1961), p. 59.

2 Miles Fairburn, 'Is There A Good Case for New Zealand Exceptionalism?', *Thesis Eleven*, no. 92 (February 2008), pp. 29–49; 'Is There A Good Case for New Zealand Exceptionalism?', in Tony Ballantyne and Brian Moloughney, eds, *Disputed Histories: Imagining New Zealand's Past* (Dunedin: Otago University Press, 2006), pp. 143–67.

3 See, for example, S. M. Lipset, *American Exceptionalism: A Double-Edged Sword* (New York: W. W. Norton, 1996); Harold Hongju Koh, 'On American Exceptionalism', *Stanford Law Review*, vol. 55, no. 5 (May 2003), pp. 1479–527. The concept and the phrase 'American exceptionalism' originated with French philosopher and historian Alexis de Tocqueville in his *Democracy in America*, first published in 1835.

4 Fairburn, *Thesis Eleven*, p. 29.

5 Ibid., p. 30.

6 John Mulgan, *Man Alone* (Hamilton: Paul's Book Arcade, 1949). For more on Mulgan, see Vincent O'Sullivan, *Long Journey to the Border: A Life of John Mulgan* (Auckland: Penguin, 2003); James McNeish, *Dance of the Peacocks: New Zealanders in exile in the time of Hitler and Mao Tse-tung* (Auckland: Random House, 2003). For Mulgan's own view of New Zealand and the characteristics of New Zealanders, see John Mulgan, *Report On Experience* (London: Oxford University Press, 1947).

7 Fairburn, *Disputed Histories*, p. 144.

8 Fairburn, *Thesis Eleven*, p. 29.

9 Raewyn Dalziel, 'New Zealand and Polynesia', in David Porter, ed., *The Oxford History of the British Empire, vol. III, The Nineteenth Century* (Oxford: Oxford University Press, 1999), p. 595.

10  R. P. Davis, 'New Zealand Liberal Legislation and Manitoba Labour, 1894–1916', in G. A. Wood and P. S. O'Connor, *W. P. Morrell: A Tribute: Essays in modern and early modern history presented to William Parker Morrell, Professor Emeritus, University of Otago* (Dunedin: University of Otago Press, 1973), p. 169.

11  D. A. Hamer, ed., *The Webbs in New Zealand 1898: Beatrice Webb's Diary with entries by Sidney Webb* (Wellington: Price Milburn for Victoria University Press, 1974); André Siegfried, *Democracy in New Zealand: translated from the French by E. V. Burns with an introduction by William Downie Stewart* (London: G. Bell & Sons, 1914); Henry Demarest Lloyd, *Newest England: Notes of a democratic traveller in New Zealand, with some Australian comparisons* (New York: Doubleday, Page, 1902); Richard Jebb, *Studies in Colonial Nationalism* (London: Edward Arnold, 1905); Albert Métin, *Le Socialisme sans Doctrines* (Paris: F. Alcan, 1910); Sydney Webb and Beatrice Webb, *Industrial Democracy* (London: Longmans, Green, 1920).

12  James Edward Le Rossignol and William Downie Stewart, *State Socialism in New Zealand* (New York: T. Y. Crowell, 1910). See also *Evening Post*, 7 January 1911, p. 9 for a review that argued the book was likely to 'place American knowledge of New Zealand on a firm basis'. See also Stephanie Dale, 'Stewart, William Downie, 1878–1949', in *Dictionary of New Zealand Biography*, vol. 3 (Wellington: Auckland University Press and the Department of Internal Affairs, 1996), pp. 488–90; Dale wrote that the circumstances surrounding the collaboration were vague, but the book 'did much to establish Stewart as a scholar both nationally and internationally'. She implied this led to his writing the introduction for the English translation of Siegfried's book. Stewart was a Reform Party politician.

13  *New Zealand Herald*, 8 January 1901, p. 5.

14  The birthplace description was in Frank Parsons, *The Story of New Zealand: A History of New Zealand From the Earliest Times to the Present* (Philadelphia: C. F. Taylor, 1904), quoted in Peter J. Coleman, 'New Zealand Liberalism and the Origins of the American Welfare State', *Journal of American History*, vol. 69, no. 2 (September 1982), p. 372; for the 'New Zealandize' campaign, see Coleman, 'New Zealand Liberalism and the Origins of the American Welfare State', p. 377. See also Coleman, 'The Spirit of New Zealand

Liberalism in the Nineteenth Century', *Journal of Modern History*, vol. 30, no. 3 (September 1958), pp. 227–35.

15  Coleman, 'New Zealand Liberalism and the Origins of the American Welfare State', p. 391.

16  'An Anonymous Proposal for the Settlement of New South Wales [Extract] [1783–1786]', in Robert McNab, ed., *Historical Records of New Zealand* (Wellington: Government Printer, 1908), p. 65. McNab put the date of the letter as being between the recognition of American independence (1783) and the decision to found a settlement at Botany Bay (1786).

17  *Morning Herald and Daily Advertiser*, 12 March 1784. See also Rüdiger Mack, 'The Mystery of the Scottish Gentleman Emigrant from 1782', *Journal of Pacific History*, vol. 32, no. 2 (December 1997), p. 248.

18  Mack, 'The Mystery of the Scottish Gentleman Emigrant from 1782', p. 248.

19  'Phillip's Views on the Conduct of the Expedition and the Treatment of Convicts', McNab, *Historical Records of New Zealand*, p. 67.

20  Robert Hughes, *The Fatal Shore* (London: Pan Books, 1988), pp. 264–65.

21  Marquis of Normanby to William Hobson, 4 August 1839, Correspondence with the Secretary of State Relative to New Zealand, 8 April 1940, House of Commons Parliamentary Papers.

22  Ibid.

23  *The Times*, 12 June 1847, p. 8.

24  While the editorialist, as was usual, was not identified, it was likely to have been either the newspaper's founder, Samuel Revans, or its first editor, William Fox, a later premier regarded as a social reformer. See Scholefield, *Newspapers in New Zealand*, pp. 24–27; Raewyn Dalziel and Keith Sinclair, 'Fox, William, 1812?–1893', *Dictionary of New Zealand Biography*, vol. 1 (Wellington: Allen & Unwin/Department of Internal Affairs, 1990), pp. 134–38.

25  For 'Parkhurst boys' figures, see *Reports Relating to Parkhurst Prison*, 1843 and 1844, House of Commons Parliamentary Papers, p. 4.

26  *Southern Cross*, 6 June, 1843, pp. 2–3. The newspaper then was edited by Scottish-born Samuel Martin, who had been the editor of the original *New Zealand Herald*, in which position he challenged the registrar of the Supreme Court to a duel over false allegations against Martin in relation to land claims. See Scholefield, *Newspapers in New Zealand*, p. 73.

27  *Report of the Select Committee on New Zealand together with the Minutes of Evidence*, 29 July 1844, House of Commons Parliamentary Papers, p. 54. For details on Brodie, see Scholefield, *A Dictionary of New Zealand Biography*, vol. 1, p. 96.

28  *New Zealand Journal*, 25 April 1846, p. 89. For Clarke details, see Scholefield, *A Dictionary of New Zealand Biography*, vol. 1, p. 159.

29  Ibid.

30  Grey and the Home Secretary, Sir George Grey, were cousins. See David Frederick Smith, 'Grey, Sir George, second baronet (1799–1882)', *Oxford Dictionary of National Biography* <www.oxforddnb.com/view/article/11533>; Peter Burroughs, 'Grey, Henry George, third Earl Grey (1802–1894)', *Oxford Dictionary of National Biography* <www.oxforddnb.com/view/article/11540>. For a similar proposal to southern Africa and a similar response, see Alan Lester, *Imperial Networks: Creating Identities in nineteenth-century South Africa and Britain* (New York: Routledge, 2001), p. 177.

31  *New Zealand Government Gazette, Province of New Ulster*, 9 March 1849, pp. 35–36.

32  Among the signatories were noted merchants from Auckland such as Frederick Whitaker, John I. Montefiore, David Nathan and James Dilworth. See *Makers of Auckland* (Auckland: Wilson & Horton, 1971).

33  *New Zealander*, 31 March 1849, p. 4.

34  Ibid.

35  The petitions and letters were included in *Convict Discipline and Transportation. Further Correspondence on the subject of Convict Discipline and Transportation* (hereafter *Convict Discipline*), 31 January 1850, House of Commons Parliamentary Papers.

36  Notes on public meeting in the School Hall, Dunedin, 26 May 1849, *Flotsam and Jetsam*, vol. 1, no. 57, Hocken Library.

37  Ibid., p. 61.

38  *Convict Discipline*, p. 123.

39  *New Zealand Spectator and Cook's Strait Guardian*, 28 November 1849, p. 3.

40  *Perth Gazette and Independent Journal of Politics and News*, 30 November 1849, pp. 2–3.

41  *South Australian News*, June 1851, p. 1.

42  *New Zealand Spectator and Cook's Strait Guardian*, 28 November 1849, p. 3.

43  C. C. Blackton, 'New Zealand and the Australian anti-transportation movement', *Australian Historical Studies*, vol. 1, no. 2 (October 1940), p. 116.

44  Ibid., p. 120.

45  Davison, Hirst and Macintyre, eds, *The Oxford Companion to Australian History*, p. 654.

46  Fairburn, *Disputed Histories*, p. 145.

47  Keith Sinclair, 'Why are Race Relations in New Zealand Better than in South Africa, South Australia or South Dakota?', *NZJH*, vol. 5, no. 2 (October 1971), p. 122.

48  'The Origins of the Māori Seats', Background Note, Parliamentary Library, 11 November 2003, p. 10 <www.parliament.nz/en-NZ/ParlSupport/ResearchPapers>; see also M. P. K. Sorrenson, 'Appendix B: A History of Māori Representation in Parliament', *AJHR*, vol. IX, H-3, B-18–21.

49  *Nelson Examiner and New Zealand Chronicle*, 5 September 1867, p. 4.

50  Scholefield, *A Dictionary of New Zealand Biography*, vol. 2, p. 34.

51  *NZPD*, 1867, vol. 1, part 1, p. 459.

52  Ibid., vol. 1, part 2, p. 816.

53  'The Origins of the Māori Seats', p. 10.

54  For Australian election background, see the website of the Australian Electoral Commission <www.aec.gov.au>; for the equivalent in Canada, see the Elections Canada website <www.elections.ca>.

55  *NZPD*, 1867, vol. 1, part 1, p. 462.

56  Keith Sinclair, 'Full circle but new links', in *In Our Time: 1870–1970 the Auckland Star Centennial Supplement*, p. 42.

57  Ibid., p. 43.

58  Ibid.

59  For analysis and comment on legislation that restricted Chinese immigration, see Nigel Murphy, *A Guide to Laws and Policies Relating to the Chinese in New Zealand* (Wellington: New Zealand Chinese Association, 1997); Moloughney and Stenhouse, 'Drug-Besotten, Sin-Begotten Fiends of Filth'; George Kay, *Seddon and Asian Immigration Legislation 1896–99*, Postgraduate Diploma in History thesis, University of Otago, 1973.

60  Belich, *Making Peoples*, p. 265. 'Kūpapa' was the term used for Māori who sided with the British forces; see John C. Moorfield, *Te Aka: Māori–English, English–Māori Dictionary and Index* (Auckland: Pearson, Longman, 2008), p. 70.

61  Scholefield, *A Dictionary of New Zealand Biography*, vol. 1, pp. 143–44.

62  N. E. Coad, *New Zealand from Tasman to Massey* (Wellington: Harry H. Tombs Ltd, 1934), p. 170.

63  W. P. Morrell, *The Provincial System in New Zealand 1852–76* (Dunedin: Whitcombe & Tombs, 1964), p. 22.

64  For a study of the capital transfer, see A. G. Bagnall, 'The Seat of Government Commission, 1864: an Australian intervention', *Turnbull Library Record*, vol. 18, no. 1 (May 1985), pp. 5–21.

65 Morrell, *The Provincial System in New Zealand 1852–76*, p. 281.

66 For a précis of the issues, see W. David McIntyre and W. J. Gardner, eds, *Speeches and Documents on New Zealand History* (London: Oxford University Press, 1971), pp. 111–14.

67 *NZPD*, 1875, vol. 1, p. 468.

68 Edmund Bohan, *Edward Stafford: New Zealand's First Statesman* (Christchurch: Hazard Press, 1994), p. 99.

69 Coad, *New Zealand from Tasman to Massey*, p. 173.

70 McIntyre and Gardner, *Speeches and Documents on New Zealand History*, p. 112.

71 A. S. Atkinson letter to C. W. Richmond, 2 August 1875, in Scholefield, ed., *The Richmond–Atkinson Papers*, vol. 2, p. 398.

72 Scholefield, unpublished autobiography, p. 62.

73 John Mackey, *The Making of a State Education System: The Passing of the New Zealand Education Act, 1877* (London: Geoffrey Chapman, 1967), p. 281.

74 Ibid., p. 283.

75 Ibid.

76 Ibid., p. 284. Chief Justice Sir Robert Stout provided a contemporary view of secular education compared with the state's role in religious education. See Sir Robert Stout, 'Religion and the State, A New Year's address delivered in the Unitarian Free Church on Sunday evening, the 4th January, 1914' (Alexandra: Alexandra Herald, 1914).

77 Jeanine Graham, 'Settler Society', in Geoffrey W. Rice, ed., *Oxford History of New Zealand*, 2nd edn (Auckland: Oxford University Press, 1995), p. 132.

78 See, for example, John Stenhouse, 'Religion and Society', in Byrnes, ed., *New Oxford History*, pp. 341–42.

79 Ian and Alan Cumming, *History of State Education in New Zealand 1840–1975* (Wellington: Pittman Publishing, 1978), p. 87.

80 Harold William Orsman, 'The Growth of Nationalism (an essay)', MS-Papers-7637, Alexander Turnbull Library, p. 4.

81 See Angus Ross, *New Zealand Aspirations in the Pacific in the Nineteenth Century* (Oxford: Clarendon Press, 1964).

82 Orsman, 'The Growth of Nationalism (an essay)', p. 5.

83 Ibid., pp. 5–6.

84 Ibid., p. 6.

85 See *AJHR*, 1893, vol. 1, A-1, A-2.

86 Knutsford telegram to Glasgow, 10 August 1892, *AJHR*, A-1, p. 11.

87 Ripon letter to Glasgow, 26 September 1892, *AJHR*, A-2, pp. 26–27.

88 For a detailed account of how and why Seddon succeeded Ballance, see R. T. Shannon, 'The Liberal succession crisis in New Zealand, 1893', in *Australian Historical Studies*, vol. 8, no. 30 (1958), pp. 183–201.

89 South Australia granted the vote to women in 1894; see Philippa Mein Smith, 'The Tasman World', in Byrnes, ed., *New Oxford History*, p. 307. Women could also vote in Wyoming in 1869, Utah in 1870, and Colorado in 1893; the standard work on the New Zealand lead is Patricia Grimshaw, *Women's Suffrage in New Zealand* (Auckland: Auckland University Press, 1972).

90 *New Zealand Graphic*, 5 August 1893, p. 63.

91 For a chronology of women's suffrage milestones, see <www.nzhistory.net/politics/womens-suffrage>.

92 Grimshaw, *Women's Suffrage in New Zealand*, p. 93.

93 *Evening Post*, 9 September 1893, p. 4.

94 Grimshaw, *Women's Suffrage in New Zealand*, p. 94. Seddon a decade later told a delegation from the Central Society for Women's Suffrage in London that the effect of the change on elections had been most gratifying: 'Both men and women felt the responsibility which was cast upon them and in that respect the granting of the franchise to women had had most beneficial results. It also had a preventative effect for it prevented a man who had the slightest stain on his moral character from becoming a candidate for Parliament because he knew that he would not have the least chance of being elected.' See *The Times*, 8 August 1902, p. 6.

95 Tony Ballantyne, 'The State, Politics and Power, 1769–1893', in Byrnes, ed., *New Oxford History*, p. 122.

96 Henry Lawson, 'The Women of New Zealand', *New Zealand Times*, 28 November 1893, reprinted in Colin Roderick, ed., *Henry Lawson: Collected Verse, vol. 1 1885–1900* (Sydney: Angus & Robertson, 1967), p. 449. For biographical details of Louisa Lawson, see John Barnes, 'Lawson, Louise (1848–1920)', in Davison, Hirst and Macintyre, eds, *The Oxford Companion to Australian History*, pp. 385–86.

97 'The Morning of New Zealand', *New Zealand Mail*, 19 January 1894; Roderick, *Henry Lawson: Collected Verse*, p. 261. For a general history of women's role in achieving the vote and later, see Sandra Coney, *Standing in the Sunshine: A History of New Zealand Women Since They Won the Vote* (Auckland: Viking/Penguin, 1993).

98 David Will M. Burn, 'The Glorious 19th', *North Otago Times*, 21 September 1893, p. 3. Burn was the youngest son of Margaret Burn, the first principal of Otago Girls' High School.

99 Orsman, 'The Growth of Nationalism (an essay)', p. 7.

100 Ibid.

101 See Guy H. Scholefield, *New Zealand in Evolution: Industrial, Economic and Political* (London: T. Fisher Unwin, 1909); *The Pacific: Its Past and Future*, PhD thesis, London School of Economics, 1919, published as *The Pacific: Its Past and Future* (London: John Murray, 1919).

102 G. H. Scholefield letter to Vance Palmer, 2 February 1955, Scholefield collection, MS-Papers-0916, Alexander Turnbull Library. See also Geoffrey Serle, 'Palmer, Edward Vivian (Vance) (1885–1959)', *Australian Dictionary of Biography* <www.adb. online.anu.edu>.

103 Of 4931 carcases of mutton shipped, only one was condemned on arrival. For background on shipments from other countries, see *Otago Witness*, 31 December 1881, p. 22. The *Brisbane Courier* remarked in 1893 that Australia 'attacked the immense difficulties of the enterprise very half-heartedly, and although it holds the historic honour of having pioneered the export of frozen meat, the substantial reward of having fought its way through all obstacles belongs to New Zealand.' See *Brisbane Courier*, 23 December 1893, p. 4.

104 *The Times*, 27 May 1882, p. 12. The letter was from William Frederick Cott, for the Bell-Coleman Mechanical Refrigeration Company.

105 Ibid., p. 11.

106 Ibid., 29 May 1882, p. 6.

107 Ibid.

108 *Evening Post*, 16 December 1881, p. 2.

109 *Evening Post*, 27 July 1882, p. 3. Barton was the second son of George Elliott Barton, lawyer, parliamentarian and Native Land Court judge.

110 Belich, *Paradise Reforged*, p. 53. Belich provides useful background on how the frozen meat trade developed and transformed New Zealand–British relations, pp. 53–70. For the development of the economic value, see J. Macdonald Holmes, 'Geographical Factors in the Foundation of New Zealand's Wealth', *The Australian Geographer*, vol. II, no. 3 (1933–35), pp. 24–36.

111 See Michael Robson, *Decision at Dawn: New Zealand and the EEC* (Wellington: Baynard-Hillier, 1972), for a recounting of the initial negotiations to secure New Zealand's farm produce trade against the trade barriers of a collective Europe.

112 Belich, *Replenishing the Earth*, p. 367.

113 See G. M. Trevelyan, *Illustrated English Social History, vol. 4 – The Nineteenth Century* (London: Longmans, Green & Co, 1952), pp. 92–94.

114 Belich, *Replenishing the Earth*, p. 470.

115 Siegfried, *Democracy in New Zealand*, p. 363.

116 Reeves, *State Experiments in Australia and New Zealand*, vol. 1, p. 68.

117 William Downie Stewart, Introduction, Siegfried, *Democracy in New Zealand*, p. x.

118 Michael King, *The Penguin History of New Zealand* (Auckland: Penguin Books, 2003), p. 259.

119 Coleman, 'New Zealand Liberalism and the Origins of the American Welfare State', p. 373. See also J. T. Paul, *Humanism in Politics: New Zealand Labour Party Retrospect* (Wellington: New Zealand Labour Party, 1946).

120 Sinclair, *Destiny Apart*, pp. 73–76. Other examples of Liberal legislation were the Land and Income Tax Act (1891), Factories Act (1891), Land and Income Assessment Act (1891), Shops and Shop Assistants Act (1894), Family Homes Protection Act (1895), Old Age Pensions Act (1898), Divorce Act (1898).

121 See *New Zealand Mail*, 11 March 1903, p. 13; Reeves, *State Experiments*, vol. 1, p. 127. Davis called the Act 'not the product of a new philosophy but the practical application of an idea already aired for some time'. He also noted Massachusetts introduced similar legislation before New Zealand. Davis, 'New Zealand Liberal Legislation and Manitoba Labour, 1894–1916', p. 174.

122 *New Zealand Graphic*, 13 November 1897, quoted in Sinclair, *Destiny Apart*, p. 74.

123 V. I. Lenin, the Russian State Archive of Socio-Political History (RGASPI), f.495, op.14, d.323, l.84, quoted in Alexander Trapeznik, 'New Zealand's Perceptions of the Russian Revolution of 1917', in *Revolutionary Russia*, vol. 19, no. 1 (June 2006), p. 70.

124 Lenin, *Collected Works, vol. 39: Notebooks on Imperialism* (London: Lawrence & Wishart, 1960), quoted in Trapeznik, 'New Zealand's Perceptions of the Russian Revolution of 1917', p. 70. Trapeznik quotes in a footnote 'one authority' as saying that Lenin was, in many instances, 'twisting Siegfried's original observations about British attitudes to New Zealanders . . . to support his own ideas about "colonial imperialism" and about the "social chauvinism" of the English-speaking working class in general'. Trapeznik, 'New

Zealand's Perceptions of the Russian Revolution of 1917', p. 75, n. 59.

125  Coleman, 'New Zealand Liberalism and the Origins of the American Welfare State', p. 374.

126  Ibid., p. 373.

127  Ibid., p. 379.

128  Henry Demarest Lloyd, 'New Zealand Newest England', *Atlantic Monthly*, vol. 84, no. 506 (December 1899), p. 793.

129  Coleman, 'New Zealand Liberalism and the Origins of the American Welfare State', pp. 385–86; Reeves visited the United States in 1899 and represented New Zealand at the International Commercial Conference in Philadelphia. He spoke to the Twentieth Century Club in Boston on compulsory arbitration, met President Theodore Roosevelt and, according to Coleman, 'granted journalists lengthy interviews so as to spread the New Zealand message as widely as possible'. Coleman, 'New Zealand Liberalism and the Origins of the American Welfare State', p. 380n. Reeves and Lloyd met on this trip, became friends and Reeves wrote on Lloyd's death in 1903 that he was 'one of those men who made him think more of mankind'. See also Keith Sinclair, *William Pember Reeves, New Zealand Fabian* (Oxford: Clarendon Press, 1965), p. 268.

130  Coleman, 'New Zealand Liberalism and the Origins of the American Welfare State', p. 380, quoting from Benjamin O. Flower, 'Premier Richard Seddon: Democracy's Lost Leader', *The Arena*, vol. 36 (August 1906), pp. 196–200.

131  Coleman, 'New Zealand Liberalism and the Origins of the American Welfare State', p. 391.

132  For example, a summary of French views of New Zealand, including Siegfried's, in the *West Coast Times*, 1 August 1905, p. 2.

133  For example, see *Southland Times*, 9 January 1901, p. 2; *Hawera and Normanby Star*, 26 February 1902, p. 4.

134  Twain comment on Davitt, see Parsons, 'Mark Twain in New Zealand', p. 59. Twain and Davitt were on the same ship that brought them from Hobart to Bluff. See also Mark Twain, *Mark Twain in Australia and New Zealand* (also published as *Following the Equator*) (Harmondsworth, Middlesex: Penguin, 1973); Shelley Fisher Fishkin (foreword), Gore Vidal (introduction) and Fred Kaplan (afterword), *Following the equator and anti-imperialist essays, Mark Twain* (New York: Oxford University Press, 1996); Lydia Monin, *From the writer's notebook: around New Zealand with 80 authors* (Auckland: Reed,

2006); Anthony Trollope, *Australia and New Zealand* (London: Chapman & Hall, 1873). For typical reporting about Twain, see *Otago Witness*, 14 November 1895, p. 37; for examples of reporting on Davitt, see *Otago Witness*, 14 November 1895, p. 2; *Evening Post*, 25 November 1895, p. 4; *New Zealand Tablet*, 29 November 1895, p. 17. Trollope and Kipling preceded the legislative changes of the 1890s. Kipling was on a recuperative holiday and made no public appearances and gave few interviews. In Melbourne on his way home, he thought New Zealand 'lovely' but questioned the high level of government and bureaucracy for such a small country. See *Timaru Herald*, 25 November 1891, p. 4; J. B. Primrose, 'Kipling's visit to Australia and New Zealand', *Kipling Journal*, issue 145, March 1963, pp. 11–16. Kipling was prevailed upon by the *New Zealand Herald* to write a short story for it and this duly appeared as 'Our Lady at Wairakei' on 30 January 1892. See Rudyard Kipling, *Our Lady at Wairakei*, with introduction by Harry Ricketts (Wellington: Mallinson Rendel, 1983).

135  *Dominion*, 21 December 1995, p. 7; *Evening Post*, 25 November 1895, p. 4.

136  Parsons, 'Mark Twain in New Zealand', p. 59.

137  Tom Brooking, *Lands for the People? The Highland Clearances and the Colonisation of New Zealand: A Biography of John McKenzie* (Dunedin: University of Otago Press, 1996), p. 269.

138  Ibid., p. 9.

139  Ibid., p. 332, n. 9.

*Five 'New Zealand for the New Zealanders'*

1  Sir John Hall, speech to the Australasian Federation Conference, Melbourne, 12 February 1890, *Official Record of the Proceedings and Debates of the Australasian Federation Conference, Melbourne 1890: Debates of the Conferences*, p. 175 <http://setis.library.usyd.edu.au> (hereafter *Official Record 1890*).

2  Geoffrey Blainey, *The Tyranny of Distance: How Distance Shaped Australia's History* (Sydney: Pan Macmillan, 2001); Blainey's central thesis is how geographical remoteness was central to the shaping of Australian history and identity.

3  *Official Record 1890*, p. 175. Hall was not quite accurate but the sense was the same. Parkes said: 'There is no obstacle in the path before us except impediments which we have created ourselves. Nature has created no obstacle.' Parkes speech to the federation

4   Ibid., p. 175.

5   Ibid.

6   Captain William Russell speech to federation conference, 11 February 1890, *Official Record 1890*, p. 129.

7   Ibid.

8   For a landmark work on the shaping of Australian identity, see Russel Ward, *The Australian Legend* (Melbourne: Oxford University Press, new illustrated edn, 1978); see also Deborah Gare and David Ritter, *Making Australian History: Perspective on the Past Since 1788* (Melbourne: Thomson, 2008), pp. 194–99. For a critique of Ward's work, see Richard Waterhouse, *The Vision Splendid: A Social and Cultural History of Rural Australia* (Fremantle: Curtin University Books, 2005). He argued there were competing sets of values in 'the Bush' and that they 'constituted a culture of consolation rather than one of celebration'; Waterhouse, *The Vision Splendid*, pp. 111–12. Ironically, the title for Waterhouse's book comes from a poem, 'Clancy of the Overflow', by one of the prime romantics of the Outback, 'Banjo' Paterson: 'And he sees the vision splendid of the sunlit plains extended, / And at night the wondrous glory of the everlasting stars'. See Rosamund Campbell and Philippa Harvie, *Singer of the Bush: A. B. 'Banjo' Paterson Complete Works 1885–1900* (Sydney: Lansdowne, 1983), p. 105. For an influential work in the United States, see Frederick Jackson Turner, *The Frontier in American History* (New York: Henry Holt & Co, 1921).

9   *New Zealand Observer and Free Lance*, 14 October 1899, pp. 2–3.

10   The *Bulletin* touted as its policy, 'Australia for the Australians'. See Patricia Rolfe, *The Journalistic Javelin, An Illustrated History of the* Bulletin (Sydney: Wildcat Press, 1979), p. 138.

11   Keith Sinclair, 'Why New Zealanders are not Australians – New Zealand and the Australian Federal Movement, 1881–1901', in Sinclair, ed., *Tasman Relations: New Zealand and Australia, 1788–1988* (Auckland: Auckland University Press, 1987), p. 90.

12   André Siegfried, *Democracy in New Zealand – translated from the French by E. V. Burns with an introduction by William Downie Stewart* (London: G. Bell & Sons, 1914), p. 334. Siegfried's work was first published in French in 1904.

13   Richard Jebb, *Studies in Colonial Nationalism*, p. 90.

14   William Pember Reeves, 'The Attitude of New Zealand', *Empire Review*, vol. 1, no. 1 (1901), pp. 111–13.

15   Reeves, *State Experiments in Australia and New Zealand*, vol. 1, p. 148.

16   Guy H. Scholefield, 'The Australasian Federation: New Zealand's Attitude', *United Empire*, vol. 3, no. 11 (1912), pp. 911–12.

17   Sinclair, *Tasman Relations: New Zealand and Australia, 1788–1988*, p. 90.

18   E. J. Tapp, 'New Zealand and Australian Federation', *Australian Historical Studies*, vol. 5, no. 19 (November 1952), pp. 244–57. Tapp traversed the whole question of the prospect of New Zealand inclusion from the earliest tentative suggestions in the late 1840s.

19   F. L. W. Wood, 'Why did New Zealand not join the Australian Commonwealth in 1900–1901?', *NZJH*, vol. 2, no. 2 (October 1968), pp. 115–29; Adrian Davy, 'New Zealand, the Australian Commonwealth and "Plain Nonsense"', *NZJH*, vol. 3, no. 2 (October 1969), pp. 190–95; Miles Fairburn, 'New Zealand and Australasian Federation, 1883–1901: Another View', *NZJH*, vol. 4, no. 2 (October 1970), pp. 138–59.

20   Geoffrey Blainey, 'Two Countries: the Same but Very Different', in Sinclair, *Tasman Relations: New Zealand and Australia, 1788–1988*, pp. 315–32.

21   Ged Martin, *Australia, New Zealand and Federation* (London: Menzies Centre for Australian Studies, 2001).

22   The Hon. Mr Justice Kirby, 'CER, Trans-Tasman Courts and Australasia', *New Zealand Law Journal* (October 1983), pp. 304–7.

23   The Hon. Justice Michael Kirby AC CMG, Presentation to Knowledge Wave 2003 – The Leadership Forum, Auckland, February 2003. Kirby related how at the time of his 1983 suggestion, Prime Minister Robert Muldoon demanded to know, 'Who is this judicial comic?' 'When I promised', Kirby said, 'that New Zealand, as part of the Australian Federation, would have two States and that bronze statues of Sir Robert would be raised from Broome to Dunedin, he was notably mollified. He left the [radio] programme declaring: "Well, we would have to negotiate the terms and conditions very carefully."'

24   *Evening Post*, 7 February 1912, p. 2; *Dominion*, 23 October 1940, p. 6. Fisher acknowledged the political difficulty of federation, and talked of closer economic ties – in effect, his suggestion was later embodied in the New Zealand–Australia Free Trade Agreement (NAFTA) in 1965 and Closer Economic Relations (CER) in 1982.

Above note 4, continuing from previous page:

conference, 10 February 1890, *Official Record 1890*, p. 41.

25  For example, Helen Irving, *To Constitute A Nation: A Cultural History of Australia's Constitution* (Cambridge: Cambridge University Press, 1999); Irving, ed., *The Centenary Companion to Australian Federation* (Cambridge: Cambridge University Press, 1999); John Hirst, *The Sentimental Nation: The Making of the Australian Commonwealth* (Melbourne: Oxford University Press, 2000); S. G. Foster, Susan Marsden and Roslyn Russell, *Federation: The Guide to Records* (Canberra: Australian Archives, 1998); Richard Cashman, John O'Hara and Andrew Honey, eds, *Sport, Federation, Nation* (Sydney: Walla Walla Press in association with the Centre for Olympic Studies, University of New South Wales, 2001).

26  Philippa Mein Smith, 'New Zealand Federation Commissioners in Australia: One past, two historiographies', *Australian Historical Studies*, vol. 34, no. 122 (October 2003), pp. 305–25.

27  Philippa Mein Smith, Peter Hempenstall and Shaun Goldfinch, *Remaking the Tasman World* (Christchurch: Canterbury University Press, 2008); Denis McLean, *The Prickly Pair: Making Nationalism in Australia and New Zealand* (Dunedin: Otago University Press, 2003). McLean had been a career diplomat for 20 years and was a Secretary of Defence.

28  Hamish Keith, *The Big Picture: A history of New Zealand art from 1642* (Auckland: Random House, 2007), p. 136.

29  Joanne Smith, 'Twelve hundred reasons why there is no Australasia: How colonisation influenced federation', *Australian Cultural History*, vol. 27, no. 1 (April 2009), pp. 35–45.

30  Ibid., p. 43.

31  Morrell, *New Zealand*, p. 86.

32  C. M. H. Clark, *Short Documents in Australian History 1851–1900* (Sydney: Angus & Robertson, 1970), p. 443.

33  *South Australian Magazine*, April and May 1842, p. 313.

34  *The Times*, 13 October 1897, p. 13. This was a phrase later attributed to the first Commonwealth Prime Minister, Edmund Barton. The irony that such a phrase automatically excluded Tasmania, quite apart from New Zealand, has seldom attracted attention.

35  Clark, *Short Documents in Australian History 1851–1900*, p. 445.

36  Ibid., p. 446.

37  Angus Ross, *New Zealand Aspirations in the Pacific in the Nineteenth Century* (Oxford: Clarendon Press, 1964).

38  Davison, Hirst and Macintyre, eds,

39  Clark, *Short Documents in Australian History 1851–1900*, p. 444; Stephen Murray-Smith, ed., *The Dictionary of Australian Quotations* (Melbourne: Heinemann, 1984), p. 212.

40  Ibid.

41  Clark, *Short Documents in Australian History 1851–1900*, p. 467.

42  *Official Record 1890*, p. 1.

43  Hirst, *The Sentimental Nation*, p. 2.

44  Alfred Deakin, *The Federal Story* (Melbourne: Melbourne University Press, 1963), p. 173. Interestingly, Deakin's book does not once mention New Zealand.

45  Stuart Macintyre, *A Concise History of Australia*, 2nd edn (Melbourne: Cambridge University Press, 2005), p. 148.

46  Clark, *Short Documents in Australian History 1851–1900*, p. 475.

47  Rolfe, *The Journalistic Javelin*, p. 279.

48  Ibid., p. 263.

49  See Mein Smith, Hempenstall and Goldfinch, *Remaking the Tasman World*.

50  I. R. Hancock, 'Cook, James Newton Haxton Hume (1866–1942)', *Australian Dictionary of Biography* <www.adb.online.anu.edu.au>.

51  John McCarthy, 'Bavin, Sir Thomas Rainsford (1874–1941)', *Australian Dictionary of Biography* <www.adb.online.anu.edu.au>; Bavin, who was knighted in 1933, was premier of New South Wales 1927–1930.

52  John G. Mulford, *Guardians of the Game: The History of the New South Wales Rugby Union 1874–2004* (Sydney: ABC Books, 2005), p. 27; S. E. Sleigh, *The New Zealand Rugby Football Annual for 1885* (Dunedin: Otago Daily Times, 1885), pp. 9, 25. Before his political life took over, Barton was also a cricket umpire; in fact, he was the only Australian prime minister to have umpired first-class matches. Barton was one of the umpires in one of international cricket's early controversies when the crowd at Moore Park (later the Sydney Cricket Ground) invaded the playing arena after disagreeing with the dismissal of a New South Wales batsman in a match against 'the Gentlemen of England'. Barton, who had not ruled on the disputed dismissal, apparently helped restore order. The incident soured relations between the England team and Australian cricket authorities and a scheduled second match against Australia was cancelled. See *The Times*, 9 April 1879, p. 10; *Argus*, 3 March 1879, p. 7; 'Edmund Barton, Australia' <www.espncricinfo.com/ci/content/player/4432.html>.

53 Bede Nairn, 'Watson, John Christian (1867–1941)', *Australian Dictionary of Biography* <www.adb.online.anu.edu.au>.

54 Bill Frindall, ed., *The Wisden Book of Test Cricket* (London: Book Club Associates, 1979), pp. 12–76; Maxwell L. Howell, Lingyu Xie and Bensley Wilkes, *The Wallabies: A Definitive History of Australian Test Rugby* (Norman Park, Queensland: GAP Publishing, 2000), pp. 8–15.

55 Bill Mallon and Ture Widlund, *The 1896 Olympic Games* (Jefferson, North Carolina: McFarland & Company, 1998), pp. 67–68. The dichotomy of New Zealand–Australia sports relationships, and their seeming contradictions to the concept of national identity, will be examined in Chapter 7.

56 Davison, Hirst and Macintyre, eds, *The Oxford Companion to Australian History*, pp. 44, 50.

57 *New Zealand Herald*, 12 September 1894, p. 5.

58 *Evening Post*, 28 December 1889, p. 3.

59 Ibid., 11 June 1896, p. 2. The Wellington branch of the association decided to follow the Australian model and set itself up as a benefit society for its members in addition to its role of promoting a New Zealand identity.

60 *New Zealand Illustrated Magazine*, 1 November 1899, p. 88.

61 *Evening Post*, 15 August 1899, p. 4. The attitude of the *Post* should perhaps be seen in the context of its opposition to the Seddon government. Its editorials were, as usual, unattributed, but a regular editorialist for 'a long period' was Arthur Atkinson, a nephew of a former premier and an ardent opponent of Seddon's. See James Hutchison, 1867–1946, Reminiscences, MS-Papers-5341, Alexander Turnbull Library; Scholefield, *The Richmond–Atkinson Papers*, vol. 2, p. 571.

62 Keith, *The Big Picture*, p. 137.

63 Sinclair, *Destiny Apart*, p. 111.

64 *Lyttelton Times*, 17 October 1888, p. 5.

65 Clark, *Short Documents in Australian History 1851–1900*, p. 455.

66 Sinclair, *Destiny Apart*, p. 110.

67 *NZPD*, vol. 50, October 23–November 10, 1884, p. 385. His geography may have been faulty, but his meaning was clear.

68 Ibid., vol. 69, August 15–September 17, 1890, p. 586.

69 Ibid.

70 'The Military Forces and Defences of New Zealand', *AJHR*, 1890, vol. III, H-10, p. 5.

71 See Irving, *The Centenary Companion to Australian Federation*, p. 416.

72 Wood, 'Why did New Zealand not join the Australian Commonwealth in 1900–1901?', p. 125.

73 Ibid., p. 126. Wood's view had partial support from another historian, M. J. B. Deaker, who argued: 'Seddon's indecision and indifference [to federation] can be attributed to the apathetic attitude with which the New Zealand public reviewed the prospect. He did not want to commit himself until he could determine the opinion of the public.' M. J. B. Deaker, 'Seddon's Contribution to Imperial Relations 1897 to 1902', MA thesis, University of Otago, 1968, p. 13.

74 Fairburn, 'New Zealand and Australasian Federation, 1883–1901: Another View', p. 158.

75 Ibid., pp. 151–52.

76 Sinclair, *Destiny Apart*, p. 122.

77 Ross, *New Zealand Aspirations in the Pacific in the Nineteenth Century*, p. 288.

78 See Ross, *New Zealand Aspirations in the Pacific in the Nineteenth Century*; C. Hartley Grattan, *The Southwest Pacific to 1900* (Ann Arbor: the University of Michigan Press, 1963); John M. Ward, *British Policy in the South Pacific 1786–1893: A study in British policy towards the South Pacific islands prior to the establishment of Governments by the Great Powers* (Sydney: Australasian Publishing Co, 1948); Niall Ferguson, *The Rise and Fall of the American Empire* (London: Penguin Books, 2005); Thomas J. Osborne, 'Trade or War? America's Annexation of Hawaii Reconsidered', *Pacific Historical Review*, vol. 50, no. 3 (August 1981), pp. 285–307.

79 Scholefield, 'The Australasian Federation: New Zealand's Attitude', p. 911.

80 *Waikato Times*, 5 January 1884, p. 3.

81 *Wanganui Herald*, 12 March 1884, p. 2.

82 Timothy McIvor, *The Rainmaker: A Biography of John Ballance, Journalist and Politician 1839–1893* (Auckland: Heinemann Reed, 1989).

83 Earl of Onslow dispatch to Secretary of State for Colonies, 21 August 1891, *AJHR*, vol. 1, A-1, p. 10.

84 *Mataura Ensign*, 1 August 1899, p. 3.

85 Morrell, *New Zealand*, p. 87.

86 *NZPD*, vol. 109, 12 September 1899, p. 194.

87 Ibid., vol. 110, 3 October 1899, p. 197; vol. 111, 29 June 1900, p. 172.

88 Ibid., vol. 113, 17 August 1900, p. 73.

89 Ibid., vol. 115, 18 October 1901, p. 439.

90 Ibid., p. 440.

91 *The Times*, 4 March 1901, p. 13.

92 Ibid. For Ross's role in the NZNA, see *Evening Post*, 11 June 1896, p. 2.

93 Report of the Royal Commission on Federation (hereafter Commission Report),

*AJHR*, 1901, A-4. It comprised Harold
Beauchamp, 41, the government appointee
on the board of the Bank of New Zealand;
Charles Bowen, 70, a member of the
Legislative Council; Thomson Leys, 50,
editor of the *Auckland Star* and said to be a
personal friend of Seddon's; Charles Luke,
46, a former mayor of Wellington; John
Millar, 46, a socialist and Liberal supporter;
Walter Reid, 61, a lawyer and member of the
Westland County Council, and chairman
of the Public Trust Office; John Roberts,
59, soldier and magistrate; William Russell,
61, leader of the opposition; and William
Steward, a Liberal MP and Speaker in the
first three years of the Liberal government.

94  The possible impact of customs regulations, given New South Wales favoured
free trade and Victoria a protectionist
policy, was frequently discussed. But the
words of Benjamin Disraeli could be borne
in mind: 'The imagination of men cannot
be set afire with customs regulations.
And men are led only by the force of the
imagination.' André Maurois, *Disraeli*
(London: Penguin Books, 1937), p. 162.

95  Commission Report, pp. 1–706; Sinclair,
*Destiny Apart*, p. 117. Counts vary but the
weight of evidence was conclusive. Some
people who appeared before the commission favoured federation under certain
conditions, some thought they would
favour it in the future but not now, some
offered no view at all, and some said they
knew nothing about it.

96  *New Zealand Observer*, 23 March 1901, p. 9.

97  Commission Report, pp. 471–706.

98  Sinclair, *Destiny Apart*, p. 118.

99  E. J. von Dadelszen, *New Zealand Official
Year-Book 1904* (Wellington: Government
Printer, 1904), p. 108.

100  Commission Report, parts XLI–XLIII.

101  Martin, *Australia, New Zealand and
Federation*, p. 126. The comment was not
quite the beginning; it was part of the
preamble and came under the heading
of 'Scope of inquiries', see Commission
Report, part X.

102  Martin, *Australia, New Zealand and
Federation*, p. 126.

103  See George Griffiths, 'Cohen, Mark
(1849–1928)', Jane Thomson, ed., *Southern
People: A Dictionary of Otago-Southland
Biography* (Dunedin: Longacre Press in
association with the Dunedin City Council,
1998), p. 98.

104  Commission Report, p. 97.

105  *New Zealand Herald*, 23 March 1900, p. 5.
See also Sinclair, *William Pember Reeves*,
pp. 290–92.

106  Sinclair, *William Pember Reeves*, p. 291.

107  Commission Report, p. 109.

108  Ibid., p. 56.

109  Ibid., pp. 105–6.

110  Ibid., pp. 282–83.

111  Ibid., p. 305.

112  Ibid., p. 324. Freeth's use of the word
'moral' could be interpreted as a reflection
on the original settlement of Australia by
convicts. A New Zealand journalist, Stella
Allan, referred to 'superior' people and this
was attributed to mean people without
'the convict stain'. See Donald Denoon
and Philippa Mein Smith with Marivic
Wyndham, *A History of Australia, New
Zealand and the Pacific* (Oxford: Blackwell
Publishing, 2000), p. 197. Although New
Zealand was not formally a penal colony,
many convicts found their way to New
Zealand; the originator of New Zealand's
colonising scheme, Edward Gibbon
Wakefield, was himself a convicted crimi-
nal. See David J. Moss, 'Wakefield, Edward
Gibbon (1796–1862)', *Oxford Dictionary of
National Biography* <www.oxford.dnb.com>;
*The Times*, 22 May 1826, p. 3; Ged Martin,
'Edward Gibbon Wakefield – Abductor and
Mystagogue' <www.gedmartin.net>.

113  Commission Report, p. 350.

114  Ibid., p. 363.

115  Ibid., p. 465.

116  Ibid., part XXXIX.

117  Ibid., part XXIV; *Otago Witness*, 15 May
1901, p. 18.

118  *The Times*, 19 August 1901, p. 5.

119  *NZPD*, vol. 116, 9 July 1901, p. 198.

120  *Evening Post*, 22 June 1901, p. 5.

121  *Graphic*, 8 April 1899, p. 432.

122  *The Times*, 1 January 1901, p. 6.

123  Rudyard Kipling, *The Complete Verse*
(London: Kyle Cathie, 1990), p. 149.
The relevant lines subsequently read: 'How
can I crown thee further? I know whose
standard flies / Where the clean surge takes
the Leeuwin or the coral barriers rise.'

124  *Bulletin*, quoted in *New Zealand Observer*,
5 January 1900, p. 4.

125  *Grey River Argus*, 9 April 1900, p. 4.

126  'Commonwealth of Australia Constitution
Act', Exhibit No. 31, Commission Report,
pp. 760–74.

127  *Official Record 1890*, p. 126.

128  Ibid.

129  Commission Report, p. 483.

130  Ibid.

131  Philippa Mein Smith, in *The Centenary
Companion to Australian Federation*, p. 404,
where she says: 'Stella Allan noted in 1900
that feminists believed New Zealand had
a separate identity, concluding that there

had "never been a genuine Federation movement in New Zealand".' Allan (née Henderson) was a New Zealand journalist who, after her marriage, moved to Melbourne and worked on the *Argus*. See Patricia Keep, 'Allan, Stella May (1871–1962)', *Australian Dictionary of Biography* <www.adb.online.anu.edu.au>. Allan's sister, Elizabeth McCombs, became the first woman member of the New Zealand House of Representatives in 1933.

132 Commission Report, p. 479. Such views were commonplace at a time of belief in what came to be known as social Darwinism, would later embody eugenics and later still, be regarded as racist. There was a belief, for example, that white people could not work in the heat of Queensland and South Pacific islanders were taken there, often illegally, for the purpose. See Ross, *New Zealand Aspirations in the Pacific in the Nineteenth Century*, pp. 71–86. This was also at a time that the Australian colonies, New Zealand, Canada and some American states had restrictive legislation against Chinese. In a New Zealand context, Brian Moloughney and John Stenhouse argued that a burgeoning nationalism lay behind the restrictive legislation. Seddon argued: 'Chinese immigration was not a good thing. New Zealand did not want her shores deluged with Asiatic Tartars.' See Moloughney and Stenhouse, 'Drug-Besotten, Sin-Begotten Fiends of Filth', p. 47; Nigel Murphy, *A Guide to Laws and Policies Relating to the Chinese in New Zealand* (Wellington: New Zealand Chinese Association, 1997), pp. 23–24; Burdon, *King Dick*, p. 43; George Kay, 'Seddon and Asian Immigration Legislation 1896–9', Postgraduate Diploma in History thesis, University of Otago, 1973.

133 Commission Report, p. 598.

134 Ibid., p. 656. See also Mein Smith, Hempenstall and Goldfinch, *Remaking the Tasman World*, pp. 40–44. Mein Smith expresses similar views in 'The Tasman World', in Byrnes, ed., *New Oxford History*, pp. 306–8.

135 Commission Report, part XXII.

136 Mein Smith, 'The Tasman World', p. 308.

137 *Official Record 1890*, p. 125.

138 *NZPD*, vol. 69, 6 September 1890, p. 586.

139 Blainey, 'Two Countries: the Same but Very Different', in Sinclair, *Tasman Relations: New Zealand and Australia, 1788–1988*, p. 321; P. A. Tomory, 'The Visual Arts', in Keith Sinclair, ed., *Distance Looks Our Way: The Effects of Remoteness on New Zealand* (Auckland: Paul's Book Arcade for the

University of Auckland, 1961), pp. 63–78. The essays in *Distance Looks Our Way* were presented as lectures in the University of Auckland Winter Lectures in 1960.

140 Blainey, 'Two Countries: the Same but Very Different', in Sinclair, *Tasman Relations: New Zealand and Australia, 1788–1988*, p. 319.

141 Ibid., p. 321.

142 Waterhouse, *The Vision Splendid*, p. 13.

143 C. E. W. Bean, *The Official History of Australia in the War of 1914–1918, vol. 1 – The Story of Anzac*, p. 46. For Bean's characterisation of 'the typical Australian', see *The Story of Anzac*, pp. 4–6.

144 John Andrews, *No Other Home Than This*, p. 300.

145 Helen Irving, 'The Imaginary Nation', in *To Constitute A Nation*, p. 25.

## Six  For God, for Queen and for (Which?) Country

1 Charles C. Bowen, 'The Battle of the Free', in Alexander and Currie, *New Zealand Verse*, pp. 8–13.

2 The war has also been known as the Anglo-Boer War, the South African War, or even as the Second Boer War, the last named being a successor to the 1880–81 Boer rebellion against British rule in the Transvaal that ended with Britain's defeat in the Battle of Majuba. See Thomas Pakenham, *The Boer War: Illustrated Edition* (London: Weidenfeld & Nicolson, 1993).

3 Richard Jebb, *Studies in Colonial Nationalism*, p. 90. See also J. D. Miller, 'Jebb, Richard (1874–1953)', *Oxford Dictionary of National Biography* <http://www.oxforddnb.com>.

4 Jebb, *Studies in Colonial Nationalism*, p. 91.

5 Sinclair, *Destiny Apart*, p. 125.

6 Jebb, *Studies in Colonial Nationalism*, p. 92.

7 Jingoism, meaning bellicose nationalism or extreme nationalism, took its name from the words of an 1878 English music-hall song that enthusiastically endorsed the possibility of war with Russia: 'We don't want to fight; but, by Jingo, if we do / We've got the ships, we've got the men, we've got the money too.' See J. M. and M. J. Cohen, *The Penguin Dictionary of Quotations* (London: Penguin Books, 1963), p. 201.

8 'The General Election, 1899', *AJHR*, 1900, H-26.

9 Malcolm Ross, *A Souvenir of New Zealand's Response to the Empire's Call* (Wellington: McKee & Co, 1899), p. 10. According to the *Observer*, Ross sent a copy of his booklet to the Transvaal president, Paul Kruger. The newspaper commented: 'It's a guinea

to a gooseberry that Paul will use up that booklet as pipe-lights for his long Dutch clay.' *Observer*, 24 February 1900, p. 3.

10 *Destiny Apart*, p. 125.

11 Phillips, *A Man's Country?*

12 Sinclair, *Destiny Apart*, p. 125.

13 D. O. W. Hall, *The New Zealanders in South Africa 1899–1902* (Wellington: War History Branch, Department of Internal Affairs, 1949).

14 See Richard Stowers, *First New Zealanders to the Boer War 1899* (Hamilton: author, 1983); Stowers, *Kiwi Versus Boer: The First New Zealand Mounted Rifles in the Anglo-Boer War 1899–1902* (Hamilton: author, 1992); Stowers, *Rough Riders at War*, 5th edn (Hamilton: author, 2008) (hereafter *Rough Riders*); John Crawford with Ellen Ellis, *To Fight for the Empire: An Illustrated History of New Zealand and the South African War 1899–1902* (Wellington: Reed, in association with the Historical Branch, Department of Internal Affairs, 1999); John Crawford and Ian McGibbon, eds, *One Flag, One Queen, One Tongue: New Zealand, the British Empire and the South African War* (Auckland: Auckland University Press, 2003).

15 The most comprehensive contemporary account was Sarah Elizabeth Hawdon, *New Zealanders and the Boer War, or Soldiers from the Land of the Moa – by a New Zealander* (Christchurch: Gordon & Gotch, 1907); Hawdon, known as Lizzie, first wrote the manuscript for a series of articles that appeared in the *Otago Witness* over several weeks in 1904. Among contemporary personal accounts were James G. Harle Moore, *With the Fourth New Zealand Rough Riders* (Dunedin: Otago Daily Times and Witness Newspapers, 1906); Joseph Linklater, *On Active Service in South Africa with 'The Silent Sixth': Being a record of events, compiled by the writer, from the time of the formation of the Regiment in New Zealand until its return from South Africa* (Wellington: McKee & Co, 1904); Trooper Frank Perham, *The Kimberley Flying Column: Boer War Reminiscences* (Timaru: author, 1957).

16 Frank Beamish letter to Minister of Defence, South African War History, 21 September 1909, AD 34 4 8015, Archives New Zealand. The file contains a chronology of the government's sometimes tortuous path toward a history.

17 Campbell also worked for the short-lived Wellington evening paper that supported the government, the *Sun* – see *Observer*, 17 May 1902, p. 5. Loughnan at the time was associate editor of the *New Zealand Times*.

See Scholefield, *A Dictionary of New Zealand Biography*, vol. 1, pp. 502–3.

18 MacDonald contributes a chapter, 'With the Main Body', in Moore's *With the Fourth New Zealand Rough Riders*.

19 Seddon letter to Minister of Defence, 6 July 1905, AD 34 4 8015, Archives New Zealand.

20 Ibid., Beamish letter to Ward, 21 September 1909.

21 Ibid., Robin letter to Allen, 19 November 1919. Robin and Allen between them also opposed the writing of any of the semi-official histories of World War I by a journalist, Malcolm Ross, who was the government-employed New Zealand official correspondent. See Ron Palenski, 'Malcolm Ross: A Forgotten Casualty of the Great War', MA thesis, University of Otago, 2007.

22 Ibid., Sir Robert Rhodes letter to Charles E. Statham, MP, 29 October 1920.

23 Ibid.

24 J. A. Shand, 'O'er Veldt and Kopje – The Official Account of the Operations of the New Zealand Contingents in the Boer War (Years 1899–1902) – Compiled from official records and field notes', qms-1790, Alexander Turnbull Library.

25 Letter from the Minister of Internal Affairs, William Parry, to J. H. E. Tilling, secretary of the South African War Veterans' Association, 27 March 1936, AD 34 4 8015, Archives New Zealand. Tilling did not serve with any of the New Zealand contingents. Born in England, he served with the Imperial Yeomanry and emigrated to New Zealand 'a year or two after the war', according to an obituary in the *Dominion*, 15 November 1939, p. 6.

26 For background on the setting up of the War History Branch, see Michael Bassett, 'An Overview of the War History Branch', lecture to Department of Internal Affairs seminar, Wellington 1997, <www.michaelbassett.co.nz/article_war.htm>; see also the *Dominion*, 22 May 1943, p. 4.

27 Kippenberger dismissed Shand's manuscript thus: 'It consists of a diffuse boastful and rambling account of the services of the New Zealand Contingents, quite unintelligible, and of long lists of names.' Ian McGibbon, '"Something of Them Here Is Recorded": Official History in New Zealand', <www.nzetc.org/tm/scholarly/tei-McGSome.html>.

28 Mulgan, *Great Days in New Zealand Writing*, p. 76.

29 *Dominion*, 10 May 1940, p. 5.

30 There is still no single book that covers the whole spectrum of New Zealand involvement in the war – politically from both

national and imperial viewpoints, militarily, or socially and culturally in terms of the impact it had within New Zealand. Readers seeking such perspectives can partly be satisfied with Crawford and McGibbon's *One Flag, One Queen, One Tongue*, which was based largely on papers presented at a 1999 symposium that marked the centenary of the war, or even the more comprehensive Australian history: Craig Wilcox, *Australia's Boer War: The War in South Africa 1899–1902* (Melbourne: Oxford University Press in association with the Australian War Memorial, 2002). Other useful academic works on the war include Kingsley D. Sampson, 'Chief Among the Children: A survey of the national self-image of New Zealanders in the years 1899–1901', MA thesis, University of Otago, 1970; Alfred J. Bathgate, 'Seddon and the Boer War Period 1899–1904', MA thesis, University of Otago, 1968; Tui Gilling, 'On Active Service: New Zealand and the South African War 1899–1902', Postgraduate Diploma of Arts thesis, University of Otago, 1990; Ian McIver, 'New Zealand and the South African War of 1899–1902: A study of New Zealand's attitudes and motives for involvement and the effect of the war on New Zealand and her relations with Britain', MA thesis, University of Otago, 1972. For general accounts of the war, see Arthur Conan Doyle, *The Great Boer War* (London: Thomas Nelson & Sons, 1903) or Pakenham, *The Boer War: Illustrated Edition*.
31 Quoted in Pakenham, *The Boer War*, p. 396.
32 *Hansard*, 23 October 1899, columns 563–64.
33 Pakenham, *The Boer War*, pp. 269–70.
34 Ian McGibbon, *The Path to Gallipoli: Defending New Zealand 1840–1915* (Wellington: GP Books, 1991), p. 115.
35 Ranfurly to Chamberlain, 27 December 1900, CO209/261.
36 Chamberlain to Ranfurly, 28 December 1900, 'Further Correspondence Relating to Affairs in South Africa', Cd547, House of Commons Parliamentary Papers.
37 Chamberlain to Ranfurly, 28 December 1900, CO209/261.
38 For biographical details of these and other Māori, see Stowers, *Rough Riders*, pp. 82–250.
39 *Observer*, 18 January 1902, p. 4.
40 Stowers, *Rough Riders*, p. 99. Klaus Loewald, 'Broughton, Edward Renata Muhunga (1884–1955)', *Australian Dictionary of Biography* <www.adb.online.anu.edu.au>; the New Zealand (Māori) Pioneer Battalion was formed on 1 September 1917, incorporating the Māori Contingent that had

been formed in 1915 and the New Zealand Pioneer Battalion of 1916. See Christopher Pugsley, *Te Hokowhitu a Tu: The Maori Pioneer Battalion in the First World War* (Auckland: Reed Books, 1995), p. 9.
41 *Te Ao Hou (The New World)*, no. 39 (June 1962), p. 63.
42 Stowers, *Rough Riders*, p. 163.
43 David Roy Simmons, 'Māori Medical Corps in South Africa during the Boer War', MS-Papers-4889, Alexander Turnbull Library.
44 Ibid. See also Stowers, *Rough Riders*, p. 55.
45 'Maori Contingent', 3 February 1902, CO209/264. A Māori detachment of 35 was among the New Zealand contingent at the coronation. See Stowers, *Rough Riders*, p. 265.
46 Scottish-born Hutcheson was one of the principal figures in the maritime strike of 1890 and was first elected to Parliament in 1896. See G. H. Scholefield, ed., *Who's Who in New Zealand* (Wellington: Rangatira Press, 1932), p. 208; *Dominion*, 7 October 1940, p. 9. Hutcheson, whose given name was John but used the hypocoristic 'Jack', should not be confused with another member of Parliament opposed to the Seddon administration, George Hutchison, who served for a time in South Africa and subsequently practised law there until 1907. See Scholefield, *A Dictionary of New Zealand Biography*, vol. 1, p. 423.
47 *NZPD*, 28 September 1899, p. 81.
48 Ibid.
49 Ibid., p. 97.
50 He was a nephew of the former premier, Sir Harry Atkinson, and of Justice William Richmond, and described by Guy Scholefield as 'a brilliant and at times bitter critic of the Seddon administration'. Scholefield, *The Richmond–Atkinson Papers*, vol. 2, p. 571.
51 The total poll nationally recorded a 74 per cent turnout. *AJHR*, 1900, H-26, pp. 3–4.
52 *New Zealand Tablet*, 19 October 1899, p. 2.
53 See Rory Sweetman, 'Cleary, Henry William, 1859–1929', in Claudia Orange, general editor, *Dictionary of New Zealand Biography*, vol. 3 (Wellington: Auckland University Press with Bridget Williams Books and the Department of Internal Affairs, 1996), pp. 101–3.
54 *New Zealand Tablet*, 19 October 1899, p. 17. The Transvaal government kept upping the period required to qualify for citizenship.
55 'Waddell, Rutherford (c1850–1932)', in Thomson, ed., *Southern People*, pp. 529–30.
56 *Outlook*, 21 October 1899, p. 1; The

Shakespearean quote was from Julius Caesar (act 3, scene 1, 273).

57 Ibid., 28 October 1899, p. 4.

58 Ibid., 4 November 1899, pp. 4–5.

59 *Otago Witness*, 30 November 1899, p. 14.

60 Dutton also served as chaplain-general in World War I. See Kieran O'Connell, "'Be Strong and Show Thyself a Man'": Christian Masculinities in Southern Dunedin 1885–1925', in John Stenhouse and Jane Thomson, eds, *Building God's Own Country: Historical Essays on Religion in New Zealand* (Dunedin: University of Otago Press, 2004), pp. 169–84; J. Bryant Haigh, *Men of Faith and Courage: The official history of the Royal New Zealand Chaplains Department* (Auckland: The Word Publishers, 1983), pp. 41, 94.

61 For Grattan Grey biographical details, see Scholefield, *A Dictionary of New Zealand Biography*, vol. 1, p. 331.

62 *New York Times*, 26 November 1899, p. 21.

63 Ibid., 24 December 1899, p. 6.

64 *Evening Star* (Dunedin), 29 January 1900, p. 1, 23 March 1900, p. 4.

65 Ibid., 29 January 1900, p. 1.

66 J. Grattan Grey, *Freedom of Thought and Speech in New Zealand – A Serious Menace to Liberty – Mr Seddon, Premier, and Mr J. Grattan Grey, Journalist – An Interesting Correspondence* (Wellington: author, 1901). The editor of the *Evening Star* at the time was Mark Cohen, and his younger brother, Albert, was the paper's parliamentary correspondent based in Wellington. George Griffiths, 'Cohen, Mark (1849–1928)', in Thomson, ed., *Southern People*, p. 98.

67 Grey letter to the Premier, 15 February 1900, 'Correspondence Between the Rt Hon the Premier and the Chief Hansard Reporter', *AJHR*, 1900, H-29, p. 3.

68 *NZPD*, 19–20 July 1900, pp. 12–53.

69 *New Zealand Free Lance*, 28 July 1900, p. 6.

70 *Evening Post*, 14 March 1900, p. 2.

71 Reeves letter to Seddon, 20 April 1900, *AJHR*, 1900, H-29, pp. 1–4.

72 *Evening Post*, 14 December 1901, p. 7.

73 Brigid Pike, 'Tasker, Marianne Allen, 1852–1911', *Dictionary of New Zealand Biography*, vol. 2, pp. 504–5.

74 *Evening Post*, 14 December 1901, p. 7.

75 Ibid.

76 *AJHR*, 1901, A1, pp. 22–23.

77 *Evening Post*, 1 November 1901, p. 5.

78 Governor's dispatches Jan–Oct 1901, original correspondence Secretary of State (CO209/202 1207), 1901 Jan–Oct dispatches, reel 2652–2653, piece 262, Archives New Zealand.

79 *Otago Daily Times*, 11 May 1900, p. 2.

80 Ibid.

81 Governor's dispatches. A transcript of the diary kept by Tasker in South Africa was published by a descendant, Paul Tasker, in 1991. He noted that within the diary was an undated newspaper clipping reporting the return to Australia of three Victorian troopers who had been sentenced to death for inciting a mutiny but who were freed on Kitchener's orders. The 'mutiny' centred on the troopers' refusal to obey the orders of a British general who called them 'a lot of white livered curs' after the Victorians were overcome in battle at Wilmansrust by an inferior Boer force. See P. M. Tasker, *A Slice of the Life of My Uncle Charlie: A Diary of Trooper C. B. Tasker, Service Number 3561, 6th Contingent, New Zealand Mounted Rifles, South Africa* (Wellington: published by the transcriber, 1991).

82 A much more celebrated case was that of Harry ('Breaker') Morant and Peter Handcock, who were executed for murder. Though Kelly-like, attempts were made to impose martyrdom on Morant, especially after a 1981 eponymous film, any objective reading of the evidence shows the British were correct. See Wilcox, *Australia's Boer War*, pp. 363–65, 367–68.

83 *Evening Post*, 9 December 1901, p. 4.

84 *New Zealand Observer*, 28 July 1900, p. 2.

85 *Evening Post*, 29 June 1900, p. 2.

86 Ibid., p. 4.

87 *Otago Witness*, 5 July 1900, p. 32.

88 *New Zealand Free Lance*, 7 July 1900, p. 6.

89 Ranfurly to Chamberlain, quarterly report, 2 July 1900, MS-Papers-6357-02, Ranfurly family: Papers, Alexander Turnbull Library.

90 The only direct New Zealand involvement in the Boxer Uprising appears to have been the murder of a Christchurch missionary, Edith Searelle, by Boxers on 2 July 1900. The Chinese government paid Searelle's mother compensation of £665 14s in July 1901. See correspondence between the Foreign Office and the Colonial Office, copied to the New Zealand Governor (CO209/202, CO209/264); for an account of Searelle's murder, see *The Times*, 29 August 1900, p. 7. A New Zealand-born journalist, Arthur Henry Adams, was sent by the *Sydney Morning Herald* and several New Zealand newspapers to cover the uprising. See Scholefield, *A Dictionary of New Zealand Biography*, vol. 1, p. 4. Dunedin-born James Waddell was an officer in French forces that formed part of the international force assembled to quell the uprising. See J. O. Lucas, G. H. Fairmaid, M. G. McInnes and W. K. Patrick, *Otago Boys' High School Old Boys' Register* (Dunedin: Otago High

School Old Boys' Society, 1963), p. 199, and Martin Windrow, *Our Friends Beneath the Sands: The Foreign Legion in France's Colonial Conquests 1870–1935* (London: Weidenfeld & Nicolson, 2010), p. 664. For a general account of the uprising, including the murder of missionaries, see Diana Preston, *The Boxer Rebellion: The Dramatic Story of China's War on Foreigners that Shook the World in the Summer of 1900* (New York: Berkley Books, 2001).

91 *Evening Post*, 20 May 1901, p. 4.
92 *Observer*, 21 December 1901, p. 2.
93 *Otago Witness*, 19 October 1899, p. 63.
94 *Evening Post*, 21 February 1902, p. 7.
95 Rudyard Kipling, 'Dirge of Dead Sisters', 1902, in Rudyard Kipling, *The Complete Verse*, pp. 175–76.
96 See Sheila Gray, *The South African War 1899–1902: Service Records of British and Colonial Women: A record of the service in South Africa of Military and Civilian Nurses, Laywomen and Civilians* (Auckland: published by the author, 1993), pp. 74–76. As with soldier numbers, the number of New Zealand nurses in South Africa varies, partly because some were part of British or Australian contingents. Gray's list seems the most comprehensive.
97 *Evening Post*, 7 February 1900, p. 4.
98 *Otago Witness*, 7 February 1900, p. 4.
99 Ibid., 15 February 1900, p. 18.
100 Diary entry 30 April 1900, diary kept by Nurse D. L. Harris of the New Zealand Contingent Whilst Serving as a Nursing Sister in South Africa April 1900–May 1901, National Army Museum: Miscellaneous Collections, Micro-MS-Coll-20-1906, Alexander Turnbull Library. The 'Mr P' referred to was Herbert Pilcher, Cape Town manager of the South British Insurance Company, who seemed to act as a general agent for New Zealanders. See *Evening Post*, 13 September 1900, p. 5.
101 Crawford with Ellis, *To Fight for the Empire*, pp. 41–42.
102 Vincent J. Cirillo, '"Winged Sponges": houseflies as carriers of typhoid fever in 19th and early 20th century military camps', *Perspectives in Biology and Medicine*, vol. 49, no. 1 (Winter 2006), p. 52.
103 *NZPD*, 29 June 1900, p. 159.
104 *New Zealand Herald*, 7 August 1900, p. 5.
105 *Press*, 24 January 1901, p. 5.
106 Joan Rattray, *Great Days in New Zealand Nursing* (London: George G. Harrap & Co, 1961), p. 128.
107 *Otago Witness*, 8 March 1900, pp. 37–38. 'Rachel weeping' was a biblical reference relating to Herod's slaying of children.

According to Matthew 2:18: 'A voice was heard in Ramah, Weeping and great mourning, Rachel weeping for her children: And she would not be comforted, because they are not.' See also Jeremiah 31:15–17: 'A voice is heard in Ramah, lamentation, and bitter weeping, Rachel weeping for her children; she refuseth to be comforted for her children, because they are not.' Holy Bible, Revised Version (London: Octopus Books, 1981).
108 Rattray, *Great Days in New Zealand Nursing*, p. 126.
109 *Observer*, 2 June 1906, p. 4.
110 Shappere was sometimes listed as Australian because, according to Rattray, her family moved to Melbourne in the 1890s. See Rattray, *Great Days in New Zealand Nursing*, p. 127; Wilcox, *Australia's Boer War*, pp. 228, 230–31. The *Observer* reported she was a matron at a leading London hospital and at a hospital in Nice built as a memorial to Queen Victoria. 'Matron Shappere stands well in the eyes of royal princesses', it said.
111 *Evening Post*, 30 September 1901, p. 5, 19 December 1901, p. 5; Stowers, *Rough Riders*, p. 53; 'New Zealand Honours – History' <www.dpmc.govt.nz>; see also Sherayl McNabb, 'Janet Wyse Mackie Williamson RRC', *The Volunteers*, the Journal of the New Zealand Military Historical Society, vol. 25, no. 2 (Boer War Commemorative Issue), pp. 67–68.
112 *New Zealand Observer*, 16 March 1901, p. 8.
113 'Banjo' Paterson, 'Our Own Flag', in Campbell and Harvie, *Singer of the Bush*, p. 686.
114 Neil C. Smith, *Australians with New Zealand Contingents to the Boer War 1899–1902* (Gardenvale, Victoria: Mostly Unsung Military History Research and Publications, 2000).
115 Stowers, *Rough Riders*, p. 175. See also John Crawford, 'The Best Mounted Troops in South Africa?', in Crawford and McGibbon, eds, *One Flag, One Queen, One Tongue*, pp. 80–81.
116 Phillips, *A Man's Country?*.
117 Ibid., p. 146.
118 Colin McGeorge, 'The Social and Geographical Composition of New Zealand Contingents', in Crawford and McGibbon, eds, *One Flag, One Queen, One Tongue*, p. 116.
119 Phillips, *A Man's Country?*, pp. 147–48. It is possible to qualify such analyses. The word 'class' in New Zealand did not have the same connotations as it did in Britain, where class was derived from birth and schooling and where there was minimal mixing between classes. Class in the New Zealand context

meant position or wealth, either inherited or acquired, but it did not prevent cross-class contact. As Sarah Hawdon noted: 'If this sending forth of sons and daughters to the scene of war does nothing else for New Zealand, it will have done much in drawing together the hearts of all classes for we have been all these two years and more united in that strongest of bonds – a common anxiety.' See *Otago Witness*, 24 August 1904, p. 69. Another point to be made in the context of the contrasting status of New Zealanders is that secondary school education in the late nineteenth century was available only to children of parents who could afford the fees. It was not until 1903 that free places were available to children who passed a proficiency examination. Since commissioned rank required a higher standard of education, it followed that those most likely to be commissioned were either from wealthy families or had been educated to a sufficient standard in Britain (where wealth also would have been a prerequisite).

120 See Stowers, *Rough Riders*, p. 191.

121 Moore, *With the Fourth New Zealand Rough Riders*, p. 17.

122 Ibid., p. 26.

123 *Otago Daily Times*, 20 November 1899, p. 5. Wilkie also served with the Ninth Contingent and was a captain in the Wellington Mounted Rifles in World War I and wrote the regiment's history.

124 Hall, *The New Zealanders in South Africa 1899–1902*, p. 69.

125 *Otago Witness*, 12 October 1904, p. 70. Kitchener would have been more familiar with New Zealand than most senior British officers because his father, Henry, moved to New Zealand in the 1860s and bought land in North Otago. His sister, Frances ('Millie'), married and settled in Kurow and her son, James Parker, served with the Second Contingent and later Kitchener's Horse. He was killed in action on 1 May 1900. A cousin of Lord Kitchener's, Henry, and four of his children were killed in a house fire in Dunedin in 1882. See Philip Magnus, *Kitchener: Portrait of an Imperialist* (London: John Murray, 1958), pp. 1–7; *North Otago Times*, 5 May 1900, p. 2; *Otago Witness*, 8 July 1882, p. 23, 29 July 1882, p. 17; *Otago Daily Times*, 17 February 1910, p. 7.

126 *Otago Witness*, 12 October 1904, p. 70.

127 R. W. F. Droogleever, *From the Front: A. B. (Banjo) Paterson's Dispatches from the Boer War* (Sydney: Macmillan, 2000), pp. 61–62.

128 Ibid., p. 150.

129 Conan Doyle, *The Great Boer War*, p. 188.

130 Ibid., p. 527.

131 *Graphic*, 8 December 1900, p. 847.

132 Wilcox, *Australia's Boer War*, p. 303. This retrospective view seems to have been drawn from the memoirs of one of the Australian soldiers, Jack Abbott, who wrote that the New Zealanders differed materially from the 'Cornstalk' (New South Wales) troops: 'However, New Zealand had her own traditions of a fierce and bloody war, which, even though it be of the last generation, is still fresh enough in the memories of the people of today to give added soldierly qualities to her sons.' J. M. H. Abbott, *Tommy Cornstalk: Being Some Account of the Less Notable Features of the South African War from the Point of View of the Australian Ranks* (London: Longman Green, 2002), pp. 219–20, quoted in John Crawford, 'The Best Mounted Troops in South Africa?', in Crawford and McGibbon, eds, *One Flag, One Queen, One Tongue*, p. 74.

133 Royal Commission on the War in South Africa, minutes of evidence, vol. 1, p. 386, quoted in McGibbon, *The Path to Gallipoli*, p. 124.

134 Quoted in Stowers, *Rough Riders*, p. 63.

135 Ibid.

136 *Illustrated London News Record of the Transvaal War 1899–1900*, p. 60.

137 *Press*, 1 January 1901, p. 10. Hales himself was an Australian.

138 *New Zealand Observer*, 23 March 1901, p. 2.

139 Stowers, *Rough Riders*, p. 223.

140 *Press*, 21 January 1901, p. 6.

141 Belich, *Paradise Reforged*, p. 79.

142 L. P. Russell letter to his mother 20 June 1901, Russell family collection, MS-Papers-3954, Alexander Turnbull Library. The New Zealander Russell met was probably Private William John Stevens Horne of the Fifth Contingent, whose address was listed as Hastings Street, Hastings. See Stowers, *Rough Riders*, p. 156.

143 Ibid., letter to mother 25 June 1901.

144 Sir William Russell was the founding president of the Hawke's Bay Polo Club in 1894. See K. M. Little, *Polo in New Zealand* (Wellington: Whitcombe & Tombs, 1956), p. 112.

145 While one consequence of death is speculation about a denied future, Lionel Phillips Russell would surely have advanced in the military that he admired so much. The male Russells had a habit of distinguishing themselves in the service of their country and of Britain. Sir William Russell was educated at the Royal Military College, Sandhurst, and twice served in New Zealand with British regiments until he took up farming in 1862. A brother, Andrew Hamilton Russell, also served with British regiments and later

became Major-General Sir Andrew and commanded the New Zealand Division in France from 1916. Their father and grandfather also had distinguished military careers. The father, Lieutenant-Colonel Andrew Hamilton Russell, was a member of the Legislative Council from 1861 until 1872 and was for a time Minister of Native Affairs. See S. W. Grant, 'Russell, William Russell, 1838–1913', in *Dictionary of New Zealand Biography*, vol. 2, p. 436; and *The Times*, 30 November 1960, p. 16.

146 Linklater, *On Active Service in South Africa with 'The Silent Sixth'*, pp. 35, 40.

147 'Paraded before lieutenant in a body and threatened to go to the commandant if he did not get us our pay. He promised us £3 so we had to be satisfied. He told us parading was against all military rules. We knew nothing about military rules, but thought it a very effective style.' Ibid., p. 75.

148 Ibid.

149 *Otago Witness*, 6 March 1901, p. 27.

150 Ibid.

151 Moore, *With the Fourth New Zealand Rough Riders*, p. 173. The word 'veldt' is spelt thus when used within quotations; otherwise, the more accepted spelling of 'veld' is used.

152 Perham, *The Kimberley Flying Column*, p. 78.

153 *Otago Witness*, 8 February 1900, p. 11.

154 Ibid. 'Galloper' in that sense was a messenger carrying orders from a commander to officers.

155 Ranfurly to Chamberlain, 14 December 1901, CO209/263.

156 McGibbon, *Path to Gallipoli*, p. 123.

157 *New Zealand Illustrated Magazine*, February 1902, p. 431.

*Seven Forging a National Identity Through Sport*

1 Michael Billig, *Banal Nationalism* (London: Sage Publications, 1995), p. 8.

2 *Otago Daily Times*, 3 January 1874, p. 2.

3 *Otago Witness*, 24 June 1908, p. 71. This report was written four months after Scott's death from mouth cancer by his former trainer, Alfred Austin, who by this time was living in London as Austin Smith. The report was an account of Scott's career and included references to his first appearance at the Caledonian sports – where Austin/Smith was a handicapper – and the apparent comment by Fergusson.

4 *Otago Daily Times*, 3 January 1889, p. 4.

5 Scott was in fact born in Lettermacaward in County Donegal in 1860 and his parents brought him to New Zealand when he was an infant.

6 *Lyttelton Times*, 6 December 1888, p. 3.

7 *New Zealand Railways Magazine*, 2 December 1935, p. 79.

8 Porritt won the bronze medal in the 100 metres in the Olympic Games in Paris in 1924; he was Governor-General of New Zealand 1967–72.

9 Innumerable books and articles have appeared on the role of sport and national identity but see in particular J. A. Mangan, *The Games Ethic and Imperialism* (London: Viking, 1986); Mangan, ed., *The Cultural Bond: Sport, Empire, Society* (London: Frank Cass, 1992); and J. Nauright, eds, *Sport in Australasia: Past and Present* (London: Frank Cass, 2000); P. C. McIntosh, *Sport In Society* (London: C. A. Watts & Co, 1963); Mike Huggins, *The Victorians and Sport* (London: Hambledon & London, 2004); Brian Stoddart, 'Sport, Cultural Imperialism, and Colonial Response in the British Empire', *Comparative Studies in Society and History*, vol. 30, no. 4 (October 1988), pp. 649–73; for a wider, non-Anglocentric view, see Richard Holt, Mangan and Pierre Lanfranchi, eds, *European Heroes: Myth, Identity, Sport* (London: Frank Cass, 2005); Jeffrey Hill, 'Cocks, cats, caps and cups: A semiotic approach to sport and national identity', *Sport in Society*, vol. 2, no. 2 (Summer 1999), pp. 1–21; David S. Forsyth, 'Empire and union: Imperial and national identity in nineteenth century Scotland', *Scottish Geographical Journal*, vol. 113, no. 1 (March 1997), pp. 6–12.

10 'The metonymic image of banal nationalism is not a flag which is being consciously waved with fervent passion; it is the flag hanging unnoticed on the public building … an identity is to be found in the embodied habits of social life. National identity embraces all these forgotten reminders.' Billig, *Banal Nationalism*, p. 8.

11 Hill, 'Cocks, cats, caps and cups', p. 3.

12 The role of the Premier, Richard Seddon, in rugby is examined in the following chapter. For how governments exploited sport for nationalistic ends, see Matti Goksøyr, 'Nationalism', in Pope and Nauright, eds, *Routledge Companion to Sports History*, pp. 267–94, especially two such disparate examples as Ireland in the nineteenth century and (the former) German Democratic Republic in the late twentieth. See also David Hassan, 'Rugby Union, Irish Nationalism and National Identity in Northern Ireland', *Football Studies*, vol. 6, no. 1 (2003), pp. 5–18. Another political advocate of the efficacy of sport was Theodore Roosevelt, who argued that

national devotion to sports would lead to
international hegemony. See Mark Dyreson,
'Sport and visions of the "American
Century"', *Peace Review*, vol. II, no. 4 (1999),
pp. 565–71.

13   Scott A. G. M. Crawford, 'A Sporting Image:
The Emergence of a National Identity in
a Colonial Setting, 1862–1906', *Victorian
Periodicals Review*, vol. 21, no. 2 (Summer
1988), pp. 56–63.

14   The study of New Zealand sports history
has sometimes been tacked on to that
of Australia and has renewed use of
the umbrella word 'Australasia'. See,
for example, Scott A. G. M.Crawford,
'Recreational and Sporting Values on
the Fringe of an Imperial Empire: the
Reshaping of a British Heritage in Colonial
New Zealand', in *Sport and Colonialism in
Nineteenth Century Australasia, Australian
Society of Sports History Studies in Sports
History, no. 1* (Sydney: Australian Society
of Sports History, 1986), pp. 65–79; C.
Little, 'Trans-Tasman Federations in
Sport – The changing relationships between
Australia and New Zealand', in Richard
Cashman, John O'Hara and Andrew Honey,
eds, *Sport, Federation, Nation* (Sydney: Walla
Walla Press, 2001), pp. 63–80; Mangan
and Nauright, eds, *Sport in Australasia: Past
and Present*.

15   Belich, *Paradise Reforged*, p. 370. Keith
Sinclair, Jock Phillips and Tom Brooking
included sport in influential works, each
using sport as a vehicle in their arguments.
Sinclair, *Destiny Apart*; Phillips, *A Man's
Country?*; Tom Brooking, *The Greenwood
Histories of the Modern Nations: The History
of New Zealand* (Westport, Connecticut:
Greenwood Press, 2004).

16   'The situation is rather like that of military,
religious and local history, which narrow-
minded academic historians avoid, and
other writers embrace with narrow-minded
fervour.' Belich, *Paradise Reforged*, p. 370;
see also Charlotte Macdonald, 'Ways of
Belonging: Sporting Spaces in New Zealand
History', in Byrnes, ed., *New Oxford History*',
p. 271.

17   Macdonald, 'Ways of Belonging', p. 271.
Macdonald's view was expressed in a
chapter dedicated to sport; the 'old'
*Oxford History of New Zealand* had no
such chapter, instead mentioning specific
sporting moments or beliefs only briefly
or in a political or wider social context.
Geoffrey W. Rice, ed., *The Oxford History
of New Zealand Second Edition* (hereafter
Rice, *Oxford History*) (Auckland: Oxford
University Press, 1992). See, for example, W.

David McIntyre, 'From Dual Dependency
to Nuclear Free', pp. 537–38: 'To many
others unconcerned with national glory
or the niceties of diplomacy, there was a
passionate identification with the country's
sporting success.' He then goes on to list
some examples of that success (without
listing the failures in the same period he
covers). For a similar approach, see King,
*The Penguin History of New Zealand*. Both
Belich and Macdonald make the point that
while hundreds of sports books have been
published in New Zealand, many of them
about the history of specific sports, trained
historians have been slow or reluctant to
pick up the challenge.

18   Late in the twentieth century Greg Ryan
became the most active of a small number
of academic historians with a professional
interest in sport: Greg Ryan, *Forerunners
of the All Blacks: The 1888–89 New Zealand
Native Football Team in Britain, Australia
and New Zealand* (hereafter *Forerunners of
the All Blacks*) (Christchurch: Canterbury
University Press, 1993); Ryan, *The Making
of New Zealand Cricket 1832–1914* (London:
Frank Cass, 2004); Ryan, ed., *Tackling
Rugby Myths: Rugby and New Zealand Society
1854–2004* (Dunedin: Otago University
Press, 2004); Ryan, *The Contest for Rugby
Supremacy: Accounting for the 1905 All Blacks*
(hereafter *1905 All Blacks*) (Christchurch:
Canterbury University Press, 2005).
A fellow Canterbury academic historian,
Len Richardson, combined with his daugh-
ter Shelley in a rare academic biography of
an individual New Zealand sportsman. Len
and Shelley Richardson, *Anthony Wilding:
A Sporting Life* (Christchurch: Canterbury
University Press, 2005). Another New
Zealand scholar, Douglas Booth, has been
influentially active especially in sports
historiography, but seldom on specific New
Zealand topics. Douglas Booth, *Australian
Beach Cultures: The history of sun, sand and
surf* (London: Frank Cass, 2001); Booth,
*The field: Truth and fiction in sport history* (New
York: Routledge, 2005); Booth, *The Race
Game: Sport and Politics in South Africa*
(London: Frank Cass, 1998); Booth and
Colin Tatz, *One-Eyed: A View of Australian
Sport* (Sydney: Allen & Unwin, 2000).
Others such as Scott A. G. M. Crawford,
G. T. Vincent and Charles Little have writ-
ten of specific sports history topics but have
seldom been published in New Zealand.
For example, Scott A. G. M. Crawford,
'Rugby in Contemporary New Zealand',
*Journal of Sport and Social Issues*, vol. 12,
no. 2 (1988), pp. 108–21; C. Little, '"Our

George": Ex-Patriot Sportsmen and the Emergence of New Zealand's National Identity', *Proceedings of Ninth International Society for the History of Physical Education and Sport (ISHPES) Seminar*, Ljubljana, 2006; G. T. Vincent, 'Practical Imperialism: the Anglo-Welsh Rugby Tour of New Zealand, 1908', *International Journal of the History of Sport* (hereafter *IJHS*), vol. 15, no. 1 (April 1998), pp. 123–40. A more recent treatise on the historiography of New Zealand sport was written by Malcolm MacLean, in which he traces developments and worries about 'nationalist shackles'. Malcolm MacLean, 'New Zealand (Aotearoa)', in Pope and Nauright, *Routledge Companion to Sports History*, pp. 510–25.

19 Erik Olssen wrote that rugby was one aspect of 'the new spirit of organisation' that pervaded all New Zealand society in the last 20 years of the nineteenth century. The 'engaging informality' of hybrid and variable rules before 1870 was replaced by order and organisation: 'The All Blacks' success [in 1905–06] in adopting specialized positional play contributed greatly to their success. The sense of national pride which the All Blacks generated helped to legitimize national structures even as the way they organized to play both reflected and reinforced the belief that specialization enhanced efficiency.' Erik Olssen, 'Toward A New Society', in Rice, *Oxford History*, p. 262. This contention is challenged in the following chapter, which shows that New Zealanders, and Māori in particular (it was the 1888 Native team that originated specialised forward positions), refined the method of playing rugby long before the 1905–06 tour.

20 MacLean cites the *New Zealand Journal of History* among publications which 'have given considerable attention to a national sporting past', but over 43 volumes since its inception in 1967 the *Journal* has included only six articles about a specific sporting topic. MacLean, 'New Zealand (Aotearoa)', p. 510. Given a justifiable concentration in the *Journal* on race relations, it seems even more surprising that scholars have written little about Māori involvement and influence in competitive sport. In addition, the historiography has almost exclusively covered sporting men, which is logical enough (if decried by postmodernist historians) when it is considered there was very little international competitive sport available to New Zealand women – or women of any other country – until well into the twentieth

century. A rare exception has been Clare Simpson's study of women cyclists and how they represented 'the New Women', but again, women's cycling in this context was a recreational pursuit – as it was also for most men – and not a competitive sporting endeavour. Clare S. Simpson, 'Respectable Identities: New Zealand Nineteenth-Century "New Women" – on Bicycles!', *IJHS*, vol. 18, no. 2 (June 2001), pp. 54–77.

21 McIntosh, *Sport In Society*, p. 54. For an appreciation of McIntosh, see Mike Huggins, 'Walking in the Footsteps of a Pioneer: Peter McIntosh – Trail Blazer in the History of Sport', *IJHS*, vol. 18, no. 2 (2001), pp. 134–47.

22 Ibid.

23 Ibid., p. 56.

24 D. H. Craven, *The Evolution of Major Games*, PhD thesis, University of Stellenbosch, 1978. Craven argued the diffusion theory for sports and that they reached the British Isles in ancient forms from the east, some originating in Asia and some in southern Europe.

25 Peter C. McIntosh, 'The British Attitude to Sport', in Alex Natan, ed., *Sport and Society: A Symposium* (London: Bowes & Bowes, 1958), p. 15.

26 Ibid., p. 17.

27 See J. A. Mangan, 'Christ and the Imperial Games Fields: Evangelical Athletes of the Empire', *IJHS*, vol. 1, no. 2 (1984), pp. 184–201.

28 This paraphrases the Edwardian poet Rupert Brooke, who wrote in 'The Soldier' in 1914: 'If I should die, think only this of me: / That there's some corner of a foreign field / That is forever England.'

29 Sir Charles Tennyson, 'They Taught the World to Play', *Victorian Studies*, vol. 2, no. 3 (March 1959), pp. 211–22.

30 Crawford, 'Recreational and Sporting Values', p. 67.

31 See David Cooper, 'Canadians Declare "It Isn't Cricket": A Century of Rejection of the Imperial Game, 1860–1960', *Journal of Sport History*, vol. 26, no. 1 (Spring 1999), pp. 51–81.

32 *Graphic*, 31 October 1891, p. 1.

33 Crawford, 'Recreational and Sporting Values', p. 68.

34 Credit for the introduction of rugby union into New Zealand is given to Charles John Monro, a son of the Speaker of the House of Representatives, Sir David Monro. The young Monro was sent to Christ's College in north London to be educated, where 'Rugby rules' were adhered to, and on

his return to Nelson in 1870 he persuaded his friends and former schoolmates to play the new game. See Ron Palenski, *Our National Game: A Celebration of 100 Years of NZ Rugby* (Auckland: Moa Publications, 1992), pp. 11–18; Clive Akers, *Monro: The Life and Times of the Man Who Gave New Zealand Rugby* (Palmerston North: author, 2008); Rex E. Wright-St Clair, *Thoroughly A Man of the World: A Biography of Sir David Monro* (Christchurch: Whitcombe & Tombs, 1971), pp. 139–40.

35  *Evening Post*, 8 February 1910, p. 11.

36  E. J. Wakefield, *Adventure in New Zealand*, vol. 1 (London: John Murray, 1845; facsimile edn, Auckland: Wilson & Horton, 1971), p. 433.

37  Ibid., p. 434. For Petre details, see Scholefield, *A Dictionary of New Zealand Biography*, vol. 2, p. 163.

38  Ibid.

39  Miriam Macgregor Redwood, *Proud Silk – A New Zealand Racing History* (Wellington: A. H. & A. W. Reed, 1979), p. 10.

40  Ryan, *The Making of New Zealand Cricket*, p. 20.

41  *Nelson Examiner and New Zealand Chronicle*, 31 July 1852, p. 90. For Redwood details, see Mollie Dickinson, 'Redwood, Henry 1823–1907', *Dictionary of New Zealand Biography*, vol. 2, p. 408.

42  Ryan, *The Making of New Zealand Cricket*, p. 27.

43  Ibid., pp. 27–28. Charles Darwin, *The Journal of a Voyage in H.M.S. Beagle* (Guildford: Genesis Publications in association with Australia and New Zealand Book Company, 1979), p. 671.

44  Ibid. See also T. W. Reese, *New Zealand Cricket 1841–1914* (Christchurch: Simpson & Williams, 1927), p. 15; *New Zealand Gazette and Wellington Spectator*, 20 February 1841, p. 2.

45  *New Zealand Gazette and Wellington Spectator*, 23 May 1840, p. 2.

46  Nancy M. Taylor, ed., *Journal of Ensign Best 1837–1843* (Wellington: R. A. Owen, Government Printer, 1966), p. 275.

47  *New Zealand Gazette and Wellington Spectator*, 20 February 1841, p. 2.

48  Reese, *New Zealand Cricket 1841–1914*, pp. 15–21.

49  For a description of cricket in early Christchurch, including team selection, see the *Press*, 23 December 1899, p. 9.

50  *Otago Witness*, 6 February 1864, pp. 1, 7–8, 11, 20 February 1864, p. 4.

51  G. J. Griffiths, *Queenstown's King Wakatip* (Dunedin: John McIndoe, 1971); *Notes on Some Early Arrivals in Otago, no. 3, W. G. Rees and His Cricketing Cousins* (Dunedin: author, 1971).

52  Wills' name has endured more as one of the founders of Australian rules football. See Greg de Moore, *Tom Wills: His Spectacular Rise and Tragic Fall* (Sydney: Allen & Unwin, 2008).

53  *Evening Post*, 12 January 1889, p. 3.

54  Mark Lamster, *Spalding's World Tour: The Epic Adventure that Took Baseball Around the Globe – and Made it America's Game* (New York: Public Affairs Press, 2006); Thomas Zeiler, 'A Night at Delmonico's The Spalding Baseball Tour and the Imagination of Empire', *IJHS*, vol. 23, no. 1 (February 2006), pp. 28–45. See also *The Times Literary Supplement*, 15 July 1960, p. 453.

55  *Observer*, 15 December 1888, p. 9.

56  *Evening Post*, 17 November 1888, p. 2.

57  For brief synopses of the history of individual sports, see Sydney P. Todd, *Sporting Records of New Zealand* (Auckland: Moa Publications, 1976). For a comprehensive background of swimming, see Baxter O'Neill, 'History of Swimming in New Zealand', Micro-MS-0421, Alexander Turnbull Library. See also G. M. Kelly, *Golf in New Zealand: A Centennial History* (Wellington: New Zealand Golf Association, 1971); Stuart Ripley, *Sculling and Skulduggery: A history of professional sculling* (Sydney: Walla Walla Press, 2009).

58  See Christopher Tobin, *John L. Sullivan and 'Maori' Slade: The forgotten and fascinating story of their world heavyweight boxing title fight* (Wanaka: Bosco Press, 2007).

59  Boxing in an ad hoc manner had made an early debut in New Zealand sport. A bare-knuckle bout on the banks of the Waimakariri River north of Christchurch in 1862 attracted a large crowd which evidently included some notable Christchurch citizens. Police also attended but were prevented from stopping the fight. Two men, Harry Jones and George Barton, were charged with 'making an affray . . . to the terror and disturbance of Her Majesty's subjects'. They were found guilty of common assault and each received a month's imprisonment. *Press* 19 July 1862, pp. 2, 4, 2 August 1868, p. 6, 6 September 1868, p. 5; *Sports Digest*, August 1962, pp. 42–45.

60  Christopher Tobin, *Fitzsimmons: Boxing's First Triple Champion of the World* (Timaru: David A. Jack and author, 2000); Gilbert Odd, *The Fighting Blacksmith: The Story of Bob Fitzsimmons* (London: Pelham Books, 1976); Brian F. O'Brien, *Kiwis With Gloves On: A History and Record Book of New Zealand Boxing* (Wellington: A. H. & A. W. Reed,

1960). New Zealand also had another world champion boxer, Aucklander Billy ('Torpedo') Murphy, in the late 1890s.

61 *New York Times*, 7 August 1883, p. 1.

62 Ibid.

63 Ibid., p. 4.

64 Slade was reported to have been 'floored' by a brick after going to Sullivan's aid in a fight outside a bar in Denver. *New York Times*, 3 January 1884, p. 1. While Slade was usually described in contemporary reports as a Māori and once as being 'a large, dark-complexioned man', there is no evidence of the racial divide that characterised boxing's early years in which white boxers generally refused to fight non-whites and forced Jack Johnson to Australia to fight for the world title. See *New York Times*, 6 August 1883, p. 5; Randy Roberts, *Papa Jack: Jack Johnson and the Era of White Hopes* (London: Robson Books, 1986); Jan Stradling, *More Than A Game: When Sport and History Collide* (Sydney: Pier 9, 2009); Nat Fleischer, *Heavyweight Championship* (London: Putnam & Company, 1950).

65 Scott Crawford, 'Joe Scott: Otago World Champion Pedestrian', *New Zealand Journal of Health, Physical Education and Recreation*, vol. 8, no. 3 (November 1975), p. 10.

66 David Grant, *On a Roll: A history of gambling and lotteries in New Zealand* (Wellington: Victoria University Press, 1994), p. 47.

67 Ibid., p. 68.

68 Ibid., p. 39. Grant argues that an anti-gambling lobby allied with the temperance campaign gradually curbed betting, resulting in the outlawing of bookmakers in 1911. Another factor was the gradual emergence of the Olympic Games and its associated 'amateur ideal'.

69 *Otago Witness*, 28 February 1889, p. 11. Scott sold his championship belt, medals and other trophies in an effort to settle debts.

70 *Sporting Life*, 18 May 1888, quoted in P. S. Marshall, *King of the Peds* (Milton Keynes: AuthorHouse, 2008), p. 677.

71 Macdonald, 'Ways of Belonging', p. 271.

72 Cuff was active in a number of sports as well as athletics. See his obituary in Arthur H. Carman and Noel S. Macdonald, *The Cricket Almanack of New Zealand 1955* (Wellington: Sporting Publications, 1955), pp. 25–26. See also Michael Letters and Ian Jobling, 'Forgotten Links: Leonard Cuff and the Olympic Movement in Australasia, 1894–1905', *Olympika: The International Journal of Olympic Studies*, vol. 5 (1996), pp. 91–110.

73 *Observer*, 7 June 1890, p. 11.

74 *New Zealand Referee*, 4 May 1888, p. 285.

75 Ibid., 26 March 1892, p. 9.

76 *Penny Illustrated Paper and Illustrated Times*, 18 June 1892, p. 392. See also Richard Cashman and Peter Sharpham, 'Symbols, Emblems, Colours and Names', in Cashman, *Sport in the National Imagination: Australian Sport in the Federation Decades* (Sydney: Walla Walla Press, 2002), pp. 58–102.

77 *Otago Witness*, 27 October 1892, p. 31.

78 See, for example, *Referee*, 22 January 1902, p. 6, giving reasons why sprinter-hurdler George Smith should compete in Britain.

79 Compounding the whole issue of whether records were legitimate or not, wherever they were set, was that there was no international governing body until the formation of the International Amateur Athletic Federation in 1913. National associations themselves determined records before this time. For comment on the machinations of Smith's 'record', see the *Referee*, 23 February 1902, p. 6; *Otago Witness*, 12 March 1902, p. 50; *Referee*, 26 March 1902, p. 6. For Smith's championship-winning race, see *The Times*, 7 July 1902, p. 7; *Referee*, 9 July 1902, p. 6; *Referee*, 20 August 1902, p. 6.

80 Peter Heidenstrom, *Athletes of the Century: 100 Years of New Zealand Track and Field* (Wellington: GP Publications, 1992), pp. 72–73. Evidence that English athletics attitudes have barely changed was provided in 2011. During the world championships in South Korea, an official appeared to err in the decathlon shot put. An English commentator remarked: 'At least when they come to London in 2012 the officials will be better.'

81 Ron Palenski and Terry Maddaford, *The Games* (Auckland: Moa Publications, 1984), p. 14. Cuff's letters to Coubertin are in the Olympic Archives, Lausanne, but Coubertin's to Cuff have not survived. For all Britain's influence in the development of modern sport, France also had an influential role, especially in the development of sport in Europe and international sport generally. Not just the modern Olympic Games originated in France, but also the Fédération Internationale de Football (FIFA), the world governing body for soccer. See, in particular, Mike Cronin and Richard Holt, 'The Globalisation of Sport', *History Today*, vol. 53, issue 7 (July 2003), pp. 26–33.

82 *Bulletin du Comité International des Jeux Olympiques* (hereafter *Olympic Bulletin*), no. 1 (July 1894), p. 1.

83 Harry Gordon, *Australia and the Olympic Games* (Brisbane: University of Queensland Press, 1994), p. 23.

84   *Olympic Bulletin*, no. 3 (January 1895), p. 2.
85   See Gordon, *Australia and the Olympic Games*; Reet and Max Howell, *Aussie Gold: The Story of Australia at the Olympics* (Albion, Queensland: Brooks Waterloo, 1988). Such was the confused nature of the organisation of the games in Paris in 1900, one New Zealander, cyclist George Sutherland, thought he did compete but his events were later deemed not to be part of the Olympic programme. See *Otago Witness*, 7 November 1900, p. 51; Olympic Museum letter to author, 22 September 1998; Bill Mallon, *The 1900 Olympic Games, Results for All Competitors in All Events, with Commentary* (Jefferson, North Carolina: McFarland & Company, 1998), pp. 79–100.
86   Quoted in Little, *Trans-Tasman Federations*, p. 67.
87   Garth Henniker and Ian Jobling, 'Richard Coombes and the Olympic Movement in Australia: Imperialism and Nationalism in Action', *Sporting Traditions*, vol. 6, no. 1 (November 1989), pp. 2–15; W. F. Mandle, 'Coombes, Richard (1858–1935)', *Australian Dictionary of Biography* <www.adb.online.anu.edu.au>.
88   While Australian cricket and New Zealand rugby retained their national identities, there was still considerable cross-Tasman sporting traffic and nationals of one country played for the national team of the other.
89   Quoted in the *Referee*, 24 September 1903, p. 6.
90   Ibid., 24 October 1906, p. 8.
91   *Otago Witness*, 23 August 1911, p. 63.
92   *The Times*, 30 October 1891, p. 3. Cooper left Adelaide for London with his father when he was thirteen.
93   *Otago Witness*, 31 August 1893, p. 34.
94   Katharine Moore, 'A Neglected Imperialist: The Promotion of the British Empire in the Writing of John Astley Cooper', *IJHS*, vol. 8, no. 2 (1991), p. 263. Moore called Cooper a 'purveyor of propaganda' and said his view of the Empire was racist, sexist and ethnocentric. Ibid., pp. 258, 266.
95   Again, a group almost totally ignored in the sparse New Zealand sports historiography, with a notable exception: Graham Langton, 'A History of Mountain Climbing in New Zealand to 1953', PhD thesis, University of Canterbury, 1996.
96   For analysis of what the natural environment came to mean to New Zealanders, especially its mountains, see Eric Pawson, 'The Meanings of Mountains', in Pawson and Brooking, eds, *Environmental Histories of New Zealand*, pp. 136–50.
97   Langton, 'A History of Mountain Climbing

98   in New Zealand to 1953', p. 29.
99   Malcolm Ross, *A Climber in New Zealand* (London: Edward Arnold, 1914), p. 21.
99   Ross letter to William Douglas, 26 November 1895, New Zealand Alpine Club records, MS1164-2/89/1, Hocken Library.
100  A. P. Harper, 'Climbing in the Alps of Switzerland and New Zealand', *New Zealand Alpine Journal*, vol. 1, no. 3 (April 1893) (Dunedin: New Zealand Alpine Club, facsimile edn, 1975), p. 136.
101  Langton, 'A History of Mountain Climbing in New Zealand to 1953', p. 102.
102  Ross, *A Climber in New Zealand*, p. 52. For Ross reference to Aorangi, see *Otago Witness*, 27 December 1894, p. 51.
103  J. M. Dixon, 'The Siege of Mt Cook', *New Zealand Alpine Journal*, vol. 1, no. 5 (May 1894) (Dunedin: New Zealand Alpine Club, facsimile edn, 1975), p. 246.
104  W. S. Green, *The High Alps of New Zealand* (London: Macmillan, 1883; facsimile edn, Christchurch: Capper Press, 1976); Green, 'Recent Explorations in the Southern Alps of New Zealand', *Proceedings of the Royal Geographical Society and Monthly Record of Geography*, vol. 6, no. 2 (February 1884), pp. 57–70.
105  *Timaru Herald*, 13 March 1882, p. 2. For a report of a celebration dinner at Coker's Hotel in Christchurch, see *Timaru Herald*, 16 March 1882, p. 3.
106  *Marlborough Express*, 29 March 1884, p. 2.
107  Green, *The High Alps of New Zealand*, preface.
108  Ross, 'Alpine Notes', *New Zealand Alpine Journal*, vol. 1, no. 6 (October 1894) (Dunedin: New Zealand Alpine Club, facsimile edn, 1975), p. 368.
109  *Otago Witness*, 27 December 1894, p. 51. The story was bylined 'by an Alpine Clubbist', but it bore the unmistakable Ross phraseology.
110  Ibid.
111  Ross, *A Climber in New Zealand*, p. 115.
112  Langton, 'A History of Mountain Climbing in New Zealand to 1953', p. 148.
113  Sally Irwin, *Between Heaven and Earth: The Life of a Mountaineer, Freda du Faur* (Melbourne: White Crane Press, 2000), p. 195.

*Eight  In Thrall to the Oval Ball*

1    E. W. Secker, 'On the Ball', New Zealand's first, and perhaps best known, rugby song. Secker, a Palmerston North accountant, wrote it in 1887. See R. H. Chester and

N. A. C. McMillan, *The Encyclopedia of New Zealand Rugby* (Auckland: Moa Publications, 1981), pp. 438–42.

2  *New Zealand Mail*, 14 March 1906, p. 19.
3  *Evening Post*, 7 March 1906, p. 7.
4  *New Zealand Mail*, 14 March 1906, p. 19.
5  *Southland Times*, 13 March 1906, p. 2.
6  George Dixon, *The Triumphant Tour of the N.Z. Footballers* (Auckland: Geddis & Blomfield, 1906); D. Gallaher and W. J. Stead, *The Complete Rugby Footballer* (London: Methuen & Co, 1906); *Why the 'All Blacks' Triumphed: 'Daily Mail' Story of the Tour* (London: Associated Newspapers, 1906).
7  *Observer*, 10 March 1906, p. 2. The team manager, George Dixon, was employed by the newspaper's publisher, Geddis & Blomfield, and managed its Wellington weekly newspaper, the *Free Lance*. See Scholefield, *Newspapers in New Zealand*, p. 93.
8  *Auckland Weekly News*, 15 March 1906, p. 31.
9  Ron Palenski, Rod Chester and Neville McMillan, *Men In Black*, 7th edn (Auckland: Hodder Moa, 2006); Billy Stead, *Billy's Trip Home: The remarkable diary of an All Black on tour* (Dunedin: NZ Sports Hall of Fame, 2005); Ryan, *1905 All Blacks*; Christopher Tobin, *The Original All Blacks 1905–06* (Auckland: Hodder Moa, 2005); John McCrystal, *The Originals: 1905 All Black Rugby Odyssey – the story of the All Black 'Originals' and their extraordinary tour of Great Britain* (Auckland: Random House, 2005). For a fictional account of the tour, see Lloyd Jones, *The Book of Fame: A Novel* (Auckland: Penguin, 2000).
10  Sinclair, *Destiny Apart*, pp. 147, 149.
11  Ibid., p. 152.
12  Phillips, *A Man's Country?*, pp. 110–11.
13  Charlotte Macdonald, 'Ways of Belonging: Sporting Spaces in New Zealand History', in Byrnes, ed., *New Oxford History*, p. 278.
14  *New Zealand Truth*, 7 June 1924, p. 4. The 'Wm Wallace' to whom the writer referred was better known as Billy Wallace, the leading points scorer on the 1905–06 tour.
15  Clive Akers, *Monro: The Life and Times of the Man Who Gave New Zealand Rugby* (Palmerston North: author, 2009); the Rev. E. Wright-St Clair, *Thoroughly A Man of the World: A Biography of Sir David Monro* (Wellington: Whitcombe & Tombs, 1971); A. C. Swan, *History of New Zealand Rugby Football Volume 1 1870–1945* (Wellington: A. H. & A. W. Reed, 1948); for Charles Monro's own words on how he introduced rugby, see *Evening Post*, 18 August 1904, p. 6; *Dominion*,

5 July 1928, p. 15. Monro was a grandson of Alexander Monro, the third of that name ('Primus, Secundus and Tertius') to hold the chair of anatomy at Edinburgh University successively over 126 years (1720–1846). Phillips, *A Man's Country?*, p. 88 and Swan, *History of New Zealand Rugby Football*, p. 1 incorrectly state that Monro was educated at Sherborne.

16  Ernest D. Hoben, 'The National Game of Maoriland', *Review of Reviews* (20 July 1895), p. 41. For details of W. L. Rees, see obituary, *Poverty Bay Herald*, 18 May 1912, p. 5; G. J. Griffiths, *Notes on Some Early Arrivals in Otago, no. 3, W. G. Rees and his Cricketing Cousins* (Dunedin: author, 1971).
17  Ryan, *1905 All Blacks*, p. 27.
18  Geoffrey T. Vincent, '"To Uphold the Honour of the Province", Football in Canterbury c. 1854–c. 1890', in Greg Ryan, ed., *Tackling Rugby Myths: Rugby and New Zealand Society 1854–2004* (Dunedin: University of Otago Press, 2005), p. 30.
19  For Sale details, see Scholefield, *A Dictionary of New Zealand Biography*, vol. 2, pp. 271–72.
20  Swan, *History of New Zealand Rugby Football*, p. 22. Later still, Drew moved to Palmerston North where he became a referee.
21  Phillips also noted that a tour in 1877 by combined Dunedin clubs was 'seminal in establishing the dominance of rugby in the south'. Phillips, *A Man's Country?*, p. 89.
22  Terry Godwin, *The Complete Who's Who of International Rugby* (Poole, Dorset: Blandford Press, 1987), p. 179. Hamersley returned to Britain in 1887 and later became member of Parliament for Mid-Oxfordshire 1910–18. He also lived in Canada where he was legal adviser to the City of Vancouver and to the Canadian Pacific Railway and apparently was instrumental in the founding of rugby in British Columbia. See U. A. Titley and Ross McWhirter, *Centenary History of the Rugby Football Union* (London: Rugby Football Union, 1971), appendix 6; *Star*, 21 April 1887, p. 4.
23  Samuel Sleigh, *Northern Tour of the Dunedin Football Club* (Dunedin: R. T. Wheeler, 1877), p. 27.
24  Hamersley was a good choice by Phillips to use as an example, however. He fitted well the image of the well-bred Englishman taking the game to the colonies. He was a solicitor and was prominent in 'volunteering' in Canterbury. He led a unit in the government attack on the Māori village of Parihaka in 1881 and, flushed with its success, offered the services of himself and his troops to the government for service

in the Sudan, an offer that was declined. Hamersley eventually got his war, serving as an artillery colonel in World War I. See *The Times*, 28 February 1929, p. 19; *Wanganui Herald*, 24 February 1885, p. 2; *Star*, 23 February 1885, p. 3.

25 Phillips, *A Man's Country?*, p. 92.

26 Phillips' argument of a rural base for rugby was challenged by Greg Ryan, 'Rural Myth and Urban Actuality – The Anatomy of All Black and New Zealand Rugby 1884–1938', *NZJH*, vol. 35, no. 1 (April 2001), pp. 60–79. While this reflected a minor skirmish between historians, any rudimentary reading of 'popular' rugby history quickly reveals the urban base of the game and the fact that All Black farmers, to give one rural occupation, were the exception rather than the rule.

27 Geoffrey Blainey, *A Game of Our Own: The Origins of Australian Football* (Melbourne: Information Australia, 1990), p. 81.

28 Ibid., pp. 80–81. One of the acknowledged founders of what is now known as Australian rules football, Tom Wills, was an early trans-Tasman traveller, but to play cricket rather than football. He travelled with the first English team to visit New Zealand, in the summer of 1864, and captained a combined Canterbury and Otago team against the English in Christchurch. See *Otago Witness*, 6 February 1864, pp. 7–8, 20 February 1864, p. 4. See also Moore, *Tom Wills*. A New Zealand Australian rules team played in the first interstate carnival in Melbourne in 1908, but its composition was mainly expatriate Australians. See *New Zealand Herald*, 14 July 1906, p. 8, 20 April 1908, p. 8; *Argus*, 19 August 1908, p. 7, 20 August 1908, p. 7.

29 Swan, *History of New Zealand Rugby Football*, pp. 37–38.

30 Ibid., p. 80.

31 Ibid., p. 83.

32 *Otago Daily Times*, 1 June 1878, p. 1.

33 Undated letter from Annabella McLean to Sir Donald McLean, McLean Papers, object 1026027, MS-Group-1551, Alexander Turnbull Library.

34 *Otago Witness*, 15 July 1882, p. 20. Given the quality of writing and the use of foreign phrases, it is possible the author was George Sale.

35 Ibid.

36 *Grey River Argus*, 24 July 1882, p. 2.

37 Mulford, *Guardians of the Game*, pp. 25–31.

38 Ibid., p. 15. For the role of Thomas Arnold and the evolution of the rugby game at Rugby School, see C. R. Evers, *Rugby: English Public Schools* (London: Blackie &

Son, 1939); Jennifer Macrory, *Running With the Ball: The Birth of Rugby Football* (London: Collins Willow, 1991). Macrory was archivist at Rugby School.

39 Mulford, *Guardians of the Game*, p. 27. Edmund Barton became the first prime minister of the Commonwealth of Australia. Lea came to be known as the 'father' of Queensland rugby. Mulford, pp. 26–27.

40 *Otago Witness*, 23 September 1882, p. 19.

41 *Evening Post*, 5 September 1882, p. 2.

42 R. H. Chester and N. A. C. McMillan, *The Visitors: The History of International Rugby Teams in New Zealand* (Auckland: Moa Publications, 1990), p. 21.

43 *Otago Witness*, 12 May 1883, p. 21. Thomas Babington (Lord) Macaulay's image came to be something of a leitmotif for British references to New Zealand in the second half of the nineteenth century, as surveyed in the introduction to this book.

44 J. O. Lucas, G. H. Fairmaid, M. G. McInnes and W. J. Patrick, *Otago Boys' High School Old Boys' Register* (Dunedin: Otago High School Old Boys' Society, 1963), p. 175; Jane Thomson, ed., *Southern People: A Dictionary of Otago-Southland Biography* (Dunedin: Longacre Press in association with the Dunedin City Council, 1998), pp. 493–94.

45 Greg Ryan argued that despite 'prevailing rhetoric, the Māori embrace of the game prior to the 1920s was comparatively limited and largely confined to an educated and acculturated elite'. See Greg Ryan, 'Athletic Warriors or a Social Elite: the Formative Years of Maori Rugby', paper presented to the Australian Society for Sports History conference, Sporting Traditions XIV, Australian Catholic University, Sydney, July 2003.

46 *Otago Witness*, 3 May 1884, p. 21.

47 Sleigh himself in his book about the tour mentions the jersey colour and the gold fernleaf, but offers no explanation. S. E. Sleigh, ed., *The New Zealand Rugby Football Annual for 1885* (Dunedin: Otago Daily Times, 1885), p. 4.

48 *Sydney Telegraph*, 14 June 1884, quoted in Sleigh, *New Zealand Rugby Football Annual for 1885*, p. 24.

49 Sleigh, *New Zealand Rugby Football Annual for 1885*, pp. 2, 21.

50 Chester and McMillan, *Encyclopedia of New Zealand Rugby*. Listed occupations for players may have been their predominant occupation later in life rather than at the time of the tour. For example, Taiaroa was listed as a solicitor but he was still only twenty-two. O'Connor was listed as

a publican, which seems unlikely at the time. The player born in India was Henry Yule Braddon, who was working in a bank in Invercargill when chosen for the tour. He was a son of the Tasmanian politician and sometime premier, Sir Edward ('Ned') Braddon. Henry Braddon remained in Sydney at the end of the tour and became a prominent businessman and financier and, like his father, was knighted. See H. McCredie, 'Braddon, Sir Henry Yule (1863–1955)', and Scott Bennett, 'Braddon, Sir Edward Nicholas Coventry (1829–1904)', *Australian Dictionary of Biography* <www.adb.online.anu.edu.au>.

51 Rugby in South Africa developed at about the same time as the game in New Zealand; and in France, it began about a decade later. See Ivor D. Difford, *The History of South African Rugby Football (1875–1932)* (Wynberg, Cape: The Specialty Press of SA, 1933), pp. 12–13; Philip Dine, *French Rugby Football: A Cultural History* (Oxford: Berg, 2001), p. 19.

52 Sleigh, *New Zealand Rugby Football Annual for 1885*, preface.

53 *Otago Witness*, 5 July 1884, p. 20; *Otago Daily Times*, 1 July 1884, p. 2.

54 Chester and McMillan, *The Visitors: The History of International Rugby Teams in New Zealand*, pp. 29–44.

55 T. R. Ellison, *The Art of Rugby Football* (Wellington: Geddis & Blomfield, 1902), p. 64.

56 Ibid.

57 *Otago Witness*, 2 March 1888, p. 27.

58 For a full account of the organisation and execution of the tour, see Ryan, *Forerunners of the All Blacks*; Ryan, '"The Originals", the 1888–89 New Zealand Native Football Team in Britain, Australia and New Zealand', MA thesis, University of Canterbury, 1992.

59 *Otago Witness*, 3 August 1888, p. 27. The article was part of a column by 'Forward', who was probably James (later Sir James) Hutchison, an Otago rugby official, a one-time president of the New Zealand Rugby Football Union and a long-serving editor of the *Otago Daily Times*. See George Griffiths, *Southern Writers in Disguise, A miscellany of journalistic and literary pseudonyms* (Dunedin: Otago Heritage Books, 1998), p. 46. The team acquired the name of 'Native' because the four additional Pākehā were said to be native-born, but they were not. One, Patrick Keogh, was born in Birmingham and another, 'Mac' McCausland, was born at Sandhurst in Victoria. See Ryan, *Forerunners of the All Blacks*, pp. 135–36.

60 Ryan, *Forerunners of the All Blacks*, pp. 141–44. Ryan argued that such was the obscurity of the team, even its itinerary was a matter of some debate. The tour manager, Thomas Eyton, recorded 80 wins from 108 matches, Ellison said 69 wins from 108, but the version most accepted is that of Arthur Swan, who recorded 78 wins, 6 draws and 23 losses from 107 matches. See Swan, *History of New Zealand Rugby Football*, p. 519; see also Thomas Eyton, *Rugby Football Past and Present: The Tour of the Native Team in Great Britain, Australia and New Zealand in 1888–89* (Palmerston North: Wm Hart, 1896), pp. 86–87.

61 *Daily Telegraph*, 28 September 1889, quoted in Eyton, *Rugby Football Past and Present*, pp. 69–72.

62 *Punch*, quoted in the *Star* (Christchurch), 3 December 1888, p. 3.

63 Eyton, *Rugby Football Past and Present*, p. 72. Four of Joe Warbrick's brothers were in the team, as were three Wynyard brothers.

64 Ibid.

65 Ellison, *The Art of Rugby Football*, pp. 65–66.

66 Undated, uncredited newspaper clipping, probably *Auckland Star*, circa 1920s.

67 *New Zealand Referee*, 4 May 1888, p. 285.

68 Camilla Obel, 'Celebration and marginalisation in New Zealand sport: the "ethnic", national Māori rugby union team', *International Journal of Sport Management and Marketing*, vol. 2, nos 1–2 (2007), p. 149.

69 The Natives assembled in Napier and played their first game there; one of the Warbrick brothers had also attended the school in Tauranga that was run by Hoben's mother. For biographical details of Hoben, see Chester and McMillan, *Encyclopedia of New Zealand Rugby*, p. 254; Ron Palenski, *All Blacks: Myths and Legends* (Auckland: Hodder Moa, 2008), pp. 88–93.

70 Ernest Denis Hoben, 'Ake, Ake, Kia Kaha', *Countess of Liverpool's Gift Book* (Wellington: Whitcombe & Tombs, 1915), p. 132.

71 Ibid. The phrase was used by a former rugby player, William McKenzie, when writing of Hoben's death. McKenzie and Hoben were journalistic colleagues in Melbourne and McKenzie wrote to Hoben's son Sydney telling him of the circumstances of his father's death: 'Even at the point of death your father still displayed his indomitable spirit – the spirit of old Rewi Maniapoto when he cried "Ake, ake, ake, kia kaha"'; McKenzie letter to Sydney Hoben, 10 February 1918, author's collection. The New Zealand team in Britain in 1905–06 was the first to use the haka most commonly known as 'the Te

Rauparaha' or 'ka māte' haka. See Wallace's memoirs, 'Reminiscences of a famous NZ international. W. J. ('Carbine') Wallace writes rugby history. Before and after the 1905 invasions', which appeared in serial form in *NZ Sportsman* over several weeks in 1932. They were reproduced as *Reminiscences of a Famous NZ International: W. J. ('Carbine') Wallace Writes Rugby History* (Dunedin: New Zealand Sports Hall of Fame, 2005).

72 Sleigh, *New Zealand Rugby Football Annual for 1885*, p. 27.

73 The Rev. F. Marshall, *Football: The Rugby Union Game* (London: Cassell & Co, 1894), p. 505.

74 Quoted in Ryan, *Forerunners of the All Blacks*, pp. 52–53.

75 Eric Watts Moses, *A History of the Proceedings of the International Rugby Football Board 1886–1960* (London: IRFB, 1960), pp. 5–8.

76 *Daily News*, 29 April 1889, p. 5.

77 Tony Collins, *Rugby's Great Split: Class, Culture and the Origins of Rugby League Football* (London: Frank Cass, 1998); Collins, *A Social History of English Rugby Union* (London: Routledge, 2009).

78 Ryan, *Forerunners of the All Blacks*, p. 120.

79 Ibid., p. 113. For the outline of the England match incident, see Collins, *A Social History of English Rugby Union*, p. 33.

80 Ryan, *1905 All Blacks*, pp. 71, 75–76.

81 Ellison, *The Art of Rugby Football*, p. 66.

82 Ryan, *Forerunners of the All Blacks*, p. 127.

83 *Silver Fern*, 1 July 1965, p. 13. Swan's series of articles about the tour continued in the publication on July 8, 15 and 22. Its place as an identity marker was borne out with Swan's comment: 'Surely, this magnificent example of courage beggars description, but it does make one proud to be a New Zealander.'

84 Beattie recorded that he later got to know one of the Native players, 'Dick' Taiaroa (a brother of the 1884 player, Jack), and stayed with him at his home in Canterbury. See Atholl Anderson, 'Beattie, James Herries, 1881–1972', *Dictionary of New Zealand Biography*, vol. 4 (Auckland: Auckland University Press with Bridget Williams Books and Department of Internal Affairs, 1998), pp. 42–43. For Taiaroa details, see Thomson, ed., *Southern People*, pp. 493–94.

85 James Herries Beattie Papers, MS-582/H/31, Hocken Library. Beattie was quoting the King James Version of Acts 17:26: 'And [God] hath made of one blood all nations of men to dwell on all the face of the earth, and hath determined the times before appointed, and the bounds of their habitation.'

86 See Ron Palenski, 'The Naming of the All Blacks: Unravelling the Myth', *Sporting Traditions*, vol. 26, no. 1 (May 2009), pp. 21–32.

87 'Billy Wallace's recollections', New Zealand Rugby Museum website <www.rugbymuseum.co.nz>.

88 Wallace died in 1972, aged 93. See Chester and McMillan, *Encyclopedia of New Zealand Rugby*, p. 205.

89 McLintock, ed., *An Encyclopedia of New Zealand*, p. 32; see Alan Turley, *Rugby: The Pioneer Years* (Auckland: HarperCollins, 2008), p. 182 for the latest example of the perpetuation of the myth.

90 Wallace, *Reminiscences of a Famous NZ International: W. J. ('Carbine') Wallace Writes Rugby History*, p. 19.

91 *Daily Mail*, 12 October 1905, p. 7.

92 *Express and Echo*, 16 September 1905.

93 Terence Power McLean (Sir Terence from 1996) (1913–2004).

94 T. P. McLean, *The All Blacks* (London: Sidgwick & Jackson, 1991), p. 12.

95 Ryan, *1905 All Blacks*, p. 78; *Southland Times*, 9 January 1906.

96 *Daily Chronicle*, 8 November 1905.

97 J. O. C. Phillips, 'Rugby, War and the Mythology of the New Zealand Male', vol. 18, no. 2, *NZJH* (October 1984), p. 96. He was referring to *Why the All Blacks Triumphed! 'Daily Mail' Story of the Tour.*

98 These were usually attributed to 'Own Correspondent' or 'By Our Special Correspondent with the Team'. Among them was Charles Rous-Marten, a New Zealander who was the London correspondent for the *New Zealand Herald*, the *Evening Post*, the *Press* and the *Otago Daily Times*. Although the players' contracts prevented them from communicating with the press, it is possible that one of their number who was a journalist, Ernest Booth, also wrote under a pseudonym.

99 *Evening Post*, 31 August 1889, p. 3.

100 Arthur C. Swan and Gordon F. W. Jackson, *Wellington's Rugby History* (Wellington: A. H. & A. W Reed, 1952), pp. 20–21; *Evening Post*, 15 February 1913; Wellington Football Club website <www.wellingtonfootballclub.org.nz/history/history.html>.

101 For example, *New Zealand Referee*, 20 July 1888, p. 103.

102 Ellison, *The Art of Rugby Football*, p. 61.

103 Eyton, *Rugby Football Past and Present*, p. 13.

104 *Evening Post*, 24 April 1893, p. 4.

105 George Henry Dixon, Tour Diary 1905-06/ Personal papers, folder 1, MS-748(1), Auckland War Memorial Museum, author's copy.

106 Ron Palenski, *The Jersey – The Pride & the Passion, the Guts & the Glory: What it means to wear the All Black jersey* (Auckland: Hodder Moa Beckett, 2001), pp. 40–41.

107 *New Zealand Observer and Free Lance*, 29 July 1893, p. 5.

108 Ibid., 15 July 1893, p. 17.

109 *Evening Post*, 28 June, 1904, p. 5.

110 See, for example, Tony Deverson, 'Sporting New Labels', *NZWords*, vol. 2, no. 1 (January 1999), p. 5.

111 The Scottish union held that the three shillings a day recompense for expenses paid to the 1905–06 New Zealand team was professionalism. See Ryan, *1905 All Blacks*, pp. 177–78; correspondence between the NZRFU in Wellington and its representative in London, Cecil Wray Palliser, copies in author's possession.

112 T. R. Ellison, 'The Prospects of a New Zealand Rugby Team Visiting England', *Wellington Rugby Annual 1898* (Wellington: Wellington Rugby Football Union, 1898), pp. 53–57. See also Marc Phillip Ellison, 'A History of the Ellison whanau of Otākou', BA Honours degree research essay, University of Otago, 2008, pp. 34–39.

*Conclusion*

1 Martin Gilbert, *Churchill: A Life* (London: Heinemann, 1991), p. 26.

2 Winston S. Churchill, *A History of the English-Speaking Peoples, vol. IV, The Great Democracies* (London: Cassell & Co, 1958), pp. 100–1.

3 *New Zealand Observer and Free Lance*, 14 October 1899, p. 2.

4 Belich, *Paradise Reforged*, pp. 29–30.

5 Arthur Marwick, *The Nature of History* (London: Macmillan, 1989), p. 328.

6 Colley, 'Britishness and Otherness', p. 311.

7 *NZPD*, 1875, vol. 1, p. 468.

8 *West Coast Times*, 7 February 1866, p. 2.

9 *Press*, 27 May 1903, p. 8.

10 Davis, 'New Zealand Liberal Legislation and Manitoba Labour, 1894–1916' in Wood and O'Connor, *W. P. Morrell: A Tribute*, p. 169.

11 Scholefield, 'The Australasian Federation: New Zealand's Attitude', pp. 911–12.

12 *The Times*, 4 March 1901, p. 13.

13 *Punch, or the London Charivari*, 11 October 1905.

14 Erik Olssen, 'God's Own Country', in Judith Binney, Judith Bassett and Erik Olssen, *The People and the Land: Te tangata me te whenua: An illustrated history of New Zealand, 1820–1920* (Auckland: Allen & Unwin in association with the Port Nicholson Press, 1980), p. 275.

15 Colley's observation when talking of British identities bears reiterating: 'In practice, men and women often had double, triple, or even quadruple loyalties, mentally locating themselves, according to the circumstances, in a village, in a particular landscape, in a region, and in one or even two countries. It was quite possible for an individual to see himself as being, at one and the same time, a citizen of Edinburgh, a Lowlander, a Scott, and a Briton.' Colley, 'Britishness and Otherness', p. 315.

# BIBLIOGRAPHY

## PRIMARY SOURCES (ARCHIVAL)

### Alexander Turnbull Library Te Puna Mātauranga o Aotearoa

Dollimore, E. S., Biographical essay of T. E. Donne, in Dennis, Lawrence Samuel (1915–2000) Papers, MS-Papers-7261-10.

Harris, Nurse D. L., Diary kept while serving as a nursing sister in South Africa April 1900–May 1901, National Army Museum (UK), Miscellaneous Collections, Micro-MS-Coll-20-1906.

Hutchison, James, 1867–1946, Reminiscences, MS-Papers-5341.

McLean, Sir Donald, Papers, MS-Papers-0032-0485.

O'Neill, Baxter, 'History of Swimming in New Zealand', Micro-MS-0421.

Orsman, Harold William 1928–2002, 'The Growth of Nationalism (an essay)', MS-Papers-7637.

Ranfurly Collection, MS-Papers-6357-06, MS-Papers-6357-02.

Russell Family Collection, MS-Papers-3954.

Scholefield, G. H., Unpublished autobiography, MS-Copy-Micro-0468.

—— Letter to Vance Palmer, 2 February 1955, Scholefield Collection, MS-Papers-0916.

Seddon Family, Papers, MS-Papers-1619-057.

Shand. J. A., 'O'er Veldt and Kopje – The Official Account of the Operations of the New Zealand Contingents in the Boer War (Years 1899–1902) – Compiled from official records and field notes', QMS-1790.

Simmons, David Roy, 'Māori Medical Corps in South Africa During the Boer War', MS-Papers-4889.

Woods, John Joseph, Papers re musical composition *God Defend New Zealand*, MS-Papers-0355.

### Archives New Zealand Te Rua Mahara o te Kāwanatanga

Governor's dispatches Jan–Oct 1901, Original correspondence Secretary of State (CO209/202 1207), 1901 Jan–Oct dispatches, reel 2652–2653, piece 262.

South African War History, AD 34 4 8015.

### Auckland War Memorial Museum Tamaki Paenga Hira

Dixon, George Henry, Tour Diary 1905–06, Personal Papers, Folder 1, MS-748(1).

### Author's Archive

McKenzie, William, Letter to Sydney Hoben.

Correspondence relating to 1905–06 New Zealand Rugby Football Union team.

### Central Library, University of Otago Te Whare Wānanga o Otāgo

New Zealand Parliamentary Debates, Various.

*Hansard*, House of Commons debates, Various.

*Appendix to the Journals of the House of Representatives*, Various.

### Hocken Collections Uare Taoka o Hākena, University of Otago

Beattie, James Herries, Papers, MS-582/H/31.

Colonial Office, Original correspondence [relating to New Zealand], 1830–1922.

Hector, Sir James, 'Extracts and notes on life of James Hector', MS-0445-1/09.

New Zealand Alpine Club records, MS1164-2/89/1.

Notes on public meeting in the School Hall, Dunedin, 26 May 1849, *Flotsam and Jetsam*, vol. 1, no. 57.

### New Zealand Sports Hall of Fame

Corlett, Yvette, Letter to author, 1 January 2002.

### Office of the Minister of Internal Affairs

'New Zealand Anthem to Rate with "God Save the Queen"', Press statement, 21 November 1977.

# Bibliography

## PRIMARY SOURCES (PUBLISHED)

Abbott, J. M. H., *Tommy Cornstalk – Being Some Account of the Less Notable Features of the South African War from the Point of View of the Australian Ranks*, London: Longman Green, 2002.

Alexander, W. F. and A. E. Currie, *New Zealand Verse*, London: Walter Scott Publishing, 1906.

Alpers, O. T. J., *Cheerful Yesterdays*, London: John Murray, 1928.

Baeyertz, Charles, *Guide to New Zealand, the most wonderful scenic paradise in the world*, Dunedin: Mills, Dick & Co, 1902.

Barton, George, *The Telegraph Libel Case. Report of Proceedings in the Resident Magistrate's Court, Dunedin, on the hearing of the charges of libel brought by the General Government of New Zealand against Mr George Burnett Barton in the case of Regina v. Barton*, Dunedin: published by the compiler, 1871.

Bathgate, Alexander, *Colonial Experiences*, Glasgow: John Machlehose, 1874; reprint Capper Press, Christchurch, 1974.

Bean, C. E. W., *The Official History of Australia in the War of 1914–1918, Volume 1, The Story of Anzac*, St Lucia, Queensland: University of Queensland Press in association with the Australian War Memorial, 1981.

Bracken, Thomas, *God's Own Country and Other Poems*, Wellington: Brown, Thomas & Co, 1893.

—— *Musings in Maoriland – A Jubilee Volume*, Dunedin: Arthur T. Keirle, 1890.

Burton, O. E., *The Silent Division*, Sydney: Angus & Robertson, 1935.

Campbell, Rosamund and Philippa Harvie, *Singer of the Bush: A. B. 'Banjo' Paterson Complete Works 1885–1900*, Sydney: Lansdowne, 1983.

Clark, C. M. H., *Short Documents in Australian History 1851–1900*, Sydney: Angus & Robertson, 1970.

Clyde, Constance, *A Pagan's Love*, London: T. Fisher Unwin, 1905.

—— and Alan Mulgan, *New Zealand, Country and People*, Auckland: Whitcombe & Tombs, 1925.

Conan Doyle, Arthur, *The Great Boer War*, London: Thomas Nelson & Sons, 1903.

Cowan, James. *The tourist resorts of New Zealand, Lake Wakatipu and its environs*, Wellington: Department of Tourist and Health Resorts, 1907.

—— *The Dominion of New Zealand; its characteristics, resources and scenery*, Wellington: Government Printer, 1911.

*Cyclopedia of New Zealand (Otago and Southland provincial districts)*, Christchurch: The Cyclopedia Company, 1905.

Darwin, Charles, *The Journal of a Voyage in HMS Beagle*, Guildford: Genesis Publications in association with Australia and New Zealand Book Company, 1979.

Deakin, Alfred, *The Federal Story*, Melbourne: Melbourne University Press, 1963.

Dixon, George, *The Triumphant Tour of the N.Z. Footballers*, Auckland: Geddis & Blomfield, 1906.

Dixon, J. M., 'The Siege of Mt Cook', *New Zealand Alpine Journal*, vol. 1, no. 5 (May 1894), pp. 245–257.

Ellison, T. R., *The Art of Rugby Football*, Wellington: Geddis & Blomfield, 1902.

Eyton, Thomas, *Rugby Football Past and Present: The Tour of the Native Team in Great Britain, Australia and New Zealand in 1888–89*, Palmerston North: Wm Hart, 1896.

Fishkin, Shelley Fisher (foreword), Vidal, Gore (introduction) and Fred Kaplan (afterword), *Following the equator and anti-imperialist essays, Mark Twain*, New York: Oxford University Press, 1996.

Gallaher, D. and Stead, W. J., *The Complete Rugby Footballer*, London: Methuen & Co, 1906.

Green, W. S., *The High Alps of New Zealand*, London: Macmillan, 1883; facsimile edition, Christchurch: Capper Press, 1976.

Grey, J. Grattan, *Freedom of Thought and Speech in New Zealand: A Serious Menace to Liberty – Mr Seddon, Premier, and Mr J. Grattan Grey, Journalist – An Interesting Correspondence*, Wellington: author, 1901.

Hamer, D. A., ed., *The Webbs in New Zealand 1898: Beatrice Webb's Diary with entries by Sidney Webb*, Wellington: Price Milburn for Victoria University Press, 1974.

Hawdon, Sarah Elizabeth, *New Zealanders and the Boer War, or Soldiers from the Land of the Moa: by a New Zealander*, Christchurch: Gordon & Gotch, 1907.

Hoben, Ernest D., 'The National Game of Maoriland', *Review of Reviews* (20 July 1895), pp. 37–46.

—— 'Ake, Ake, Kia Kaha', *Countess of Liverpool's Gift Book*, Wellington: Whitcombe & Tombs, 1915, pp. 129–133.

Horsman, E. A., ed., *The Diary of Alfred Domett 1872–1885*, London: Oxford University Press, 1953.

Hyde, Robin, *Journalese*, Auckland: National Printing Company, 1934.

Jebb, Richard, *Studies in Colonial Nationalism*, London: Edward Arnold, 1905.

Khaldūn, Ibn, *The Muqaddimah: An Introduction to History*, translated by Franz Rosenthal, Princeton: Princeton University Press, 1967.

Kipling, Rudyard, *The Complete Verse*, London: Kyle Cathie, 2006.

—— *Our Lady at Wairakei*, with introduction by Harry Ricketts, Wellington: Mallinson Rendel, 1983.

# Bibliography

Lawlor, Pat, *Confessions of a Journalist*, Wellington: Whitcombe & Tombs, 1935.

Le Rossignol, James Edward and William Downie Stewart, *State Socialism in New Zealand*, New York: T. Y. Crowell, 1910.

Linklater, Joseph, *On Active Service in South Africa With the 'Silent Sixth': Being a record of events, compiled by the writer, from the time of the formation of the Regiment in New Zealand until its return from South Africa*, Wellington: McKee & Co, 1904.

Lloyd, Henry Demarest, *Newest England: Notes of a democratic traveller in New Zealand, with some Australian comparisons*, New York: Doubleday, Page, 1902.

McIntyre, W. David and W. J. Gardner, eds, *Speeches and Documents on New Zealand History*, London: Oxford University Press, 1971.

McKinlay, Ernest, *Ways and By-Ways of a Singing Kiwi: With the N.Z. Divisional Entertainers in France, Belgium, Germany, 1916–1919*, Dunedin: David M. Lister, 1939.

McNab, Robert, *Historical Records of New Zealand, vol 1*, Wellington: Government Printer, 1908.

Marshall, the Rev. F., *Football: The Rugby Union Game*, London: Cassell & Co, 1894.

Marshall, John, *Memoirs, Volume One: 1912 to 1960*, Auckland: Collins, 1993.

Métin, Albert, *Le Socialisme sans Doctrines*, Paris: F. Alcan, 1910.

Moore, James G. Harle, *With the Fourth New Zealand Rough Riders*, Dunedin: Otago Daily Times and Witness Newspapers, 1906.

Mulgan, Alan, *The Making of a New Zealander*, Wellington: A. H. & A. W. Reed, 1958.

Mulgan, John, *Man Alone*, Hamilton: Paul's Book Arcade, 1949.

—— *Report On Experience*, London: Oxford University Press, 1947.

New Zealand Press Association, *Memorandum of Association and Articles of Association of New Zealand Press Association Ltd*, Wellington: NZPA, 1960.

Perham, Trooper Frank, *The Kimberley Flying Column: Boer War Reminiscences*, Timaru: published by author, 1957.

Reeves, The Hon William Pember, *State Experiments in Australia and New Zealand*, 2 vols, London: George Allen & Unwin, 1902.

—— 'The Attitude of New Zealand', *Empire Review*, vol. 1, no. 1 (1901), pp. 111–113.

'Report of the Intercolonial Conference of Surveyors', *The Surveyor*, Journal of the Institute of Surveyors, New South Wales, vol. 5, no. 12 (12 December 1892).

Roderick, Colin, ed., *Henry Lawson: Collected Verse, vol 1 1885–1900*, Sydney: Angus & Robertson, 1967.

Ross, Malcolm, *Tourists Guide Book to the Lakes District of Otago*, Dunedin: New Zealand and South Seas Exhibition, 1889.

—— *Aorangi; or, The Heart of the Southern Alps, New Zealand*, Wellington: Government Printer, 1892.

—— 'Alpine Notes', *New Zealand Alpine Journal*, vol. 1, no. 6 (October 1894), pp. 366–368.

—— *A Souvenir of New Zealand's Response to the Empire's Call*, Wellington: McKee & Co, 1899.

—— *The Duke in Southern Isles: New Zealand's Loyal Welcome*, Wellington: McKee & Co, 1901.

—— *A Climber in New Zealand*, London: Edward Arnold, 1914.

Ross, Mrs Malcolm (Forrestina Ross), *Round the World With a Fountain Pen: The Log of a Lady Journalist*, Wellington: Blundell Brothers, 1913.

—— *Mixed Grill*, Wellington: Whitcombe & Tombs, 1934.

Rousseau, Jean Jacques, *The Confessions*, London: Penguin, 1960.

Scholefield, Guy H., ed., *The Richmond-Atkinson Papers*, 2 vols, Wellington: Government Printer, 1960.

Shillaber, Benjamin, *Life and Sayings of Mrs Partington and Others of the Family*, New York: J. C. Derby, 1854.

Siegfried, André, *Democracy in New Zealand – translated from the French by E. V. Burns with an introduction by William Downie Stewart*, London: G. Bell & Sons, 1914.

Sleigh, S. E., ed., *The New Zealand Rugby Football Annual for 1885*, Dunedin: Otago Daily Times, 1885.

—— *Northern Tour of the Dunedin Football Club*, Dunedin: R. T. Wheeler, 1877.

Stead, Billy, *Billy's Trip Home: The remarkable diary of an All Black on tour*, Dunedin: New Zealand Sports Hall of Fame, 2005.

Tasker, P. M., *A Slice of the Life of My Uncle Charlie: A Diary of Trooper C. B. Tasker, Service Number 3561, 6th Contingent, New Zealand Mounted Rifles, South Africa*, Wellington: transcriber, 1991.

Taylor, Nancy M., ed., *Journal of Ensign Best 1837–1843*, Wellington: R. A. Owen, Government Printer, 1966.

Thomson, A. S., *The Story of New Zealand*, vol. III, part II, London: John Murray, 1859.

Trollope, Anthony, *Australia and New Zealand*, vol. II, London: Chapman & Hall, 1873.

—— *The New Zealander*, Oxford: Clarendon Press, 1972.

Turner, Frederick Jackson, *The Frontier in American History*, New York: Henry Holt & Co, 1921.

Twain, Mark, *Mark Twain in Australia and New Zealand* (also published as *Following the Equator*),

Harmondsworth, Middlesex: Penguin, 1973.
Varley, Isabella, *Ivy Leaves: A Collection of Poems*, London: Simpkin Marshall, 1844.
Vogel, Sir Julius, *Anno Domini; or, Woman's Destiny*, London: Hutchinson & Co, 1889.
Wakefield, E. J., *Adventure in New Zealand*, vol. 1, London: John Murray, 1845; facsimile edition, Auckland: Wilson & Horton, 1971.
Wallace, Billy, *Reminiscences of a Famous NZ International: W. J. ('Carbine') Wallace Writes Rugby History*, Dunedin: New Zealand Sports Hall of Fame, 2005.
Webb, Sydney and Beatrice, *Industrial Democracy*, London: Longmans, Green, 1920.
*Why the 'All Blacks' Triumphed: 'Daily Mail' Story of the Tour*, London: Associated Newspapers, 1906.
Woolford, John and Karlin, David, *The Poems of Browning*, vol. II, London: Longman, 1991.


## NEWSPAPERS / MAGAZINES

*Argus*, 1879–1908
*Auckland Star* (also *Evening Star*), 1892–1970
*Auckland Weekly News*, 1906
*Brisbane Courier*, 1893
*Bulletin*, 1900
*Daily Mail*, 1905
*Daily News*, 1889
*Daily Telegraph*, 1889
*Dominion*, 1939–1995
*Evening Post*, 1866–1915
*Evening Star* (Dunedin), 1900–1963
*Express and Echo*, 1905
*Graphic* (UK), 1899–1900
*Grey River Argus*, 1882–1911
*Hawera and Normanby Star*, 1902–1904
*Illustrated London News*, 1888
*Lyttelton Times*, 1888
*Marlborough Express*, 1878–1884
*Mataura Ensign*, 1899
*Morning Herald and Daily Advertiser*, 1784
*Nelson Evening Mail*, 1878
*Nelson Examiner and New Zealand Chronicle*, 1844–1868
*New York Times*, 1883–1914
*New Zealand Free Lance*, 1900–1904
*New Zealand Gazette and Wellington Spectator*, 1840–1841
*New Zealand Graphic*, 1893–1900
*New Zealand Herald*, 1901–1963
*New Zealand Illustrated Magazine*, 1899–1902
*New Zealand Journal*, 1846
*New Zealand Listener*, 1940
*New Zealand Mail*, 1894–1906
*New Zealand Observer* (also *New Zealand Observer and Free Lance*), 1888–1906
*New Zealand Railways Magazine*, 1935
*New Zealand Referee*, 1888
*New Zealand Spectator and Cook's Strait Guardian*, 1849
*New Zealand Tablet*, 1880–1899
*New Zealand Times*, 1893
*New Zealand Truth*, 1927
*New Zealander*, 1849
*Otago Daily Times*, 1868–1910
*Otago Witness*, 1851–1911
*Penny Illustrated Paper and Illustrated Times*, 1892
*Perth Gazette and Independent Journal of Politics and News*, 1849
*Poverty Bay Herald*, 1912
*Press, the*, 1861–1901
*Progress*, 1905–1906

# Bibliography

*Referee* (Sydney), 1902–1906
*Saturday Advertiser and New Zealand Literary Miscellany*, 1876
*Silver Fern*, 1965
*South Australian Magazine*, 1842
*Southern Cross*, 1843
*Southern News and Fouveaux Straits' Herald*, 1861
*Southland Times*, 1901–1906
*Sporting Life*, 1888
*Sports Digest*, 1962
*Sports Special*, 1908–1929
*Star*, the, 1893
*Sydney Telegraph*, 1884
*Taranaki Herald*, 1868–1899
*Te Aroha News*, 1887
*The Times* (London), 1826–1927
*The Times Literary Supplement*, 1960
*Timaru Herald*, 1878–1891
*Tuapeka Times*, 1876–1878
*Waikato Times*, 1884
*Wanganui Herald*, 1884–1885
*Wellington Independent*, 1866
*West Australian*, 1894
*West Coast Times*, 1866–1905

## SECONDARY SOURCES

### Online

*Australian Dictionary of National Biography* <www.adb.online.anu.edu.au>.
Australian Electoral Commission <www.aec.gov.au>.
Background note, 'The Origins of the Māori Seats', Parliamentary Library, November 2003, p. 10 <www.parliament.nz/en-NZ/ParlSupport/ResearchPapers>.
Bassett, Michael, 'An Overview of the War History Branch', Lecture to Department of Internal Affairs seminar, Wellington 1997 <www.michaelbassett.co.nz/article_war.htm>
*Dictionary of Canadian Biography Online* <www.biographi.ca>.
Dobson, Edward, 'On the present state of Applied Science in the Canterbury Province', Address to the annual meeting of the Philosophical Society of Canterbury, 5 November 1866, *Transactions and Proceedings of the Royal Society of New Zealand 1868–1961*, vol. 1, 1868 <http://natlib.govt.nz/volume. rsnz_01/rsnz_01_00_001580.html.
'Edmund Barton, Australia' <www.espncricinfo.com.au/Australia/content/player/4432.html>.
Elections Canada <www.elections.ca>.
Harvey, D. R., 'Newspapers', in Keith Maslen, ed., *Book & Print in New Zealand: A Guide to Print Culture in Aotearoa*, Wellington: Victoria University Press, 1997 <www.nzetc.org/tm/scholarly/tei-GriBook. html>.
'History of New Zealand Coinage', Reserve Bank of New Zealand website <www.rbnz.govt.nz/ currency/money/0094086.html>.
House of Commons Parliamentary Papers <http://parlipapers.chadwyck.co.uk>.
Jolliffe, William, 'The Evolution of the Penny Postage in New Zealand', Paper read to the Philatelic Society of New Zealand, 5 October 1911 <http://www.philatelicdatabase.com/new-zealand.html>.
King, Thomas, 'On New Zealand Mean Time, and on the Longitude of the Colonial Observatory, Wellington, with a note on the Universal Time Question', *Transactions and Proceedings of the Royal Society of New Zealand 1868–1961*, vol. 35, 1902 <http://natlib.govt.nz/volume.rsnz_35_00_005180. html>.
McGibbon, Ian, '"Something of Them Here Is Recorded": Official History in New Zealand', <www. nzetc.org/tm/scholarly/tei-McGSome.html>.
Martin, Ged, 'Edward Gibbon Wakefield: Abductor and Mystagogue', <www.gedmartin.net>.
'New Zealand Flag', Ministry for Culture and Heritage <www.mch.govt.nz>.
'New Zealand Honours: History', Department of the Prime Minister and Cabinet <www.dpmc.govt. nz>.

# Bibliography

*New Zealand Railways Magazine*, <www.nzetc.org/tm/scholarly/tei-corpus-railways.html>.

*Official Record of the Proceedings and Debates of the Australasian Federation Conference, Melbourne 1890: Debates of the Conferences* <http://setis.library.usyd.edu.au>.

*Oxford Dictionary of National Biography*, Oxford, Oxford University Press <http://oxforddnb.com>.

*The Journals, Detailed Reports, and Observations relative to the Exploration by Captain Palliser of that portion of British North America which, in latitude, lies between the British Boundary Line and the height of land or watershed of the Northern or Frozen Ocean respectively, and, in longitude, between the western shore of Lake Superior and the Pacific Ocean During the Years 1857, 1858, 1859 and 1860, presented to both Houses of Parliament 1863* (Paper 3164), House of Commons Parliamentary Papers <http://parlipapers.chadwyck.co.uk>.

Wallace, Billy, 'Recollections', New Zealand Rugby Museum <www.rugbymuseum.co.nz>.

Wellington Football Club <www.wellingtonfootballclub.org.nz/history/history.html.

Women's suffrage <www.nzhistory.net/politics/womens-suffrage>.

## Theses

Bathgate, Alfred J., 'Seddon and the Boer War Period 1899–1904', MA thesis, University of Otago, 1968.

Craven, D. H., 'The Evolution of Major Games', PhD thesis, University of Stellenbosch, 1978.

Davis, George Frederick, 'Anzac Day meanings and memories: New Zealand, Australian and Turkish perspectives on a day of commemoration in the twentieth century', PhD thesis, University of Otago, 2008.

Deaker, M. J. B., 'Seddon's Contribution to Imperial Relations 1897 to 1902', MA thesis, University of Otago, 1968.

Ellison, Marc Phillip, 'A History of the Ellison whanau of Otākou', BA Honours degree research essay, University of Otago, 2008.

Gibbons, Peter, '"Going Native": A case study of cultural appropriation in a settler society, with particular reference to the activities of Johannes Andersen in New Zealand during the first half of the twentieth century', PhD thesis, University of Waikato, 1992.

Gilling, Tui, 'On Active Service: New Zealand and the South African War 1899–1902', Postgraduate Diploma of Arts thesis, University of Otago, 1990.

Helm, A. S., 'The Early History of South Island Telegraphs', MA thesis, Victoria University of Wellington, 1951.

Hocken, A. G., 'The early life of James Hector, 1834 to 1865: The first Otago Provincial Geologist', PhD thesis, University of Otago, 2007.

Kay, George, 'Seddon and Asian Immigration Legislation 1896–99', Postgraduate Diploma in History thesis, University of Otago, 1973.

McIver, Ian, 'New Zealand and the South African War of 1899–1902: A study of New Zealand's attitudes and motives for involvement and the effect of the war on New Zealand and her relations with Britain', MA thesis, University of Otago, 1972.

Palenski, Ron, 'Malcolm Ross: A Forgotten Casualty of the Great War', MA thesis, University of Otago, 2007.

Ryan, Greg, '"The Originals", the 1888–89 New Zealand Native Football Team in Britain, Australia and New Zealand', MA thesis, University of Canterbury, 1992.

Sampson, Kingsley D., 'Chief Among the Children: A survey of the national self-image of New Zealanders in the years 1899–1901', MA thesis, University of Otago, 1970.

## Articles, Addresses

Armstrong, Meg, '"A Jumble of Foreignness": The Sublime Musayums of Nineteenth-Century Fairs and Expositions', *Cultural Critique*, no. 23 (Winter 1992–1993), pp. 199–250.

Bagnall, A. G., 'The Seat of Government Commission, 1864: An Australian intervention', *Turnbull Library Record*, vol. 18, no. 1 (May 1985), pp. 5–21.

Baker, William J., 'William Webb Ellis and the Origins of Rugby Football: The Life and Death of a Victorian Myth', *Albion: A Quarterly Journal Concerned with British Studies*, vol. 13, no. 2 (Summer 1981), pp. 117–30.

Ballantyne, Tony, 'The State, Politics and Power, 1769–1893', in Giselle Byrnes, ed., *New Oxford History of New Zealand*, Melbourne: Oxford University Press, 2009.

Ballon, H. C., 'Sir James Hector, M.D., 1834–1907', *Canadian Medical Association Journal*, vol. 87 (14 July 1962), pp. 66–73.

# Bibliography

Beaglehole, J. C., 'The Development of New Zealand Nationality', *Journal of World History*, vol. II, no. 1 (1954), pp. 106–23.

Bell, Avril, 'Dilemmas of settler belonging: roots, routes and redemption in New Zealand national identity claims', *Sociological Review*, vol. 57, no. 1 (February 2009), pp. 145–62.

Blackton, C. C., 'New Zealand and the Australian anti-transportation movement', *Australian Historical Studies*, vol. 1, no. 2 (October 1940), pp. 116–22.

Blake, Kevin S., 'Colorado Fourteeners and the Nature of Place Identity', *The Geographical Review*, vol. 92, no 2 (April 2002), pp. 155–79.

Bond, Ross, 'Belonging and Becoming: National Identity and Exclusion', *Sociology*, vol. 40, no. 4 (2006), pp. 609–26.

Boos, Florence S., 'The Poetics of the Working Classes', *Victorian Poetry*, vol. 39, no. 2 (Summer 2001), pp. 103–09.

Booth, Douglas, 'Healthy, Economic, Disciplined Bodies, Surfbathing and Surf Lifesaving in Australia and New Zealand, 1890–1950', *New Zealand Journal of History*, vol. 32, no. 1 (April 1998–99), pp. 43–58.

Brittan, Alice, 'Australasia', in John McLeod, ed., *The Routledge Companion to Postcolonial Studies*, Milton Park, Oxfordshire: Routledge, 2007, pp. 72–82.

Brookes, Rod, 'Newspapers and national identity: The BSE/CJD crisis and the British press', *Media Culture Society*, vol. 21 (1999), pp. 247–63.

Broughton, Henare, 'Te Hakituatahi o Aotearoa: 1835 (First Flag of New Zealand)', *New Zealand Official Yearbook 2002*, Auckland: David Bateman, 2002.

Cashman, Richard and Peter Sharpham, 'Symbols, Emblems, Colours and Names', in Cashman, ed., *Sport in the National Imagination: Australian Sport in the Federation Decades*, Sydney: Walla Walla Press, 2002.

Cerulo, Karen A., 'Symbols and the World System: National Anthems and Flags', *Sociological Forum*, vol. 8, no. 2 (June 1993), pp. 243–71.

Champlin, Carroll D., 'The Cultural Contribution of International Expositions', *Phi Delta Kappan*, vol. 20, no. 4 (December 1937), pp. 115–17.

Chan, Adrian, 'New Zealand, the Australian Commonwealth and "Plain Nonsense"', *New Zealand Journal of History*, vol. 3, no. 2 (October 1969), pp. 190–95.

Chapman, Sir Frederick, 'The Interest and Value of New Zealand History', Inaugural lecture, New Zealand Historical Association (Otago branch), 21 June 1928, Dunedin: Otago Daily Times and Witness Newspapers, 1928.

Cirillo, Vincent J., '"Winged Sponges": houseflies as carriers of typhoid fever in 19th and early 20th century military camps', *Perspectives in Biology and Medicine*, vol. 49, no. 1 (Winter 2006), pp. 52–64.

Clifford, James, 'Taking Identity Politics Seriously: The Contradictory, Stony Ground', in Paul Gilroy, Lawrence Grossberg and Angela McRobbie, eds, *Without Guarantees: Essays in Honour of Stuart Hall*, London: Verso Press, 2000, pp. 94–112.

Cole, Douglas, 'The Problem of "Nationalism" and "Imperialism" in British Settlement Colonies', *The Journal of British Studies*, vol. 10, no. 2 (May 1971), pp. 160–82.

Coleman, Peter J., 'New Zealand Liberalism and the Origins of the American Welfare State', *Journal of American History*, vol. 69, no. 2 (September 1982), pp. 372–91.

—— 'The Spirit of New Zealand Liberalism in the Nineteenth Century', *Journal of Modern History*, vol. 30, no. 3 (September 1958), pp. 227–35.

Colles, H. C., 'National Anthems: Their Birth and Parentage', *Musical Times*, vol. 55, no. 860 (1 October 1914), pp. 609–11.

Colley, Linda, 'Britishness and Otherness: An Argument', *The Journal of British Studies*, vol. 31, no. 4 (October 1992), pp. 309–29.

Cooper, David, 'Canadians Declare "It Isn't Cricket": A Century of Rejection of the Imperial Game, 1860–1960', *Journal of Sport History*, vol. 26, no. 1 (Spring 1999), pp. 51–81.

Cowan, James, 'Sir Joseph Ward: A Statesman of New Zealand and the Empire', *New Zealand Railways Magazine*, vol. 11, issue 2 (1 May 1936), pp. 17–20.

Crawford, Scott A. G. M., 'Joe Scott: Otago World Champion Pedestrian', *New Zealand Journal of Health, Physical Education and Recreation*, vol. 8, no. 3 (November 1975), pp. 111–13.

—— 'Recreational and Sporting Values on the Fringe of an Imperial Empire: The Reshaping of a British Heritage in Colonial New Zealand', in *Sport and Colonialism in Nineteenth Century Australasia – Australian Society of Sports History Studies in Sports History No 1*, Sydney: Australian Society of Sports History, 1986, pp. 65–79.

—— 'A Sporting Image: The Emergence of a National Identity in a Colonial Setting, 1862–1906', *Victorian Periodicals Review*, vol. 21, no. 2 (Summer 1988), pp. 56–63.

# Bibliography

—— 'Rugby in Contemporary New Zealand', *Journal of Sport and Social Issues*, vol. 12, no. 2 (1988), pp. 108–21.

Cronin, Mike and Richard Holt, 'The Globalisation of Sport', *History Today*, vol. 53, issue 7 (July 2003), pp. 26–33.

Daley, Caroline, 'Selling Sandow: Modernity and Leisure in Early Twentieth-Century New Zealand', *New Zealand Journal of History*, vol. 34, no. 2 (October 2000), pp. 241–61.

Davis, R. P., 'New Zealand Liberal Legislation and Manitoba Labour, 1894–1916', in G. A. Wood and P. S. O'Connor, *W. P. Morrell: A Tribute: Essays in modern and early modern history presented to William Parker Morrell, Professor Emeritus, University of Otago*, Dunedin: University of Otago Press, 1973, pp. 169–83.

Davison, Graeme, 'Punctuality and progress: The foundations of Australian standard time', *Australian Historical Studies*, vol. 25, issue 99 (1992), pp. 169–91.

Day, Patrick, 'Julius Vogel and the Press', *Turnbull Library Record*, vol. 19, no. 2 (October 1986), pp. 103–22.

Deverson, Tony, 'Sporting New Labels', *NZWords*, vol. 2, no. 1 (January 1999), p. 5.

Dyreson, Mark, 'Sport and visions of the "American Century"', *Peace Review*, vol. 11, no. 4 (1999), pp. 565–71.

Ellison, T. R., 'The Prospects of a New Zealand Rugby Team Visiting England', *Wellington Rugby Annual 1898*, Wellington: Wellington Rugby Football Union, 1898, pp. 53–57.

Fairburn, Miles, 'New Zealand and Australasian Federation, 1883–1901: Another View', *New Zealand Journal of History*, vol. 4, no. 2 (October 1970), pp. 138–59.

—— 'Is There A Good Case for New Zealand Exceptionalism?', in Tony Ballantyne and Brian Moloughney, eds, *Disputed Histories: Imagining New Zealand's Past*, Dunedin: Otago University Press, 2006, pp. 143–67.

—— 'Is There A Good Case for New Zealand Exceptionalism?', *Thesis Eleven*, no. 92 (February 2008), pp. 29–49.

Forsyth, David S., 'Empire and union: Imperial and national identity in nineteenth century Scotland', *Scottish Geographical Journal*, vol. 113, no. 1 (March 1997), pp. 6–12.

Gibbons, Peter, 'Cultural Colonization and National Identity', *New Zealand Journal of History*, vol. 36, no. 1 (2002), pp. 5–17.

Goksøyr, Matti, 'Nationalism', in S. W. Pope and John Nauright, eds, *Routledge Companion to Sports History*, London: Routledge, 2010.

Graham, Jeanine, 'Settler Society', in Geoffrey W. Rice, ed., *Oxford History of New Zealand*, second edition, Auckland: Oxford University Press, 1995.

Green, W. S., 'Recent Explorations in the Southern Alps of New Zealand', *Proceedings of the Royal Geographical Society and Monthly Record of Geography*, vol. 6, no. 2 (February 1884), pp. 57–70.

Grimshaw, Patricia, 'Women Campaign for the Vote', *New Zealand's Heritage: The making of a nation*, vol. 4, part 47, Wellington: Paul Hamlyn, 1972, pp. 1295–300.

—— 'Tasman Sisters: Lives of the "Second Sex"', in Keith Sinclair, *Tasman Relations: New Zealand and Australia, 1788–1988*, Auckland: Auckland University Press, 1987, pp. 224–45.

Hall, David, 'The age of exhibitions', *New Zealand's Heritage: The making of a nation*, vol. 4, part 47, Wellington: Paul Hamlyn, 1972, pp. 1312–16.

Harper, A. P., 'Climbing in the Alps of Switzerland and New Zealand', *New Zealand Alpine Journal*, vol. 1, no. 3 (April 1893), pp. 134–42.

Harvey, David, 'Between Space and Time: Reflections on the Geographical Imagination', *Annals of the Association of American Geographers*, vol. 80, no. 3 (September 1990), pp. 418–34.

Harvey, D. R., 'Circulation Figures for some Nineteenth Century New Zealand Newspapers', *Archifacts*, 1988/4 and 1989/1, pp. 20–29.

—— 'Towards a Bibliography of New Zealand Newspapers', Bibliographical Society of Australia and New Zealand *Bulletin*, vol. 11, no. 2 (August 1989), pp. 41–49.

—— 'Editors and Compositors: Contemporary Accounts of the Nineteenth-Century New Zealand Press', Bibliographical Society of Australia and New Zealand *Bulletin*, vol. 14, no. 3 (April 1991), pp. 103–13.

—— 'Economic Aspects of Nineteenth-Century New Zealand Newspapers', Bibliographical Society of Australia and New Zealand *Bulletin*, vol. 17, no. 2 (second quarter 1993), pp. 55–78.

—— 'The Power of the Press in Colonial New Zealand: More Imagined than Real?', Bibliographical Society of Australia and New Zealand *Bulletin*, vol. 20, no. 2 (second quarter 1996), pp. 131–45.

Hassan, David, 'Rugby Union, Irish Nationalism and National Identity in Northern Ireland', *Football Studies*, vol. 6, no. 1 (2003), pp. 5–18.

Hempenstall, Peter, 'Getting Inside the Tasman World: A Case for Remembering Local Histories

# Bibliography

in New Zealand, Australia and the Southwest Pacific', The Jim Gardner Lecture, Canterbury History Foundation, 2009, p. 4.

Henniker, Garth and Ian Jobling, 'Richard Coombes and the Olympic Movement in Australia: Imperialism and Nationalism in Action', *Sporting Traditions*, vol. 6, no. 1 (November 1989), pp. 2–15.

Hill, Jeffrey, 'Cocks, cats, caps and cups: A semiotic approach to sport and national identity', *Sport in Society*, vol. 2, no. 2 (Summer 1999), pp. 1–21.

Holcroft, M. H., 'Mud Pools and Mountain Views', *New Zealand's Heritage: The making of a nation*, vol. 5, part 67, Wellington: Paul Hamlyn, 1972, pp. 1868–72.

—— 'Baeyertz of the *Triad*', *New Zealand's Heritage: The making of a nation*, vol. 5, part 69, Wellington: Paul Hamlyn, 1972, pp. 1924–28.

Holmes, J. Macdonald., 'Geographical Factors in the Foundation of New Zealand's Wealth', *The Australian Geographer*, vol. II, no. 3 (1933–35), pp. 24–36.

Hooker, Brian, 'New Light on the Mapping and Naming of New Zealand', *New Zealand Journal of History*, vol. 6, no. 2 (October 1972), pp. 158–67.

Huggins, Mike, 'Walking in the Footsteps of a Pioneer: Peter McIntosh: Trail Blazer in the History of Sport', *International Journal of the History of Sport*, vol. 18, no. 2 (2001), pp. 134–47.

Hutchison, I. G. C., 'Scottish Newspapers and Scottish National Identity in the Nineteenth and Twentieth Centuries', Address to the 68th International Federation of Library Associations and Institutions, Glasgow, August 2002.

Jarvie, Grant, 'Sport, nationalism and cultural identity', in Lincoln Allison, ed., *The changing politics of sport*, Manchester: Manchester University Press, 1993, pp. 58–83.

Kirby, The Hon. Mr Justice Michael, 'CER, Trans-Tasman Courts and Australasia', *New Zealand Law Journal* (October 1983), pp. 304–7.

—— Presentation to Knowledge Wave 2003: The Leadership Forum. Auckland, February 2003.

Koh, Harold Hongju, 'On American Exceptionalism', *Stanford Law Review*, vol. 55, no. 5 (May 2003), pp. 1479–527.

Kwasitsu, Lishi, 'The production of the *Nelson Examiner* in the context of the early New Zealand press', *Turnbull Library Record*, vol. 19, no. 2 (October 1986), pp. 123–40.

—— 'News reporting on the *Nelson Examiner, 1842–1847*', *Turnbull Library Record*, vol. 20, no. 1 (May 1987), pp. 31–43.

Letters, Michael and Ian Jobling, 'Forgotten Links: Leonard Cuff and the Olympic Movement in Australasia, 1894–1905', *Olympika: The International Journal of Olympic Studies*, vol. 5 (1996), pp. 91–110.

Little, C., 'Trans-Tasman Federations in Sport: The changing relationships between Australia and New Zealand', in Richard Cashman, John O'Hara and Andrew Honey, eds, *Sport, Federation, Nation*, Sydney: Walla Walla Press, 2001, pp. 63–80.

—— '"Our George": Ex-Patriot Sportsmen and the Emergence of New Zealand's National Identity', *Proceedings of Ninth International Society for the History of Physical Education and Sport (I SHPES) Seminar*, Ljubljana, 2006.

Lloyd, Henry Demarest, 'New Zealand Newest England', *Atlantic Monthly*, vol. 84, no. 506 (December 1899), pp. 789–94.

McCrone, David, Robert Stewart, Richard Kiely and Frank Bechhofer, 'Who are we? Problematising national identity', *The Sociological Review*, vol. 46, no. 4 (November 1998), pp. 629–52.

Macdonald, Charlotte, 'Ways of Belonging: Sporting Spaces in New Zealand History', in Giselle Byrnes, ed., *The New Oxford History of New Zealand*, Melbourne: Oxford University Press, 2009.

McIntosh, Peter C., 'The British Attitude to Sport', in Alex Natan, ed., *Sport and Society: A Symposium*, London: Bowes & Bowes, 1958, pp. 13–24.

Mack, Rüdiger, 'The Mystery of the Scottish Gentleman Emigrant from 1782', *Journal of Pacific History*, vol. 32, no. 2 (December 1997), pp. 243–49.

Mangan, J. A., 'Christ and the Imperial Games Fields: Evangelical Athletes of the Empire', *International Journal of the History of Sport*, vol. 1, no. 2 (1984), pp. 184–201.

—— and John Nauright, eds, 'Sport in Australasian Society Past and Present', *International Journal of the History of Sport Special Issue* (June–September 2000).

Mein Smith, Philippa, 'New Zealand Federation Commissioners in Australia: One past, two historiographies', *Australian Historical Studies*, vol. 34, no. 122 (October 2003), pp. 305–25.

—— 'The Tasman World', in Giselle Byrnes, ed., *New Oxford History of New Zealand*, Melbourne: Oxford University Press, 2009.

Mellini, Peter and Roy T. Matthews, 'John Bull's Family Arises', *History Today*, vol. 37, issue 5 (May 1987), pp. 17–23.

# Bibliography

—— 'From Britannia to Maggie: The Fall and Rise of John Bull's Descendants', *History Today*, vol. 38, issue 9 (September 1988), pp. 17–23.

Milne, John, 'Civil Time', *Geographic Journal*, vol. 13, no. 2 (February 1899), pp. 173–94.

Mitchell, Ross, 'Sir James Hector', Canadian Medical Association *Journal*, vol. 66 (May 1952), pp. 497–99.

Moloughney, Brian and John Stenhouse, 'Drug-Besotten, Sin-Begotten Fiends of Filth', *New Zealand Journal of History*, vol. 33, no. 1 (April 1999), pp. 43–64.

Moore, Katharine, 'A Neglected Imperialist: The Promotion of the British Empire in the Writing of John Astley Cooper', *International Journal of the History of Sport*, vol. 8, no 2 (1991), pp. 256–69.

Obel, Camilla, 'Celebration and marginalisation in New Zealand sport: the "ethnic", national Māori rugby union team', *International Journal of Sport Management and Marketing*, vol. 2, nos 1–2 (2007), pp. 146–59.

O'Connell, Kieran, '"Be Strong and Show Thyself a Man": Christian Masculinities in Southern Dunedin 1885–1925', in John Stenhouse and Jane Thomson, eds, *Building God's Own Country: Historical Essays on Religion in New Zealand*, Dunedin: University of Otago Press, 2004.

Oliver, W. H., 'New Zealand About 1890', Macmillan Brown Lectures, 1972.

Olssen, Erik, 'God's Own Country', in Judith Binney, Judith Bassett and Erik Olssen, *The People and the Land: Te tangata me te whenua: An illustrated history of New Zealand, 1820–1920*, Auckland: Allen & Unwin in association with the Port Nicholson Press, 1990, pp. 253–75.

—— 'Toward A New Society', in Geoffrey Rice, ed, *The Oxford History of New Zealand*, second edition, Auckland: Oxford University Press, 1995, pp. 254–84.

Osborne, Thomas J., 'Trade or War? America's Annexation of Hawaii Reconsidered', *Pacific Historical Review*, vol. 50, no. 3 (August 1981), pp. 285–307.

Palenski, Ron, 'The Naming of the All Blacks: Unravelling the Myth', *Sporting Traditions*, vol. 26, no. 1 (May 2009), pp. 21–32.

Parsons, Coleman O., 'Mark Twain in New Zealand', *South Atlantic Quarterly* (Winter 1961), pp. 51–76.

Pawson, Eric, 'Local times and standard time in New Zealand', *Journal of Historical Geography*, vol. 18, no. 3 (1992), pp. 278–87.

—— 'The Meanings of Mountains', in Pawson and Tom Brooking, eds, *Environmental Histories of New Zealand*, Melbourne: Oxford University Press, 2002, pp. 136–50.

Phillips, J. O. C., 'Musings in Maoriland – or was there a *Bulletin* school in New Zealand?', *Australian Historical Studies*, vol. 20, no. 81 (October 1983), pp. 520–35.

—— 'Rugby, War and the Mythology of the New Zealand Male', *New Zealand Journal of History*, vol. 18, no. 2 (October 1984), pp. 83–103.

Pickles, Katie, 'Colonisation, Empire and Gender', in Giselle Byrnes, ed., *The New Oxford History of New Zealand*, Melbourne: Oxford University Press, 2009, pp. 219–41.

Potter, Simon J., 'Webs, Networks, and Systems: Globalization and the Mass Media in the Nineteenth- and Twentieth-Century British Empire', *Journal of British Studies*, vol. 46, no. 3 (July 2007), pp. 621–46.

Primrose, J. B., 'Kipling's visit to Australia and New Zealand', *Kipling Journal*, issue 145, March 1963, pp. 11–16.

Rabel, Roberto, 'New Zealand's Wars', in Giselle Byrnes, ed., *New Oxford History of New Zealand*, Melbourne: Oxford University Press, 2009.

Reid, Donald M., 'The Symbolism of Postage Stamps: A Source for the Historian', *Journal of Contemporary History*, vol. 19, no. 2 (April 1984), pp. 223–49.

Reid, J. C., 'A False Literary Dawn', *New Zealand's Heritage: The making of a nation*, vol. 4, part 57, Wellington: Paul Hamlyn, 1972, pp. 1593–96.

Rosie, Michael, John MacInnes, Pille Petersoo, Susan Condor and James Kennedy, 'Nation speaking unto nation? Newspapers and national identity in the devolved UK', *Sociological Review*, vol. 52, no. 4 (November 2004), pp. 437–58.

Ryan, Greg, 'Anthropological Football: Maori and the 1937 Springbok Rugby Tour of New Zealand', *New Zealand Journal of History*, vol. 34, no. 1 (2000–01), pp. 60–79.

—— 'Rural Myth and Urban Actuality: The Anatomy of All Black and New Zealand Rugby 1884–1938', *New Zealand Journal of History*, vol. 35, no. 1 (April 2001), pp. 45–69.

—— 'Athletic Warriors or a Social Elite: The Formative Years of Maori Rugby', Paper presented to the Australian Society for Sports History conference, Sporting Traditions XIV, Australian Catholic University, Sydney, July 2003.

Schneider, Edgar W., 'The Dynamics of New Englishes: From Identity to Dialect Birth', *Language*, vol. 79, no. 2 (June 2003), pp. 233–81.

# Bibliography

Schneider, William, 'Colonies at the 1900 World Fair', *History Today*, vol. 31, issue 5 (May 1981), pp. 31–36.

Scholefield, Guy H., 'The Australasian Federation: New Zealand's Attitude', *United Empire*, vol. 3, no. 11 (1912), pp. 911–12.

Searelle, Pamela, 'Samuel Turner, Mountaineer', *New Zealand's Heritage: The making of a nation*, vol. 6, part 78, Wellington: Paul Hamlyn, 1972, pp. 2164–66.

Shannon, R. T., 'The Liberal succession crisis in New Zealand, 1893', *Australian Historical Studies*, vol. 8, no. 30 (1958), pp. 183–201.

Sharkey, Michael, 'David McKee Wright, Māorilander', *Journal of New Zealand Literature*, no. 10 (1992), pp. 35–55.

Simpson, Clare S., 'Respectable Identities: New Zealand Nineteenth-Century "New Women" – on Bicycles!' *International Journal of the History of Sport*, vol. 18, no. 2 (June 2001), pp. 54–77.

Sinclair, Sir Keith, 'Full circle but new links', *In Our Time: 1870–1970 the Auckland Star Centennial Supplement*, pp. 39–46.

—— 'Why are Race Relations in New Zealand Better than in South Africa, South Australia or South Dakota?', *New Zealand Journal of History*, vol. 5, no. 2 (October 1971), pp. 121–27.

—— 'Towards 1990 – Nation and Identity', Hocken Lecture, 1988, Dunedin: Hocken Library, 1990.

Skilton, David, 'Tourists at the Ruins of London: The Metropolis and the Struggle for Empire', *Cercles*, no. 17 (2007), pp. 93–119.

Smith, Joanne, 'Twelve hundred reasons why there is no Australasia: How colonisation influenced federation', *Australian Cultural History*, vol. 27, no. 1 (April 2009), pp. 35–45.

Spence, Andrew, 'What "Kiwi" Means', in R. A. Barr, *With the British Rugby Team in Maoriland*, Dunedin: Otago Daily Times and Witness Newspapers, 1908, pp. 54–55.

Stafford, Jane, 'Alfred Domett, Robert Browning and a Dream of Two Lives', *Journal of New Zealand Literature*, no. 21 (2003), pp. 32–53.

Stenhouse, John, 'Religion and Society', in Giselle Byrnes, ed., *New Oxford History of New Zealand*, Melbourne: Oxford University Press, 2009.

Stoddart, Brian, 'Sport, Cultural Imperialism, and Colonial Response in the British Empire', *Comparative Studies in Society and History*, vol. 30, no. 4 (October 1988), pp. 649–73.

Stout, Sir Robert, 'The Rise and Progress of New Zealand', in Thomas Bracken, *Musings in Maoriland: A Jubilee Volume*, Dunedin: Arthur T. Keirle, 1890.

—— 'Religion and the State, A New Year's address delivered in the Unitarian Free Church on Sunday evening, the 4th January, 1914', Alexandra: Alexandra Herald, 1914.

Tapp, E. J., 'New Zealand and Australian Federation', *Australian Historical Studies*, vol. 5, no. 19 (November 1952), pp. 244–57.

Tennyson, Sir Charles, 'They Taught the World to Play', *Victorian Studies*, vol. 2, no. 3 (March 1959), pp. 211–22.

Thompson, Andrew, 'Nations, national identities and human agency: putting people back into nations', *The Sociological Review*, vol. 49, no. 1 (February 2001), pp. 18–32.

Torsella, Joseph M., 'American National Identity, 1750–1790: Samples from the Popular Press', *Pennsylvania Magazine of History and Biography*, vol. 112, no. 2 (April 1988), pp. 167–87.

Trapeznik, Alexander, 'New Zealand's Perceptions of the Russian Revolution of 1917', *Revolutionary Russia*, vol. 19, no. 1 (June 2006), pp. 63–77.

Trudgill, Peter, Elizabeth Gordon, Gillian Lewis and Margaret Maclagan, 'Determinism in new-dialect formation and the genesis of New Zealand English', *Journal of Linguistics*, no. 36 (2000), pp. 299–318.

Vincent, G. T. and Toby Harfield, 'Repression and Reform: Responses within New Zealand Rugby to the Arrival of the 'Northern Game', *New Zealand Journal of History*, vol. 31, no. 2 (October 1997), pp. 234–50.

—— 'Practical Imperialism: The Anglo-Welsh Rugby Tour of New Zealand, 1908', *International Journal of the History of Sport*, vol. 15, no. 1 (April 1998), pp. 123–40.

—— '"To Uphold the Honour of the Province", Football in Canterbury c. 1854–c. 1890', in Greg Ryan, ed., *Tackling Rugby Myths: Rugby and New Zealand Society 1854–2004*, Dunedin: University of Otago Press, 2005.

Walker, H. de R., 'Australasian Extensions of Democracy', *Atlantic Monthly*, vol. 83, no. 499 (May 1899), pp. 577–85.

Wood, F. L. W., 'Why did New Zealand not join the Australian Commonwealth in 1900–1901?', *New Zealand Journal of History*, vol. 2, no. 2 (October 1968), pp. 115–29.

Zeiler, Thomas, 'A Night at Delmonico's: The Spalding Baseball Tour and the Imagination of Empire', *International Journal of the History of Sport*, vol. 23, no. 1 (February 2006), pp. 28–45.

# Bibliography

**OTHER PUBLICATIONS**

Akers, Clive, *Monro: The Life and Times of the Man Who Gave New Zealand Rugby*, Palmerston North: author, 2008.

Allison, Lincoln, *The changing politics of sport*, Manchester: Manchester University Press, 1993.

Anderson, Benedict, *Imagined Communities: Reflections on the Origins and Spread of Nationalism*, London: Verso Books, 2006.

Andrews, John, *No Other Home Than This: A History of European New Zealanders*, Nelson: Craig Potton Publishing, 2009.

Arnold, Rollo, *New Zealand's Burning: The Settlers' World in the Mid 1880s*, Wellington: Victoria University Press, 1994.

Bailey, Rona and Herbert Roth, eds, *Shanties by the way: A selection of New Zealand popular songs and ballads*, Christchurch: Whitcombe & Tombs, 1967.

Bassett, Michael, *Sir Joseph Ward, A Political Biography*, Auckland: Auckland University Press, 1993.

Bayly, C. A., *The Birth of the Modern World 1780–1914*, Oxford: Blackwell Publishing, 2004.

Belich, James, *Making Peoples: A History of the New Zealanders From Polynesian Settlement to the End of the Nineteenth Century*, Auckland: Allen Lane, the Penguin Press, 1996.

—— *Paradise Reforged: A History of the New Zealanders From the 1880s to the Year 2000*, Auckland: Allen Lane, the Penguin Press, 2001.

—— *Replenishing the Earth: The Settler Revolution and the Rise of the Anglo-World, 1783–1939*, Oxford: Oxford University Press, 2009.

Billig, Michael, *Banal Nationalism*, London: Sage Publications, 1995.

Blainey, Geoffrey, *A Game of Our Own: The Origins of Australian Football*, Melbourne: Information Australia, 1990.

—— *The Tyranny of Distance: How Distance Shaped Australia's History*, Sydney: Pan Macmillan, 2001.

Bohan, Edmund, *Edward Stafford: New Zealand's First Statesman*, Christchurch: Hazard Press, 1994.

Bohlman, Philip V., *The Music of European Nationalism: Cultural Identity and Modern History*, Santa Barbara: ABC/CLIO, 2004.

Booth, Douglas, *The Race Game: Sport and Politics in South Africa*, London: Frank Cass, 1998.

—— and Colin Tatz, *One-Eyed: A View of Australian Sport*, Sydney: Allen & Unwin, 2000.

—— *Australian Beach Cultures: The history of sun, sand and surf*, London: Frank Cass, 2001.

—— *The field: Truth and fiction in sport history*, New York: Routledge, 2005.

Brenchley, Fred and Elizabeth, *Myth Maker*, Milton, Queensland: John Wiley & Sons, 2005.

Brooking, Tom, *Lands for the People: The Highland Clearances and the Colonisation of New Zealand: A Biography of John McKenzie*, Dunedin: University of Otago Press, 1996.

—— *The Greenwood Histories of the Modern Nations: The History of New Zealand*, Westport, Connecticut: Greenwood Press, 2004.

Burdon, R. M., *The Life and Times of Sir Julius Vogel*, Christchurch: The Caxton Press, 1948.

—— *King Dick: A Biography of Richard John Seddon*, Wellington: Whitcombe & Tombs, 1955.

Byrnes, Giselle, ed., *The New Oxford History of New Zealand*, Melbourne: Oxford University Press, 2009.

Carlyle, Thomas, *On Heroes, Hero-Worship and the Heroic in History*, Whitefish, Montana: Kessinger Publishing, 2006.

Carman, Arthur H. and Noel S. Macdonald, *The Cricket Almanack of New Zealand 1955*, Wellington: Sporting Publications, 1955.

Cashman, Richard, John O'Hara and Andrew Honey, eds, *Sport, Federation, Nation*, Sydney: Walla Walla Press in association with the Centre for Olympic Studies, University of New South Wales, 2001.

Chester, R. H. and N. A. C. McMillan, *The Visitors: The History of International Rugby Teams in New Zealand*, Auckland: Moa Publications, 1990.

Coad, N. E., *New Zealand from Tasman to Massey*, Wellington: Harry H. Tombs Ltd, 1934.

Coleman, Peter J., *Progressivism and the World of Reform: New Zealand and the Origins of the American Welfare State*, Lawrence, Kansas: University Press of Kansas, 1987.

Colley, Linda, *Britons: Forging the Nation 1707–1837*, New Haven: Yale University Press, 2005.

Collins, Tony, *Rugby's Great Split: Class, Culture and the Origins of Rugby League Football*, London: Frank Cass, 1998.

—— *A Social History of English Rugby Union*, London: Routledge, 2009.

Condliffe, J. B., *Te Rangi Hiroa: The Life of Sir Peter Buck*, Christchurch: Whitcombe & Tombs, 1971.

Coney, Sandra, *Standing in the Sunshine: A History of New Zealand Women Since They Won the Vote*, Auckland: Viking/Penguin, 1993.

Crawford, John with Ellen Ellis, *To Fight for the Empire: An Illustrated History of New Zealand and the South African War 1899–1902*, Wellington: Reed, in association with the Historical Branch, Department of Internal Affairs, 1999.

Crawford, John and Ian McGibbon, eds, *One Flag, One Queen, One Tongue: New Zealand, the British Empire and the South African War*, Auckland: Auckland University Press, 2003.

Cryer, Max, *Hear Our Voices We Entreat: The Extraordinary Story of New Zealand's National Anthems*, Auckland: Exisle Publishing, 2004.

Curthoys, Ann and John Docker, *Is History Fiction?*, Sydney: University of New South Wales Press, 2006.

Dalziel, Raewyn, *Julius Vogel: Business Politician*, Auckland: Auckland University Press/Oxford University Press, 1986.

—— 'New Zealand and Polynesia', in David Porter, ed., *The Oxford History of the British Empire, vol III, The Nineteenth Century*, Oxford: Oxford University Press, 1999, p. 595.

Davison, Graeme, *The Unforgiving Minute: How Australia Learned to Tell the Time*, Melbourne: Oxford University Press, 1993.

Day, Patrick, *The Making of the New Zealand Press 1840–1880: A Study of the Organizational and Political Concerns of New Zealand Newspaper Controllers*, Wellington: Victoria University Press, 1990.

de Moore, Greg, *Tom Wills: His Spectacular Rise and Tragic Fall*, Sydney: Allen & Unwin, 2008.

Denoon, Donald and Philippa Mein Smith with Marivic Wyndham, *A History of Australia, New Zealand and the Pacific*, Oxford: Blackwell Publishing, 2000.

Difford, Ivor D., *The History of South African Rugby Football (1875–1932)*, Wynberg, Cape: The Specialty Press of South Africa, 1933.

Dine, Philip, *French Rugby Football: A Cultural History*, Oxford: Berg, 2001.

Droogleever, R. W. F., *From the Front: A. B. (Banjo) Paterson's Dispatches from the Boer War*, Sydney: Macmillan, 2000.

du Fresne, Karl, *The Dom 1907–2007: A Century of News*, Wellington: Dominion Post, 2007.

Evers, C. R., *Rugby: English Public Schools*, London: Blackie & Son, 1939.

Ferguson, Niall, *The Rise and Fall of the American Empire*, London: Penguin Books, 2005.

—— *Empire: How Britain Made the Modern World*, London: Penguin Books, 2008.

Fischer, David Hackett, *Albion's Seed: Four British Folkways in America*, New York: Oxford University Press, 1989.

Fleischer, Nat, *Heavyweight Championship*, London: Putnam & Company, 1950.

Foster, S. G., Susan Marsden and Roslyn Russell, *Federation: The Guide to Records*, Canberra: Australian Archives, 1998.

Frindall, Bill, ed., *The Wisden Book of Test Cricket*, London: Book Club Associates, 1979.

Gare, Deborah and David Ritter, *Making Australian History: Perspective on the Past Since 1788*, Melbourne: Thomson, 2008.

Glue, W. A., *New Zealand Ensign*, Wellington: Government Printer, 1965.

Goldie, Terry, *Fear and Temptation: The image of the Indigene in Canadian, Australian, and New Zealand Literatures*, Montreal: McGill-Queen's University Press, 1989.

Gordon, Harry, *Australia and the Olympic Games*, Brisbane: University of Queensland Press, 1994.

Grant, David, *On a Roll: A history of gambling and lotteries in New Zealand*, Wellington: Victoria University Press, 1994.

Grattan, C. Hartley, *The Southwest Pacific to 1900*, Ann Arbor: University of Michigan Press, 1963.

Gray, Sheila, *The South African War 1899–1902: Service Records of British and Colonial Women: A record of the service in South Africa of Military and Civilian Nurses, Laywomen and Civilians*, Auckland: author, 1993.

Greenhalgh, Paul, *Ephemeral Vistas: The Expositions Universelles, Great Exhibitions and World's Fairs, 1851–1939*, Manchester: Manchester University Press, 1988.

Griffiths, George, *Notes on Some Early Arrivals in Otago, No 3: W. G. Rees and His Cricketing Cousins*, Dunedin: author, 1971.

—— *Queenstown's King Wakatip*, Dunedin: John McIndoe, 1971.

—— *The National Anthem*, Dunedin: Granville Books, 1977.

Haigh, J. Bryant., *Men of Faith and Courage: The official history of the Royal New Zealand Chaplains Department*, Auckland: The Word Publishers, 1983.

Hall, D. O. W., *The New Zealanders in South Africa 1899–1902*, Wellington: War History Branch, Department of Internal Affairs, 1949.

Heidenstrom, Peter, *Athletes of the Century: 100 Years of New Zealand Track and Field*, Wellington: GP Publications, 1992.

Hirst, John, *The Sentimental Nation: The Making of the Australian Commonwealth*, Melbourne: Oxford University Press, 2000.

—— *Sense & Nonsense in Australian History*, Melbourne: Black Inc Agenda, 2006.

# Bibliography

Hobsbawm, Eric and Terence Ranger, *The Invention of Tradition*, Cambridge: Cambridge University Press, 2003.

Hocking, Geoff, *The Australian Flag*, Melbourne: Five Mile Press, 2002.

Holt, Richard, J. A. Mangan and Pierre Lanfranchi, eds, *European Heroes: Myth, Identity, Sport*, London: Frank Cass, 2005.

Howell, Maxwell L., Lingyu Xie and Bensley Wilkes, *The Wallabies: A Definitive History of Australian Test Rugby*, Norman Park, Queensland: GAP Publishing, 2000.

Howell, Reet and Max, *Aussie Gold: The Story of Australia at the Olympics*, Albion, Queensland: Brooks Waterloo, 1988.

Huggins, Mike, *The Victorians and Sport*, London: Hambledon & London, 2004.

Hughes, Robert, *The Fatal Shore*, London: Pan Books, 1988.

Hughes-Warrington, Marnie, *Fifty Key Thinkers on History*, Oxford: Routledge, 2008.

Hunter, Ian, *Age of Enterprise: Rediscovering the New Zealand Entrepreneur 1880–1910*, Auckland: Auckland University Press, 2007.

Irving, Helen, *To Constitute A Nation: A Cultural History of Australia's Constitution*, Cambridge: Cambridge University Press, 1999.

—— ed., *The Centenary Companion to Australian Federation*, Cambridge: Cambridge University Press, 1999.

Irwin, Sally, *Between Heaven and Earth: The Life of a Mountaineer, Freda du Faur*, Melbourne: White Crane Press, 2000.

Jones, Lloyd, *The Book of Fame: A Novel*, Auckland: Penguin, 2000.

Keith, Hamish, *The Big Picture: A history of New Zealand art from 1642*, Auckland: Random House, 2007.

Kelly, G. M., *Golf in New Zealand: A Centennial History*, Wellington: New Zealand Golf Association, 1971.

Kertzer, David L., *Ritual, Politics and Power*, New Haven: Yale University Press, 1988.

King, Michael, *The Penguin History of New Zealand*, Auckland: Penguin Books, 2003.

Knight, Hardwicke, *Photography in New Zealand: A Social and Technical History*, Dunedin: John McIndoe, 1971.

Lamster, Mark, *Spalding's World Tour: The Epic Adventure that Took Baseball Around the Globe – and Made it America's Game*, New York: Public Affairs Press, 2006.

Lawlor, Pat, *Books and Bookmen*, Wellington: Whitcombe & Tombs, 1954.

Lester, Alan, *Imperial Networks: Creating identities in nineteenth-century South Africa and Britain*, New York: Routledge, 2001.

Lipset, S. M., *American Exceptionalism: A Double-Edged Sword*, New York: W. W. Norton, 1996.

Little, K. M., *Polo in New Zealand*, Wellington: Whitcombe & Tombs, 1956.

Loughnan, R. A., *The Biography of Sir Joseph Ward*, Wellington: New Century Press, 1929.

McClure, Margaret, *The Wonder Country: Making New Zealand Tourism*, Auckland: Auckland University Press in association with the New Zealand Tourism Board and the Ministry of Culture and Heritage, 2004.

McCrystal, John, *The Originals: 1905 All Black Rugby Odyssey – the story of the All Black 'Originals' and their extraordinary tour of Great Britain*, Auckland: Random House, 2005.

McGibbon, Ian, *The Path to Gallipoli: Defending New Zealand 1840–1915*, Wellington: GP Books, 1991.

McIntosh, P. C., *Sport In Society*, London: C. A. Watts & Co, 1963.

Macintyre, Stuart, *A Concise History of Australia*, second edition, Melbourne: Cambridge University Press, 2005.

McIvor, Timothy, *The Rainmaker: A Biography of John Ballance, Journalist and Politician 1839–1893*, Auckland: Heinemann Reed, 1989.

MacKenzie, John M., 'Empire and Metropolitan Cultures', in Andrew Porter, ed., *The Oxford History of the British Empire, vol III, The Nineteenth Century*, Oxford: Oxford University Press, 1999.

Mackey, John, *The Making of a State Education System: The Passing of the New Zealand Education Act, 1877*, London: Geoffrey Chapman, 1967.

McLean, Denis, *The Prickly Pair: Making Nationalism in Australia and New Zealand*, Dunedin: Otago University Press, 2003.

McLean, T. P., *The All Blacks*, London: Sidgwick & Jackson, 1991.

Macleod, Jenny, *Reconsidering Gallipoli*, Manchester: Manchester University Press, 2004.

McLeod, John, ed., *The Routledge Companion to Postcolonial Studies*, Milton Park, Oxfordshire: Routledge, 2001.

McNeish, James, *Dance of the Peacocks: New Zealanders in exile in the time of Hitler and Mao Tse-tung*, Auckland: Random House, 2003.

# Bibliography

Macrory, Jennifer, *Running With the Ball: The Birth of Rugby Football*, London: Collins Willow, 1991.

Magnus, Philip, *Kitchener: Portrait of an Imperialist*, London: John Murray, 1958.

Mallon, Bill, *The 1900 Olympic Games, Results for All Competitors in All Events, with Commentary*, Jefferson, North Carolina: McFarland & Company, 1998.

—— and Ture Widlund, *The 1896 Olympic Games*, Jefferson, North Carolina: McFarland & Company, 1998.

Mangan, J. A., *The Games Ethic and Imperialism*, London: Viking, 1986.

—— ed., *The Cultural Bond: Sport, Empire, Society*, London: Frank Cass, 1992.

—— and J. Nauright, eds, *Sport in Australasia: Past and Present*, London: Frank Cass, 2000.

Marshall, P. S., *King of the Peds*, Milton Keynes: AuthorHouse, 2008.

Martin, Ged, *Australia, New Zealand and Federation*, London: Menzies Centre for Australian Studies, 2001.

Martin, John E., *The House: New Zealand's House of Representatives 1854–2004*, Palmerston North: Dunmore Press, 2004.

Marwick, Arthur, *The Nature of History*, London: Macmillan, 1989.

Marx, Anthony W., *Faith in Nation – Exclusionary Origins of Nationalism*, Oxford: Oxford University Press, 2003.

Maurois, André, *Disraeli*, London: Penguin Books, 1937.

Mein Smith, Philippa, Peter Hempenstall and Shaun Goldfinch, *Remaking the Tasman World*, Christchurch: Canterbury University Press, 2008.

Monin, Lydia, *From the writer's notebook: Around New Zealand with 80 authors*, Auckland: Reed, 2006.

Morehead, Alan, *Rum Jungle*, London: Hamish Hamilton, 1953.

Morrell, W. P., *The Provincial System in New Zealand 1852–76*, Dunedin: Whitcombe & Tombs, 1964.

—— and D. O. W. Hall, *A History of New Zealand Life*, Wellington: Whitcombe & Tombs, 1957.

Morris, Ewan, *Our Own Devices: National Symbols and Political Conflict in Twentieth-Century Ireland*, Dublin: Irish Academic Press, 2005.

Moses, Eric Watts, *A History of the Proceedings of the International Rugby Football Board 1886–1960*, London: IRFB, 1960.

Mulford, John G., *Guardians of the Game: The History of the New South Wales Rugby Union 1874–2004*, Sydney: ABC Books, 2005.

Mulgan, Alan, *Great Days in New Zealand Writing*, Wellington: A. H. & A. W. Reed, 1962.

Murphy, Nigel, *A Guide to Laws and Policies Relating to the Chinese in New Zealand*, Wellington: New Zealand Chinese Association, 1997.

Natan, Alex, ed., *Sport and Society: A Symposium*, London: Bowes & Bowes, 1958.

Nathan, Simon and Mary Varnham, eds, *The Amazing World of James Hector*, Wellington: Awa Press, 2008.

Natusch, Sheila, *Southward Ho!: The Deborah in Quest of a New Edinburgh 1844*, Invercargill: Craig Printing and Southland Frozen Meat, 1985.

O'Brien, Brian F., *Kiwis With Gloves On: A History and Record Book of New Zealand Boxing*, Wellington: A. H. & A. W. Reed, 1960.

Odd, Gilbert, *The Fighting Blacksmith: The Story of Bob Fitzsimmons*, London: Pelham Books, 1976.

Olssen, Erik, *Building the New World: Work, politics and society in Caversham 1880s–1920s*, Auckland: Auckland University Press, 1995.

O'Neill, R. B., *The Press 1861–1961*, Christchurch: Christchurch Press Company, 1963.

O'Sullivan, Vincent, *Long Journey to the Border: A Life of John Mulgan*, Auckland: Penguin, 2003.

Pakenham, Thomas, *The Boer War: Illustrated Edition*, London: Weidenfeld & Nicolson, 1993.

Palenski, Ron, *Our National Game: A Celebration of 100 Years of NZ Rugby*, Auckland: Moa Publications, 1992.

—— *The Jersey: The Pride & the Passion, the Guts & the Glory: What it means to wear the All Black jersey*, Auckland: Hodder Moa Beckett, 2001.

Palenski, Ron and Terry Maddaford, *The Games*, Auckland: Moa Publications, 1984.

Pascoe, John, ed., *Mr. Explorer Douglas*, Wellington: A. H. & A. W. Reed, 1957.

Paul, J. T., *Humanism in Politics: New Zealand Labour Party Retrospect*, Wellington: New Zealand Labour Party, 1946.

Phillips, Jock, *A Man's Country? The Image of the Pakeha Male: A History*, Auckland: Penguin, 1987.

Pope, S. W. and John Nauright, eds, *Routledge Companion to Sports History*, Oxford: Routledge, 2010.

Potter, Simon J., *News and the British World: The Emergence of an Imperial Press System*, Oxford: Oxford Historical Monographs, the Clarendon Press, 2003.

Pound, Francis, *The Invention of New Zealand: Art and National Identity 1930–1970*, Auckland: Auckland University Press, 2009.

# Bibliography

Preston, Diane, *The Boxer Rebellion: The Dramatic Story of China's War on Foreigners that Shook the World in the Summer of 1900*, New York: Berkley Books, 2001.

Pugsley, Christopher, *Gallipoli: The New Zealand Story*, Auckland: Hodder & Stoughton, 1984.

—— *Te Hokowhitu a Tu: The Maori Pioneer Battalion in the First World War*, Auckland: Reed Books, 1995.

—— *The Anzac Experience: New Zealand, Australia and Empire in the First World War*, Auckland: Reed, 2004.

Rattray, Joan, *Great Days in New Zealand Nursing*, London: George G. Harrap & Co, 1961.

Redwood, Miriam Macgregor, *Proud Silk – A New Zealand Racing History*, Wellington: A. H. & A. W. Reed, 1979.

Reese, T. W., *New Zealand Cricket 1841–1914*, Christchurch: Simpson & Williams, 1927.

Reeves, William Pember, *The Long White Cloud (Ao Tea Roa)*, London: George Allen & Unwin, 1934.

Renwick, William, ed., *Creating a National Spirit: Celebrating New Zealand's Centennial*, Wellington: Victoria University Press, 2004.

Rice, Geoffrey W., ed., *The Oxford History of New Zealand, Second Edition*, Auckland: Oxford University Press, 1992.

Richardson, Len and Shelley, *Anthony Wilding: A Sporting Life*, Christchurch: Canterbury University Press, 2005.

Ripley, Stuart, *Sculling and Skulduggery: A history of professional sculling*, Sydney: Walla Walla Press, 2009.

Roberts, Heather, *Where Did She Come From? New Zealand Women Novelists 1862–1987*, Wellington: Allen & Unwin/Port Nicholson Press, 1989.

Roberts, Randy, *Papa Jack: Jack Johnson and the Era of White Hopes*, London: Robson Books, 1986.

Robinson, Howard, *A History of the Post Office in New Zealand*, Wellington: R. E. Owen, Government Printer, 1964.

Robson, Michael, *Decision at Dawn: New Zealand and the EEC*, Wellington: Baynard-Hillier, 1972.

Rockel, Ian, *Taking the Waters: Early Spas in New Zealand*, Wellington: Government Printing Office Publishing, 1986.

Rolfe, Patricia, *The Journalistic Javelin, An Illustrated History of the* Bulletin, Sydney: Wildcat Press, 1979.

Ross, Angus, *New Zealand Aspirations in the Pacific in the Nineteenth Century*, Oxford: Clarendon Press, 1964.

Ryan, Greg, *Forerunners of the All Blacks: The 1888–89 New Zealand Native Football Team in Britain, Australia and New Zealand*, Christchurch: Canterbury University Press, 1993.

—— *The Making of New Zealand Cricket 1832–1914*, London: Frank Cass, 2004.

—— ed., *Tackling Rugby Myths: Rugby and New Zealand Society 1854–2004*, Dunedin: Otago University Press, 2004.

—— *The Contest for Rugby Supremacy: Accounting for the 1905 All Blacks*, Christchurch: Canterbury University Press, 2005.

Rydell, Robert W., *All the World's A Fair: Visions of Empire at American International Expositions, 1876–1916*, Chicago: University of Chicago Press, 1984.

Said, Edward W., *Orientalism*, London: Penguin, 2003.

Sanders, James, *Dateline-NZPA: The New Zealand Press Association 1880–1980*, Auckland: Wilson & Horton, 1980.

Scates, Bruce, *A New Australia: Citizenship, Radicalism and the First Republic*, Cambridge: Cambridge University Press, 1997.

Schivelbusch, Wolfgang, *The Railway Journey: The Industrialization of Time and Space in the 19th Century*, Berkeley and Los Angeles: University of California Press, 1986.

Scholefield, G. H., *New Zealand in Evolution: Industrial, Economic and Political*. London: T. Fisher Unwin, 1909.

—— *The Pacific: Its Past and Future*, London: John Murray, 1919.

—— *Newspapers in New Zealand*, Wellington: A. H. & A. W. Reed, 1958.

—— ed., *Who's Who in New Zealand and the Western Pacific*, Wellington: Rangatira Press, 1932.

Sharp, Iain, *Real Gold: Treasures of Auckland City Libraries*, Auckland: Auckland University Press for Auckland City Libraries and the Auckland Library Heritage Trust, 2007.

Shaw, Martin and Henry Coleman, *National Anthems of the World*, London: Blandford Press, 1963.

Sinclair, Keith, *Imperial Federation: A Study of New Zealand Policy and Opinion 1880–1914*, London: Athlone Press and the University of London, 1955.

—— ed., *Distance Looks Our Way: The Effects of Remoteness on New Zealand*, Auckland: Paul's Book Arcade for the University of Auckland, 1961.

—— *William Pember Reeves, New Zealand Fabian*, Oxford: Clarendon Press, 1965.

—— *A Destiny Apart: New Zealand's Search for National Identity*, Wellington: Unwin Paperbacks in association with the Port Nicholson Press, 1986.

# Bibliography

——— ed., *Tasman Relations: New Zealand and Australia, 1788–1988*, Auckland: Auckland University Press, 1987.

Smith, David and Gareth Williams, *Fields of Praise*, Cardiff: University of Wales Press, 1980.

Smith, Neil C., *Australians with New Zealand Contingents to the Boer War 1899–1902*, Gardenvale, Victoria: Mostly Unsung Military History Research and Publications, 2000.

Sobel, Dava, *Longitude: The True Story of a Lone Genius Who Solved the Greatest Scientific Problem of His Time*, London: Harper Perennial, 2007.

Sorrenson, M. P. K., *Maori Origins and Migrations: The Genesis of Some Pakeha Myths and Legends*, Auckland: Auckland University Press/Oxford University Press, 1979.

Stern, Fritz, *The Varieties of History From Voltaire to the Present*, London: Meridian Books, 1957.

Stowers, Richard, *First New Zealanders to the Boer War 1899*, Hamilton: published by the author, 1983.

——— *Kiwi Versus Boer: The First New Zealand Mounted Rifles in the Anglo-Boer War 1899–1902*, Hamilton: published by the author, 1992.

——— *Rough Riders at War*, fifth edition, Hamilton: published by the author, 2008.

Stradling, Jan, *More Than A Game: When Sport and History Collide*, Sydney: Pier 9, 2009.

Swan, A. C., *History of New Zealand Rugby Football, Volume 1, 1870–1945*, Wellington: A. H. & A. W. Reed, 1948.

——— and Gordon F. W. Jackson, *Wellington's Rugby History*, Wellington: A. H. & A. W Reed, 1952.

Titley, U. A. and Ross McWhirter, *Centenary History of the Rugby Football Union*, London: Rugby Football Union, 1971.

Tobin, Christopher, *Fitzsimmons: Boxing's First Triple Champion of the World*, Timaru: David A. Jack and author, 2000.

——— *The Original All Blacks 1905–06*, Auckland: Hodder Moa, 2005.

——— *John L. Sullivan and 'Maori' Slade: The Forgotten and Fascinating Story of their World Heavyweight Boxing Title Fight*, Wanaka: Bosco Press, 2007.

Tosh, John, *The Pursuit of History*, London: Pearson Education, 2006.

Trevelyan, G. M., *Illustrated English Social History, Volume 4 – The Nineteenth Century*, London: Longmans, Green & Co, 1952.

Turley, Alan, *Rugby: The Pioneer Years*, Auckland: HarperCollins, 2008.

Various authors, *Makers of Auckland*, Auckland: Wilson & Horton, 1971.

Verry, Leslie, *Seven Days a Week: The Story of Independent Newspapers Ltd*, Wellington: INL Print, 1985.

Ward, John M., *British Policy in the South Pacific 1786–1893: A study in British policy towards the South Pacific islands prior to the establishment of Governments by the Great Powers*, Sydney: Australasian Publishing Co, 1948.

Ward, Russel, *The Australian Legend: new illustrated edition*, Melbourne: Oxford University Press, 1978.

Waterhouse, Richard, *The Vision Splendid: A Social and Cultural History of Rural Australia*, Fremantle: Curtin University Books, 2005.

Wilcox, Craig, *Australia's Boer War: The War in South Africa 1899–1902*, Melbourne: Oxford University Press in association with the Australian War Memorial, 2002.

Williams, John F., *Anzacs, the Media and the Great War*, Sydney: University of New South Wales Press, 1999.

Wilson, A. C., *Wire & Wireless: A History of Telecommunications in New Zealand 1890–1987*, Palmerston North: Dunmore Press, 1994.

Windrow, Martin, *Our Friends Beneath the Sands: The Foreign Legion in France's Colonial Conquests 1870–1935*, London: Weidenfeld & Nicolson, 2010.

Wolfe, Richard, *Well Made New Zealand: A Century of Trademarks*, Auckland: Reed Methuen, 1987.

Wright, Ed, *Lost and Found in History: Ghost Colonies – Failed utopias, forgotten exiles and abandoned outposts of empire*, Sydney: Pier 9, 2009.

Wright-St Clair, Rex E., *Thoroughly A Man of the World: A Biography of Sir David Monro*, Christchurch: Whitcombe & Tombs, 1971.


## GENERAL REFERENCE

Bagnall, A. G., *New Zealand National Bibliography*, vol. 3, Wellington: Government Printer, 1972.

Beck, Emily Morison, ed., *Bartlett's Familiar Quotations: A collection of passages, phrases and proverbs traced to their sources in ancient and modern literature*. Boston: Little, Brown, 125th anniversary edition, 1980.

Chester, R. H. and N. A. C. McMillan, *The Encyclopaedia of New Zealand Rugby*, Auckland: Moa Publications, 1981.

# Bibliography

Cohen, J. M. and M. J., *The Penguin Dictionary of Quotations*, London: Penguin Books, 1963.

Davison, Graeme, John Hirst and Stuart Macintyre, *The Oxford Companion to Australian History*, revised edition, Melbourne: Oxford University Press, 2001.

Godwin, Terry, *The Complete Who's Who of International Rugby*, Poole, Dorset: Blandford Press, 1987.

Griffiths, George, *Southern Writers in Disguise, A miscellany of journalistic and literary pseudonyms*, Dunedin: Otago Heritage Books, 1998.

Holy Bible, Revised Version, London: Octopus Books, 1981.

Lucas, J. O., G. H. Fairmaid, M. G. McInnes and W. J. Patrick, *Otago Boys' High School Old Boys' Register*, Dunedin: Otago High School Old Boys' Society, 1963.

McLintock, A. H., *An Encylopaedia of New Zealand*, 3 vols, Wellington: R. E. Owen, Government Printer, 1966.

Moorfield, John C., *Te Aka, Māori-English, English-Māori Dictionary and Index*, Auckland: Pearson, Longman, 2008.

Murray-Smith, Stephen, ed., *The Dictionary of Australian Quotations*, Melbourne: Heinemann, 1984.

*New Zealand Official Year Book*.

Oliver, W. H. and Claudia Orange, general editors, *The Dictionary of New Zealand Biography*, 5 vols, 1990–2000.

Orsman, H. W., ed., *Dictionary of New Zealand English*, Auckland: Oxford University Press, 1997.

Palenski, Ron, Rod Chester and Neville McMillan, *Men In Black*, seventh edition, Auckland: Hodder Moa, 2006.

Scholefield, G. H., *A Dictionary of New Zealand Biography*, 2 vols, Wellington: Department of Internal Affairs, 1940.

Thomson, Jane, ed., *Southern People: A Dictionary of Otago-Southland Biography*, Dunedin: Longacre Press in association with the Dunedin City Council, 1998.

Todd, Sydney P., *Sporting Records of New Zealand*, Auckland: Moa Publications, 1976.

Znamierowski, Alfred, *The World Encyclopedia of Flags: The definitive guide to international flags, banners, standards and ensigns*, London: Hermes House, 2002.

# INDEX

Page numbers in **bold** refer to illustrations.